"Millennial's, You Have The Power To Change The World"

Millennials

"Your Time Has Come"

Stephen A Vigiano

outskirts
press

Outskirts Press, Inc.
http://www.outskirtspress.com

ISBN: 978-1-9772-5111-4

Outskirts Press and the "OP" logo are trademarks belonging to Outskirts Press, Inc.

PRINTED IN THE UNITED STATES OF AMERICA

INTRODUCTION

IF you can dream it, you can become it. If it can be imagined, it can be achieved! Wisdom is something we must share with our children. As a father of three and a grandfather, it's my belief as parents and grandparents we must understand that the life lessons we teach our children will shape their world. Why do I believe this? Because I have lived it, we are a product of the people who bring us into this world and the environment and society we grow up in. We don't get to paint the ideal picture of a world we would like to live in, even though we are born with a blank canvas that can be painted to reflect our hopes and dreams. We are brought into this world in a state of pure innocence, with no thought of what is right or wrong, good or evil. So many of us are at the mercy of our parents or a guardian who has raised us from birth. If our parents were kind, compassionate and taught us how to learn the importance of kindness, integrity and empathy, then our children would have a much greater chance to succeed in life. A chance to realize their own hopes and dreams, not the dreams that were placed in their minds by us. The importance of human relationships and how we are treated and how we treat others can bring out the best in mankind. Then there is the opposite side of life which seems to have taken away so much of mankind's hope for a world that embraces human dignity. How the current state of the world can shatter their hopes and dreams, how it can impact their lives in ways we never could have imagined. The first seven years of a child's life are the most crucial to their emotional and mental wellbeing. It is at this stage of their development that will shape who they are and what they may become. The world they are exposed to can be filled with love and encouragement or it can be filled with fear and abuse, which can destroy a child's self-esteem. The results of that kind of upbringing may be the reason we have so much hatred and violence in our world today. We as a society are so focused on our physical healthcare, but we are neglecting the most important aspect of living a joyful, happy and healthy life. The care of our minds. We must first cure mental health in order to cure the body. Many doctors say that they see patient's that show no signs of physical ailments, but believe their symptoms are brought on by the state of our mental health. Anxiety, depression and feelings of fear are killing our world. When we cure the mind, we will cure the body. Understanding how the mind controls the body is the start to healing, we must learn to remain calm during these emotional storms life throws our way. Without hope for change, all we are left with is despair and lost dreams!

There is a great need to release all the toxic thoughts in our minds on a daily basis. Holding on to these negative thoughts will cloud your mind and create a destructive cycle; leading to breakdowns of the mind and body.

By learning to control your thoughts rather than letting your thoughts control you, the connection between the mind and body will once again be in harmony.

It is my hope that you take the time to review the time you are given on this Earth and ask yourself, "Did I dream big, did I follow my dreams and passions and leave the world a better place than I found it?"

Embracing change is all about a dream I have for future generations of our world to embrace positive change and carry the torch of humanity into a future that will create a world where everyone matters.

We all need people in our lives that we can believe in; men and women we can model ourselves after. We need people whom we can trust to tell us the truth about things we need to hear and learn, while encouraging us to think big thoughts and to have big dreams. In turn our lives will reflect those dreams and hopes we were put on this Earth to discover.

What is the secret to life? Is it to take a moment to reflect on the things you have done and then ask yourself "Did I make a difference?" Showing compassion and empathy towards others will never diminish your self-worth; it will only increase it. Every day we are given opportunities to positively impact the lives of those we touch along life's journey. Life is an incredible opportunity to change the world through kindness and to use our creative thinking that will lead to a better world. It is in our thoughts that our dreams are created. Our hope for the future of mankind can become a reality. So don't avoid the future, embrace your future.

"Putting off an opportunity that is presented to you today, thinking it can wait until tomorrow causes more regrets and heartache then you could ever imagine. We have a choice when opportunity comes knocking at our door, we can seize the moment or we can simply ignore the signs. Life is about taking a leap of faith knowing there will be someone there to catch you when you jump"

"Measure a person, not by what they have done for themselves, but by what they have done for others"

Stephen A Vigiano

To my friend and mentor
Irwin Pfeffer
"Thank you"

The following quote gives my life meaning

The Gift

"*It has taken me a lifetime to understand the simple life lessons taught by the greatest thinkers throughout the history of our world. The constant theme was how our thinking affects our outcomes in life. Each day when we awaken we are given three options of thought that could determine the meaning of our lives. These options are the past, the present and the future. Our yesterday's are gone forever, today is all we have because tomorrow may never arrive. Most of what we fear and worry about resides in our tomorrow's. This to me is what causes so much anxiety and stress in our world. Then there is today, if we open the gift that is today and live in the present moment, we will bring more hope, joy and meaning to our lives. Today is a gift that so many of us never open*"

Stephen A Vigiano

FOREWORD

By
Troy Vigiano

My father has written many messages to future generations, but this books main message is to inspire millennials, Gen Z, and all future generations to take back our power from the status quo, the wealthy elite class of our society. We cannot wait any longer to take back our world from those people in power who continue to destroy our planet and ruin the lives of so many members of our society and especially our generation, where so many of us are burdened with debt and a future world filled with doubt and uncertainty. All this is being done while these elite members of this nation simultaneously are lining their pockets from that collective misery that is produced by unfettered corporate influence. It is my hope that this book's message will inspire younger generations to correct the mistakes of our ancestors and create a nation that truly cares about the equality for all of its people and the re-establishment of human kindness and empathy as the main driver of human innovation.

The destruction of our planet has been an ongoing problem since humans began congregating en masse, but did not turn to catastrophic levels until the forefathers of capitalism (the industrialists), who were also large proprietors of wage slaves, began producing mass quantities of products. Mass production from the past 400 years has caused pollution to rise immensely and the damage that comes with it have been amplified because of so many centuries of un-regulated corporate greed and their compounding effects on the environment. The wealthy individuals and corporations do not care that they are slowly killing the planet because they know that they will be long gone by the time climate change becomes a life threatening issue.

Why do we continue to put faith in the status quo to fix the world's problems, when they are knowledgeable of what has been happening and they still choose to do nothing? We are already living in the next great extinction and it is largely in part to climate change being accelerated by this same corporate greed that has been destroying peoples' lives for profits for centuries. The Earths plant ecosystem has lost over 90 % of all of our known species and we have lost up to 70% of Earths known vertebrae mammals in the past century alone. The planet we call home is dying. We have to stand up and fight for what is right. It's up to us and future generations to stop this madness from continuing and from ever happening again.

My father's book is meant to be a guide in leading us to this perspective and to show that despite the odds, we cannot give in to our fears of the current status quo. We must conquer these fears and use our collective strength to unify our nation and put an end to this imbalance of wealth and power. We must focus on the true problems that are destroying this country: such as a stagnate unlivable minimum wage, corporate influence in our lives, our world being destroyed for profits, the ascending level of homeless individuals, and the lack of opportunity for current and future generations to safely start their own families or even feel comfortable to live on their own without financial assistance.

My father's wisdom that is written in this book is about inspiring us to overcome the many obstacles and challenges we are currently facing; he is giving us a roadmap on how we can change this nation and move the world safely into the 21st century. We are now the largest generation in the United States of America and we can no longer stand by and watch this nation and the world crumble before our very eyes. The time to take action is now.

"Millennials, Your Time Has Come" is a call to action; to redirect our energies in positive ways that will bring this nation out of the grips of poverty and ignorance that has held it back for the past 400 years. The new movement will be focused on the true meaning of "Life, Liberty and the pursuit of Happiness". We will no longer be dominated

by the few who feel it is their birthright to hold us in the bondages that they themselves have created for the people of this nation.

When we understand that we have the *"Power"* to do this, it is then that we will change the course of history and give our generation and future generations a chance to not only survive, but for the first time in this nations short history the opportunity to thrive and succeed.

Troy Vigiano

TABLE OF CONTENTS

A special thank you to my daughter Kylie Kelley for doing such a wonderful job with the final edits to this book you are about to read!

Chapter One

WHEN WE CHANGE OUR THINKING WE WILL CHANGE THE WORLD

WHAT WILL THE future look like for our children and grandchildren? Will it be a world filled with hope that gives them the opportunity to realize their dreams and what they are passionate about? Or will it be a world driven by the mistakes of past generations? Will we continue down this road of the self-destruction of our planet or will we get our thinking right and make positive changes to the world we live in for future generations?

The only way to change our view of the world is to change the way we see the world; we can no longer live in a time tunnel from the past that has carried over to the present. Living in the past is what impedes the future.

Future generations should not be guided by the thinking of past generations. It is the thoughts and actions of this current generation in power that has removed so much hope for the future generations of mankind, they deserve so much more than what they are about to receive from the current generation in power.

When will we change our thinking? When will we see the world through the eyes of love? It takes no effort at all to be hateful and thoughtless. It takes great courage to be kind, considerate and to show compassion and empathy towards everyone who comes into your life. To be self-ish or to be selfless, that is the question that really must be answered by current and future generations. When we change the world to reflect a more selfless and thought-ful generation of future Americans, we will create a world based on equality, one where no person is more important than any other human being on planet Earth.

This morning I asked my sons who are both millennials and college graduates this question. If you could change one thing in our world, what would it be and why would you like to see it change? It took a while for them to re-spond to this thought provoking question as it dawned on me that there is no simple answer and that the answers would vary based on their life experiences and their view of the world and what the future could look like if the changes they dreamed of could become a reality. My Son Troy, 24, who is two months shy of being an official millennial is very passionate about the human conditions we live in and the imbalance of wealth in this nation. Here is what he told me.

"I would change how this world demands so much from the common people. People work 60 hour plus work weeks just to get by while there are only a small percentage of people who barely have to lift a finger. The rest of society chugs along doing hard labor just so the rich and powerful can continue to live their multimillion dollar lifestyles.

I want everyone to have the same equal opportunities that I was led to believe was reality. Eliminating poverty and limitless greed from our society would be my dream for the future of mankind".

My son Troy graduated with a degree in social sciences from St. Mary's College in the San Francisco Bay area. He is passionate about equal rights for all of the citizens of this country and the world.

My other son Evan who is 28 and is a graduate from the University of San Francisco in the Bay area agrees with his younger brother Troy but adds his own thoughts on what changes he feels the country needs in order to progress beyond its current limitations and limiting beliefs we have lived by for centuries.

"I think I would have to agree with Troy on the wealth gap being one of the biggest problems in our country and the world. I would like to see more equal opportunities for those who are less fortunate and financial education. Understanding the importance of investing/saving are things people with money have the luxury to teach their kids that others don't. Most of my generation will be in debt half their lives with student loans and their mortgages, that is if their fortunate enough to get a loan for a down payment on a home.

I would also say our education system needs a major overhaul, not only because of the debt burden, but just everything from American history curriculum to making kids take the same classes through high school.

Someone who struggles in math and has a creative mind shouldn't be forced to pass AP Calculus just to be able to get into the college they want to attend. Our education system should be tailored to help kids understand the real world they are about to enter and who they want to be as a member of society".

My son Evan graduated with a degree in business management and just like his brother Troy knows that as a society we can and must do better for the future generations of this world. They both feel that it is up to their generation to change the direction we are heading towards.

I have often said that my generation, the baby boomers,

are the generation of *ME* and *I*, that we sailed the ship that I call the "USS Humanity" towards the setting Sun, a place filled with empty promises and regrets from a generation who took advantage of this planet and quite possibly put us all on a path to destroying our planet.

Finally, I posed the same question to my daughter Kylie who is 32 and has three young children knowing that her viewpoint may be different than her two younger brothers. This was her reply: "It's not just one thing. It starts at home and teaching our kids how to treat everyone with kindness and fairness. On another scope, I think your first book helped me to realize that not every person questions what goes on in politics. I think it's every Americans responsibility to care".

It is my faith in my children's generation, the millennials, who now number 72.1 million citizens of this nation (and as of July 1st 2019 are now the largest generation in America) will soon become the new captains of this ship.

They will sail it towards the rising sun; where each new sunrise brings hope for the changes this country needs and restores our faith in humanity.

My generation abused this planet and suppressed the majority of the people who live and work in the United States of America. Greed seemed to be the driving force in my generation that was and still is in power.

With greed comes compromise and with compromise you lose the most precious character trait to being a human being; you lose your integrity. It's a part of your DNA whether you realize it or not and once you compromise it for money and status as a politician or leader of society you have turned your back on the people you serve and the country you once believed in.

With change comes a new beginning for our country, positive change will lead us out of the darkness that now clouds our judgment and reasoning minds.

To change the world we must first change the way we think and view society. The present view is through a lens that has somehow distorted the truth and is based on falsehoods from leaders who have lost all semblance of reality.

How could this happen in America? Who's to blame for the downfall and destruction of the planet and the truth that is being covered up with so many false beliefs from leaders who forgot who elected them and who no longer serve the hard working people of this country. Instead they seem to now be serving a cult that has been tucked away in the closet since the beginning of this nation.

They are straying away from the Constitution that they took an oath to uphold and they have lied to the American people when they swore to defend the Constitution with their right hand on the Bible.

It seems to me that the oath these representatives took is no longer serving the best interest of the people. It has become an oath to an ideal that is moving us away from a democratic society to one of authoritarian rule.

When I see what direction our world is going in I often say a little prayer to remind me that there are things I can change and things that are out of my control. The key to this prayer is understanding the difference between the two. We so often waste our time and energy on the things we cannot change and do very little about the things we have control over.

I believe we must focus more on what we can change and let go of the things that our out of our control. Believe it or not, we the people of this country have so much more power then we think we have. Elected officials in the Congress, the Senate and our Presidential leaders think we don't see how they conduct themselves and if they are truly serving us or if they are only serving themselves. Well I am here to tell the people of the United States of America this is something that is within our control, although the leaders of our country would have us believe and think that they control us, when in reality we are the ones in control.

We have the one thing they need to survive in this political quicksand. We have the freedom to choose who we put in office, we have the power to change the political landscape of America it's called, "The Vote".

Although the current leaders want you to think that your vote doesn't count and that you are powerless to change this nation into one that we all will be proud to live and work in, they will do their very best to suppress our right to vote and make it difficult to find the time to cast our ballots. Why do you think that is? Could it be that since the beginning of this great nation that was the plan all along? With the objective to control the direction of the United States of America for the purpose of those in power and those who maintained the highest levels of wealth in our country.

I believe that every time the people of this land who suffer from suppression, racism and never being given the same opportunities that the higher earning select few had, those in power tried to control the narrative by feeding us small amounts of hope that things would change and that our lives would somehow get better.

Then after the dust had settled, we would be taken by these leaders back to where we started. They managed to squelch the fire, to put down the rebellion of thousands of Americans who peacefully protested the inequity and injustices that they have had to endure since the first day the British Commonwealth set up shop in this country.

For a nation that is barely 400 years in the making, we have made great strides in technology and turning grassland and open spaces into giant cities and concrete towers, but we have failed miserably to grow the human spirit of those who have lived in a world that kept most people in this country in the bondage of hatred, violence and being held back.

We talk about human rights being the fabric of our nation, it is written into the Constitution and the Declaration of Independence. Since when was the pursuit of happiness only reserved for the top percentage of privledged citizens in this country? Why have we not lived up to the meaning of these sacred documents? Perhaps it is because nobody reads them anymore, especially those with whom we elect to serve our country in what is supposed to be in the best interest of the people. What happened to that catch phrase "We the People" in these documents? It now should read "Us in Power".

Can we change this warped and outdated way of running this country? If so, when will we do it? We have many leaders in our government who are in their 60's, 70's and 80's, baby boomers who have been in these positions of power for decades. I would like to know the genius who decided that a President can only serve two terms but a Senator or Congressman can serve for decades.

Does anyone realize that so many of these lifetime politicians who have served this country for two, three, or even four decades may have become complacent and only care about the title, money and power the office brings to them? What if they see the world they live in now, the 21st century, as they did the world they grew up in back in the sixties?

This book is about changing the way we see the world; to evolve with this ever changing planet and society we live in. We can't operate our lives and this country from a place that no longer exists and no longer serves the wellbeing of mankind. That place is from the distant past decades ago, perhaps even from centuries ago. What has really changed in the way this country is run? We have lived through the Civil War, the Spanish Flu, World War I and World War II, the Korean War, the War in Vietnam and countless wars since then.

We have lived through a once in a lifetime pandemic in the 21st century which we ignored in the beginning, hoping it would just miraculously disappear and has killed millions of innocent people on our planet. Over the last hundred years we have polluted this planet and created nuclear weapons that puts us on the brink of extinction.

For What? What purpose have the above things been done for? To advance mankind into the future or to slowly destroy everything that is good and right about being a human being? As I said we must change the way we do things in order to change the way we will shape the future of this country and the world. Let's look at the alternative to change which is simply doing nothing, watching the world as we know it being slowly destroyed before our very eyes. The problem is to the naked eye which most of us see through; climate change is invisible.

Even when the scientists show documented proof that our world is changing and that it may be uninhabitable within the next century, people of great ignorance refuse to face the facts and in many cases those people are the ones who wield great power in this corrupt political system that has been in place since the beginning of this nation.

It seems to me and many people of integrity and compassion in this country, that if we allow those in power to go down this self-destructive path, then we have no one to blame but ourselves. We the people have the power of the vote to remove those political figures who serve only themselves and somehow forgot who elected them. We must take back our power from these bad actors and recast the political landscape of America to reflect the people it was originally designed to serve!

Never again will we be fooled into thinking that several hundred men and women in the congress and the senate have eminent domain over the rest of us. They are a product of the wealthy cowards, the one percent that buy their way into taking control of the political landscape of this country. The time has come to rethink the structure of modern American politics that is still operating out of a system that was created in 1776 by a select group of men from Great Britain who came over to create the United States of America in their image. It is apparent how little has changed over the past 246 years.

Chapter Two

THE FUTURE WILL BE DRIVEN BY CHANGE

THE FOUNDATION OF change is the belief that you have the power to change things and the faith to believe in what has yet to come. Faith is the fuel that ignites the flames of optimism. Although faith may not be seen to the naked eye it is a belief that can be seen in our imaginations.

We have the power to heal ourselves and to heal the world. That power lies in the part of our mind that many of us seldom use. The experts say that as human beings we only use a small percentage of the human brain, about 10 percent of the brains capabilities. Well, it seems to me that when we are able to figure out a way to tap into the unused potential of that 90 percent of our brain, it is then that we will begin to change and transform the world. That change will lead to a world that will cure disease, course correct our planet and climate change, feed every child and adult on this planet and put pure drinking water in every household on Earth with a goal of ending poverty and ignorance on this planet.

With these changes that our untapped mind will create and manifest in the world will come a renewed faith that mankind can change and transform this planet. With a new beginning that will once and for all put the past mistakes of our ancestors behind us, a distant memory of how things used to be. We will create our own new memories of what the world's true potential could be. It is time to change the course of humanity and right our past wrongs to reshape our future destiny!

We are all given gifts we are born with. How do we discover these natural gifts and talents, how do we nurture them? How do we apply them to find fulfillment in our lives? Can we be like the caterpillar that morphs into something as beautiful as a butterfly?

Of course we can, if we understand how powerful our minds are when it comes to creating our own destiny. By nurturing these gifts we are born with we can uncover the secret to success and bring more joy to our lives. These gifts allow us to grow both mentally and spiritually as human beings. We expand our life's "Toolkit" and keep on adding to it as we pursue our personal journey towards growth and reaching our true potential.

Our life's journey is a never ending one filled with triumphs and failures. In my view there really are no failures in life; these are simply opportunities for growth and uncovering the gifts you were born with. We can use these gifts, talents and our innate will to overcome any challenges or obstacles that life throws our way.

There is nothing more satisfying then turning one of life's perceived failures into a major success. We have it within ourselves to break through the noise, to persevere and use our minds and the gifts we were born with to triumph over all odds no matter how difficult the challenge may seem to you.

The only way you will lose the battle is if you give up. The sad thing is so many of us give up just before we make a major breakthrough that would take us to victory over that monumental challenge that we have faced.

Always remember that giving up is a choice. It takes no courage or fortitude to give up; it takes great courage and a strong will to keep on going until you have overcome any difficulties you will face in this lifetime. Believe it or not, you are stronger then you think, we are all equipped with the gifts and guts to overcome everything that life can throw our way! Never give up and never give in to a perceived weakness. Any weakness can be turned into a strength if you believe in yourself and your ability to learn and grow throughout your lifetime.

As I said, the growth of any human being is in how they map out the journey. The journey is not a straight line from birth to death, it is the lifeline that tells our story that resides between those two dates.

We have a birth date, a journey in the middle and an ending date, the day we die.

The journey tells the story of our lives, not only to ourselves but to the rest of the world. How do you want to be remembered? Did you fulfill your potential, did you open the gifts you were given at birth that would show the world your magnificence?

We seldom think about our lives in the sense that we will all leave behind a legacy, our life story. We may get to the end of our life's journey and look in the mirror for one last time and ask ourselves this: Did my life have meaning? What did I stand for and did I make a difference in the world and in the lives of those I had the privledege to touch?

Wow, what a dramatic way of thinking about our lives in terms of the ups and downs, the good times and the bad times. That life certainly does not look like a straight line does it. That means to me that our lifeline is not a straight line either when you really think about it. That lifeline represents the beginning point of our lives all the way to the end point of our existence. I don't think anyone on this earth has or will ever live a life that is in a monotone straight line. It is our destiny to have many life experiences that will be highs and lows. I believe as we open up our natural born gifts and realize our full potential the highs will overshadow the lows and our path to living a life of purpose and dream fulfillment will lead us to our final destination.

Today is a gift we must open and explore, it is not in our yesterdays that we will find happiness and it is not in the undiscovered tomorrows that we will find fulfillment. It is only in today where we will find the God given gifts that will lead us into tomorrow, which when discovered will ultimately change the world!

We all have these gifts within us, but you must reach for them in order to discover them. Let them take us to wherever we want to go. Instead of saying *NO*, we simply say *YES* and hold the belief that we can make it happen.

The story of your life is locked in all of this! Unlock your story and you will find the meaning of your life!

When we fail to progress or to keep moving forward through positive change, we as a society have doomed ourselves to failure. Life on this planet has been a series of continuous change and evolving to where we are now. Without change we as a species would still be where we started, when man first stepped foot on this planet, living in caves.

To me, life is about leaving a legacy. It's about how much you have given and how little you have taken. When we give of ourselves with no thought of what is in it for us, we enrich our own lives so much more then we realize. In doing so we make the world we live in a better place.

Can you imagine if we all had a sense of giving and not taking? What would that world look like? How would that change the imbalance we now see in this country? We would leave the world better than we found it, it's that simple.

I believe that a shift like that in our thinking could change the course of human history. We live in a world where we have lost sight of the simple life lessons we were taught as children: kindness towards others, compassion and empathy towards the world and everything that lives and breathes on Earth.

My son Troy and I were discussing the state of our country and he pointed out that as a nation, people need to strengthen their critical thinking skills and be able to recognize the gravity of all the bad things happening in this country and around the world! Just because something isn't happening to us or is not affecting us doesn't mean it shouldn't matter! Our society in general has rewarded the wealthy people of this country. It's been proven through academic studies that high paying CEO's and executive positions are filled by the more sociopathic people in society. Their traits which are deemed socially detrimental are regarded as top leadership credentials because society has long been about bottom line profits. These type of people thrive on capitalist cultures that demand inhumane levels of personal sacrifice because they care more about their image and reputation then they care about other people and relationships. They have been rewarded for their selfish behavior for decades. History has proven they will not change. We have to hold them accountable and to a higher standard if we wish to see positive change in our society. It's like the kid in school who always cheats on all his exams and never gets caught. He's never experienced the feeling of being exposed for his lack of morals and ethics and how his achievements are not really his own. So why would he ever stop cheating? The answer is he won't, not until people like that are held accountable for their actions.

That is what the elite one percent are, a bunch of spoiled kids with no real understanding of the people and societies that surround them. They don't understand the suffering they cause and they don't care because they are like spoiled brats. Selfish, until they've been taught why what they are doing is wrong and how their actions are affecting others. It's basic human decency that should be almost as applicable as common sense. Unfortunaly, not for these people.

"Most children are more socially aware then the 1%, who dominate our country, we must hold these rich and powerful people accountable, and we will!"

Troy Vigiano

What a powerful statement from a 24 year old young man who sees the world as it is, not as so many of us in this country have created in their minds that has no resemblance to the real world we live in. How did we, the United States become the Divided States of America? That is the biggest question facing our country in the early part of the 21st century.

It seems that the two party system that was designed by our government to balance out the decisions that affect this nation have gone off the rails. They seem to have been overtaken by the massive amount of ego driven individuals who forgot the oath they swore on a Bible when they took office. I can honestly say that I do not recognize the government anymore; it seems to have lost its way to power and greed. This to me is a reality check for everyone who lives in what was once called a democracy. How soon we have forgotten that the United States of America was formed so that its citizens could break away from the tyranny of Great Britain that was ruled by a King. We created a new world as it has been described in the history books where we could live in the freedoms of democracy. But are we really free? I believe if we go back and examine our short history we will discover so many periods in time where the cruelty and injustices that so many of our citizens had to endure was not in the best interest of all who lived here. It seemed to favor only a small majority of those privledged men who set out to build what is now known as the United States of America.

What was the original purpose of the early settlers of this country? It seemed to me that the wealth imbalance in the country started the day they landed their ships in this new world and took their first steps on North American soil. There seems to be a pattern that was carried over from Great Britain that they wanted to get out from under. It was a pattern of a tiered system of government.

Yes, there has always been a pattern in our world where we have lived in a tiered system that holds people back and suppresses them to live their lives in favor of the wealthy and bounds the poor in chains that are not of their own making.

Go back in history to the Roman Empire and you had rulers at the top a "Cesar" and human slaves at the bottom along with so many different levels of wealth and power in between these two tiers of existence. What has changed since the days when a man who once walked this earth preaching about love and the brotherhood of man, Jesus Christ, who to this day is the most revered person who ever graced this planet? In my eyes, not much. Fast forward though history and tell me what you see? There has always been a pattern throughout the world where there are those at the bottom, which seemed to be the masses who do the bulk of the labor in the world, those in the middle who do the bidding of those at the top who run the world with such titles as King, President or as so many leaders of the world we will simply call Dictators or Tyrants.

That is why anyone who looks at the past to determine the future of our civilization must realize that men like Hitler and Stalin from WWII (who for a brief moment in history threatened the balance of power in the free world with the threat of world dominance) did not survive. Throughout the history of the world these tyrants and those who have come before them have destroyed themselves because of their own vanity and unhinged minds that stood for everything that was wrong with being human. Their lust for power and dominance over the world was what led to their downfall. These men who would take away our rights and freedoms may have been put in power as a reminder of what we detest most about being human, demons from the dark side of humanity put there to wake us up out of the coma of complacency that we seem to have fallen into as a nation.

How does this great nation that our founding fathers described in the Declaration of Independence or the Constitution of the United States of America compare now in the 21st century, to the past British Empire that was ruled by a King? I will give you my perspective on that question: not much in the ways of human dignity. As a society based on technology we have made great strides, but as a society based on human rights we are not that much better than the King of Great Britain which we fought to free ourselves from.

The system of government is broken. I beg to ask this question, when was our system of government ever not broken? We have been fighting amongst ourselves since the beginning of time and it has carried over to the birth of a nation known as the United States of America. Who gave the privledged white man the right to place others into bondage and slavery? Who had the right to say who could prosper and who should live a life with no hope for advancement towards the direction of their hopes and dreams? Who has the right to tell you how to live your life in what is supposed to be a free society? In this imbalanced world we now live in, no one should have that right and no one (including our government) should have the power to destroy a human beings right to a better life for themselves and the people they love.

This is my argument for *CHANGE* in our world and especially in this country. We are heading on a collision course that could end all human life on this planet. We are a nation that just seems to be unable to do what is in the best interest of its people.

We are a nation that has lost its way to greed and corruption. If the two party system doesn't work then why do we keep doing what we are doing that has never served the majority of the people in this country and only works for the few who seem to think, "If it's not broken then why would we want to fix it?". That to me is the true definition of insanity.

Now comes the big question, how do we move forward with a country that is on the brink of a cultural and quite possibly a political revolution? Are we heading back to the beginning of this countries existence where we will no longer have a President, but will have a King and his Parliament to rule over the land?

There would no longer be a need for a President. We would be taken back to a time where the leader of the United States of America calls them self "A King". An authoritarian ruler with total power over its people, who puts us in a system that strips every American of their human rights and civil liberties!

Prisons will become dungeons, the White House will become a castle with a moat around it and a drawbridge that only allows a select few in for an audience with the King and his Court. I know this all sounds like a fantasy that I've created in what many would believe to be an over stimulated imagination. After watching the regressions in this country and the movement that is taking place to suppress the majority of the hard working people of this nation by both verbal and non-verbal threats from the leaders of our society, I don't think I'm that far out of line.

Change is the basic component for the evolution of the world and all life on this planet. When we look back over the history of the world what has really changed besides the modern movement to technology and the destruction of our planet? Let's look at the evolution of mankind, since the beginning there were the strong and then there was the weak among us. The strong became the leaders and the weak became subservient to the leaders. Tell me, how much has that changed over the past 2022 years since the death of Jesus Christ?

I still see a world where the rich and powerful members of society rule and the suppressed people of the world remain under the guiding hands of those in power. As far as human dignity goes, have we really advanced the human condition from the Roman Empire to the current world we live in? We are living in a world where the leader of the free world once told a foreign dictator "my button is bigger than yours". Has this world come down to which country has the most nuclear weapons and who will be the first to press the Big Red Button?

That again is an example of just how far we haven't come as a society and the ignorance of the human race. The word humane has no relation to the word human. I know, they are two different words with two different meanings, but think about how much better the world would be at solving our problems if our leaders and their people looked at the world through the eyes of being more humane. The word humane in Webster dictionary means, having or showing compassion or benevolence. The formal meaning is even better, intended to have a civilized or refining effect on people.

We are given a great opportunity every single day of our lives and that is to positively impact the lives of the people we meet. We all have a responsibility to leave the world a better place. It takes hard work and courage to make a difference; it takes very little effort on one's part to be selfish and show your cowardice to the world around you. It seems to me that it is the ordinary people of this planet who show the most courage and have to overcome so many things that are not in their favor. In turn, they must conform to leaders who in many cases represent the worst human qualities of the world!

It also shows how the people of this country who occupy the ivory towers of society show a lack of moral conscience and a great deal of self-importance which in my mind shows a complete lack of intestinal fortitude "Courage". It's so easy to act tough when you are in a position of power, which takes no spine at all.

But when you are living in poverty and life keeps on

beating you down at every turn and you show up every day with the courage to go on, that is the true essence of a human being and represents the best qualities in all of us.

I so admire the people of this great nation who fight for what they believe in and always look to do the right thing, regardless of the consequences. Then there are the so called "Leaders" of this country who hide behind a glass tower that is ready to crumble beneath their very feet. They walk the sacred halls of Congress with great bravado with their egos and ignorance on full display. The problem is, they are like driving in rush hour traffic stuck in a gridlock of their own making.

They talk the big talk, but unfortunately they forget how to put one foot in front of the other to walk a fine line of significance, doing things that actually benefit the people who elected them. We must rethink our future so we can realize that we as a nation haven't progressed much in a humanitarian way. Yes, we have changed the landscape of this nation cosmetically, but human injustice is as bad today as it was during the Civil War. It has simply been masked over now because those who still live in a world powered by violence, hatred and injustice are still the ones in power who do their best to create civil unrest in this nation.

I am afraid it may be too late for my generation, the boomers, to right the wrongs of the last 246 years. It will be up to future generations who soon will be in power to change the destiny of the United States. Millennials will be confronted with this monumental task of changing our world and asked to bring back the balance of humanity for the first time in our country's history. Our country has masked over its fatal flaws with lies, deceit and putting a band aid over the open wounds that the leaders of this nation have inflicted on its people. It is now time to unearth the tragedy of American politics and our history of inequities so we can finally let the healing of our nation begin!

I listen to my sons Troy and Evan because they are both millennials and they both see the future of our world quite a bit differently then it currently is. I believe it will be their generation's destiny to reshape this country which will be the catalyst that reshapes the world.

The founding fathers spoke of a perfect union when they referred to this country. In my view and in the view of my son's, we are far from being a perfect union. I believe in the future generations of this nation and see us forming a perfect union to reflect a new society, one based on human dignity and elevating the human condition to one of equality through social justice reform. The one emotion that seems to be holding us back is the fear of changing long standing beliefs that have been passed down from prior generations. These fears can become our reality if we think about them long enough. The truth is, what we think about we bring about. How could it be otherwise?

The society we live in today is a photograph of the painted pictures from the minds of past generations.

The only way to alter our society is to change the current picture we have painted that displays this imbalanced top down country and world we currently adhere to and live in. Every chapter in history that contained dramatic changes in the world was led by a movement that was so strong that no power on Earth could hold it back. We have seen throughout history that movements based on violence are done for all the wrong reasons, but movements done by fighting for a cause that is right and just, that's bigger than all of humanity is worth fighting for.

The sanctity of human life and human rights is worth fighting for and in some cases worth dying for. The past few years of this country's history are proof that we have not progressed in human rights as far as the leaders of our nation would like us to believe.

The past several years have simply ripped off the giant band aid that was covering up the mistakes that were made to downplay human rights and the wounds inflicted by the suppression of the hard working people of color in America. It was by those whom we elected to do the exact opposite, whose job it was to create a world where everyone, regardless of the color of their skin, gender or religious beliefs were given the same opportunity to wealth and happiness that the top one percent were given. It is time that this pyramid of wealth be turned upside down so the few at the top can now see the world through the eyes of the hundreds of millions of people it has held captive in a prison of poverty. A world they created by taking away our rights to freedom and the pursuit of happiness we were all promised. I don't think they would survive for long if they were subjected to a life of poverty. They have lost sight of doing an honest day's work. Could you imagine them getting a blister on their manicured hands from manual labor?

Their ego driven desires to control the world and the minds of those of us who live under their self-serving ideologies will soon come to an end. These leaders cling onto their human frailties, they have a fear of failure not only of themselves, but of those around them that they put in positions of authority.

This may come down to the failure of our educational system in this country; an educational system that has failed to produce human beings who can think for themselves. The whole purpose of getting an education is to expand the mind to a state of independent growth and give the individual a new way of thinking for themselves that is independent from the constant brainwashing that is forced upon us by the leaders of society.

By becoming educated and being able to think and act for ourselves we take control of our lives and can set a new course for expansion that is independent from what our government and society thinks our life's journey should be. When we become acquainted with the powers that our minds possess and nurture that power we will become independent and creative thinkers. We can now be capable of solving complex personal problems as well as problems that have plagued mankind for centuries. When we get our thinking right we will get our lives right which in turn will get the world we live in on a path to enlightenment; something we will all have a hand in creating.

Chapter Three

HOW FAR HAVE WE REALLY COME?

WE LIVE IN a world that is on edge, a world that seems to be rather lopsided and out of balance. Why is it that throughout the history of the world there seems to be an organizational chart for humanity? Going back thousands of years you will see a world that had Rulers who would sit on a throne and wave their hand to those who served them. This was the highest form of suppression in history, the chosen few lived in a kingdom or a palace while the masses lived in slavery. Those who labored for these rulers often died from lack of food and water, but many died from the physical abuse of the manual labor they were forced to perform for these cowards who disguised themselves as Kings.

Now, let's move to more modern times. The 21st century has arrived and we still see similar patterns of suppression in the world and here in the United States of America. Many citizens were led to believe that this nation was one of prosperity with such words as life, liberty and the pursuit of happiness for all of its people.

Looking back at our short history, I fail to see that those who wrote the Declaration of Independence really understood how those words of freedom and liberty were not written for so many people of this country who were considered different because of the color of their skin or the language they spoke.

What were they afraid of? Why did these early leaders hold back everyday people who had every right to the pursuit of happiness that they wrote about in these documents that would shape this nation?

I believe it was their own insecurities and fears that one day they would be in the minority and the common man, woman and child who did not look like them would someday make up the majority of the citizens of the United States of America. They did their best to suppress and hold them down through the eyes of prejudice, hatred, and slavery.

We are now in a crisis for the identity of a nation that has been in denial ever since it broke away from the tyranny of King James of Great Britain.

Are we truly a democratic society as we move into the early part of the 21st century, or are we a democracy disguised as the very thing we fought against back in the early part of this country's history when we were 13 colonies trying to create a new life, free from the tyranny of British rule?

It seems that our newly formed government back in the days of the Declaration of Independence was really geared for the select few in power and that creating a president to lead this new nation was very similar to the very world they fought to be free from. Did we go from a King to a President and just change the rules of governing the people, where those in power could craft the new laws and rules that the citizens of this new world had to adhere to and had no say in?

And did these new laws that were created apply to everyone or just to the people who built this country with slave labor and the removal of human rights?

Did the leaders of the newly formed free world have exempt status from the laws and rules that the masses had to conform to? Now that I look back over our history, how far have we really come as a society? We have made great advances in technology, but we have made little progression in what will be vital to our future, EQ Emotional Quotient, otherwise known as emotional intelligence. It is an amazing statistic that many of the leaders of this country and CEO's of major corporations have very low levels of emotional intelligence and that the studies find more midlevel managers have a much higher level of EQ.

It also shows that just because someone has a high IQ it does not mean that their higher level of intelligence comes with a higher level of EQ based on compassion, empathy and an understanding of the human conditions we live in.

Why is it that we see so many leaders of this country say one thing one day and then make a 90 degree turn in their thinking a day later? Does being a politician in office become a game of changing your mind so you can get enough votes to stay in power? Even if it means compromising your integrity and disavowing the oath of office you took in order to save your political career at all costs?

Why then did you swear your allegiance to the Constitution of the United States of America on a Bible? Have they ever thought about the consequences of their actions in relationship to those they were elected to serve; or the inactions they took when it came time to uphold their end of the bargain?

So my question to those in power and those who seek to remain in power in this great nation is this: How far have we come from the beginning in regards to the words which may ring hollow now, that we all have the right to life, liberty and the pursuit of happiness?

Do we *ALL* have that right or has it been taken away from

the majority of the people of this country? The wealth disparity in the United States of America is appalling. If we are the one nation that all other countries look to for guidance and leading the way to equality and freedom, what message are we really sending to the world? We will never send the right message until we rewrite the message to reflect a new America based on the equality of all of its citizens.

I believe the next great generation, one of the largest generations in the history of this country, will rewrite the message. They are young, they are the most diverse generation in the history of the United States of America and they are called by one name, millennials (of which I am so proud to be the father of three.) This is a new generation that will change the landscape of humanity. They will think of things that are far outside of the comfort zones of the current leaders of this nation. They are not happy with this imbalanced tower of humanity where the one percent have it all and the rest have to struggle just to feed their families and put a roof over their heads. The idea that we can create a more level playing field to overcome the inequity of this wealth gap that has been a part of our society since the beginning of time can and will be done by these young Americans who do not see the need to suppress the lives of others. It's called freedom.

I would be curious to see what millennials think about the political structure of this nation and what they would do to change things.

I believe they are not too happy with its current structure and the segregated roadmap that our politicians have gone down over the past 246 years. They have witnessed the same things that have held back this country from realizing its full potential since the time they could comprehend what was going on in the world.

What have they witnessed over their lifetimes? What examples of democracy and human dignity have they observed from the current generation in power? To think that an entire generation feels betrayed by elected officials in this country who have failed to live up to the oath they took to uphold the Constitution.

When I speak to my sons' Evan and Troy their biggest concerns are "How can I make a life for myself and raise a family when I have thousands of dollars in student debt and may not even qualify for a home loan?"

It almost sounds like going to college to further your education is a financial burden that many of these bright young Americans can't get out from under.

That to me is one of the most counterproductive aspects of living in this country.

I once asked my oldest son Evan to research what the average reading level was in this country and he came back with this startling news. The average reading level in the United States of America was that of a sixth grader according to the Literacy Project. It also shows that the majority of Americans stop reading after the age of eighteen. The only things they read are the books and reports they have to learn from in order to get a passing grade in school or to complete a project at work.

I ask myself this question all the time, is lifelong learning only relegated to the field of employment we are in or should it be about more than just work?

Shouldn't we take a deeper look at the one word that really represents lifelong learning? If our focus is only on our work, will we ever truly look for and find the meaning of what we are meant to learn here on Earth?

This may be why so many of us are just getting by, doing just enough at our jobs that will keep us employed. Can advancing our knowledge be the key to advancing our lives in a more meaningful way that goes beyond our careers? I have never let my career define me as a man. We are so much more than the title on a business card. We have the unlimited potential to be and do anything that we set our minds to and are willing to work hard for. I only know that hope without a plan is simply wishful thinking. I truly believe that if we have faith in an idea and then take action towards making the idea a reality, it can be the catalyst to the change we desperately are seeking in the world.

"Thoughts are fleeting but paper never forgets". What does

that have to do with what I am saying about the hopes and dreams I have for future generations? It has everything to do with setting goals and then taking the action steps that are needed to achieve your goals and dreams for a brighter future for all of your fellow citizens. A goal that is not written out is simply a flashing thought that passes through your conscious mind like a split second picture in time.

The chances of you acting on any idea that is not first written down on paper is reduced to a fleeting thought, a thought that will be lost in the winds of your vacant memory.

The first thing anyone must do to achieve their goals in life is to write them down on a piece of paper. Then stick that piece of paper on the mirror in your bathroom and on the refrigerator in your kitchen so you can be reminded of the goal several times a day. It is the repeated act of seeing your goals in writing that sets off the cybernetic mechanism in the brain that sets your goal seeking process in motion.

How can this be so? Because the three V's of action are now the dominant focus of your mind. Remember, nothing in this world was ever created without it first being conceived in the mind.

The first V is to verbalize the idea you are thinking about and writing it down on paper. The second V is to visualize the idea, to see yourself already achieving the goal.

The third V, which takes a great deal of imagination, is to vitalize your goal, by acting *"AS IF"* it has already happened. You need to see yourself already living the desired outcome of your goal.

So, what does this have to do with changing the landscape of America? How do we reshape the world and our country to reflect a world that we have envisioned, not a reflection of the world we are currently living in? A world you do not wish to inherit from the generation that is currently in power. A world with such horrible and inhumane living conditions that we are no longer willing to accept.

The current conditions of our society only reflect the thinking of past generations who have built the United States of America into the image of those in power and those who have set the rules for life in this country. Looking back over our short history I do not see how the majority of our citizens who have been made to suffer from the ideologies of those whom we elected into positions of power over the past 246 years truly reflects what we, the people they are elected to serve really desire.

I am puzzled how the state of our union has been handed over to a President, Vice President and a Congress (made up of 435 elected members) and a Senate (made up of 100 elected members) with the power to make life altering decisions for the people of this country which now numbers over three hundred and thirty one million people. We also have 9 lifetime Supreme Court Justices with the political power to change the course of this nation's history.

Those in these positions of great power will tell the people that if you do not like the way we run the country then you have the power of the *VOTE* to change the landscape and future of America. All this is done while the true motives of these people in power has always been to suppress the voting rights of its people either through voting restrictions due to the color of your skin or the origin of your sex.

(To think that Women and African Americans who lived and worked in this country were denied the right to vote back in the early part of the 20th Century and to see to this very day in the year 2022 how the right to vote in this country is still being regulated by certain political parties in the United States of America.)

When a political party continually tries to remain in power by changing voting laws and trying to control who can and cannot vote in this country, how far have we really come since the early 1900's?

When will the day come where the voice of the people of America rings loud and clear through the sacred halls of the Capitol buildings in Washington D.C.? When will those whom we elect stop their internal fighting and petty grievances long enough to change how we operate this nation and start to focus on how they can enrich the lives of those they were elected to serve?

Those boomers who are now in power are in the twilight of their political careers and whether they realize it or not in the final stages of life on planet Earth. I wonder if it has ever occurred to them that life comes with an expiration date and that date is something we are often blindsided by. We have such a short time on this Earth, but so many of us think we are immortal beings that are focused on the body and have lost sight of the eternal part of us which is our soul. Our bodies last for just so long, but our souls are eternal!

So it is my hope that my generation rethinks its current business and life model for future generations with the goal of changing what we can change before the hourglass of time has run out on us. To right the wrongs of our past that were selfish and served only those in power and wealth. To start a new process of working for the future generations of this world by changing the way we think and act towards the planet and of course towards each other.

Change is a part of the evolution of mankind and our planet. We must move this nation in a new direction, one that serves the people and no longer serves the privledged few who are in power and have set the course of history up until now. A course where "We the People" have had very little say in the direction we have gone down as a nation.

It is time for "We the People" to take back what is our natural birthright, to finally have a voice in the direction of our country's future which will ultimately reflect a new direction for the world!

Change our attitudes of mind and we will change the world! A positive mental attitude is the accumulation of our hopes, dreams, and beliefs that when you combine these three powerful emotions together we are left with *FAITH* and faith is what can motivate us all to rise up as one and change this nation's thinking!

One of the most profound actions regarding a positive mental attitude towards every situation or perceived crisis that comes our way is that every one of us has the ability of adopting a positive attitude and using it for the sole purpose of enriching our lives and the lives of others.

It is our mind that will allow us to master fear, ignorance, and poverty; the three things that the leaders of this country want us to focus our thinking on. If you think in negative terms you will bring about negative conditions in your life, if you think in positive terms your results will be positive. The mind hears phrases with such words like, I can't do it, I can't afford that and I will never be good enough. I am telling you all right now to please stop this way of thinking and use your mind to override this self-defeating negative talk that has held you back since your childhood. From this moment forward, speak to yourself only in positive terms and please respect the person you are and the person you wish to become.

I wish we could all be given a mental and emotional release from all the negative garbage that society has forced into our minds. We are a product of mind conditioning by those whom we call the leaders of modern society!

Whether we realize it or not we were all born with a natural mental filter. A filter designed by our creator to sort through the mental and emotional garbage that is shoved down our throats and placed into our conscious minds. We have the power to not allow these negative thoughts to enter our subconscious mind where they will most likely ferment and eventually take over our way of thinking.

When the falsehoods that we are subjected to on a daily basis are not filtered out through the reasoning mind, we then become the product of another human being's thinking and cult of personality. We become zombies who follow a leader or group of leaders who have brainwashed us into their way of thinking and their way of living which has no benefit for us and every benefit for them.

The problem with this is that they have all the power and they have all the money. They use their power and influence to suppress the majority of the people they are supposed to represent and lead. Why are we still living in an archaic world that believes that we have a house of representatives whose job it is to represent the people of this great nation and so called democratic society?

Those whom we elected no longer adhere to the basic fundamentals of human decency, they only do what is in their own personal best interest or what is in the best interest of their political party to remain in power at all costs.

Now comes the brainwashing of the people of this nation who have fallen prey to those in power who could care less if you have a roof over your head or can provide food and clean water for your family. They are too busy fighting over Constitutional Amendments and Bills that would move this country in a new direction where the wealth gap would be reduced and where human rights and the education of our children would be at the top of their political agenda.

Unfortunately for them, doing the right thing for the people of this nation would take great effort and sacrifice on their part. I can assure you that that is not in their political blueprint, although it should be. That is why I am convinced that once these aged politicians are retired and have passed on through history, the next generation, the millennials and generations beyond them will get it right for the first time in this nation's short history.

Why do I believe that so strongly? Because of the history of the United States of America. They will have learned from the mistakes of past generations on how not to treat this planet. They will learn from our past mistakes how not to treat the people of this nation that have always been driven by social injustice, hatred, and violence. We are the ones who got it wrong, the current generation in power. We are the ones who had tunnel vision and were blind to our own egos and reckless abandonment of morals and values. We lost our way and could never find our way back out of the darkness that we alone created!

Chapter Four

MILLENNIALS WILL
CHANGE THE WORLD

WHAT A BOLD statement to make by a man who is a part of a generation that has been steering the "ship of life" in this country towards what could possibly be the end of civilization. My generation the baby boomers may go down in the history books as the only generation to be leaving future generations less than we were given. We were given a world that was free of the hatred and senseless killings of millions of human beings by a madman named Adolf Hitler. It's hard to imagine that was less than 100 years ago. Our parents fought and defeated one of the worst human beings ever to be born in the history of mankind. So what did my generation do with this new found freedom? We became a generation of entitlement that created a new world of concrete and mortar. We polluted our waters and air all in the name of progress. I don't think we ever considered that what we were doing to this beautiful planet would negatively affect future generations. Even if we knew that what we were doing was not in the best interest of our long term health as a society, I don't think it really mattered to those in power who were making these life altering decisions. Maybe because they knew that by the time the damage was noticeable to the naked eye, they would be long gone, buried beneath a mantle of pollution they perpetrated on us. All the time knowing that we had no say in the destruction of the planet.

We have had how many years to get this thing we know as life right since the boomers took over the world? The answers will not come from my generation; it will come from the generation that will soon be taking over the United States of America, the millennials (who now number 71.2 million citizens of this nation). They will be the ones who will study history and look back over the past generations time in power and come to their own conclusions as to how the world got off track and went down a road of greed and corruption. Our flat out selfishness had no boundaries or governor to keep us in check. Was my generation really doing good things for the planet and its inhabitants or were we knowingly doing these things that would end up destroying the planet? Good question... That all depends on what we consider right and wrong. Those are two ideals that we must examine before we are to consider the future destiny of this planet and the billions of people who inhabit it.

History has a way of documenting the good things we do as human beings and also the bad things we have done as human beings. Many of them have been done by sole individuals as well as entire civilizations.

We can start at the separation of the timeline of humanity 2022 years ago where we went from BC to AD. We now live in the timeline of 2022 AD. AD means after the death of Jesus Christ.

The death of a man, who to this very day is still the most revered person who has ever walked on this planet. Jesus Christ was a simple man who spoke of love and the brotherhood of man at a time when his fellow citizens lived in the inhumane conditions of slavery, poverty, and crucifixion because of their religious beliefs.

It is my firm belief that Christ came at a time when the world was filled with hatred, violence, and a tiered system of humanity that suppressed human rights and human dignity.

He was so far ahead of his time in the simple concept of human rights and the freedoms that all men, women and children on Earth deserved. That we are all equal in the eyes of God. Christ spoke of the importance of loving your neighbor as you would love yourself, simple truths that we should all live by.

Fast forward to the 21st century. The words and actions of Jesus Christ are now being challenged by a nation that has lost its way to the politically twisted minds of a select few individuals whom we have voted into power.

Leaders who may never even have heard of Jesus Christ and his profound words of human kindness and unconditional love. Even if they did, they were not adhered to by these leaders who have betrayed their oath of office which should be based on leading from a place of kindness, compassion and trust.

Who can we trust to lead us into the unknown future? I can assure you that it will not be my generation who has led this country down a dark path of selfish greed and corruption. It will be a new generation of thinkers and doers who will lead this nation out of the dark ages and into the future.

That's right, it will be the generations of the future not the generations of the past. Millennials will change the course of history and right the wrongs of previous generations to create a world where they will want to live in and raise their children.

I believe that they will step back, take a deep breath and call a time out. They will then rethink their options on the environment, equality and the human conditions that mankind has been forced to live in since this nations inception. A world where human life was discarded if it did not fit into the plans of these leaders of past generations who used hatred and violence to maintain order.

They will, for the first time look outside of their own egos and see that there is a better way of life on this planet and that living in a tiered society with this lopsided organizational chart for humanity is not working.

They will restart the world with a level playing field where everyone has the ability to get into the game of life and be given the chance to pull themselves up and out of poverty. Finally, this nation will lift the vail of suppression and secrecy from its people and remove it for all time.

Your mind is the gatekeeper to the future, whatever your mind can conceive and believe is possible, it can bring to reality. I believe that the human mind is the last untapped resource on Earth. It is not what lies underneath the oceans and it is not going to be found on another planet in another universe.

I think the billions of dollars we are spending on space exploration is a wonderful thing, but looking to solve the problems that face mankind will not be discovered on a space station or another planet before the destruction of our planet takes place. Can we solve the real-time problems we face on Earth that exist at this very moment before we try to solve problems that have yet to arrive in space exploration. What if it took a thousand years to discover life on another planet at a cost of trillions of dollars? With the environmental experts predicting that climate change may destroy this planet within the next few generations, who will be around to welcome these new lifeforms when they arrive to find a planet that is no longer inhabited by human life?

So can we put the exploration of outer space on the back burner for a short while so we can fix the problems that are threatening life as we know it now on Earth? Think of how we could use those trillions of dollars to balance out the wealth gap in this country. To take us out of the dark ages as far as human rights and the dignity of mankind is concerned and elevate everyone in this nation out of the roots of poverty, prejudice, and work to create higher levels of education.

We have it within our power to change this nation, to create a civilized world where everyone matters. A world were no man, women or child is left behind. Where the air and water is crystal clear and free of manmade pollutants that are destroying our climate and the environment.

It has been the wrong thinking of men who have created this imbalanced world we live in today, no one else! Man has driven us to the brink of extinction and there is no one to blame but ourselves. Unfortunately, the big decisions were made by the few who somehow were put in power and took control of our lives.

I wonder what it is that motivated these men to serve only themselves and by doing so relegated the rest of us to reside in the lower class tiers of society.

We were supposedly given *"free will"* in what was once called the land of the free and the home of the brave. We even have those words ring out loud in the Star Spangled Banner which was based off a poem that was written back in 1814 by Francis Scott Key.

Have we as a nation lived up to those famous words written by Francis Scott Key which are the foundation of the Star Spangled Banner and the pillar of democracy since the war of 1812?

With the history of this great nation, I believe we have never lived up to those famous words "Land of the Free". As a nation we have always been suppressed and held down by those whom we have put in power. We have had our freedom to choose the life we seek to attain removed and replaced with conditions that served only the wealthy and powerful people of this nation. Our freedoms were removed from the freedoms that were written by the founding fathers when they spoke of "Life, Liberty and the pursuit of Happiness".

Perhaps it was the 56 men who signed the Declaration of Independence who got the message wrong. Maybe it was meant at the time for themselves, men in power and men who had British blood coursing through their veins. Men who looked and unknowingly may have acted just like the King they wanted to escape from.

They came to America to pursue a new life, one that would free them from the tyranny of a King and a way of life that they were forced to live under back then.

But did Thomas Jefferson and John Adams represent a variety of the citizens of the thirteen colonies back in the summer of 1776 when they decided their case for liberty? They had one motive and that was to convince the thirteen colonies that the time had come for the thirteen Colonies to declare their independence from King James and to never pay taxes to Great Britain again.

So my question is this to the men who wrote the Declaration of Independence: how did those of different origins, color, and races factor into the decision to separate from Great Britain? What would be the fate of the Native American, Indians, or the slaves that you brought over in chains on ships from Africa? Did you somehow forget to include them in the future plans for the thirteen colonies or were they to be looked upon as a means to your own personal ends?

It looks to me like prejudice, discrimination and racial inequality started before this nation ever began. It was sewn into the fabric of this country by a group of privledged men who created the United States of America.

Bigotry and racism were there from the beginning. We never evolved into the hatred, violence and racism that exists in this country today because it has been here all along since the beginning of this countries existence.

That is why we have never become a nation that welcomes a diverse population of its people who should feel included and no longer excluded from having a say in the future direction of this country.

It was a nation created by a group of men who are the descendants of a world that was ruled by a King where the people lived in a tiered system of government. That sounds eerily similar to how the United States of Americas system of government and hierarchy still exists today.

We no longer live under the rule of a King, we have a President who is our "Commander in Chief." The working class are now the middle class while the poor remain in poverty. The wealth gap is now larger than ever while the majority of the citizens of this nation remain suppressed by our government. In 2022 one percent of the population still holds the majority of the wealth in this country.

So how much longer are future generations of this nation going to take this imbalance of wealth and power before they realize that the time for change has come. The next generation will be the generation that changes history. It will be the millennials who will take control of this country and lead this nation and the world towards positive change.

It was the baby boomers who failed to learn from the past and get it right. We were a generation of entitlement who took more than we gave back to the world and this nation. We were given so much by our parents' generation who knew the meaning of struggle and the value of a dollar bill. They sacrificed themselves for us "the baby boomers" so we could have a life that was better than our parents had. Why then did we not learn from the wonderful example they showed us on the values of perseverance and living a life with integrity?

In a sense we followed the patterns and lifestyles of the men who wrote the Declaration of Independence and who fought to free themselves from the tyranny of a King. They tried, but failed to create a world that was based on liberty and justice for all of its citizens.

I'm afraid in those many years that followed 1776 we have failed as a society to move past this hierarchy of humanity that still puts a certain race at the top and all other races of color at the bottom. My generation could not get it right when it came to human rights just as their parents before them and their parents before them could not conceive of a world without hatred and violence towards people who did not look or speak like them.

This is the saddest part of our history and it goes against everything that is good and right about being a human being and living on this planet. When will this stop? When will we say "Enough is Enough" that we can no longer tolerate this dark world of hatred and violence towards millions of innocent people who have done nothing wrong except being born into a world that only recognizes them for what is on the outside. We must begin to judge all people on the merits of their character and no longer by the color of their skin.

I know that enlightenment is a word the leaders of the world don't understand, but it is a word that will change the way the world looks at future generations who will take our place when our time on this planet is over. That is when the world we live in will be free of all the pettiness that comes from being human. A world that lives up to the home of the free; where we are all entitled to life, liberty and the pursuit of our own version of happiness, not a version of happiness that was created in the mind of someone else.

The millennials will be the generation that rewrites the Declaration of Independence and updates the Constitution to reflect the 21st century. I find it hard to believe that these two documents that were written hundreds of years ago by people who had owned slaves and lived a life of privledege have remained relatively untouched by the generations that followed them.

We have made Amendments to the Constitution over the years, but why have we not taken the time to take a hard look at the Declaration of Independence and update it to reflect the current society we now live in. These documents were written by a group of men who represented their roots in British heritage and an unchanged way of life that they carried over from Great Britain to the new world. Not to offend anyone reading this, but the people that they wanted to separate themselves from were of one race (Caucasian). These documents were never written with people of color in mind, how could they have been when they were enslaved by the men who wrote these documents at the time of their writing. That is reason enough for future generations to reexamine these two documents and rewrite them to reflect equality. We offend others with our own racial bias, why not take the time to understand and get to know the other person before you judge them. Judge them by their character not by the color of their skin.

The Declaration of Independence was drafted by a committee of five men in June of 1776 and ratified on July 4th 1776 our day of Independence. The Constitution of the United States of America was written also by a group of privledged men in 1787. It was ratified in 1788 and put into operation in 1789 and said this: We the people of the United States, in order to form a more perfect union, establish justice, insure domestic tranquility, provide for the common defense, promote the general welfare, and secure the blessings of liberty to ourselves and our posterity, do ordain and establish this Constitution for the United States of America. In the pictures that show the signing of the Constitution every person is Caucasian, there are no Women, Native Americans or African Americans, in fact there were no people of color who had anything to do with the drafting of the Constitution of the United States of America. That was because at the time of its writing slavery was still in existence. Can we look back over time and see a pattern has been formed that started long before we became the thirteen colonies and long before the first ship arrived on this North American continent? What would that pattern of life look like if it was really exposed for what it truly was and still is to this day in the 21st century? The pattern is the abuse of power by one group of human beings over another group of human beings by way of forcing the lower classes of society to become servants to this designated higher class. Over the past 400 years this nation has masked over these patterns of abuse and inequality over the middle class and the poor people of this country by the wealthy citizens of this nation. On the outside they appeared to care about the pain and suffering they inflicted on the majority of the citizens of the United States of America, but that was simply a ruse to get us to think that as their wealth increased so would their generosity and the quality of our lives.

My son Evan told me just last night that one member of his generation holds 98 percent of the wealth in the millennial generation. That is quite different from the current generation in power, where there are more billionaires than ever in the history of this country.

The millennials only have to dethrone one individual. It may be possible that they can convince this person of great wealth to give back for the betterment of mankind and the citizens of this country whom he made his vast fortune off of.

Think of how this one person could change the course of history and go down as one of the greatest humanitarians of his generation. No one person can spend that amount of money on material things, but the internal wealth he will have derived from giving his fortune away to preserve the world. By being the catalyst for the changes that need to happen in order to move the world forward, to push through climate change and restore human equality. It all comes down to taking personal responsibility for the future of this planet and the continuation of life. No one wants to raise their children in a controlled environment where you can't step outside without wearing some sort of a spacesuit to protect you from a toxic environment. Millennials, this is your time, this is your call to action. Do you have the courage and are you up for the task that awaits you?

Chapter Five

Life Is A Journey
Not A Destination

So many of us see life as a destination and never think about the journey we take to reach that destination. I can only say from a long life of experience that the destination is a series of desired goals and the journey is the process of how you took action towards attaining those goals.

Goal attainment is the secret to living a successful life. It can also be the attainment of the dreams you created in your mind that can lead you to a life well lived, a life that brings you fulfillment and joy.

When I was in my twenties I had no idea what setting a goal meant. I simply worked hard and believed that things would turn out well for me in my life. Then during a business class I met a man who changed my life and showed me the power of the mind and how the mind in his own words was a "billion dollar computer" that we as human beings seldom use and do not know how to tap into. I found his educational seminars on the power of the mind to be so interesting that I hung on to every word he spoke and took notes so I would not forget.

He spoke of goals as if they were the secret to living a successful life, not only in business but in our personal lives. He told us that the mind is so powerful that whatever we think about we can manifest through the repeated act of visualization, which will bring the goal to reality.

I had never heard of such things before. We were never taught the power of the mind in high school and beyond. It seems now as I look back at my schooling that my generation was not equipped for success as we moved into our adult lives and the world of work.

So, when I attended this class on motivation and the power of the mind to bring your goals and dreams to reality, I went from the unknown to an awakening that changed my life.

This life coach taught me how to tap into the part of the mind that could control future outcomes in my life. I first thought how can that be possible? He told us that the experts say we only use about 10 percent of our minds capacity.

If that was the case then why hasn't anyone figured out how to tap into the other 90 percent of the mind? Wow, could you imagine what great progress we could make in correcting our climate crisis, ending disease as we now know it, cleaning up our air, water and feeding every human being on this planet!

This journey that I started over three decades ago continues to this day. I am constantly amazed at how the mind can create the inside world we live in as well as the external world we wish for in the future. The mind is the last great unexplored resource known to mankind.

You will find that by training your mind to set goals and to see yourself attaining these goals you will open up your life to a whole new world of possibilities. Here is what I learned from this life coach during that week which transformed my life and my thinking about how the mind works.

The first thing is this, if you have a thought come into your mind that has significant meaning and is a goal or life task you wish to accomplish, write it down on a piece of paper. Why do this you may ask? Because as this wise man stated to the class "Thoughts are fleeting but paper never forgets". What does that mean to someone who is seeking to attain a goal or fulfill a dream of theirs? It means that if you have a goal and you do not write it out on paper you will eventually forget the goal and it will become just another wish that flows out of your conscious mind into a place that I like to call the land of lost dreams.

The process of goal attainment has a formula that I was taught and have used to achieve many of the dreams that I've pursued over the course of my life since the time I took this class in mindfulness and how to use the power of the mind.

The technique I was taught was termed the three V's of Action.

Number One: Verbalize your goal
Number Two: Visualize your goal
Number Three: Vitalize your goal

What does this mean, verbalize, visualize and then to vitalize your goals? It simply means that there is a formula for success that is controlled by our minds to achieve the goals we desire.

To verbalize our goal we must first have a goal that has taken over our thinking and has become so important to your future that you can't get it out of your mind. That goal must then be written out on paper with a list of things you must do to get you to the completion of the goal. This includes setting a date you believe you will accomplish the goal.

The next step is to visualize the goal you have written down on paper, to actually see yourself completing each and every step it will take you to arrive at the date you set for the completion of the goal. The last thing you must do is to vitalize the desired goal by acting "AS IF" it has already happened. This is the most crucial part of goal setting and attaining what you want in life. If you can assume that you are already living the desired outcome you wrote down describing the goal and the journey you took to achieve the goal your subconscious mind will bring the goal to reality. How do I know this works? I will give you some examples of how it has worked in my life. During the seminars, the life coach asked us to write down a two year goal and a five year goal that we wished to achieve. This was in August of 1989 and my two year goal was to become a member of the PGA of America and if I were to pass the final exam I would be on my way to achieving my dream and making it a reality.

So I wrote down a two year goal of becoming a PGA member with a date of August 1991. I was elected to PGA membership on February 1st 1991 having achieved the goal six months early. When I got to the five year goal I kept thinking about a position I wanted to get in the golf industry. I have been a PGA golf professional for most of my adult life and at the time of this educational seminar I was just getting started in my career. I was working as an assistant golf professional at a small private Country Club in my hometown of Camarillo, CA. at the time of this seminar. There was a large developer at the time who was planning a new ultra-modern Country Club with million dollar estates and condominiums surrounding the golf course. There was a rendering of the new clubhouse and course on the front cover of the local newspaper that described this 50 million dollar land development project which included a private Country Club. Now when the instructor asked us to write down our five year goal with the date it was to be completed, I wrote down on my note pad that I would be the Director of Golf at this new Country Club by August of 1994. The date I wrote this goal was August of 1989. I had no idea how I would make this five year goal happen. When I got back home to Camarillo from the class I attended in Arizona, I picked up the local paper with the rendering of the new Country Club, cut it out and taped it to my refrigerator with these words inscribed on it, "I will be the Director of Golf at Spanish Hills Golf & Country Club by August of 1994" and every day I would take the time to read my 5 year goal over and over again until I started to see myself accepting the job and signing an employment contract. That started in August of 1989 and I continued to stay focused on the rendering and the words I inscribed on that newspaper clipping to remind me of my long term goal. Honestly, I must admit that prior to going to Arizona to attend that business seminar I had no idea what a goal even was, let alone how to attain it. That trip changed my life!

In May of 1994 I accepted the position of Director of

Golf at Spanish Hills and signed a contract for more money than I ever dreamed was possible. I stayed there for over five years. Then in the middle of my career in golf I changed direction and I took a job working for a friend of mine who owned a BMW Dealership in Camarillo, CA. I had no idea how to sell cars or any real knowledge of the car industry but my friend just told me to learn everything I could and work harder and smarter than everyone else and he would promote me through the ranks. That was in 1999 and I again set a 2 year goal of being the top salesperson in the store by 2001 and making a six figure income that year. In 2001 I was not only the number one salesperson, I was named employee of the year and did something no other salesperson in the history of that BMW Dealership had ever done. I won the highest sales award that BMW North America had, "The Grand Travel Award" given to the top client advisors in sales volume and customer satisfaction from BMW Centers all across North America.

The prize included an all expense trip with other award winners and several of BMW's upper management to Munich, Germany. My wife and I flew out of LAX to JFK in New York and from there flew to Budapest, Hungary where we joined the other BMW award winners on a private cruise up the Blue Danube to Munich Germany while stopping along the way to see the beauty of other countries. We spent 5 days in Munich which culminated in going to celebrate in Germany's biggest annual celebration,

Octoberfest. This is where the goal was achieved and had exceeded anything I could have ever imagined. Oh, and by the way I did make a six figure income that year. We even extended our trip to spend 5 more days visiting France and that was one of the most memorable experiences of my life. My memories of Paris will remain with me for the rest of my life.

So, set big goals that will bring your life joy and fulfillment, write them down on paper, create a series of tasks you need to do to attain your goal and don't forget to assign a date that you will achieve the goal. Finally you must see yourself as if you have already achieved the goal and act the part of the person you have visualized in your mind. If it can work for me I know it will work for all of you who are reading this book. I have been asked before about, what if I don't achieve my goal by the date I set, does it mean that I should abandon the goal all together and start a new one? The answer is no you do not abandon the goal you just set a new date that you wish to complete the goal. Only abandon the goal if the goal is no longer something you want to attain. If that is the case then just modify the goal to match you newest desire for how you want your life to move forward.

Always remember goals are personal, be careful who you share your goals and dreams with, there are people out in this world that would like nothing better than to destroy your dreams and do their best to hold you back from a life that only you can imagine. I hope this section helps you understand that you all have been given a great gift, but the problem I see is that so few of us have opened up this wonderful gift. That gift is the enormous potential we all have to think and use the power of our minds to change our lives and to change the world. This is a part of the journey that can be taken by those who have the courage to take that first step and who discover that there is a soulful connection between our minds and our hearts and that is Love. What are the two most powerful emotions that we possess as human beings inhabiting this Earth with billions of other people? That would be the emotions of love and fear. Love comes from the connection we all have to our hearts. For me, fear was when I became disconnected from my heart and worried about the things that had not yet arrived in my life. The fear of the unknown was my biggest fear and the things I could imagine in my mind that were mental disasters of my own making that scared the hell out of me. There was a point in my life that fear had such a tight grip on my mind that I could hardly stand the thought of going outside! I created a self-imposed prison for myself that originated in my own mind.

When fear is turned into anxiety you will end up destroying your physical health because of the enormous stress you placed upon your mental health.

This is why I pray that your generation does something my generation has failed to do; connect the mind and the heart and consider them as equal partners in the health and wellbeing of all human beings on this planet. What exactly do I mean by this? I mean that when we improve our mental health we will improve our physical health which will raise our sense of wellbeing. It's that simple.

When I learned how to control my thoughts my body healed by itself in a miraculous way that went beyond what I thought was humanly possible.

At the early age of 5 my mother took me for my first day of kindergarten and I had my first panic attack. It was an out of body experience even at such an early age. It was so bad that the school Principal thought it was better for me to skip a year and start school when I turned 6. The next panic attack came at the age of 12 when I was scheduled to go to a summer ice hockey camp. I got so anxious I could not eat for two days. I managed to have enough courage to overcome the fear and go to the camp. It changed my life. I ended up loving it, they even asked me to stay on to be a camp counselor for the 6 to 9 year olds that were attending the hockey camp that summer. I ended up working at the skating rink throughout high school and became an all-star defenseman in the Metropolitan Junior Ice Hockey League. Unfortunately it did not end there. When I was 23 and had moved to California, again I felt the overwhelming fear of life which came in the form of major panic attacks which eventually led me to the hospital with a bleeding ulcer. The doctors said the illness was all in my mind. I asked them, how can my mind make me so sick? The answer to that was discovered when they ordered me to be evaluated by a psychiatrist at the UCLA Medical Center.

It was there that I was diagnosed with what was termed panic disorder and was told that I had a chemical imbalance in my brain; possibly from a traumatic brain injury when I was a child. I had told the doctor that at the age of three I was playing superman with my brother and thought I could fly down a stairway that was 20 feet high with metal surrounding the steps. I was told that after flying down the staircase and hitting the floor that I landed on my head and my nose had been broken. Back then you were expected to tough it out, even though I was only three years old at the time. I was given an ice bag and a band aid to recover.

Playing ice hockey, I can remember at least two times when I was struck in the head and may have suffered a concussion from the blows. Perhaps those were concussions that I was never aware of. Back then they seldom worried about getting hit in the head. So after my visit to UCLA I was given medication to help with the panic attacks and medicine to help balance out the chemicals in my brain for the bouts of depression and sadness I was suffering from. I can say that it took some time for me to regain some sense of normalcy, if there even is such a thing. With medication and help from a wonderful friend who just happened to be a doctor of mental health, I have been able to live a fulfilling life. I also found that meditation, exercise, and the self-care of my body and mind became a priority for me. I was raised in a family that believed in God and being a good person towards others. This became the most important part of my life. Up until I found out how my mind created such fearful thoughts which gave me an ulcer, I had no idea the power our mind has over our bodies. I knew I was not alone when it came to the sadness that invaded my mind and left me with such a feeling of emptiness. It was the moment that I started to take care of my mind that I started to take proper care of my body. I asked the doctor about that when he said my illness was all in my head.

He said that more than 50% of the people in this hospital are here because of some form of mental health issue that has manifested into a health issue of the body. You who are reading this book now know more about me then most of the people who are close to me in my life. Why would I share such personal stuff with you at this late stage of my life? Because I don't want any of you to have to go through what I experienced. Forty years ago the science of the mind and how it affected the human body was just starting to be explored. No one ever told me that when I connect my heart and my mind through love that it would lead me to a more happy and healthy life. That is why this is so important for me to speak from the experiences of my own personal battle with mental health that I have had to deal with and overcome. No one can enjoy the journey when they are battling mental health issues. The fact is that one out of every five adults will suffer from some form of mental health problem in their lifetime. I believe that mental health issues come from our failure to seek proper medical evaluations of our brain and a better understanding of the negative reactions the brain has towards fears that are both real and imaginary. Let us look at fear for what it really is, it is a state of mind that is controlled by your emotions and imagination. It wasn't until I understood my mental health and got the proper treatment that it was possible for me to overcome the feelings of fear that manifested into panic attacks and uncontrolled feelings of sadness. Now (many decades later) I can say that the fear still comes in small manageable waves, but they are simply ripples and no longer tidal waves of emotions and sadness that can render a human being into a state of paralysis. When you transform your fears into faith, you will arrive at a point in your life where you can finally take possession of your mind. I have found that when I have mastered my own mind I am now able to master my outside world. Little things that used to really bother me no longer do. Finally, as you grow older and wiser learn to keep an open mind to the things that are new to you and especially to the new people you will meet along the journey. To me it has always been the beginning point of the journey that I have undertaken followed by the actual journey itself which has led me to the final destination. Remember to take time to enjoy the journey, you earned it.

It is like having a life altering goal that you have set for yourself. With the beginning point being the actual setting of the goal with specific details on how you will go about attaining the goal a (to do list) and putting an ending date as to when you will achieve the goal. You then must use the three V's of action to bring your goal to reality. Once again I want to emphasize that so many of us fail to write down our goals and take the action steps needed to achieve the goal. You must set the goal first, take the necessary action steps you need to bring the goal to reality, then act and see yourself as if you have already achieved the goal.

It is then that you have given yourselves the best chance to change your lives, to change your destiny and to rewrite the history of the world. It's sad that you have been handed a world on the brink of destruction especially when it was a world you had no say in creating.

That is why you must change the future direction of mankind from where the current generation has taken us, to a new vision; a destination that only your generation can create. All you need to do is write down a new set of goals for the future of mankind then put a new date on when you want the world to reflect the vision you have for what is possible when we get our thinking right. Set the goals, make a plan, and then set the dates that you wish to accomplish all the changes you want to see take place in this world within your lifetimes. Build a world that you will be proud of; a world that is free of hatred and violence. A world that is powered by love and human kindness for everyone. I know you may be thinking, "Is a world like that even possible? Is it too late to reverse the damage that previous generations have done to our planet? It is never too late unless you give up and give in. The end of the world should not be at the hands of man, it should come from our Creator or by Mother Nature. We should never have been put on a course that would lead us to the destruction of this planet. The word modern progress took hold of this nation in the latter part of the 19th century when the industrial revolution was taking over the United States of America. It only took us a hundred years to get to a place where the scientist and environmental experts are predicting the end of mankind through climate change. This is the 21st century and we had to have a courageous young woman from Sweden named Greta Thunberg who as a teenager become the most recognized leader of climate change and the leading environmental activist in the history of the world. Greta is not a millennial, she is a part of the next generation that will follow the millennials. This gives me great hope and faith in the future of mankind to understand and see the problems facing the world; to find real-time solutions to these problems that are threatening life as we know it. There needs to be more young people in our world who see the world the way Greta Thunberg sees it. Where are the climate activists in the United States who are willing to fight for what they believe in? Nothing changes until you change your thinking and look at the world and its problems through your faith in humanity. Only love can overcome the hatred and ignorance that has engulfed our nation and the world. Are we that tainted as human beings that we have lost all sense of reality towards being human, have we forgotten the difference between good and evil? Or have we just turned our backs on human kindness and human dignity? What has become of mankind that we have lost such morals and valued emotions as compassion, empathy, and kindness? Is it that we as parents have gotten so lazy that we did not see the point in teaching our children the values we grew up with? Did the quest for money and power overtake whatever goodness we were born with and leave us looking in the mirror wondering how could we have been so selfish and thoughtless towards the future generations of the world?

Chapter Six

EDUCATION IS THE KEY TO OUR FUTURE

HOW IT IS possible that the richest country in the world with what many would think to be the finest educational system on Earth could have an average reading level of a twelve year old. That seems unimaginable in a country that the world looks upon as the greatest nation in history.

In my own family my grandfather who was born in 1901 never got past the third grade and went to work for his father at a very early age. He lived through the Spanish Flu, WWI, the Great Depression, and of course WWII. That seems like so much for one generation to have to endure. The thing about my grandfather was that he worked hard and believed in himself, knowing that he would be successful and take care of his family. His goal was to be successful in business and raise his 4 children during those dramatic changes in our country. He was a self-educated man who was one of the smartest men I have ever known.

My grandfather started out with a horse and carriage giving taxi rides in New York City's Central Park. He turned that small business into the largest limousine service in the State of NY by the time he was fifty years old. He had a dream (Goal) of owning a ranch in upstate NY and he realized that dream in the early 1950's.

My grandfather retired to his dream home and ranch where he and my grandmother lived until they reached the final destination on their amazing journey of life. My grandmother was a big influence in my life. She always displayed love, compassion and human kindness towards everyone who came into her life regardless of the color of their skin, religious beliefs or financial status.

My grandfather showed me that if you believed in your dream and worked hard you could do and have anything in life that you had a great desire for.

I was so blessed to have such role models when I started on my life's journey.

The lessons I learned from my grandmother on human relations and the lessons I learned from my grandfather on the pursuit of a dream and a work ethic that to this day I have seldom seen matched in any other human being was the foundation of who I am today and what I believe is a vital part of how we as parents should approach how we raise our own children.

Education is knowledge and knowledge is the key to freeing yourself from the bondage of poverty that holds you back in life. So, if the average reading level is that of a sixth grader, the future of our country could be in jeopardy. How can we raise the level of education in this country so that future generations have been educated to lead through wisdom and right decision making?

It must start with this nation's political position on the roots of proper education for our children. The idea that a child doesn't have to start school until the age of 5 is no longer working. The development of a child starts the day they are born. The experts declare that from birth to the second grade is the most crucial time in the development of a child's life. With that said, we must change the way we look at the education of our children and reevaluate their educational timeline. We should start our children in preschool at the age of two and then they advance into kindergarten at the age of five followed by the first grade until they graduate from high school. We must make preschool free for every child in this country with the goal of raising the level of education to new standards that reflects the world of technology that these new citizens of the world will be entering.

Two year colleges should also be free of tuition as well as trade schools that will bring more qualified young men and women to the workforce. These measures will ensure that the changes we make as a nation will be for the benefit of everyone and serve this country well.

It seems that most children are more socially aware then the wealthy in this country. A child understands that doing good things can be rewarded and unfortunately a person of great wealth may have lost sight of this great truth. That truth has been around since the beginning of time. Do good things for others; never do bad things. Doing bad things get you in trouble and doing good things are what build your character and shape you into a person of integrity.

I wonder if as human beings; do we ever take into account the environment we grow up in and the environment we raise our children in. If we grow up without love and kindness and are forced to live in a world that lacks most of the material necessities of life and we accept these conditions as a permanent way of living, is it possible that our children will grow up to accept these same conditions as well?

Could it be that the conditions of life that we grow up with determine our life's journey?

This is why how we change the way we educate our children in the future is so vital to helping them to succeed where their parents may have been held back because of the lack of education that was never afforded to them. If life is a journey and you don't like the way the journey is going which means you certainly don't like the destination you are heading towards, simply change direction and chart a new course with a newly designed destination that matches up with your new goals and desires.

This is called independent creative thinking and it is a gift that we are all born with, it is also known as free will. You have the freedom to choose your own personal journey with goals and dreams designed by only you. It is called your life's story and it must only be written by you. Unfortunately, so many of us become the victims of another human beings way of thinking and follow a story written by them that is designed to suppress us and control our thinking. This is called brainwashing and is also a form of human conditioning that bombards us with so many falsehoods that we fall prey to the lies we are told.

When this happens we give our personal power away to someone whom we may never even meet, someone who either by birthright or by election has been put in a position of great power over our nation and its citizens. A nation that is vulnerable to the motives of these leaders and elected government officials.

Imagine if we were to advance the education of future generations of America where they could no longer be programed and conditioned by the false statements of the leaders of this nation, it is then that we would regain our personal power through education and the expansion of our minds. Which in its own right is the key to being able to think for oneself and no longer be misguided by false leaders who think they know what is best for the people they lead. Leadership should not be something you're born into it is something that you earn by showing great courage and integrity.

My children's generation known as the millennials will learn from the past when it comes to the future education of their children, knowing that the more educated they are and the more we teach them simple lesson of right and wrong the better off the world will be. It may also be the key to closing the wealth gap and raising millions of people in this country out of the darkness of poverty and abuse. Taking them to a new world based on equality and a balance of wealth never before seen in this nation. It is sad to me to see so many of the wealthiest people in this country (some of which are born into wealth) contribute and give back so little for the betterment of the society that helped them acquire their wealth.

When the one percent use their wealth to enrich the lives of those less fortunate, it is only then that they will open up their hearts of stone and remove the invisible walls that have divided them from the rest of society. It is then that the world will be given a chance to heal the wounds and scars of the past.

We all have a stake in the future destiny of the world, we do not have to keep sailing this giant ocean liner of humanity off the edge of a giant waterfall that will end civilization as we now know it. We have the ability to place a new captain and crew on board this new ship of life and sail it towards a brighter future. One filled with the hopes and dreams of future generations and the promise of a new and better life for all who inhabit the Earth.

Our minds control our destiny and our children need to have their minds filled with the knowledge that will take them into the 22nd century and beyond. That is why the conditioning of our minds must be re-evaluated and examined to understand what needs to be changed in our habitual thinking patterns.

No one else can reprogram their mind but you. If we get our thinking right we will have a greater chance of getting our children's thinking right. Remember that what we think and how we react towards life will be a model for how we raise our children and they may grow up mirroring the things we do and say and therefore we may never give them the chance to become independent and creative thinkers of their own choosing.

We all have it within our power to educate ourselves on mistakes and situations that have held us back in the past. We can change our thinking and refuse to accept anything that has negatively impacted us up until this point in our lives.

Change the perception of the thing that is keeping you stuck in life, that you no longer want in your life and you will have the power to change everything. You can rewrite your own story. You can look at this change as the movie of your life and know that you are the star of the show; you are the writer of your life's movie, the producer, the director and most importantly the editor of the movie of your life. No longer will you act out a movie of your life that was written by someone else. If you want the movie of your life to win an academy award then it must be your story not a story that was written by someone else.

The beautiful thing about the movie of our lives is that we have the power to edit the script. If there are some bad actors in your movie, you have it within your power to cut them out of the script and leave them on the cutting room floor.

Wow! What a wonderful and refreshing way to rethink our lives and how we can conceive of new trails to blaze and how we are responsible for our life's story. You can then pass the wisdom you've learned over the course of your lifetime down to future generations. Let them know that they are no longer tied to old paradigms from the past that are no longer serving them. Let them see how you broke free from the chains of hatred and violence that have been a way of life in our country for centuries. Those people in power who had decided everything for us, forcing us to conform to their way of thinking and did their best to strip us of our dignity who created a country that was based on lies, cruelty and the suppression of human rights. They are now feeling the pressure from people who will no longer tolerate this way of life. They have no idea how strong our faith is and the power of the human spirit to overcome the hardships of life that are put upon us.

They can't see the faith we have in ourselves and the power of an entire generation to unite for a common cause. My faith in my children's generation is stronger than it has ever been, knowing what I now know compared to what I was told to believe as a child. Could it be that it is my generation the baby boomers that are suffering from a lack of reading skills? Could it be possible that we are the ones who have come to accept that we will never change and there is no point to lifelong education? That we were the generation who thought we knew everything there was to know about life and that at some point in our lives we decided there was nothing left for us to learn.

The root of ignorance is complacency; it is that simple. When you think you have learned all there is to know you are on a path to nowhere and your journey will end in disappointment and regret. You can't pass down what you don't know, therefore don't ever think that knowledge is over the moment school ends, it is not. It is at that moment that you graduate from high school or college that the learning process actually begins. Never stop learning, it is the key to human growth and the key to a brighter future for yourself and your children.

Give them the tools of education so they can think and reason for themselves and you will have given them the keys to a life well lived and a brighter future!

Education is the key to change simply because education involves using your mind every day. The mind is like a muscle; if you neglect it over a long period of time it will atrophy and become weak. The mind, if not used to think and grow on a daily basis will become a vacuum of empty space, a place that is spent living out past memories that should have been let go of a long time ago.

A great thinker of the 20th century discovered a profound truth about the mind and its power to change your life. He said whatever you plant will grow and become a reality. He said if you plant roses in your garden, you will get roses and see the different varieties and the beauty of a rose. On the other hand if you plant nothing in your garden you will grow weeds. So what was the metaphor to this as it relates to our minds?

If you plant great thoughts in your mind through education and your imagination you will achieve great results. On the other hand if you plant nothing in your mind, your mind will be an empty void and you will accomplish very little over your lifetime. That great thinker and philosopher was Napoleon Hill who wrote a book titled Think and Grow Rich.

His genius was in high demand by the leading giants of the industrial world at the time. He taught them that if you can conceive of an idea and believe in it, you would achieve it. Once again the power of the mind to create wealth and change in our world has been around for centuries, the problem is this. The average reading age in this country is twelve years old and the majority of us stop reading the moment we leave school. This may be why the words of a great man like Napoleon Hill have never been read by the millions of people in this country who need to start reading again. Dale Carnegie wrote one of the most influential books in the history of the world "How to Win Friends and Influence People" it sold over 30 million copies.

He wanted to teach the art of public speaking and how it could influence the speaker's chances of advancing their careers in both business and life.

This book is one of the most important books that I have ever read. If you want to make friends and learn how to influence others in your favor, you need to read this book. This is just another great example of how reading can change your life and set your mind in motion. Education is our future and it will give you the tools you will need to change the world.

Change your thinking by using your mind to go from a negative world to a world of endless possibilities and remember, nothing in life can happen until our thinking makes it so. Let's take this bit of advice my grandmother gave me as a child, "Mind your Mind". Be the change that you want to see in the world!

Chapter Seven

———⌁———

CHANGE IS THE KEY TO UNLIMITED POSSIBILITIES

WHY WOULD I write a book about change and what is it that I hope to accomplish? I believe that it should never be about those in power; it should be about the people they are elected to serve, the citizens of the United States of America. That is why I am writing this book, it is not so much about what I think and believe it is about what the future generations of this country come to believe as their truths.

What I hope to get out of writing this book is to inspire an entire generation to realize that they have the power to change history. My generation is simply holding on to the torch of life just waiting to pass in on to the millennial generation; hoping to see if they can be the change that the world is needing so desperately. The future will be in your hands and the past will be written to tell the story of a generation that lacked self-control, a group of leaders that will be known for its lack of doing the right thing for its people and never understanding the real meaning of human dignity and our right to freedom and equality.

The civil rights act of 1964 was supposed to give every human being living in the United States of America the freedom to pursue what the Constitution had written as its foundation for human rights. It starts out saying "We the people of the United States, in order to form a more perfect union, establish justice and tranquility" *OK* stop right there. Justice for who? Those in power and wealth did form a perfect union and established justice and tranquility only for those who could afford it. I believe those who drafted this document that is the foundation of modern politics and the basis for life in this country may have missed something. They may have left out a large population of citizens of the United States of America.

As I said, google the Constitution and just take a moment to read the names of the men of wealth and power who signed their names to it, many of whom were slave owners. It was written by Thomas Jefferson in large part. The picture of these men gathered in a room where the document was signed and put in place shows only men of a certain race and status in this country. There are no Women, no Native American Indians, and how could there be any African Americans when they were being used as slaves for these men of privledege who stood in that room writing a document that would soon set the direction for an entire nation?

The word civil rights did not exist when the Constitution was written and unfortunately it was only written for those select few privledged citizens of this newly formed nation they had envisioned for themselves.

The treatment of the citizens of the United States of America from the day the thirteen colonies annexed themselves from the tyranny of British rule has not changed much. We passed the Civil Rights Act in 1964 which prohibited discrimination on the basis of race, religion, gender, or ethnicity towards any citizen of this nation. Has the Civil Rights Act ever lived up to its promise to protect the people of this nation who still fight against discrimination?

I am here to tell my children and their generation that our history is tainted by these men who looked for great wealth and unlimited power over the people of this nation with a document that only served them and their families. It did not serve the people whom they considered to be beneath them. They wanted to get out from under a King's rule, from a country that placed its citizens in classes based on status, wealth and their place in society.

It seems to me that they may have unknowingly carried that same ruling system of government from the country they fled from Great Britain over to the new world by also categorizing its people in different classes based on their wealth, status, and unfortunately the color of their skin.

Look at us from the early 1900's to today, we still have classified our citizens as upper class, middle class, lower class and those who live in poverty. That to me does not resemble a civil rights or human rights movement towards equality for all. So who has taken away the basic rights from so many people of this nation? Could it go as far back as the Declaration of Independence? Which starts out with these noble words that should have been written for all the citizens of this country but unfortunately were not?

"We hold these truths to be self-evident, that _all men_ are created equal, that they are endowed by their creator with certain unalienable rights that amongst these are Life, Liberty and the pursuit of Happiness" that to secure these rights, governments are instituted among men, deriving their just powers from the consent of the governed—that when any form of the government becomes destructive of these ends, it is the _right of the people_ to alter or abolish it, and to institute a new government laying its foundation on such principles and organizing its power in such a form, as to them shall seem most likely to affect their safety and happiness.

Please take a moment to reread those sacred words above and know that they were written for the citizens of the United States of America, therefore let us fast forward to the current state of this country in the 21st century. The question facing all of the citizens of America is this: Are we in 2022 enjoying those most precious rights of happiness and safety in the current climate we are living in during the worst pandemic the world has seen in over 100 years that has taken over 800,000 lives in this country?

This document talks about when any form of government becomes destructive of these ends, it is the right of the people to alter or abolish it. Are we seeing a pattern in our government that has remained intact for centuries? Has the current government of the United States or past governments that had previously been in power since the writing of the Declaration of Independence ever lived up to the meaning of this document that was written as a blueprint for the freedom and happiness of all of its citizens? If not, then why in the 246 years since it was written have we not looked at this document which was written by the privledged men of that generation and maybe think about updating it to reflect the current world we now live in? Would redefining our failed government into a governing body that truly reflects the needs of all of its people be a step in the fair and equal treatment of everyone who lives and breathes in the United States of America? Can we make the needed progress that so many people have died for?

That sounds like the words we would all love to hear at the birth of a new nation that would reflect our dreams for the future of this planet. We must envision a brighter future for everyone who lives in the United States of America, in a nation that is united and no longer divided into classes of its citizens that are strictly based on wealth, education and the color of your skin.

It is also evident to those who have read this document that the meaning of these phrases are up for debate, but nevertheless, this declaration has served to justify the extension of American political social democracy since it was written.

This takes us to today 2022 and our members of Congress, the Senate and our President and Vice President who must take an oath of office and be sworn in by either a Supreme Court Justice or by the Vice President of the United States of America.

The oath goes something like this, remembering that they must put their right hand on the Bible and swear an oath of allegiance to uphold and defend the Constitution of the United States of America. This is the oath of office they take, "I do solemnly swear that I will faithfully execute the office of the President of the United States and to the best of my ability to preserve, protect and defend the Constitution"

That example is for the highest office in the land, but it is also used as an oath to uphold and defend the Constitution by those in the Congress and the Senate. That is part of their job description even if many of them have never read their own job description that is providing they even have one. I have never seen an actual job description for any of these public servants and quite frankly I've never seen such a group of elected officials in my life especially in this time of upheaval who can't get anything of significance accomplished unless it is done by one single political party that is in power and can use the Presidents power of the office to bypass the other party in the Senate to pass a bill. What is the purpose of having two political parties if neither side can work together in the spirit of cooperation and doing what is in the best interest of the people of this country?

They seem to have a job that has no rules, regulations or any direction from the top. It seems like we put a bunch of independent contractors in the capitol and none of them know how to read a blueprint, let alone understand the reason they were elected in the first place; which is to represent the people who elected you.

The Senate looks like a retirement home where a bunch of Senior Citizens are still living from the past memories of their youth back in the 1960's. Talk about taking a walk down memory lane. This is why we must change the system. A system that has been broken in a country that still remains the same as the day they wrote the Declaration of Independence and the Constitution. A system that was written with only one class of its citizens in mind, which was and still is the upper class, the rich and powerful members of our society who dominate this country.

I don't think my generation has enough time to right the wrongs of the past 400 years, but it is my hope that some of us boomers realize that we are still a part of the decision making process in the United States of America. We have a choice to make. Do we sit back and remain silent until our time runs out or do we stand up and fight for future generations who will be taking over this country!

Change really is the key that unlocks all human progress, it is what got us to the place we are now which may not be in the best interest of the longevity of the human race. It will be the changes that are made starting right now in 2022 that will determine the fate of mankind.

What is it that I want to see changed in this country before I reach my final destination, remembering that I am still on my own personal journey that I have written for myself? I want to see the world come full circle in so many ways. Can we address climate change so that our children don't have to be forced to live in an environmentally controlled living space for the remainder of their lives? How about cleaning the water while we are in the process of cleaning our air. When will we stop building and start preserving the land and other natural resources on this planet?

While all this is taking place can we really do something about human rights based on the true meaning of both the Constitution and the Declaration of Independence? Can we finally in the short history of the United States of America live up to the meaning of civil rights for everyone living in this country?

Can we teach our children kindness and compassion from the time they take their very first breath so they can be the ones who change the dynamics of racism, hatred, and violence in this nation? Let's allow them to create a world based on love, human kindness and compassion towards each other.

Judgement is the worst quality any human being can have and yet we all judge one another whether we realize it or not. Judgement can lead to resentment of others and resentment can lead to anger towards others which can ultimately lead to violence towards others. When we figure out how to remove judgement from our DNA we will move to a world that is driven by compassion and ideals that work in the best interest of all life on this planet. Change is seeing the world as it could be not as it currently is.

The other negative aspect of being human is that of not taking responsibility for your actions and blaming anyone or anything for the bad things you have done to others. When we stop blaming others for the problems that we as individuals and as a society have created we will no longer need to use lies and excuses for the problems we now face.

Blame and judgement are what I like to call life's scapegoats and may be at the root of so many of the problems that have faced the world since the beginning of time. I know that no one human being has ever lived a perfect life. We have all done some bad things in our lives that we have come to regret.

The thing is, did we learn from these mistakes and missteps or did we continue to go on doing things that could eventually get us in trouble and ruin our lives or even worse the lives of others? If the answer is yes and you continued to go down that road of self-destruction than you only have yourself to blame.

Unfortunately, in so many cases we start to live the lies we say and do our best to convince others that we are telling the truth when we know that the truth could be our downfall and as individuals we could end up in a court of law and also in the court of public opinion. I wonder which court is more important to the perpetrator of such lies. If the person is unknown to the world then I am sure it would be the court of law. If the person is someone who is in a position of great power, perhaps a political figure, than I am certain it would be the court of public opinion.

Through the advent of social media and television news media, the truth as we know it has become a political statement of which side you are on. It is no longer about the real things that are happening in the world or in this country, it's become a mechanism for planting the seeds of lies and mistrust in the people of this country who never got their reading level past the sixth grade. Propaganda is a dangerous weapon in the hands of evil doers who prey on the uninformed!

I know that is a harsh statement to make, but what if I am right. What if that alone is enough for future generations to arm their children with an education that will shield them from the falsehoods of the media that is poisoning our minds by the rich and powerful people of America through the means of social media being used as a tool to control our minds with these mind viruses?

If you want to fix the wealth gap look no further than the world of misinformation that we have let permeate our minds which have somehow been fed a virus of ransomware that has taken over our thinking and created a world where we have lost control of our minds to a corrupt mental virus that was created to keep the growth of society in check.

We fought a civil war from 1861 – 1865 that was between Northern and Pacific States and Southern States that voted to secede from the Confederate States of America. It was also at this time that the President of the United States of America, Abraham Lincoln, who is regarded as one of America's greatest heroes wrote the Emancipation Proclamation that declared forever to free those African Americans who were slaves within the Confederacy in 1863.

Lincoln did not live to see the results of his dream come to fruition. He was assassinated on Good Friday, April 14th 1865 by John Wilkes Booth who was believed to be helping the South, a sympathizer of the Confederacy.

The Republican Party was known as the Party of Lincoln, but as with anything that has its roots in history, the Party of Lincoln could never finish the job that Abraham Lincoln set out to do.

Free all the people of this country and remove the chains and shackles from those living in slavery that Lincoln was willing to risk his life and the lives of the northern armies for. It wasn't until June 4th of 1919 that women were given the right to vote.

And it wasn't until the Voting Rights Act of 1965 that was enacted by President Lyndon Johnson that change started to take place for African Americans in this country. It was echoed across our nation by one of the greatest men in the history of this country, a man who led the Civil Rights Movement, Reverend Martin Luther King Jr. A great man who died fighting for what he and so many others believed in. Take a moment to listen to Dr. King's speech from August 28th 1963 that was given at the

Lincoln Memorial in Washington D C which should have changed the course of history in this country. His "I have a dream speech" should have moved this nation out of the darkness of hatred and racial inequality, it was the seed of an Amendment that should have changed how African Americans are viewed in this nation. Unfortunately the 15th Amendment rang hollow throughout the land and remains that way into the 21st century. It was their fight for civil rights that created the 15th Amendment of the Constitution which prohibited the federal government and each state from denying a citizen the right to vote based on that citizen's race, color or previous condition of servitude.

So the title of this chapter is "Change is the key to unlimited possibilities".

Describing the civil war and the hopes of a President who wanted a nation free from slavery, where human rights were put in place for everyone not just for the powerful and privledged citizens of the states that were divided by ideologies of bigotry and racism. Lincoln was brave and took bold action even though he was fought at every turn. Lincoln knew that those human rights were stripped away by the people who supposedly came to this country to start a new world, but somehow ended up a divided nation.

Have we ever really come to the conclusion that as a nation we have never been united as one people under God, where the pursuit of life, liberty and real happiness is a reality for everyone who lives in America? We have made some progress in human rights and the civil rights of our citizens, but we still have a long way to go towards the equality of every human being who lives in this country. It is partially due to the hatred and ignorance of so many people in a nation that has held back the Civil Rights Movement and continues to do so into the 21st century.

We are on the brink of a new form of civil war where a certain group of American citizens feel it is their natural birthright to suppress human rights and hold onto a way of life that reverts back to the days of the confederacy.

As a country have we lost our way to the point where we may once again start a civil war with those who are still living in a past they can't escape from? A past that has separated our citizens by the color of their skin from a time of unfiltered rule by a group of people who felt the righteousness of their privledged lives?

A privilege that came with a price. It was the price of human life and human decency that showed little if any regard for the sanctity of human life.

So how do we change the world, how do we change the mistakes of the past so we can create a new future? A future that finally overcomes the frailty of the human ego, a world that can finally see through the vails of secrecy that those in power hide behind? We must first change our perception of the world we live in and come up with a worldview that embraces our differences. A world that no longer punishes a human being for no fault of their own other than being born into a certain race, religion or a world of poverty that has tried to strip them of their right to live a life that reflects equality. To a life of happiness and prosperity that we have spoken about since the beginning of the United States of America. This is called change which means to evolve into a new way of thinking and doing. If as a civilization we had failed to change and evolve over the course of history, we would still be living in caves.

We need to plant the seeds of possibilities now and let future generations nurture them and watch them grow into what is possible, ideas that will reflect everything that is right and decent in the world. We can no longer sit back and watch the world as we know it crumble before our very eyes.

We can never progress when we are living from the memories of the past, which impedes our progress towards a brighter future. We have progressed so far as a nation when it comes to all the modern achievements that man has produced over the past hundred years. Technology and the advancements in modern medicine are incredible and will continue to evolve. My concern (as I have stated after giving you a short history lesson in the human rights aspect of the United States of America) is that we have failed to overcome one of the fatal flaws this country has ever known. That is the failure to treat every citizen of the United States of America as an equal and intrical part of our society. We have failed to be genuine in our written and spoken words that are meant to uphold the civil rights of everyone who was born on American Soil!

We have planted the seeds of change during President Abraham Lincoln's time in office when he abolished slavery and we have planted the seeds of change during President Lyndon Johnson's time in office with the Civil Rights Act of 1964 and the Civil Rights Movement. I am hopeful that we will plant new seeds of justice in 2022 with the George Floyd Policing Reform Act and Equal Voting Rights for all of our citizens. That of course will depend on the courage of those elected officials in the House and Senate of which many have betrayed their oath of office and have left bloodstains on the Bible and the Constitution they swore to defend and uphold.

It seems to me that there are so many who serve this country in positions of political power that will die with a conscience that is marred with guilt for the things they failed to do and remained silent over. What a terrible way to die knowing that you failed your country and you failed yourself.

I tell you now that nothing in our world will ever change without someone who possesses great passion, who has the courage it will take to change the way we think about any given subject. It can be a life subject, a worldly subject or any subject that forces us to rethink the way we have done things in the past and to think of new ways to progress the world and this nation to a better place.

As I have said so many times, "What we think about, we bring about" think in negative terms and you will bring about negative conditions in your life, think in positive terms and you will bring about positive conditions in your life.

Try this sometime, when you're angry and upset, just go ahead and smile. That's right break open a big smile on your face. It will be a forced smile at first, but after a few moments your anger will dissipate and the smile on your face will become real. The simple act of smiling changes the chemistry in your brain to bring a sense of joy to your life. A smile can be the emotional change that we may all need to embrace as we move out of a world of hatred and violence into a newly changed world powered by the greatest emotion of all, *LOVE!* Love is powered by your connection to your heart. Love will bring you peace of mind, something that so many of us have never truly embraced. You must remember the most important aspect of love and that is loving yourself. If you do not like the person who is staring back at you in the mirror, your lack of love for others will be difficult to hide. Self-love is the greatest love of all. How can you love anyone else if you do not love yourself? Even though we come with many faults as human beings, failing to love yourself should not be one of them. Could it be a child's upbringing that will shape their perception of themselves, which may determine if they love themselves or dislike themselves and mirror their dislike of themselves to the rest of the world?

I am convinced that it is the early years of our life that will shape our thoughts and our view of the world. We are a product of the world we are raised in and we may take on the characteristics, mannerisms, and beliefs of our parents and family members. The beliefs of our loved ones can be based on the truth or on the falsehoods that our parents adopted and were led to believe were true in their childhood. This makes me ask this question, are we a society that has been brought up to believe what past generations pass down to us, their life's experiences that are no longer relevant to the world we are about to enter?

Will we ever break the chains of hatred in this country we now live in before it's too late to do something about it? God, I hope so. We have it within us to reshape the world. It is called *"FAITH"* and faith is inspired by love and the emotions of compassion, empathy and hope. There can only be change when the will of the people is greater than any one individual or group of individual's in this country. Only then will we see a revolution of change that will spark an entire generation to move away from the current ways of thinking that are destroying our planet, to a new and better way for the world to exist. It is people who change the world, not the world who changes people. When we get our thinking right by the act of rethinking the current ways of life as we know it, we will change the world and our perception of life on this planet. Without change we will continue to live in the darkness with no hope of what is truly possible!

Chapter Eight

THE FUTURE IS IN YOUR HANDS

WHAT DOES THE future look like if we continue to go down the current path that this country and the world are heading on? Are the scientific experts right when they talk about the rapid changes that are taking place to our climate? If they are correct, will their predictions of life on Earth as we know it be gone in the next few generations of mankind?

That to me is something no generation in the history of the world should have to be subjected to. The next great generation known as the millennials should never have been put in this situation in the first place.

Looking back over the past 120 years when this country started an industrial revolution there seemed to be no end in sight as to how much those generations of the past could build on this planet. They built railroads that went across this country. They built factories that popped up all over the Northeastern parts of the United States of America.

In New York City they erected Skyscrapers all over Downtown Manhattan. You had the richest men in America trying to outdo one another as Titans of Industry and in the construction of these giant towers of humanity. Ford became one of the richest men in the world when he mass produced the automobile, then came a man named DuPont who bought out General Motors with the goal of taking down the Ford Motor Company. By the early 1920's there were more than 20 million automobiles on the road and Ford and GM had built the largest automobile factories in the world. This was just adding to the growing and unforeseen pollution and destruction of this planet!

Then we had Walter Chrysler who was considered to be a part of the three big auto makers during the twenties build the largest skyscraper in the world in Downtown Manhattan only to be outdone by Mr. DuPont whose ego was so large that he had to outdo The Chrysler Building in size and scope by erecting the largest building in the world which he named The Empire State Building.

It seems to me that these great titans of industry had huge egos and that they were only motivated by wealth and outdoing their competition.

Next to come was the birth of aviation which became in high demand when the United States Post Office realized that the airplane could carry more mail by the pound and deliver the mail at the fastest rate of time the post office had ever seen. Up until then the mail was sent out by trains and automobiles.

Here again we had two titans of industry fighting for these highly profitable government contracts from the United States Post Office.

The Ford Aviation Company had been first to act, seizing the bulk of these government contracts and making a fortune in the process. Then a young man who was a skilled pilot and had just begun to build his aviation empire got into the mix. He did it by changing the dynamics of the plane's engine. He invented an airplane engine that was no longer water cooled, it was the first air cooled engine and it allowed him to remove over two hundred pounds of space in his new airplanes that could be used to carry more mail then the Ford planes could. He presented his new plans to the government and won a very lucrative contract that would earn his new company over five million dollars a year. That young man's name was Boeing and he created one of the largest companies in the history of aviation.

So what does this short history lesson have to do with the climate crisis the world is facing in 2022? These titans of the industrial age had no idea that what they were doing to modern civilization would (over the next 120 years) do such damage to the environment. They wanted to modernize the industrial world with a new vision for life on this planet. Ford wanted a car in every driveway, Boeing was the father of the modern airplane and now 100 years later the modern jets that fly billions of people all around the world every year.

The Industrial Revolution was the spawn of change that created the start to the destruction of our planet. Change leads us to what is possible in the world, unfortunately that change can either be for the benefit of mankind or it could be used for the willing destruction of the planet which can lead to the taking of human life in mass quantities.

We have seen what man was capable of doing over the past one hundred plus years and we are now seeing the results that the industrial revolution did in creating the uneven wealth gap in the United States of America. It was during this time period that men such as Ford, DuPont, Chrysler, Andrew Carnegie, Rockefeller, and JP Morgan had accumulated the majority of the wealth in this country.

This was the beginning of the wealth gap in this country although, for all intent and purposes it started the moment we stepped foot on this new continent. These men started to accumulate more wealth than they could ever spend and used their vast fortunes to grow even richer.

The only difference is we are now witnessing these new titans of industry in the 21st century who are making their vast fortunes from modern technology.

The richest men in the world are the ones who created and advanced the human race into the world of computers, cell phones, social media and the internet.

There may be no end to the unlimited possibilities that this technology revolution can take. I can only hope that we do not get caught up in this new way of life and forget some of the basic principles and of what it means to be human.

The future of mankind holds such great possibilities. What will the world look like one hundred years from now?

Looking back over the past one hundred plus years, if you were to chronology this timeline in picture form it would be a sequence of major changes that have taken place in the world. Pictures that showed the world not as it was, but as it was capable of becoming.

These were human beings with great vision who had the willpower to overcome failure while never losing sight of the big picture that was a burning desire within them. Every one of these great industrial giants were visionaries who created ideas in their minds that would change the world and our way of living for generations to come.

This is the message I want future generations to understand. Look back over the past one hundred plus years to see the evolution of capitalism and industry and examine the best and the worst of that time period. Determine how much you can learn from the past that will benefit mankind moving forward. Then create a new world that captures the visions, hopes and dreams of your generation. Once you have the vision, take action to bring your vision to reality. A vision without an action plan is simply a wish.

There can be no wishing that things will change, you must take bold steps if you want to change the world and have it reflect the hopes and dreams of your generation. Learn from past generations' mistakes and do not repeat them. Improve upon them. Everything you do moving forward must be examined from the endpoint and beyond, no longer just from the beginning of the project.

That is what the industrialists of the past did. They only looked at the vision and the final results of achieving the goals they set. They never looked 20, 50, or 100 years down the road to see if what they were creating was going to negatively impact the planet and life as we know it. How could they possibly have known?

They were only motivated by money and the status that wealth brought to them. They never gave much thought as to how this industrial revolution would take its toll on the Earth. One of the good things to come out of this massive change in this country was that these titans of industry created millions of jobs for the citizens of the United States of America and that stimulated an economic growth that this country had never seen before.

It was also during WWII that the German Army was in the process of creating an atomic bomb. This prompted President Roosevelt to begin the process of making our own version of a bomb known as "The Manhattan Project". This bomb would have catastrophic consequences if unleashed upon mankind. The United States Government used the desert areas of New Mexico as a test site for the first atomic bomb; it proved to be successful and was ready to be used if needed.

Nearing the end of the war after the United States and its Allies defeated the German Army and the death of Adolph Hitler by suicide, the only remaining obstacle to ending the war was the fight against the Empire of Japan.

It was during this time that the nation mourned the death of President Roosevelt and Vice President Harry Truman took over as our President.

It was Truman's decision to end this war in either two ways. He could send hundreds of thousands of American troops over to fight Japanese forces and risk the death of thousands of American lives or he could end the war with Japan by a nuclear attack. Truman chose the option of dropping two Atomic Bombs on Japan. The first was on Hiroshima and the second bomb was dropped on Nagasaki.

The war was over in an instant. The aftermath of the nuclear fallout is still being felt to this very day. The testing of atomic bombs and the nuclear waste that came from them and the bombs that were dropped on Japan have forever changed this planet.

Combine the effects of the Industrial Revolution and the lasting impact that the nuclear fallout has taken on this planet and you get a better picture of what has caused the climate to change and the results we are now witnessing.

Why does this matter? I believe that as a planet and as a civilization we are at a breaking point when it comes to the possibilities of World War III. That war will not end well for mankind. If the leaders of the world who start WWIII have the capability of launching nuclear missiles at one another, the world as we know it will no longer exist.

The only remaining people on this planet will be the leaders who made the decision to drop these nuclear bombs in the first place from a secure location that was built to withstand the impact and aftermath of a nuclear invasion.

Why should these leaders of the world have the ability to determine who should die and who should live knowing that they may be the only ones left to survive?

In the United States of America do we throw diplomacy out the window, sit in our homes and wait for the end of the world to come? Knowing that a select group of human beings have the ability to destroy all life on this planet is scary to me and should be to all of you. That way of thinking may have worked back in WWII with Harry Truman, but I think as a nation we need to rethink the power we bestow on any one individual or group of individuals in our country.

If we are to die as a nation it should not be at the hands of a select group of people making that decision; it should be made with one thing in mind. That nuclear war must be avoided at all costs.

Finally, if that were to ever happen by a foreign adversary, we would no longer have to be concerned about global warming and saving the planet. The future of this planet and the well-being of all living creatures on it would cease to exist.

We must take a step back and look at where we have come from and look at where we are now with the hope of changing future outcomes so that we never get to a place where nuclear weapons are even an option.

This is why the current generation in power must stop doing what we have done in the past that was so destructive to our planet and civilization. That includes the suffering of so many people in the United States who have lived through the ugliness of hatred, violence and racism as we march into the 21st Century.

The current generation in power who are mostly boomers need to realize that their time as leaders is coming to an end and they must let go of their ego's and selfishness which has gotten in the way of this nation's progress towards human rights and the freedoms which we are all entitled to.

Leave the state of the union better than you found it! Spend the rest of your time as public servants, serving the public and not your own political ambitions.

Remember this, that when all is said and done, what do you want to be remembered for? You can go out a hero or you can go out a zero, it is totally your choice. We all have choices in our lifetime, we can live a life of integrity and compassion towards each other or we can be ruthless towards one another and live a life filled with a self-glorified ego that serves only ourselves.

It is never too late to rewrite history, to take us in a new direction. One that serves the best interest of future generations. The current generation in power has the ability to build a new bridge to the future if they choose to do so!

It is very important that the next generation, the millennials, are prepared and ready for the challenges that await them because the time to prepare is now.

Life is not a dress rehearsal, it is a moment by moment sequence of events that requires your complete attention. We can't survive if we only have a small percentage of the millennial generation being the ones participating in the future direction of America. We need all hands on deck! So if you want to correct climate change, see equal justice for every person who lives in this country, stamp out racism, discrimination, poverty, and ignorance for good in this nation, then get up take a stand and do something about it.

Change bad habits into habits that are constructive and will move mankind forward in the pursuit of happiness and a free world which you will be proud of and want to raise your children in. With hope comes faith and faith can move mountains. Faith combined with taking action can create changes in our society that will last forever. Make the changes in the world that are a reflection of the vision you have seen regarding this planet and our society.

I am counting on you to gather together for a cause that is bigger than yourself, a cause that will unite this country and no longer divide it.

It can be done, why do I know that? Because of my faith in all of you to get it right! Life will always be an experiment in human behavior and the evolution of mankind. We have seen the great progress of technology in the 21st century, but we still haven't solved the conflicts that reside in the human mind that result in mental health issues. When we prioritize mental healthcare our physical health will improve. You will live a better quality of life then previous generations and you will live a longer and more productive life as you transition with age.

Get ready to change the world one idea at a time. Turn your ideas into visions, take the necessary action to bring your visions to reality. Know this, that the mind is the last great frontier facing mankind, focus on what your mind is capable of doing and never on the things that you do not want to happen.

So many of us focus our thoughts on things we don't want to happen and manage to bring those negative visions to reality. So if you can imagine it, you can achieve it. If you can dream it, you can become it. You are what you think about all day long, so think about what you want to accomplish and who you would like to be, because the person you become is a reflection of your thoughts and beliefs.

Someone recently told me that they felt the current generation, the boomers, were made up of 80 percent workers and twenty percent fluff and that the millennials were fifty percent work and fifty percent fluff. He then stated that the generation that will follow them will be eighty percent fluff and twenty percent work.

I am not in agreement with his way of thinking, but he

himself is of the generation that followed my generation the boomers and I know this man to be a very hard worker who is a devoted family man. He says that many in his generation were handed down wealth that did not come with a price that included the understanding of hard work to get ahead in life. He also thinks that future generation (of which the millennials are next in line behind his generation) are the generation that has been given everything without having to work for it.

I hope the above statement gets your attention, because it certainly has gotten mine. I can only hope to inspire you all to prove him wrong. To go out and fight for what you believe in and show future generations that will follow you that you have the mental and emotional strength to change the world and you have the physical strength to move this planet forward.

Don't think you can do it with your minds alone because that would be wishful thinking. It will take great minds to create a new vision for the world, but you must take it one step further. You must take your vision for the future and put it in motion. The only way to put a plan in motion is to take action. It will never get done without your entire generation buying into the dreams and visions the new leaders of this nation have planned for its citizens.

With no stated plan of action to set in motion, you will be like a ship of fools steering the ship of humanity in a never ending circle, watching the sunset and the sunrise until the end of time comes or perhaps until the end of your time on Earth arrives. If you can keep your minds and hearts open to the possibilities that life has to offer, you will change the world!

I want to take a moment to remind you all that change is an internal job; it does not come from the surface of our being. That is why you must continue to explore the inner most regions of the human mind. I believe it is there that you will find the answers to the mysteries of life on this planet.

We were put on this Earth to evolve and grow, in order for us to do that we must embrace change in the world and more importantly in ourselves.

Change does not take place overnight, it is a long and slow process that happens over years, decades and centuries and will continue until the end of time.

Progress is the cause and effect of change. We can never get to where we wish to go if we do not progress and make the necessary changes along the way.

I will challenge you, the millennials to change the way you think about life on this planet and to see a new vision that will bring a better way of living for everyone who exists and will soon exist on Earth. The future generations that follow you will be your children and grandchildren.

Think of them when you make decisions that will affect the future of this nation and the world!

I have faith that your generation will turn the ship of life around and point it in the direction that you have envisioned for this planet. Yours will be a generation of thinkers and doers despite what others say about what you may contribute to the future of mankind and the healing of our planet. The most important thing is the healing of the hearts and minds of everyone living on Earth. You must rid the world of hatred and the inhumane treatment of other human beings, and animals that exist on Earth. This is what needs to take place in order to heal this planet and moving us to a place of love. Love is the catalyst that will change hatred into kindness, compassion, and empathy towards others.

When we cleanse our minds and the way we have thought over the past 2022 years since the death of Jesus Christ to reflect a world that he himself believed in and died for, it is then that we will have reached a level of enlightenment that would match the intention of our Creator.

We were given free will, the right to think and do as we wished, provided we did not do things that were detrimental to society and other human beings. It may be that the free will we have been given has been abused by those who have ruled over us in fear and tyranny, men who put themselves above all others.

That way of life still exists in many parts of the world in the 21st century. So, what can the people of the United States of America do to move the world out of this way of thinking and living and into a world where the free will of mankind is used for the betterment of society and the world we live in?

In order for us to do this we must push past this outdated political system that has been in place since the Declaration of Independence and the Constitution.

We must revise these documents to reflect the current state of America that we live and work in as we move into the middle of the 21st century. It will take a concerted effort by an entire generation. I am talking directly to the generation that all three of my children are included in, millennials. It is within your power to change these documents to reflect the modern world you will soon create.

Think about this, those two documents that were written with the intention of being the foundation of our democracy by the founders of this nation, were written 246 years ago, we are now in the 21st century!

There have been several Amendments to the Constitution since its inception, of which many may no longer reflect our way of life in the 21st Century. Back when it was written we had two sides of society. One side trying to preserve a way of life from the beginning of this country's existence, a side that annexed itself from the Union of Northern and

Pacific States that was known as the Confederate States.

A group of privledged white men who didn't do very much manual labor on their own, they relied on slaves to do most if not all of the heavy lifting. A group of men who had little regard for human life and the human suffering that they were causing to other people who just didn't look like them.

And yet, there was another side of this nation, men who fought to win the civil war and bring an end to slavery and the inhumane sufferings that were taking place in the south. Lincoln had a dream of creating a more perfect union for all the citizens of this country, not just those privledged men of that time period but for the African Americans who were brought over in the bondage of slavery!

That is why we should never sit back and live out of the past memories of those privledged men who wrote the Constitution and the Declaration of Independence. We must fight for the true meaning of these documents. That this is the land of opportunity and that every citizen has the right to life, liberty and the pursuit of happiness regardless of the color of your skin, religious beliefs or gender!

Looking over this timeline in our history I think as a nation we have failed to live up to either one of these documents that were written for just one class of the citizens of this country and we also failed to live up to the promises that these two documents were designed to accomplish.

I don't have all the answers to the problems that face this nation, but I do have faith in the millennial generation and generations that will follow them. I know that they will have the courage to do what my generation failed to do; that is to right the wrongs of past generations all the way back to the days that Jesus Christ graced this Earth with his wisdom, compassion and presence.

Who is to say that future generations of this country can't sit down in peace and figure out what is truly best for all concerned. To watch them remodel our systems of government to reflect a fair and equitable way of making decisions?

Who is to stop them from reframing the Constitution to reflect the people (and when I say the people I mean all the people of this country) regardless of the color of your skin, religion, sexual orientation, or any other way in which you choose to live your life on this planet.

My generation will be dead and gone by the time you take over, but that doesn't mean that your generation can't start the wheels of change in motion right now.

I hope that those of you who are reading this understand that you are the future of this country and the world and you all have the power to create change. How can that be done you may ask? Because as those who are currently in power age and their numbers dwindle, your voices will grow and your numbers will increase to the point where it will be your voices that will guide this nation. It will be your voices that will resonate through the halls of Congress.

It will be your voices that will speak the truth to this nation. The future of this country must be based on truth, it can no longer be dominated by lies. Those were the methods used by cowards, leaders who thought of themselves and Sovereign Rulers, Modern Dictators. Your generation will reshape the world to where kindness and compassion are a normal way of life. Remember that nothing will happen until you have an overwhelming desire to change the world.

Chapter Nine

───⟨≈⟩───

Be the Change You Want To See In the World

THIS BOOK HAS been part history lesson, part inspirational and hopefully part motivational for the next generation of leaders in this nation. The words above were spoken by Gandhi, a man who sought change through nonviolence. We have spoken about the creation of the United States of America and how we got to where we are today in the year 2022 as a society. The messages in this book are about embracing the challenges you will face in the future. It has been proven that when we change our thinking we change our attitudes towards life. Nothing great was ever produced without a creative vision and the actions that were taken to bring that vision to reality.

To be the change you want to see in the world, you must act according to the creative thinking that will make those changes possible. Without creative thinking there can be no vision and without a vision there can be no positive change in the world; leaving very little hope for the world's survival.

Remember the three V's I wrote about that will guide you to the changes you wish to see in the world and in yourself. Verbalize your idea, that means when you say it in your mind take out a piece of paper and write that thought down. A thought is merely a wish until it is written down on paper because paper never forgets!

Visualize your thought and see yourself actually becoming what you have envisioned in your mind. The act of visualization brings your goals and dreams to reality. Vitalize your goal, this means you must act "As If" it has already happened.

The key to goal setting is to follow up your written goals by taking the necessary action steps on your to do list to bring the goal to reality, make sure you set a date that you want to achieve the goal. If an entire generation can change the world within their lifetimes for better or worse, isn't it at least worth trying? The millennial generation will soon be running this nation and the world. It is now time for positive change, because without change we can never advance humanity to a place it has never been before and that is a place of world peace.

I know that many in my generation are fed up with this political system that has never worked for the betterment of all this nation's citizens. It won't change until someone decides to rethink this two party system of Democrats and Republicans. If we do not make these changes to our political two party system I don't see us progressing as a nation anytime soon.

Speaking of history, did you know that when the Founding Fathers wrote the Constitution of the United States of America they had no intention of having a two party political system?

That's right, This two party system was created by a political controversy in the 1790's that saw the emergence of this two party political system, the Federalist Party and the Democratic-Republican Party that were centered on the different views of the Federal Government.

1790 was a long time ago and the Federalist Party did not last for very long which ended up splitting the two parties that were left into what we now know as the Republican and Democratic Parties. That is how we created this political system we now live in. I ask this question to the future generations of America, What can be done to correct this imbalance of power in our nation?

Is it possible for us to go back to the original thinking

of our Founders and have a one party system? Can it be built on the premise of one single house of representatives elected by the people of this nation whose sole purpose is to be public servants to the citizens of America?

I can only imagine the pushback your generation will get from those in my generation who still serve in positions of power. They will fight what they cannot control. My generation will hold onto power until they take their last breath on this earth so your generation needs to prepare itself for a fight!

It will be your minds that will create a new vision for this country and how you see our government moving forward. Nothing will ever get done until you change the way you look at life and how we have done things for the past several hundred years. As Dr. Wayne Dyer (who is one of my literary heroes) often said "When you change the way you look at things, the things you look at change" he was talking about so much more than material things, the things that could only be seen by the naked eye. He was talking about the unseen things of the future that were visions created in our subconscious minds, the part of the mind where all creation comes from.

Millennials, you will only have yourselves to blame if you fail to move this nation in a new direction, a direction that will be created by your generation that will serve future generations and all the world. The only way you can fail is if you sit by and do nothing while the world crumbles beneath your feet.

I have complete faith in your generation that you will not repeat the mistakes of past generations and that you will have observed us and learned from the mistakes we made. Positive change will become a key part of your generation.

The only way you change the world is to change your view of the world. I have often said that we are all destined to paint a picture of our lives and that we are given a blank canvas of which we may or may not have control over the final portrait. So many of us in my generation have had the portraits of their lives painted by someone else or by the society we grew up in, never having the ability to paint our own picture that would show the story of our lives.

I do know this, it is within every human beings power to rewrite their own story if it is not going the way you have envisioned it. Life is a day to day, moment by moment experience, it is not a story that is written in stone that is a permanent reminder of the history of your time spent on Earth.

So get out a new storyboard that is blank and a whole new set of watercolors and turn the current story of your life into a beautiful story filled with all the things you want to accomplish and the visions you created in your imagination.

You are the author of the story of your life, no one else. So if you want to be the change you want to see in this world you must first work on changing yourself through the process of reprogramming your mind to match the changes you want to see in your life and the world moving forward.

Trust me, you all can get there if you can remember that the destination is the final vision of what you have painted in your mind and the journey is what action steps you took that got you there, it is called your lifetime!

The government you are currently living in is antiquated and broken, so it is up to all of you to repaint the picture of this nation and rewrite the laws of humanity.

You can rewrite the Constitution to reflect the new age you are about to enter. You have the right to remove this two party system that was never written into the Constitution by the Founding Fathers of this nation.

You also have the right to love one another and create a world that is free of hatred and the pettiness and frailties that come from being human. When we all become more tolerant of each other's faults and less judgmental of those acquired faults that come from being human, we will change the course of history.

Only you can change your life and by course correcting your thinking you will not only treat yourself better you will change how you act towards others. We do not need to take away our free will we must change its direction towards a free will that is based on love, compassion, and the brotherhood of mankind. These are the seeds we need to plant in the minds of human beings, seeds of a changing world that will reflect our progress in human rights and human dignity.

I do know that the human mind does not like being controlled by the voice of fear. You can listen to the voice of fear and live your life in a place that will take away your desires for living or you can listen to the voice of faith, the voice of inspiration which will free you from the bondage of fear and anxiety.

It is in our faith that we will create the changes that will be needed to save this planet from self-destruction. What we pass down to our children must be better than what our parents passed down to us. There is a progression in evolution that must now be used for the betterment of mankind. It should never again be misused for the personal gains of a select few who created this lopsided tower of humanity where the wealthy live at the top of the tower and the rest of us live on the ground floor. Who do you think built this tower of humanity? It was not the wealthy, they wouldn't know a hammer and shovel if it hit them in the head. It was the blood, sweat and tears of the working class citizens of this nation that built the United States of America, not those privledged few of great wealth.

If we are going to flip over this tower of humanity to reflect the birth of a new nation it can only be done with all of our hearts and minds in the right place. It must be a place that reflects love, compassion and the belief that all human beings are created equal.

No one person on this planet is more important to the future of mankind than any other human being on this Earth. I know that it will not be my generation that will flip this tower over because it was my generation that built this tower. When all is said and done, our faith in humanity may be all we have left to change the world. We must have faith in the human spirit so we can create a life that brings us fulfillment and joy. If we do not seek to pursue the happiness that is our God given right, we will never become the best versions of ourselves. You can't fail the world, you can only fail yourself because you didn't try. Maybe you never felt the need to change your life or to change your habits of thought. It is this complacency in our thinking that is killing mankind!

I believe the key to life is loving yourself. How can you love others if you do not love yourself? You can't because you will always put roadblocks between you and the emotion of love. Loving yourself is the secret to finding meaning to your life. Love is the human emotion that will restore the spirit of humanity we once had, something we have strayed away from. Faith will lead us to a future that is fueled by love for our fellow citizens. It is in understanding these emotions that will allow us to better understand the human conditions we currently live in and wish to change. I have faith that the world will change and bring with it the hope for a brighter future. A future where the motivating factors on this planet are human compassion and a better understanding of life as we know it. A world where doing good things for others is commonplace instead of a rarity in life.

To someday see a world that has matured to a point where our right to human dignity is written into the new Constitution of the United States of America. There has to come a time when the world is free of sin and hatred, but that will take a giant shift in our thinking. As I said we need a new plan because faith without a plan is merely a wish and we know where that will get us, nowhere. Nowhere is not an option nor is it a destination on Earth.

Faith combined with creative thinking followed by taking action is the key that will unlock the future potential of mankind. This is how we will progress and this is the catalyst to change that the world it is in dire need of. It will be up to future generations to buckle down and make these needed changes that must take place in order for the Earth to survive!

The future of mankind now hangs in the balance; it is caught between two generations that do not see the world the same way. We must move away from the current ways of thinking that are destroying the planet. A world that is fueled by hatred, violence and racial bias towards people of color in this nation. The time has come to seek the truth and realize that unless we change our current ways of thinking the world as we know it will no longer exist.

So the predictions from the past that told of the end of the world which have yet to come true will have to make way for the self-destruction of this planet that was no one's fault but our own. This is something we have within our power to avoid, the end of the world should not happen as a result of the mistakes made by man!

You must be the change that you want to see in this world if you want to save the Earth and life as we know it. What is it that separates the ordinary from the extraordinary in life? It is human character, it is the beliefs that are programed into our minds by the people who raised us and the environment we grew up in? Those beliefs can stay with you for the rest of your life if you let them. They will define you to the world and display your character and the traits you convey to others such as compassion, love, and human kindness. It can also show the world your disdain for human life through the hatred and violent acts you do towards others. Maybe during your early development as a child you were abused and grew up in an environment that didn't treat you fairly. If you grew up with no feelings of love and security in your life you could be living with a deep seated resentment for the world and life in general.

You have the ability to change your life if you choose to do so, it will not be easy and will take great courage and conviction to believe in yourself when others don't. It is within all of us to evolve into the person we have envisioned in our hearts and minds. Use the three V's method if you want to get out of this self-defeating world that you were forced to grow up in. You have the key to get out of that world and get to a new place in life. Create a world that matches your new way of thinking. The key is your mind, educate yourself, never stop learning and growing as a human being. Education is the key to the freedom you seek, it is only when you change the way you think that you will change your life.

We all have a need to feel appreciated, loved, and valued as human beings. I know that if you always do your best and do more then you are asked to do with integrity, you will get to where you want to go. Never compromise your values and always do the right things in life no matter what. Doing bad things and compromising yourself for greed and the pursuit of wealth is a path to a life of emptiness. It is when you give and share what you have that life will give you back so much more than money can buy. Stand up for what you believe in even if you know that others will hurl hateful criticism towards you. Know that their words come from a place of insecurity, vanity, and judgement; not from a place of love and human kindness.

Know the difference between right and wrong, good and

evil and then you will understand the meaning of life which is to do as much good in this world as you possible can until you make your final curtain call.

Our lives are a presentation to the world of who we are and what we choose to believe in. Discovering who we are is the journey of life and it could ultimately lead you to why we exist on Earth and what purpose we serve in the short time we live on this planet. I truly believe that when we discover who we are we will then know why we exist. Don't be the person who compromises yourself for greed and power, a person who shows little regard for the rights of others.

That person will separate themselves from their true authentic self, the person they were meant to be not the false person they are now portraying.

These types of people lose themselves to the truth and move into a false reality of their own making; a reality that no longer takes responsibility for their acts of cruelty against their fellow human beings and the world.

These people who just happen to be in positions of great power have lost all sense of right from wrong and good from evil. They have compromised their thinking for power and greed. They spill their false sense of reality onto us thinking that what they say will change the thinking of those they are elected to serve. That they have the cowardice to lie in a public forum with no sense of shame for their failure to tell the truth. What a violation of their oath of office. If they can lie with their right hand on the Bible then I guess not telling the truth in a public speech is no big deal. What's to become of this nation? It is up to you, the next generation who will be taking over, what are you going to do to make things right?

The worst thing you can do is go down a road we created that is riddled with lies, deceit and the excuses we have made for decades of human failure. You must take full responsibility for your thinking and your actions. It seemed that my generation played the blame game and we blamed the blight of this nation and the world on things that we said were out of our control. The only thing that was out of control was us. We lost ourselves in what the world will someday look back upon as the industrial revolution that became the world of modern technology.

We lost touch with the human spirt. We were taken over by a modern world that had no boundaries and removed all its guardrails and limits in the name of progress. As a society we have moved away from the finest qualities that make us human, like integrity, compassion and a world filled with humor. Why do I include humor in this equation? Because without humor no one on this earth would understand the healing power of laughter. Laughter brings with it a smile to our faces that changes the chemistry in our brains and can take us from an unhappy place in our minds to a place of joy!

I see so many people in this world who are unhappy and seem to be going through the motions of life. This is why there is so much tension in the world and why we see so much hatred and violence. Life tests us every single day. It tests our courage to see if we have the guts and integrity to do the right thing even if it can cost you everything in life.

We all have the power to start over again and regain the things we may have lost by failing to tell the truth and doing the right thing. The loss of your integrity because you compromised yourself may be hard to overcome and difficult to go back to the way you once were. You can go down the road of greed and compromise and you will find it a lonely road to take. Throughout the history of mankind those who have used their power for evil and selfish greed had the people they tried to control take them down. Eventually even the worst human beings on this Earth are removed from their positions of power by a society that understands and never takes their freedoms and liberties for granted. A society that will not be ruled by any one person or organization.

I can't emphasize enough that you are the keeper of the kingdom of your mind, the gatekeeper to your thoughts. Our minds are very susceptible to all kinds of people who want to dominate your thinking and bend your will to their way of thinking. I implore you to never let anyone else do your thinking for you because if you do you have given away your personal power over your mind. No one has the right to control your mind even though there are people and leaders throughout history who have been driven by this concept. The time for us being brainwashed by people in positions of authority must come to an end. If we wish to turn things around and change this nation we must take back control of our minds and learn how to think for ourselves.

There are too many mind viruses bombarding civilization in the 21st century. There are so many lies floating around that are taken as the gospel truth. The truth is, with the advent of social media and cable news channels that are bending and manipulating their First Amendment Rights (which is the freedom of speech) we have seen an explosion of falsehoods and fabricated stories that have us spiraling out of control. We are becoming a byproduct of these mind viruses that are being broadcasted through these forms of communication and the media.

I wonder if these people who are broadcasting these falsehoods have figured out what few of us are yet to understand and that is this. If you see something for an extended period of time you will eventually believe the subliminal messages that are being transmitted to the conscious mind and absorbed by the subconscious mind. In other words that is the essence of mass marketing and propaganda. You see the commercial over and over again until you end up buying the product and believing that it is actually doing some good for you; regardless if the product can actually do what it claims to do.

It is no different with the lies that are being broadcasted by social media and the news networks of the world. If the lie is watched over a sustained period of time you will either turn the message off or you will eventually receive the message into your mind and believe it to be real and factual, a form of brainwashing.

This brings me back to our children and future grandchildren. Will their learning environment be positive or will it be negative? That is a question that you must have only one answer to. Their world will be one of positive learning and a better understanding of life on this Earth. They must be taught the difference between right and wrong, good and evil if we want them to progress beyond this world of the media controlling our thinking. Are we really using technology for the good of mankind or is it being used to take us to a place we never intended to go. I am talking about a one Way Street designed to take away our creative ability to think and reason for ourselves.

We can no longer keep exposing our children to this make believe world we currently live in. They must no longer be exposed to all the things that those who control the media are trying to brainwash us with. They deserve better from us and they must not be a product of what they see on television or read on their cellphones and laptops. I can't tell you how to raise your children but I can hopefully nudge you in a new direction, one that looks a lot different than what we are now seeing in our society.

What I am trying to point out is that the more we expose our children to all the negative aspects of life the less chance you will have to make the needed changes you want to see in the world. We can't change this country when the world is filled with such negative messaging that is permeating and poisoning our minds. It is your children's future that must be considered. They must not come into a world that still looks like the world we are currently living in. That world must change in order for your generation and your children's generation to have any chance of progressing and evolving into a world that has corrected climate change and has a government that finally works for the people and no longer for the few select individuals who are trying to control the world.

It is up to us as parents and grandparents to change our way of thinking if we want them to survive. We must change the way we live our lives so we can be better examples than the ones we are currently presenting to future generations of the world. Whether we realize it or not they look to us for guidance and they also look to us as examples of what they should be when they grow up. If we have compromised our values and morals and live a life based on lies and corruption, what do you think the chances are that they too will follow in our footsteps? The chances are much greater than you may think or believe!

The only way we can change our current mindset is to change our attitudes towards life. That will happen when we stop blaming others for our failures and take responsibility not only for our own lives but for the future of humanity. Always remember it is not what happens to you in life, it is how you react to it. There is a saying I have lived by for most of my adult life "Act, don't react, you have the power to choose" what exactly does that mean? For me it meant that I had a choice as to how I dealt with everything that seemed at the time to be a misfortune or a failure in my life. I had the free will to choose to give up or to go on, no one else could make that choice for me.

By reacting to the so called bad things, I found that it just made them worse. If on the other hand I looked at this as an opportunity which I could learn and grow from, I took action to solve the problem or the negative situation. I was learning to train my mind to act in a positive or neutral way as opposed to reacting in a negative way that might hurt others and could possibly destroy my own life.

Think of this as you move forward with your life. Everything that you see in the world was once imagined in the mind of a human being. It started out as a thought and by the power of creation they turned that thought into reality. So many of the things we see today had many failures before they were created. The people who created them were visionaries. They did not quit when they failed, they kept on trying until they achieved the results they desired.

Thoughts that are driven by action have created the world we are now living in and it will be the thoughts of future generations that will make the world of tomorrow.

When the thinking of mankind reflects the best of being human the world will revert to a place where no one is left behind. A world where every human being is valued and appreciated for their uniqueness. We will then care for everyone who lives and breathes on this planet in equality, where doing the right thing by all of us is a common occurrence.

That world exists. It is in the minds of everyone who is living on Earth whether they realize it or not, but unfortunately there are so many of us who have lost sight of that beautiful picture of what life on this planet should look like.

That world is real, it just may be through the course of history those in power lost their souls to a world they created through the sufferings of others! There is hope, I have complete faith that future generations will create a new world, the world I have been writing about in this book. This new world will be guided by decency and fueled by compassion towards our fellow human beings. A world without blame, excuses and judgement which have caused so many problems in our world throughout the course of history.

It would be a world that would showcase everything that

is right with the world and the best qualities of being human. It all starts with love and our understanding that we are all different and unique in our own ways. No two people on this planet are identical in their makeup or DNA. We must embrace our differences if we are to get to a place where we are mature enough to all get along with one another and for the first time in the history of the world a place where we will all live in peace and harmony.

Is that even possible? We will never know if we don't try. Filling our hearts with love and compassion must be passed down to future generation and so on, we must get to a point where love, compassion, and the sanctity of human life are a normal way of living. We must try to create a positive form of conditioning of the human mind. By taking it to a place where being selfless is a normal way of life. It can be done through the process of lifelong learning and raising our emotional intelligence.

Giving is the highest form of being a human being, it is the greatest gift we will possess in our lifetime whether we realize it or not. Those who have discovered the power of giving are the ones who will change the thinking of an entire generation and generations to come. Remember that when you give, it is best to keep the gift to yourself and never share it with others. To share it, is to boast and feeds the ego, it also takes away from the meaning and intent of the gift you gave to someone who needed it at the time.

Love is the most precious gift of all and it is the one gift that guarantees happiness and the gift that will change the world. Be the change you want to see in the world starting right now by sharing the love that is within you and don't forget that when you smile you light up the world!

Chapter Ten

_____

BRIDGES UNITE US
WALLS DIVIDE US

THROUGHOUT THE HISTORY of the world walls have been built to keep people we don't like on the other side, The Great Wall of China, The Berlin Wall and the U S Border Wall which separates our country from Mexico just to name a few. We do this in many respects to protect ourselves from unwanted strangers, people whom we don't even know and people we may fear.

As human beings we also build imaginary walls in our minds designed to protect us from the unknown. Those fears are the worst kind because whether we know it or not fear (either real or imagined) can do great emotional damage to our minds which can cause a physical breakdown of our bodies.

We all have the ability to change the lives of the people we meet every day. The opportunity will always present itself if you take down the mental and emotional barriers you have built up in your mind to shelter yourself from others. Our lives will change when we start to build emotional bridges between ourselves and the rest of the world, it is then that we will tear down these invisible walls of hatred that are destroying our lives and the world we live in.

Look at life as a gift to be shared with others, perhaps even with strangers we will meet along our life's journey. We have the power to do random acts of kindness and when we do that we brighten up other people's lives in a way that is certain to increase our own feelings of self-worth.

One thing to remember is that when we do something nice for someone else we must never reveal the act of kindness to others. The secret to kindness and its power to change lives is that you must keep the act of kindness to yourself.

Why is it so important to tear down the walls of humanity which are designed to keep people out and replace them with bridges that will allow people in? Because if you build a bridge you have embraced change and when you build a wall you've embrace the hatred and violence of past generations who were the architects of these walls that did nothing to advance humanity and only held the world back.

If we are to embrace the changes the world is in such desperate need of it must start in our minds. We can no longer embrace the way we have done things in the past, we must look for new and better ways of protecting this planet and life as we hope it could be in the future.

When we realize what great opportunities we have to change this country we will open up our minds with ideas that will build emotional bridges designed to unite this nation. The future is filled with the waters of uncertainty and right now those waters are murky and filled with fear, hatred and violence.

Belief is one of the most powerful thoughts any human being can have, nothing ever happens until you make it happen through the power of belief.

My goal in life is to inspire future generations to understand that there is "Magic in Believing". It is a catalyst to positive change and the secret sauce that will benefit mankind and has the power to change future outcomes.

One of the guaranteed certainties in life is that life detests inactivity in a person with a healthy mind and life has little rewards for the person who uses their mind as nothing more than an empty space between their ears. If the power of the mind is neglected by future generation of this nation there will be many walls to defend, walls that will separate our society and tear down the bridges of humanity that are designed to unite us.

So let's build more bridges and tear down these walls of hatred that have divided this nation since the beginning. There is no better time than now to understand that we have the power to change the world. In this nation we must finish what Abraham Lincoln set out to accomplish and that is to tear down the invisible walls of hatred, violence and racial inequality in the United States of America. We have had over 140 years to improve upon what Lincoln, Johnson, and Dr. Martin Luther King Jr. set out to do and that is to build a world where every human being is valued and judged by the content of their character, not by the color of their skin.

My generation tried and failed at this monumental task of ending bigotry and racial injustice during our time when we were in a position of power to do something about it. In all honesty, my generation never really put in the effort it would have taken to change the suffering and violent acts of racial hatred in this country. We kept shouting about the Second Amendment Rights of every citizen in the United States and why owning guns was in the best interest of this nation. The Second Amendment reads exactly like this and was written in 1789.

Amendment II: A well-regulated Militia, being necessary to the security of a free state, the right of the people to keep and bear arms, shall not be infringed.

The Second Amendment provides U.S. citizens the right

to bear arms......Having just used guns and other arms to ward off the British Soldiers, the Second Amendment was originally created to give citizens the opportunity to fight back against Great Britain and King James who was unfairly taxing them.

I want you all to take a deep breath and go back and reread the Second Amendment and try to imagine the war against the British by the thirteen colonies that settled here in the new world, which is now known as the United States of America. Those early settlers had guns and rifles that used a single lead ball inside its chamber that was filled with gun powder and set in motion by using a flintlock to propel the bullet. Muskets and hand guns that shot only one single bullet, take a moment to digest that picture of self-defense and fighting a war for freedom.

Now fast forward in time to the 21st century where every day it seems like some mentally deranged human being (mostly murderous men) who are filled with hatred and want to take revenge on the people who have wronged them go out and buy a military style assault weapon. There is no background check, no waiting period and they can buy a thousand rounds of ammunition for this weapon of mass destruction, no questions asked. I just can't see the resemblance between a single shot musket from the 1790's and an assault weapon from the 21st century. With that said I am speaking to the future generation of leaders in this nation about amending the Constitution of the

United States of America.

My recommendation is to start with the Second Amendment of the Constitution. It was never written to give American citizens the right to bear military style weapons that could kill hundreds of people in a matter of minutes. It was never meant for the mentally ill or the deranged people of this country to have an open invitation to own these guns. I get that what I am saying will ruffle the feathers of the NRA which is one of the most corrupt organizations in the history of this nation. There are also some people in this country who are still living in a time warp from the days of the confederacy, with many of them now feeling that they are in the minority of this country and it scares the hell out of them!

I believe the majority of the people in this country would like to see stricter gun laws put in place that would allow the government to amend the Constitution's Second Amendment, sensible new laws that reflect the current world we live in. Why do we continue to allow our citizens to defend themselves and their civil liberties with military style assault weapons and body armor? This goes beyond all human reasoning.

If you want to own a handgun to protect your civil liberties, fine? But, why would anyone need to own an automatic weapon to protect themselves? I understand you want to protect your family and property from intruders, but does it have to be with these weapons of mass destruction?

If we do not change the system then more innocent people will keep on dying.

Thousands of people die from gun violence every year. In 2018 data from the Center for Disease Control's National Statistics reported 38,390 deaths by firearms of which 24,432 were by suicide. 13,958 were homicides. The U.S. has had 225 mass shootings in 2021 as of May 28th with more than 17,000 people dying from gun-related violence so far. Need I go on!

It is apparent to me that my generation has had ample time over the past 40 years to fix this problem, but have failed to do much about it. Could it be because they chose the money from gun lobbyist over the safety of human life? In many ways I am ashamed of my generation and how they behaved over their time in power. It will be up to the millennial generation to put an end to this madness that has simply gotten out of control. Yes, gun control is out of control in this country and there doesn't seem to be any one group of people who have the power or the courage to change it or even seem to want to end the senseless gun-related violence and gun-related suicides in our country any time soon.

Suicide has taken a grip on this country the likes of which we have never seen before. The number one cause of death in our veterans is suicide, the number one cause of death in men over the age of 60 is suicide and the number two cause of death in young Americans from the ages of 12 to 22 is suicide.

That alone is reason enough to want to fix the mental healthcare system in America. Mental health can no longer be swept under the rug in our society. Many of the gun-related deaths in this country are related to mental health issues in one form or another. I have stated many times in this book that the health of the body is directly related to the health of the mind.

Having one month dedicated each year to recognize mental healthcare is not enough. We need the government to take mental healthcare seriously and put the needed money into research and the development of new treatments that will help cure the mind and alleviate so many problems in the world that are caused by mental health issues.

I will share with you my journey to get out from under the grips of my own personal mental health issues. I have suffered from depression and anxiety my entire life. I am still waiting on scientist to come up with new and safer medications than the ones I am currently taking. I have been taking the same medication for my depression for over 25 years and a different medication for my anxiety for that same period of time in my life. I can only think that my medication for depression is not a cure, it is a band aid for covering up the real problem. When a doctor tells you that you have a chemical imbalance in your brain and that your brain lacks certain chemicals in order for it to function properly and they can only correct the problem with synthetic drugs that speaks volumes about the progress we have made in mental healthcare.

When a doctor prescribes a pill to calm your mind down from the panic attacks you are experiencing and the pill is simply a quick fix to the problem and not a long-term solution, we need to find a better way to cure the health of the mind that goes beyond simply masking the problem with drugs and alcohol.

What would the world look like if we were able to get a handle on mental health and find long lasting cures for depression, anxiety, and the long list of mental health issues that continue to plague our society? What would happen to this country if we could spot and address the mental health crisis of people of all ages that are considering taking their own lives through the act of suicide?

What would happen to the people of this country who commit these crimes against humanity known as mass murder? What would happen to the thousands of other people in the United States who commit gun-related homicides if they were all to get the mental health care treatments that could help heal their mental health issues and return their minds to a safer place; a place that has a better understanding of compassion and empathy towards others?

Think of this regarding mental healthcare, if we have 330,000,000 people living in this country, what is the percentage of people who suffer from some form of mental health issue? I can tell you from my own personal experience that more than half the people I have met in my lifetime have had some form of mental health issues that manifested in some form of substance abuse. How many people do you know that have issues or problems that they have trouble dealing with either mentally or emotionally? What is happening to the millions of Americans who have no access to healthcare let alone mental healthcare?

Who is going to give them a magic pill to end their pain and suffering? The answer is no one is coming to the rescue because our government has shown very little capacity for caring for people with mental health issues. This is evident in how our government treats our war heroes, our veterans who have served this country in times of war. When will the mental healthcare of our veterans be a major priority for the government that seems to have abandoned these great men and women in their darkest hour? Those men and women who believed in something greater than themselves, which was to defend this country from all enemies and defend the Constitution of the United States of America?

When will we make mental healthcare a top priority in this country instead of spending so much money on the development of nuclear weapons that are designed to end all life on this planet? There may come a time when we no longer need to worry about the Second Amendment of the Constitution.

So let's stop building walls, whether real or imaginary that are dividing this country and dividing the world into a place that threatens our democracy and ultimately is threating all life on this planet.

We have left future generations with a lot of problems that need to be solved. These problems will take much thought and great courage to solve and overcome. The millennial generation will have to face things that prior generation either ignored or just didn't understand when it came to the preservation of life on this planet.

Your generation will have so many challenges, but I know you are equipped to take them on; even if it is one massive challenge after another.

I wish to give you some advice on moving this country forward and that is this. Many of you have seen to do lists before and some of us use them and some of us don't. A to do list is very important for your generation to grasp and take hold of because if you do not prioritize your to do list that will save this planet and improve the quality of life for everyone on it, you may end up just spinning your wheels, just like the current generation in power has been doing for decades.

Many people write their personal to do list all wrong. They put the easy things that are usually fun to do at the top and the hardest things they need to accomplish at the bottom. This may be why we have failed as a nation to get stuff done. The people whom we have elected can't seem to get their priorities sequenced in their order of importance. They do the easy work that has very little consequences or impact on our way of life in this country. They have a habit of putting the critical stuff on the back burner hoping that we as a nation will somehow come down with the biggest case of mass amnesia the world has ever known and simply forget about the dire predicament we are in as a nation.

The government now reminds me of two mice in a cage running lap after lap on their little Ferris wheels, working so hard at something that ends up getting them nowhere. Two political parties that now resemble two mice running franticly in circles ending up doing very little to move mankind forward and doing its best to keep us stuck in a never ending revolving door we know as life in this country.

So let us understand where our priorities should be, not where society wants them to be. Our nations to do list must take a hard look at what is important to the continuation of life on this planet. This includes climate change, the inequality of human life, mental healthcare and the lack of education in this country.

I do not want to make the list too long otherwise you may not know where to start because the hardest thing for any nation to do is to start a project and see it through to completion.

I deliberately left off the list the biggest issue my sons Evan and Troy had and that was reducing the wealth gap in this country because it seems to me if we do not address climate change and this planet becomes unlivable over the next one hundred years there will be no one left to spend the money!

Also, if we do not address mental healthcare and the advanced education of the people of this nation we will never close the wealth gap in the United States of America. Education and more focus on the mental healthcare of Americans will level the playing field in this country once and for all, which in turn will raise this nation out of poverty and into prosperity.

So it seems to me like your generation has inherited a real mess from the current generation in power of which I am sad to say I am one of them. But no task is too great if you put your collective minds towards the vision you have for the future of this country and follow through on the action steps you will need to take towards the completion of these monumental tasks.

This is why I titled this book *"Millennials, Your Time has Come"* it's because you have the power to change the world. Life in itself is a progression of the mind and body towards the unknown future. Nothing will ever happen until you change the way you perceive the current conditions in this country and the world. My generation has only embraced the material wealth changes in this country, we never have embraced the needed changes that must be addressed towards the current living conditions in this country to better reflect a more just system of equality and human rights. That is one of the greatest challenges we face as a nation.

So tear up the current blueprint for life that is being handed over to your generation and rewrite it to match your future destiny. Change the patterns of life that we have adhered to for centuries and rebuild this nation into one that serves the people and reflects the true intentions of those two documents we hold so dear to our hearts, the Constitution and the Declaration of Independence.

Your time has come to re-examine the current ways of life in this country and the laws and restrictions that have been placed on our society over the past two hundred and forty six years. Change is what fuels progress, we can no longer sit by and watch the world slowly destroy itself without taking action.

Seek a new vision for this country and the world, make the needed plans for change and then carry out those plans by taking action to complete them. When you do that as a nation the world will follow your lead and you will be the generation that saved the world by pulling in the reins of hatred, violence and ignorance that rears its ugly head in America and the world!

This can be done if you continue to build bridges and stop building walls that have been visible to the eyes of the world. Let them stand as a reminder of history. The walls that have done the most damage to society are the invisible walls of hatred, violence, and ignorance! It is these walls that must come down in order to move your generation forward. You must build new bridges that will unite the world!

A whole new world awaits you all if you will only embrace change and understand that change is really the only path we have to progress as human beings and change is the catalyst towards the evolution of mankind, our world, and life on this planet.

Millennial's your time is *NOW*! The challenges that are being put before you are many and this will be no easy task for your generation to change this country and ultimately change our world. I have faith in you and faith can move mountains, I know you can do it! It was my generation who took away your ability to create wealth and prosperity in this country. We were the ones who shackled your generation down with a burden of debt that you were never prepared for. Now that many of you are out of college you must suffer from the mistakes of a generation that failed you both financially and emotionally. You're education will pay off in the long run because you are the smartest generation in the history of this country. When you see injustice you won't close your eyes to it like we did, you will stand up and fight for what you believe in. My final request for you is this, embrace the challenges that face you, fight back with all your mind and all your heart, use love over hate, change yourselves and you will change the world!

Embrace the 21st Century!

"As we get a little older and a little wiser, we are given opportunities to pass along the wisdom we have acquired to those who are just getting started on their life's journey. When given the chance, take the time to positively impact the life of another human being through kindness and generosity and you will positive

Impact the future of the world"

Stephen A Vigiano

MY FINAL THOUGHTS

Dreams are what activate the creative side of our minds to see things that are not visible to the conscious mind. It is in our dreams either at night when we are sleeping or by day when we gaze off into the distance and take our creative minds to another place in time (which is known as daydreaming) that we will build the bridges of humanity that will unite our country and will over time tear down the invisible walls of ignorance and hatred that continue to divide this nation.

I am a dreamer who always looks on the brighter side of life and does my best not to judge another person without walking a mile in their shoes while doing my utmost to try and see the world through the eyes of the other person.

Why should we take the time to see the world through the eyes of those we meet along the journey, people we meet on a daily basis? Perhaps it is because we are so wrapped up in our own world that we fail to take the time to notice the world around us and the beauty and diversity of humanity.

There is so much more to life than many of us could ever imagine, it is out there ready to be explored and expanded upon. We have it within our power as human beings to change the course of history and to rebuild this nation into a country that can be reimagined through love and a renewed faith in democracy.

We did not start out as a nation fueled on violence and hatred for one another! We were designed to form a nation that would represent a perfect union, where every citizen of the United States was given the right to freedom, the pursuit of happiness, and the right to choose a life that only they could imagine.

Unfortunately those words were written by that first generation of Americans who broke away from the rule of King James of Great Britain and were written only for one select group of privledged citizens of the thirteen colonies. It was never designed for the Native American Indians who were the rightful owners of all the land that would become the United States of America. And we must never forget the biggest injustice this country has had to endure since its inception and that was the slavery of African Americans that were brought over in chains.

How is it possible that any one race of human beings could justify their ego driven sense of superiority over other races who simply did not look like them. The arrogance of those men who started this nation is still being felt today in the 21st century.

If we are a country made up of immigrants, then why is it that we have never lived up to those famous words "land of the free and the home of the brave"?

We have evolved into the land of the suppressed and the home of the rich and powerful who in my opinion are just coward's hiding behind their wealth!

Something has to change in order for the world as we know it to survive the greed and thoughtlessness of past generations. The future of our world will rest with one new generation known as the millennials and the generations to follow them.

What a huge burden my generation has bestowed on future generations to clean up. Where do they start? How will they overcome and fix the many challenges that they will face once the boomers are no longer in power?

How will they navigate the waters of hatred, violence and ignorance as well as the mistrust that is being handed over to them?

I believe in this new generation, that they will be the ones to figure out what we failed to understand which is no one class of people in this country is more important than any other! This imbalanced world we now live in that is destroying the climate and the air we breathe and the water we drink is on the brink of extinction.

The millennials are going to have to rise up to the occasion and they will. They will not sit back and watch what we did to destroy their future continue. They are smarter and more compassionate then we are and will prove it once they take over this ship of humanity and sail it towards the rising sun with a promise of renewed hope, no longer sailing it towards the setting sun that is filled with regrets and broken promises, a direction it has sailed in since this nation's inception!

The world has always had an organizational chart for humanity where the people were defined by wealth and titles at the top of the chart and the rest of its citizens at the bottom who suffered from these leaders self-absorbed ideologies of greed and excess!

This new generation is going to finally tear down these imaginary walls that have divided this country and rebuild this nation and our world to look like them, a generation that is filled with a diverse group of Americans who understand that we are all different and unique in our own ways. They will see the world as it could be, not as it currently is, being run by a generation that lives in the past.

They will put an end to wars and the taking of human lives by suicide. They must end this senseless violence that has plagued this nation since the beginning. They will be the generation that cracks the mental health code by discovering natural ways to cure the mind. We must find cures for the mind for those who are suffering so badly from mental health issues that their only escape is to take their own lives by suicide, it is then that we give them back the will to live!

That is why I wrote this book; it is to open up the eyes of future generations to what is possible and to challenge them to change the world!

There are so many people who have come into my life that have helped me shape my views of the world. I must first thank God and my Lord and Savior Jesus Christ. You do not have to believe in them, but you must believe in something in order to have the faith to change yourself and the world around us.

My belief is that nothing is impossible in this lifetime and at any given moment we have the ability to change ourselves and our world. We are presented with many challenges and it is how we react to these challenges that will shape our destinies.

To my three children Kylie, Evan, and Troy whose generation gives me hope for the future of mankind. They are my reason for pushing myself to go beyond the limits and boundaries that life and society tries to bottle us up in.

They are a part of the next great generation that will change the course of history and rewrite the future of this nation and the world! They will no longer see the need to live in a world that is dominated by a select few who have lost their integrity and have been swallowed up in a world of greed and corruption.

They will find cures for the mind and body that will cure the soul of this nation of all that is wrong with it. They will end injustice, racism and the unfair treatment of our fellow citizens who have had to endure such treatment since those men of privledege first set foot on this land.

I pose this question to the millennial generation, all seventy one million of you! "What if" you all decided to register as Independents at the ballot box? What would that do to those in power in Washington DC? Could you be the first generation to elect an Independent President and Vice President who are no longer affiliated with either political party?

Time is the most precious commodity in our lives, it is not the material things that will bring you peace of mind and happiness. It is what you think and how you spend your time that will determine your success in life. Time is the one thing you can't get back, yet it seems to be the one thing we waste the most.

The boomers have left you at an inflection point with so many hurdles and challenges that you must overcome. I believe you must tackle climate change first because without correcting our climate to make this planet livable, the other challenges will not matter.

Then you must decide to take on the greatest challenge of being human and that is the mental health crisis that is killing the people of this country. You must then work on creating a nation that has removed racial injustice and poverty the *things that have created this huge wealth gap in America. Only then through education and by creating equal opportunities for every citizen in this nation will we rise above the hatred, violence, and poverty in America.*

Finally, when love overcomes hatred and we see compassion overcome violence we will see a new world that represents everything that is right about being human.

Every day is truly a wonderful opportunity to change our world through kindness, compassion, and the gift of love. So next time you see someone who is struggling in life stop and take a moment to lift them up through a random act of kindness and remember to keep the good deed to yourself and watch your own self-worth grow, it is in the act of giving that we receive the most satisfaction in life!

Millennials!

"Do it now, don't wait until it's too late"

Here's your to do list for the 21ˢᵗ Century

Address climate change!
End racial injustice!
Make mental healthcare a top priority!
Educate our children!
Create a unified government that works for all of its people!
Teach your children kindness, compassion and love!
Be the change you want to see in this nation!

*"Our only limitations are the ones we
create or permit others to establish for us"*

*With love
Stephen A Vigiano*

CPSIA information can be obtained
at www.ICGtesting.com
Printed in the USA
BVHW040040200422
634749BV00007B/127

Hitler's Panzers

Hitler's Panzers

The Complete History
1933–1945

Anthony Tucker-Jones

Pen & Sword
MILITARY
AN IMPRINT OF PEN & SWORD BOOKS LTD.
YORKSHIRE – PHILADELPHIA

First published in Great Britain in 2020 by
PEN & SWORD MILITARY
An imprint of
Pen & Sword Books Ltd
Yorkshire – Philadelphia

Copyright © Anthony Tucker-Jones 2020

ISBN 9781526741585

The right of Anthony Tucker-Jones to be identified as Author
of this work has been asserted by him in accordance
with the Copyright, Designs and Patents Act 1988.

A CIP catalogue record for this book is
available from the British Library

Typeset in 10.5/13 Ehrhardt by Vman Infotech Pvt. Ltd.
Printed and bound in the UK by TJ International Ltd, Padstow, Cornwall.

Pen & Sword Books Ltd incorporates the imprints of Pen & Sword
Archaeology, Atlas, Aviation, Battleground, Discovery, Family History,
History, Maritime, Military, Naval, Politics, Social History, Transport,
True Crime, Claymore Press, Frontline Books, Praetorian Press,
Seaforth Publishing and White Owl
For a complete list of Pen & Sword titles please contact

PEN & SWORD BOOKS LTD
47 Church Street, Barnsley, South Yorkshire, S70 2AS, England
E-mail: enquiries@pen-and-sword.co.uk
Website: www.pen-and-sword.co.uk

Or

PEN AND SWORD BOOKS
1950 Lawrence Rd, Havertown, PA 19083, USA
E-mail: Uspen-and-sword@casematepublishers.com
Website: www.penandswordbooks.com

Contents

List of Plates

18. Not a tank but an early model turretless assault gun based on the Panzer III known as the Sturmgeschütz III Ausf B armed with the 75mm StuK37 L/24 gun.

19. Sturmgeschütz III Ausf F armed with the more powerful 75mm StuK40 L/43 or L/48 gun somewhere in Russia.

20. StuG III lost in Italy. Guderian viewed the assault gun, intended to support the infantry, as a defensive weapon that dissipated the offensive capabilities of his panzers.

21. GIs posing with a StuG III Ausf G captured during the fighting in Normandy.

22. More StuG III Ausf Gs, this time serving in Italy. Panzers were in very short supply during the Italian campaign.

23. The howitzer version of the StuG III known as the StuH42.

24. The Panzer IV Ausf A, developed at the same time as the Panzer III, was intended as a support tank. However, its larger turret meant it could be upgraded with a larger gun for tank-to-tank combat.

25. Panzer IV Ausf D destroyed in Libya.

26. Panzer IV Ausf Es on the way to the Eastern Front and an uncertain fate.

27. British soldier examining a Panzer IV Ausf H captured in Italy.

28. Factory-fresh Panzer IVs.

29. Panzer IV Ausf J in Poland fitted with Schürzen side plates designed to ward off bazooka fire.

30. This derelict Panzer IV was a casualty of the fighting in Normandy.

31. The StuG IV was very similar to the StuG III.

32. The Hummel 150mm self-propelled gun used a hybrid Panzer III/IV chassis.

33. The second version of the Panzer V, confusingly known as the Panther Ausf A.

34. The third and final model Panther, designated the Ausf G.

35. Panther Ausf A captured in Normandy.

36. Another Panther Ausf A knocked out in Normandy.

37. Fighting in Poland, this Panther served with the 5th SS Panzer Division in the summer of 1944.

38. Another Panther serving with the 5th SS Panzer Division.

39. Two snow-covered Panthers lost during the Battle of the Bulge.

Introduction

It all began in Poland. The world watched as Polish cavalry charged German metal boxes mounted on tracks. These boxes had rotating turrets armed with machine guns that simply mowed the Poles down. The elite Pomorske Cavalry Brigade, trapped in the Polish Corridor between Germany and East Prussia, suffered such a fate. Trying to break out, they had bravely charged General Heinz Guderian's panzers. Their trumpets sounded and their pennants fluttered in the wind as they galloped forward. It did not take long for men and beasts to be reduced to bloody obscenities. Guderian recalled they 'suffered tremendous losses'.

Poland, like Britain and France, had a proud cavalry tradition but was much slower in acknowledging that the day of the horse as a weapon of war was almost over. Polish intelligence knew the Germans had panzers, but they wrongly believed these were dummies made of wood and cardboard. The Poles had tanks but not many so it had fallen to the dashing cavalry to try and stop Hitler's Blitzkrieg in September 1939. Their swords and lances had little impact on armour plate. They were massacred and Poland's armies were swiftly surrounded and overwhelmed.

Britain and France had known that Hitler possessed panzers since the mid-1930s but had chosen to ignore the impending danger. After all, at the time there were much more pressing matters such as the Spanish Civil War and the Japanese invasion of China. There is a popular misconception that Hitler's panzers emerged fully formed in 1939 to sweep all before them in Europe and the Balkans. This is far from the truth as Hitler's very first two tanks, the Panzer I and Panzer II, were little more than lightly-armed training vehicles designed to get round the military restrictions of the Treaty of Versailles.

Attempts at providing a battle tank with the subsequent Panzer III went far from smoothly. It was initially armed with a 37mm gun, whereas British tanks had a 40mm, the heavier French tanks a 47mm or even a 75mm gun and Soviet tanks a 45mm gun. To make matters worse, the Soviets were in the process of developing the KV-1 and the T-34 which were both armed with a much more powerful 76.2mm anti-tank gun. Likewise, the early Panzer IVs with a short-barrelled 75mm gun were really designed as support weapons due to its lower muzzle velocity (good for firing high-explosive but not anti-tank rounds).

The upshot was that Hitler's panzers were in imminent danger of losing the tank arms race almost from the very beginning. Fortunately, as an interim solution the later versions of the Panzer III were up-gunned with 50mm guns. This enabled the Panzer III to remain Hitler's workhorse for another two years while his tank designers sought a winning combination of armour and firepower with the Panzer IV, Tiger and Panther.

It was during the mid-1930s that Hitler's fledgling Panzerwaffe envisaged a 15-ton panzer, armed with a 37mm or 50mm armour-piercing gun, as the basic tank for the developing panzer divisions. It was proposed that this 'light' tank be supplemented by a medium 18-ton tank armed with a 75mm gun and this developed into the Panzer IV. From the start Guderian wanted a 50mm gun installed in the Panzer III, but in an effort to get production underway without interdepartmental disagreement the smaller 37mm gun, which was the standard infantry anti-tank gun, was accepted. It would not be until after the French campaign that the 50mm gun began to be fitted to the Panzer III.

Guderian wrote afterwards:

> We had differences of opinion on the subject of gun calibre with the Chief of the Ordnance Office and with the Inspector of Artillery. Both of these gentlemen were of the opinion that a 37mm gun would suffice for the light tanks, while I was anxious that they be equipped with a 50mm weapon since this would give them the advantage over the heavier armour plate which we expected soon to be incorporated in the construction of foreign tanks. Since, however, the infantry was already equipped with 37mm anti-tank guns, and for reasons of productive simplicity it was not considered desirable to produce more than one type of light anti-tank gun and shell. General Lutz and I had to give in.

During the 1920s Guderian had joined the staff of the Inspector of Motorized Troops, working with Major Lutz. Once Hitler was in power the Führer set up an Armoured Troops Command under General Lutz with Guderian as his chief of staff. Both were avid enthusiasts of the panzer concept and the need for hard-hitting armoured divisions. They enjoyed Hitler's full support. Guderian was then given command of the newly-established 2nd Panzer Division in 1935 but he continued to work closely with Lutz over the development of the Panzerwaffe. Guderian did not get the chance to impress upon Hitler the need for the 50mm gun again until after the Polish campaign.

The Panzer III and IV were given entirely different guns which performed very different tasks. A small-bore weapon with a high muzzle velocity has a long range, accuracy and penetrating power. In addition, the higher velocity makes it easier to hit moving targets. Such penetrating power is only useful against other tanks and concrete emplacements. A larger bore gun is less effective except at short range. The stubby 75mm KwK37 L/24 (KwK – Kampfwagenkanone or tank gun) gun fitted to the early Panzer IV had a low velocity which made it ideal for firing high-explosive shells capable of destroying soft targets. The short range made it unsuited for tank-versus-tank combat.

The small bore of the 37mm KwK L/46.5 fitted to the Panzer III had all the characteristics of a high-velocity gun, but was less effective against infantry and towed anti-tank guns. This was why Guderian really wanted the bigger high-velocity 50mm gun as it would be able to fire a high-explosive shell big enough to do the same job as the L/24. Larger high-velocity guns were effectively dual role weapons and they gave a tank commander an advantage over his opponents.

The earlier Panzer I and II light tanks, armed with nothing heavier than machine guns or a 20mm cannon respectively, were considered as no more than stopgaps. The prototypes for the new 15-ton tank were codenamed Zugführerwagen (platoon commanders' vehicle – abbreviated as ZW) and tested in 1936–7. The Panzer III became a medium tank as the Panzer I and II weighed about 5 tons and 9 tons respectively.

Whilst the Panzer IV proved to be Hitler's rock throughout the Second World War, during the opening stages of the conflict the more numerous Panzer III acted as his beast of burden. It was in the service of Rommel's tough Afrika Korps that the Panzer III is perhaps best remembered. For a time, it provided Rommel with a stand-off kill capability that the British could not match, although ultimately it was Rommel's towed anti-tank guns that proved the greatest threat to British armour.

After the invasion of the Soviet Union it was evident the Red Army's T-34 tank outmatched both the Panzer III and IV. To counter it the Germans designed the Tiger and the Panther but these were never built in decisive numbers. In contrast German factories churned out almost 30,000 Panzer IIIs and IVs including their numerous variants.

While the Panzer III was a reasonably good design at the start of the war, once it began to encounter better-armed enemy tanks, it soon became clear that its 37mm and 50mm guns were inadequate. The Panzer III turret would not permit a larger-calibre gun. In the meantime, the Panzer IV, Hitler's trusty workhorse, was up-gunned with a powerful long-barrelled 75mm gun and the Panzer III was subsequently given over to turretless assault gun production, mounting a version of the same weapon. It was in the latter guise that the Panzer III really made its greatest contribution to Hitler's war effort and undoubtedly helped prolong the conflict until 1945, even though his armed forces had already been decisively defeated on all fronts in mid-1944.

The development of the Panzer III and Panzer IV was quite remarkable in light of the Germans having such limited experience of tanks. Both turned out to be highly flexible combat vehicles. They shared many common features with the layout and sub-components. In the case of some, such as the hull machine-gun mounting, access hatches and visors, they were interchangeable. This made field maintenance much easier.

The myth of the invincible Tiger has developed over time, with it being considered the deadliest tank of the Second World War. At the time British and American tankers developed 'Tiger anxiety'. The reality is somewhat different; with only 1,354 Tiger Is and around 500 Tiger IIs ever built they were never going to make anything more than a local impact on the conduct of the war. In contrast the Panzer III/IV, M4 Sherman and T-34 were produced in the tens of thousands. Almost 6,000 Panzer V Panthers were manufactured and this was an immediate contemporary of the Tiger. Variants of the Tiger were built in even more limited numbers: there were only seventy-seven Jagdtigers, eighteen Sturmpanzers and ninety Jagdpanzer Elefants. Recovery vehicles consisted of just three Bergepanzer Tiger I and three Bergepanzer Elefant.

The German High Command without a doubt squandered its opportunities with the Tiger. Rather than equip an entire panzer division with it, the Tigers were dissipated into penny packets amongst the German Army and Waffen-SS. Because there were so few of them they were formed into independent tank battalions that gave a very powerful tactical blow, but lacked a greater strategic punch.

Hitler, always his own worst enemy, could not wait to get the Tiger into action and pointlessly committed a few first at Leningrad and then in Tunisia where the local terrain did not allow it to play to its strengths. It also meant that the Allies soon became aware of the presence of a formidable new German panzer. Similarly, at the Battle of Kursk, which is often cited as the Tiger's finest moment, again there were too few. Likewise, the impact of the subsequent Tiger II in Normandy, the Battle of the Bulge and at Budapest/Lake Balaton was very limited.

The paucity and deployment of the Tiger was to be a cause of rancour amongst Hitler's senior generals. Guderian, father of Hitler's panzer forces and Inspector General of Armoured Forces, was dismayed at how they were wasted at Leningrad and in Tunisia thanks to the Führer's impatience. He was very vocal in his post-war criticism of Hitler's treatment of the Tiger. In North Africa they became an issue of contention between Generals Rommel and von Arnim in the dying days of the Nazi campaign in Tunisia.

It is notable that Field Marshal Erich von Manstein, in his memoirs *Lost Victories*, and General Reinhard Gehlen, in *The Gehlen Memoirs*, make no mention of the Tiger's role or impact at Kursk – the Nazis' last major offensive on the Eastern Front. If anyone was to sing its praises, it would have been Manstein who commanded Army Group South with such incredible flare and Gehlen who was in charge of intelligence on the Eastern Front. As far as they were concerned it was just another panzer. Ultimately they had much bigger strategic axes to grind.

Panzer corps commander General von Mellenthin was complimentary of the Tiger's role at Kursk: 'the spearhead of the wedge was formed by the heaviest tanks, and the Tigers proved their worth against the Russian anti-tank fronts organized in depth'. While the Tiger may have done sterling work, the reality was that it was unable to completely cut through the Soviet defences or help stave off Hitler's inevitable defeat at Kursk. Instead it was compelled to cover the German retreat.

Ultimately it was a handful of extremely tough German tanks aces such as Johannes Bölter, Otto Carius, Kurt Knispel, Martin Schroif and Michael Wittmann who achieved incredible success with the Tiger against remarkable odds that really sealed the tank's all-pervading reputation. It was the likes of Michael Wittmann who fearlessly knocked out enemy tank after enemy tank that erroneously convinced many Allied tankers that the Tiger was all but invincible. Wittmann's eventual death clearly signalled that this was not the case.

PART I

DESIGNING TRACTORS

Chapter 1

Goodbye Versailles

The Panzer I and II light tanks were never really intended for combat operations. They were designed to give the German Army something to train with and to develop the tactics and organization of their new armoured units. These tanks were essentially a quick fix while the heavier Panzer III and IV were being built. When war broke out in Europe Hitler had insufficient numbers of the latter and was forced to deploy the two initial models. Whilst not as famous as Hitler's subsequent panzers, these tanks played a vital role in his early Blitzkrieg campaigns both in the West and the East. They were also instrumental in the development of his Panzerwaffe.

This situation came about because in the 1930s Germany faced a growing technology gap when it came to tanks. Ever since the Kaiser's defeat in the First World War the Germans had been forbidden from utilizing tanks. In the meantime, Britain, France and the Soviet Union forged ahead with their own rudimentary armoured forces. To compound matters, Germany's experiences with tanks in the First World War had been extremely limited, having belatedly built a few lumbering A7Vs.

Nonetheless throughout the late 1920s the German military were not idle. Guderian, one of the founders of the Panzerwaffe, explained:

> I first became interested in tanks in 1922, when I held an appointment in the *Inspektion der Kraftfahrtruppen* (Inspectorate of Motorized Troops) in the old Reichswehr Ministry. From that date I began to study the experience with tanks during World War I and the progress made after that war in foreign armies, with the result that I became employed as a teacher of tank tactics in 1928.

Also in the late 1920s the Germans secretly built themselves half a dozen prototype 19-ton medium tanks codenamed the 'Grosstraktor' or Big Tractor. Although only armoured with mild steel its main weapon was a 75mm gun. Thanks to an agreement with the Soviet government they were subsequently shipped to Kama for tests on the basis it was outside the Armistice control area. Several prototypes of a second design armed with a 75mm and 37mm gun were also produced, though neither went into mass production.

Despite the restrictions of the Treaty of Versailles, Germany secretly conducted extensive tank trials abroad, most notably in the Soviet Union and Sweden. These are little-known and largely forgotten episodes. Ironically the Soviets willingly aided the Germans as both countries were considered international pariahs. Cooperation started in 1926 when Moscow agreed to allow Germany to establish the Kama tank training school in Kazan. To conceal its true purpose, it was officially known as the Heavy Vehicle Experimental and Test Station.

It was opened for business three years later when it started taking not only German officers, but also German designers and engineers. The school was under Major Ritter von Radlmeier assisted by Captain Charles de Beaulieu. The tank development work was overseen by Captain Pirner. His brief was to ensure good mobility, ground clearance and engine efficiency for future vehicles. For the Germans arriving in the middle of Soviet Tatarstan it must have felt like another planet. Germany had two other bases: one to train the air force some 300 miles south-east of Moscow at Lipetsk and another experimenting with chemical warfare at Tomka.

Crucially this relationship gave German manufacturers their first taste of producing tanks since the First World War. Daimler-Benz, Krupp and Rheinmetall-Borsig were instructed to covertly produce two prototypes apiece of the Grosstraktor in 1925, but it took five years before they were all ready. Depending on the number of machine guns the prototypes were known as the Grosstraktor I and II. One type, as well as a fully-rotating turret housing the main armament, featured a machine-gun turret mounted on the rear of the hull. Getting these tanks to Kazan almost 445 miles east of Moscow was no easy task. It was also difficult to keep them hidden from prying eyes. Shipped east by rail it is almost certain that Soviet military intelligence crawled all over them at every opportunity.

Some members of the Soviet General Staff struggled to understand why they were welcoming ideological enemies into their midst. What Stalin got in exchange was the know-how for high-quality steel making. He also received advice on how to build artillery, aircraft and tanks. In particular Soviet aircraft had a nasty habit of falling from the sky on a daily basis.

Although junior Red Army officers did attend training courses at Kama, on the whole the Soviets sent their men to the Red Army Armour Centre at Voronezh. Ultimately Stalin was only prepared to permit the sharing of ideas to a certain degree. The Soviets were already pressing ahead with their own tanks based on British and French designs. This signalled to the Germans that they were facing a potential arms race with the Soviet Union.

These Kama trials proved crucial in helping develop the later Panzers. It also meant that the Red Army was aware that Germany was looking to develop a medium tank armed with a 75mm gun. Quite what the Red Army and the local Tartars thought of the Grosstraktor is not recorded. However, it is evident that the Soviet T-28 medium tank which appeared in the early 1930s was influenced by the Grosstraktor. It is unclear if the German tracked 37mm self-propelled anti-tank gun and 77mm self-propelled gun prototypes developed in the late 1920s were also sent to the Soviet Union.

At the same time during the 1920s Krupp acquired a majority share in the Swedish company Landsverk. The German engineer Otto Merker was sent to start designing both tracked and wheeled armoured vehicles in 1929. That year Guderian spent four weeks in Sweden with a Swedish tank unit. 'Colonel Burén gave me a most friendly welcome,' he recalled. There Guderian was able to watch a version of the German Leichter Kampfwagen (LK) II light tank being put through its paces by Swedish company commander Captain Klingspor. Inspired by the British Whippet tank, two prototypes had been built in Germany at the end of the First World War but never saw combat.

The Germans had been impressed by the Whippet's manoeuvrability and its relatively good speed. Mud chutes down the side also helped prevent clogging of the tracks and wheels which reduced maintenance. However, the Whippet's fixed turret formed by a raised superstructure at the back was far from ideal. The initial LK I design had a rotating turret, but the Germans decided this would slow production. Instead they reverted to the fixed style turret on the LK II. This tank proved to be more agile and faster than the Whippet.

After the war enough parts for ten LK IIs were covertly shipped to Sweden which used them to create its very first tank formation. Five tanks were built armed with a 37mm gun or two machine guns. The design then went into production as the M/21 powered by a German engine. Intriguingly Guderian said he got 'to see the latest German tank . . .'. This was rather telling and presumably referred to the upgraded M/29.

Guderian got to drive one during Swedish military exercises. This confirmed that having the engine and transmission in the front was not a satisfactory arrangement. The Germans had already come to the same conclusion ten years earlier. They had designed a LK III with the engine located to the rear. This allowed for a better central fighting compartment but a prototype was never completed. Also experiments with the Whippet and LK II showed that the unsprung wheels limited speed and gave the crew an extremely uncomfortable ride.

Interestingly, Josef Vollmer, who had designed the LK I, went to Sweden to develop a new light tank. His work resulted in the Landsverk 10 or M/31 with a turret armed with a 37mm gun. This bore a passing resemblance to Hitler's subsequent Panzer I built by Krupp, amongst others. Again this tank was powered by a German engine. Guderian does not record whether he met Merker and Vollmer, but as the Swedes were in the process of upgrading the M/21, design issues would have been discussed. Soviet intelligence was tipped off that the Germans were looking at light tanks. Krupp and Rheinmetall-Borsig were in the process of secretly developing a prototype 'leichtertraktor' or light tank, though a turreted version with a 37mm gun did not appear until 1934. By this stage the Red Army was being equipped with the T-27 tankette.

Men such as Guderian began to develop the concept of mobile warfare employing motorized and armoured troops. This began to involve employing dummy tanks, as Guderian recalled:

> During the summer of 1932 General Lutz for the first time organized exercises involving both reinforced infantry regiments and tank battalions – the latter, of course, equipped with dummies . . . For the first time since the signing of the Treaty of Versailles there appeared at that year's manoeuvres German armoured reconnaissance cars built, according to our specifications, of steel armour plate mounted on the chassis of a six-wheeled lorry. School children, accustomed to stick their pencils through the canvas walls of our dummies in order to have a look inside were disappointed this time . . .

Guderian was not distracted by the traditionalists. 'There was considerable unobjective criticism on the part of the cavalry, but our success was so obvious that not much notice was taken of this petulance.' Indeed, Guderian soon found many of the younger cavalry officers coming over to his way of thinking.

In terms of getting their tank programme underway the Germans did certainly not hang about. In 1932 the German Army Weapons Office (Heereswaffenamt) bought a Vickers Carden-Loyd IV tankette chassis from Britain. During the late 1920s and early 1930s Carden-Loyd had begun developing a series of two-man light reconnaissance tanks. These were ideal for patrolling the borders of Britain's vast empire.

The German Weapons Office's stated intention was to assess the chassis' suitability as a possible carrier for a 20mm anti-aircraft gun. Instead they decided they would draw on it to produce a light training tank. To meet the requirement for a 5-ton tank with twin machine guns in a fully traversing turret, Krupp designed a chassis largely copied from the Carden-Loyd. This beat four other designs on offer. Then in December 1933 Kassel received an order to build three running prototypes. In the meantime, Daimler Benz was given the contract to build the superstructures and the turrets. The vehicles were completed in February 1934.

Guderian observed:

> When we drew up the long-range plans we were well aware that years must pass before our new tanks would be ready for action. The Carden-Loyd chassis, which we purchased in England, was suited to this purpose; it was actually intended as a carrier for a 20mm anti-aircraft gun. It was

true that nothing larger than machine guns could be mounted in any turret that this vehicle could carry. But with this disadvantage, it could be ready for action by 1934 and it would at least serve as a training tank until our real combat tanks began to appear. So the supply of this item of equipment, which was designated the Panzer I was ordered. Nobody in 1932 could have guessed that one day we should have to go into action with this little training tank.

These developments continued especially once Hitler came to power. He publicly rejected the military restrictions of the Treaty of Versailles in early 1935 when he announced German rearmament. Guderian noted:

> In June 1934, a Command of '*Kraftfahr-Kampftruppen*' (Motorized Fighting Troops) was established, which later was given the title of '*Kommando der Panzertruppen*'. I became Chief of Staff of this Command. Under the direction of General Lutz, we carried out the first manoeuvres of a panzer division at Munsterlager in July, 1935 – with complete success.

General von Thoma, who after Guderian was the most famous of the initial panzer leaders, was overjoyed, saying 'It was wonderful to have real tanks for the first time in 1934, after being confined to tactical experiments with dummies for so many years'. The day of the tank was at hand. On 15 October 1935 Hitler's very first three panzer divisions were established.

Officially prevented from possessing armoured fighting vehicles, Hitler's Germany had begun secretly producing turretless tracked 'agricultural tractors' for training purposes. These quickly evolved into to the Panzer I and Panzer II light tanks and laid the foundations for the medium Panzer III, IV and Panther and heavy Tiger. The Panzer II armed with a 20mm gun first appeared in 1937. Although both were phased out of active service by the middle of the Second World War, self-propelled gun variants continued to see combat until the very end on all fronts.

The birth of modern armoured warfare was rudely heralded by Hitler's Blitzkrieg (Lightning War) against Poland in 1939 when his panzers overwhelmed the Polish Army. Just a few years before this though a number of European powers had already cut their teeth in the developing art of tank warfare during the Spanish Civil War of 1936–9. In this conflict neither of the protagonists had any indigenous tank capability, forcing them to rely heavily on external suppliers. This enabled Germany, Italy and the Soviet Union to use the conflict as a valuable testing ground for all manner of military equipment – but in particular tanks, aircraft and artillery.

During the early 1930s Germany secretly designed its 'training' tank which became the PanzerKampfwagen (PzKpfw) IA followed by the IB; in total nearly

2,500 were built. The much more numerous IB had a more powerful engine and weighed 5.7 tons, with a turret mounting two machine guns. Several hundred of both types were sent to Spain.

The Spanish Civil War proved invaluable for the development of Germany's panzer forces. At the time a colonel, von Thoma, a veteran of the First World War, commanded the panzer group in Spain where his advisors trained Franco's Nationalist tankers and gained combat experience. Thoma created four tank battalions each of three companies with fifteen Panzer Is per company and thirty anti-tank companies each with six 37mm guns. Officially the instructors handed the tanks over to the Nationalist crews. However, von Thoma managed to take part in 192 tank actions during his time in Spain.

Late in the autumn of 1937 large-scale exercises were conducted before Hitler and senior foreign dignitaries. The fledgling tank troops were involved including the 3rd Panzer Division and 1st Panzer Brigade. Guderian recalled:

> On the last day of the manoeuvres a final attack was mounted for the benefit of the foreign guests; all the available tanks took part in this, under my command. It was an impressive spectacle even though the only tanks we then had were the Panzer I.

These manoeuvres were held at Neustrelitz and reportedly involved around 800 tanks, which seems a suspiciously inflated number. Amongst the guests were Field Marshal Sir Cyril Deverell, the British Chief of the Imperial General Staff, and Marshal Pietro Badoglio, Chief of the Italian General Staff. Neither seemed inclined to point out that this 'impressive spectacle' was clearly in violation of the Treaty of Versailles, which Hitler had so openly rejected three years earlier. Such diplomatic niceties were pointless as German tanks were already at war in Spain.

At the luncheon afterwards Guderian noted that the British delegation seemed more interested in Italian tanks and they expressed the view that the tank was very much an infantry support weapon. Although Deverell was alert to the growing military threat posed by Germany, he was at loggerheads with the Secretary of State for War over defence spending, especially on tanks, and was subsequently sacked. Guderian was keen to talk to Badoglio whose forces had been using light tanks against tribesmen in Ethiopia.

To be fair the Panzer I was not a very big tank – it did not look particularly menacing. To the British it was comparable to their range of three-man light tanks that were entering service, which were only armed with machine guns. These were fine for scouting and security duties but little more. The British though were also developing cruiser tanks armed with 2pdr (40mm) guns. What they did known in any great detail was that the Panzer II, III and IV armed with 20mm, 50mm and 75mm guns were all just going into production. Nonetheless Guderian remembered that 'the conversation was an animated one'.

There was another reason that the foreign visitors were not unduly alarmed by the Panzer I. Guderian, that ardent tank enthusiast, may have painted a rather excessively rosy picture of the proceedings in order not to dent his optimism but General Nehring recalled that the whole thing was almost a shambles as many of Guderian's tanks ran out of fuel or broke down. Guderian cryptically admitted 'Supply and repair facilities were found to be insufficient'. The high-ranking German spectators were as a result critical of the new panzer arm. These shortcomings were to be a problem the following year during the Austrian Anschluss.

By the end of 1937 the Spanish Nationalists were still very weak in armour and the Republicans' Soviet-supplied tanks remained very much superior to the Panzer I and Italian Fiat-Ansaldo tankettes. To help offset this all the Nationalists could do was make use of captured Soviet tanks. Nor was the Nationalist deployment of armour any better than the Republicans. By the end of 1938 the Republican Army had just 50 tanks left, Franco by contrast having 300. On 3 January 1939 Nationalist forces crossed the Ebro and the Republican front collapsed, at the end of March Franco marched triumphantly into Madrid marking the end of the war.

During the conflict tanks were largely confined to an infantry support role following the French doctrine, which greatly reduced their offensive value. The Panzer I was mainly deployed during a period when there were limited tank-to-tank and anti-tank engagements. The use of tanks in Spain was never really decisive. Despite the Nationalists' lack of effective tanks or anti-tank guns, the Republicans were unable to exploit their superior Soviet armour. Air power and artillery emerged as the key to the war. Nevertheless, both Germany and the Soviet Union drew important lessons from their experiences.

Von Thoma fully understood the shock value of massed tanks as an offensive rather than supporting weapon. He recalled:

> General Franco wished to parcel out the tanks among the infantry – in the usual way of the generals who belong to the old school. I had to fight this tendency constantly in the endeavour to use the tanks in a concentrated way. The Francoists' successes were largely due to this.

Thus the very beginnings of Blitzkrieg were born in part thanks to the Panzer I.

Chapter 2

Going Farming

The two initial models of Panzer I came in a number of different guises. The first batch of just fifteen Ausf (Model) A Ohne Aufbau (literally 'without turret') were simply tracked training vehicles for Hitler's fledgling Panzerwaffe. These were followed by 818 Ausf A machine gun-armed light tanks, utilizing the same chassis but with the addition of a rear idler and turret, which were built from July 1934 to June 1936. The follow-on model, the Ausf B, was produced from August 1935 to June 1937 with 675 built. Manufacture was spread across Daimler-Benz, Henschel, Krupp-Gruson and Maschinenfabrik Augsburg-Nürnberg (MAN). At 40km/hr these light tanks were relatively fast but very poorly armed.

The Ausf A Ohne Aufbau, known as the Krupp Tractor, was the vehicle that laid the very foundations for Hitler's powerful panzer force. It was officially designated an agricultural tractor (Landwirtschaftlicher Schlepper or LaS for short) to conceal Germany's secret tank programme in complete defiance of the Treaty of Versailles. This explicitly forbade Germany from owning or building tanks or other armoured fighting vehicles.

Despite these restrictions the German Army's Motorized Instruction Command (Kraftfahrlehrkommando) requested in the early 1930s a fully-tracked vehicle for training purposes. The rest of Europe was busy developing tanks and the German military did not want to be left behind. During the First World War Germany had almost completely ignored the new-fangled weapons being produced by the British and French.

In response Krupp designed its turretless tractor which lacked a super-structure, turret and armament. The 'Tractor' was powered by a Krupp M305 60hp petrol engine (at 2,500rpm) giving a top speed of 37km/hr and a range of 145km. The gearbox offered five forward and a single reverse gear. The vehicle weighed 3.5 tons and was just over 4m long and 2m wide. It only required two crew.

The Krupp design featured a fully-tracked armoured hull, with a suspension comprising four road wheels, a front sprocket and a fifth larger road wheel that acted as the rear idler. Above the four main road wheels were three return rollers. To improve the ride and the vehicle's performance the first road wheel was attached to a coil spring and hydraulic shock absorber. The other four including the idler were fitted in pairs with leaf springs supported by a distinctive horizontal girder.

Five companies (Daimler-Benz, Henschel, Krupp-Gruson, MAN and Rheinmetall-Borsig) were invited to produce three vehicles each. The intention being that they would all gain production experience. Production ran from February to April 1934. This initial model Panzer I was sent to the very first two panzer regiments, Kraftfahrlehrkommando Zossen and Ohrduf, in the spring of 1934 so they could conduct fully-tracked armoured vehicle training.

The 'Tractor' was only the first stage in creating a tank force. The decision had already been taken to take the training vehicles a step further by building a follow-on type with an armoured superstructure and a turret armed with a machine gun. Krupp had been instructed to build 135 but by January 1934 the orders had risen by another 450.

This light tank was called the MG Panzerwagen or armoured machine-gun tank. However, for simplicity it was re-designated the Panzer I Ausf A (i.e. Model A) or 1A LaS Krupp. It was the first German tank to go into mass production in July 1934. It had the same suspension and hull as the ohne Aufbau, but with a superstructure built out over the tracks and with a turret offset to the right. The position of the latter permitted space for the driver's access hatch to the left. The turret was armed with two coaxial 7.92mm MG13 machine guns mounted in an internal moving gun mantlet. These had 1,525 rounds of ammunition. For access the turret had a single semi-circular hatch that opened forward. Turret traverse was by hand.

Visibility was good, with six vision ports in the turret and five in the super-structure. Powered by the same engine, the ventilation proved poor, leading to overheating. This was overcome by the installation of an air-scoop louvre on the rear deck, plus two scoops were added at the back to deflect exhaust fumes. The armour was 13mm throughout except for the upper surfaces which were 8mm. The Ausf A, like its predecessor, only required two crew, with one acting as driver and the other the commander/gunner. Understandably the weight increased considerably to 5.4 tons.

Rheinmetall-Borsig did not seem to have been involved in its manufacture. Kraftfahrlehrkommando received its first Ausf A in September 1934. By the summer of 1935 it had 475. General von Thoma stated 'in 1934 our first tank battalion was formed, at Ohrdruf, under the name "Motor-Instruction Commando". I was in charge of it. It was the grandmother of all the others.'

According to Colonel (later General) Walter Nehring, another panzer aficionado, in 1934 the tanks had no radios. All command and control between the crews had to be conducted visually employing signalling flags. Initially many of the tanks companies had few actual tanks and training was conducted using Rubezahl tractors and Carden-Loyd tracked carriers, the more fortunate ones getting to use prototype medium tanks returned from Kama and the Krupp tractors. During 1939 and 1940 the Ausf A saw combat in Poland and France respectively. The 40th Panzer Battalion used it during the invasions of Denmark and Norway. It also saw service in North Africa and Finland.

Although the second model Panzer I was very similar to the first, there were a number of telltale differences. One of the major faults identified with the Ausf A was the Krupp engine. While it had been adequate for the training vehicle the added weight on the light tank meant that it was underpowered. The extra strain also meant that the engine still had a habit of overheating. The solution was to install a Maybach NL38TR 100hp (at 3,000rpm) engine. While generally known as the Ausf B it was also referred to as the 1B LaS May.

The new engine was not the only change with the Ausf B. The light armoured tracked command vehicle based on the Panzer I, known as the Kleine Panzerbefehlswagen, had a lengthened chassis to accommodate extra radio equipment. This chassis and the modified suspension was used on the second type of Panzer I. To facilitate this lengthening a new road wheel was added, making five in total, and an additional return roller making four in total. The idler was elevated so that it no longer acted as a road wheel. The forward road wheel, as on the Ausf B, was cushioned by a coil spring, while the leaf springs on the other four road wheels were supported by a girder. The problem of overheating was addressed by redesigning the rear deck so that louvres drew air into the water-cooled engine and its radiator. The upper part of the tank, namely the superstructure, the turret and armour, remained the same as the Ausf A.

Krupp experimented with installing its air-cooled M601 diesel engine in the Panzer I producing at least two prototypes. The LKB1 utilized the Ausf A while LKB2 used the Ausf B. It was not put into service because it provided insufficient power. In 1937 Krupp also developed a prototype LKA for the export market. While it had a similar superstructure and turret layout, it had a completely different suspension arrangement to the A and B models. This comprised front drive sprocket, four road wheels, a level idler and two return rollers.

Predictably the infantry and cavalry inspectorates felt they should keep control of the new tanks and the supporting anti-tank guns and motorized infantry. The supporters of the panzer forces saw this as a wasteful dispersion of the tank which they argued should be deployed en masse to conduct deep penetration operations. After the exercises held at Lüneburg in 1938 General of the Artillery Ulex turned to Nehring and said 'What the Herr Oberst says may be well and true, but if ever we use these tanks in action, we will do so in the way we think fit.'

The Ausf B was issued to the panzer units from 1935 until 1940. By early 1941 the Panzer I was being phased out of front-line service. However, the Ausf B was issued to the self-propelled anti-tank gun battalions for use by the company and battalion commanders. Not surprisingly by late 1943 the commanders were complaining that the Panzer I was not longer fit for purpose as a command vehicle.

The very belated Ausf C and F were the rarest models of the Panzer I and they saw very little combat. Just forty Ausf C were built by Krauss-Maffei as a light tracked reconnaissance vehicle from July to December 1942. Notably it was completely different from the A and B and featured five overlapping road wheels with torsion bar. It was capable of an impressive 79km/hr. The F also built by KM was intended as a heavily-armoured infantry assault tank with just thirty produced from April–December 1942. The extra armour slowed it to 25km/hr.

Limited numbers of Panzer I variants included self-propelled guns, bridge-layers, command vehicles, ammunition carriers, flamethrowers and repair and maintenance vehicles. The most notable was the Panzerjäger I designed as a mobile anti-tank gun platform armed with a Czech-built 47mm gun, which saw action in France, North Africa and Russia. This made the best use of the Ausf B chassis and because of its widespread deployment it was extensively photographed.

The Panzer II light tank was up-gunned from the Panzer I's machine guns to a 20mm cannon. In many ways the early series Panzer II looked like an enlarged Panzer I with similar suspension. Just seventy-five of the initial Ausf a/1-a/3 were built from May 1936 to February 1937. Even fewer Ausf b were produced with just twenty-five appearing from February to March 1937. They were no faster than the Panzer I. These early Panzer IIs were little more than trials and training tanks, although they did see combat.

The original plans for re-equipping the German Army had been based on deploying medium tanks armed with shell-firing guns. These would evolve as the Panzer III medium tank and the Panzer IV medium support tank. They were expensive, however, and took longer to produce than light tanks. In the meantime, it was decided to build a 10-ton tank as an interim measure to supplement the 6-ton Panzer I.

This was required to support the Panzer I by providing a light tank that could fire both armour-piercing and high-explosive rounds. The proposal for the 2cm MG Panzerwagen was rather rushed, with the remit issued by the Waffenamt in July 1934 and the soft steel prototypes appearing in October 1935.

Prototype vehicles for this new specification were produced by Krupp, Henschel and MAN. The designs were developed in part from Krupp's Panzer I Ausf A/B and its LKA export model. Krupp designed its LKA II by fitting a larger turret which had very similar specifications to the Panzer II. However, it was the MAN version that was chosen for production.

The suspension on the MAN design comprised six road wheels either side mounted in pairs on leaf springs. The latter were supported by a horizontal girder giving it a similar appearance to the Panzer I. Whereas the Panzer I Ausf B had four return rollers the Panzer II Ausf a only had three. The rapid expansion of Hitler's panzer divisions plus growing international tensions resulted in the MAN prototypes being ordered in batches of twenty-five for the a/1, a/2 and a/3 rather than the normal two or three. These were built by MAN and Daimler Benz.

After trials with the first ten Panzer II Ausf a/1 the rubber-tyred cast rear idler was abandoned in favour of a welded one. The a/2 was fitted with a fireproof engine compartment wall. Also a larger port was fitted beneath the engine to improve access to the fuel pump and oil filter. On the Ausf a/3 the suspension springs were improved and a larger radiator was fitted.

The Ausf a was powered by a Maybach HL57TR engine, with six forward and one reverse gear. It had a slightly better range than the Panzer I, at 200km. The turret featured a split hatch and dummy commander's periscope cover that was characteristic of the models before the Ausf C. Armament consisted of the 20mm KwK30 L/55 gun and one MG34. It carried 180 20mm rounds and 2,250 rounds for the machine gun.

While the main armament was a considerable improvement on the Panzer I's machine guns, it was still not terribly effective. Although the rate of fire was good, it could only reach 600m. It was criticised for only being able to fire armour piercing ammunition. However, the Panzer II carried both the panzergranate solid shot armour-piercing shell and the sprenggranate high-explosive shell. The Pzgr, while armour-piercing, also contained a small high explosive charge. Nonetheless, the armour-penetrating capabilities of these small 20mm rounds was not very good. The standard towed anti-tank gun was the 37mm weapon.

This early model Panzer II was almost 2 tons heavier that the Panzer I and required three crew, commander/gunner, loader/radio operator and driver. The latter's position was set forward of the turret, with the superstructure front plate angled back to the right. The driver was served by a forward facing vision port and a second facing to the right and a third to the left.

It was first sent to the panzer regiments in the spring of 1936. Initially it was issued to the platoon and company commanders but as more became available they were used to form a full platoon in each company for tank-to-tank combat. The Ausf a series saw action in Poland, but were relegated to reconnaissance work during the invasion of the West.

The Ausf b was the second model in the developmental series of the Panzer II and externally looked very similar to the Ausf a. Internally though it was greatly improved. Key amongst these improvements was a better engine in the Maybach HL62TR, which required a strengthening of the mountings for the motor, transmission and final drives. In the engine compartment cooling and ventilation was enhanced and a new type of exhaust muffler was fitted.

Externally it was fitted with a new drive sprocket, wider road wheels and return rollers and wider tracks. The springs were improved to stop slipping or damage and brackets were introduced to strengthen support for each pair of road wheels. The rear track fenders were hinged to stop clogging with dirt and stones. The Ausf b was issued to units in the same way as the Ausf a.

The Panzer I and II were not really what the likes of Lutz, Guderian, Nehring and Thoma wanted. They were after something much bigger and more powerful. After Lutz and Guderian returned from the Soviet Union in the spring of 1934 an order had been placed for a 24-ton medium tank. This was modelled after the early Soviet style with a 75mm and 37mm gun and three machine guns mounted in multiple turrets. Known as the Neubaufahrzeug, the contract was awarded to Rheinmetall-Borsig and was a development of the company's earlier Grosstraktor. Just a handful of this type of tank was produced before the project was abandoned. Instead it had been decided to rely on the Panzer I and II.

After their experiences with the Panzer II Ausf a and b the specialists of Waffenprüfamt 6 (the Weapons Department or Heereswaffenamt responsible for tank and armoured fighting vehicle procurement – Wa Prüf 6) presented numerous reasons why this tank should not go into mass production. However, as Nehring pointed out, although it was unsatisfactory in some areas, ultimately it was the only one readily available and was suitable for the task in hand. Hitler was insistent that his tank force be expanded as rapidly as possible leaving them with little option. Guderian had no choice but to pressure the Wa Prüf 6 representative warning 'Don't you raise difficulties – I must have those tanks'. After that the Panzer II went into production.

The Ausf c was the last model in the developmental series. Not only did it have an entirely different type of suspension, it also had a more powerful 6.2-litre engine, which had first been used in the Ausf b. This gave it a far better performance than its predecessors and formed the design basis for all subsequent models of Panzer II. Confusingly the Ausf c went into full production as the Ausf A from July 1937. The B was produced from December 1937 and the C from June 1938. Over 1,100 were built in total and along with the subsequent Ausf F were the most common type of Panzer II.

Because very few Panzer IIIs and IVs were available, in 1938 in theory a panzer battalion comprised three companies of Panzer Is and one company of Panzer IIs. This gave a total of 80 and 16 respectively, so a panzer division had 340 Panzer Is and 64 Panzer IIs. However, such numbers were never put into the field and the panzer divisions' tank strength dwindled as the Second World War progressed, ranging from 300 to 150 tanks. By the end of 1938 some seventeen panzer regiments had been formed.

The German tank arm was originally based on seven motorized battalions or Kraftfahrtruppen of the Reichsheer. These though were heavily reinforced in the mid-1930s by units drawn from the cavalry and infantry. The first three panzer divisions each consisted of a panzer brigade of two tank regiments and a rifle brigade normally made up of a single rifle regiment. The infantry element was drawn from the cavalry as well as the line infantry (in contrast the motorized divisions were former infantry units), formed into regiments of two battalions. Initially lorry-borne so they could provide close support for the tanks, these were effectively dragoons and played to the cavalry's desire to be fully mobile.

Reconnaissance vehicles were needed for both the motorized infantry divisions (which later became panzergrenadier divisions) and the panzer divisions. These were provided in the form of armoured cars of varying sizes. Some thought was also given to adapting the Panzer II to this role by increasing its speed. The problem was that the average armoured car could managed 80km/hr, twice the speed of the Panzer II.

The Ausf D and E were developed to give the cavalry a light tank capable of pursuit, with a top speed of 55km/hr. Built by MAN the entire hull, superstructure and suspension were different from the normal Panzer II, though the turret remained the same. They had only four large double-tyred road wheels and dispensed with the return rollers. Just forty-three were built from May 1938 to August 1939, sufficient for a single battalion. In contrast, the FAMO produced Ausf F was the final model of the regular style Panzer II series with 524 built from March 1941 to December 1942.

As early as 1940 it was recognized that the Panzer II was outdated as a combat tank. However, its development as a reconnaissance vehicle was continued fruitlessly for the next three years. The final three types of Panzer II to appear were designed for a reconnaissance role, but bore little resemblance to the previous models and were produced in very small numbers.

The Ausf G was another attempt to increase the Panzer II's speed. It had a completely redesigned suspension, five pairs of overlapping road wheels, sprung on torsion bars. As with the D, E and F the hull front was box shaped but lacked hatches. Just twelve were built by MAN from April 1941 to February 1942 and none saw combat. Twenty-seven Ausf G turrets were used for fortified positions. The similar-looking Ausf J, also built by MAN, saw twenty-two produced from April to December 1942 and half-a-dozen served with 12th Panzer on the Eastern Front. MAN also built 100 Ausf Ls from September 1943 to January 1944. Known as the Lynx, this saw combat on the Eastern and Western Fronts.

The Panzer II was used for a variety of different tasks, which included flamethrowers and self-propelled guns, such as the very successful Marder II and Wespe armed with a 76.2mm anti-tank gun and 105mm light howitzer respectively. Over 850 Marder were produced, 675 Wespe and some 150 flamethrowers. Other specialized variants were produced in much smaller quantities and many got little further than the drawing board.

Chapter 3

We Need a Tank Killer

It was always intended that the main combat tank of Hitler's panzer divisions would be armed with a 50mm armour-piercing gun, plus a coaxial turret machine gun and a front hull machine gun. The specification issued by the Army Weapons Office in 1935 was for a tank no heavier than 24 tons (so Germany's bridges could cope). The actual requirement was for a 15-ton tank with a top speed of 40km/hr with a five-man crew (driver, hull gunner/radio operator, commander, gunner and loader). The basic design of the tank was broken down into four major sub-assemblies; the hull, front superstructure, rear superstructure and turret.

Initially five firms were invited to come up with designs for the Panzer III, and three prototypes were produced. The contract was won by Daimler-Benz from a specification drawing on the best elements of all three prototypes. For convenience the main armament was accepted as a 37mm gun, which was already in production for the infantry anti-tank companies. But to keep Guderian happy this was on the condition that the turret ring be large enough to permit an up-gunning to a 50mm gun at a later date (the 50mm PaK38 anti-tank gun did not appear until 1940). This was an important decision as it enabled the Panzer III to stay in service for at least two years longer than would otherwise have been possible.

Only a very few initial production models of the Panzer III armed with a 37mm KwK L/46.5 gun were built during 1937–9. The Ausf A had just ten produced, the B and C only fifteen each, the D ran to thirty and E just under 100. Due to problems with their suspension and the thinness of their armour the A, B and C, after seeing action in Poland, were swiftly withdrawn from combat units in February 1940. The D model also fought in Norway before being withdrawn. The service life of the E was extended by up-gunning it with the desired 50mm gun.

The Ausf A was initially known as the 3.7cm Geschütz-Panzerwagen (Vs Kfz 619) (Armoured Gun-tank) (Trial Vehicle). To conceal its subsequent development, the tank was dubbed Zugführerwagen or platoon commander's vehicle. The Ausf A went into production as a development series in 1937. Five of the 1 Serie Zugführerwagen (1st Series Platoon Commander's Vehicle) had been produced by early May 1937.

After five attempts with the Panzer III during 1937–8, it seemed as if the designers had finally got it right with the Ausf E. The plan was to build almost 700 under the designation Ausf F, but in light of the improved Ausf G and H about to be produced with a schedule that would overlap the F order was cut by some 250 tanks. The Panzer III was in very short supply by 1939 and it was clear Daimler-Benz could not cope on its own, so contracts were issued to Altmärke Kettenfabrik GmbH (Alkett), Fahrzeug und Motorenbau GmbH (FAMO), Henschel, MAN, Mühlenbau und Industrie AG (MIAG), Maschinenfabrik Niedersachsen-Hanover (MNH) and Wegmann to form a production group. The guns were built by Karges Hammer and Garnh and major sub-assemblies were manufactured by Deutsche Edelstahlwerke.

Whilst some Allied intelligence reports apparently made reference to a Panzer III Ausf I, this was not a production designation actually employed by the Germans. Instead they skipped a model. The Panzer III Ausf J finally reversed the frustrating trend of its predecessors in that orders were increased and not cut (a fate which had befallen the Ausf F, G and H). Two variants of the Ausf J were built totalling some 2,616 tanks, making it the most numerous Panzer III. The Ausf J first went into production in March 1941 armed with the standard 50mm KwK38 L/42 gun but from December 1941 was also produced in parallel with the long-barrelled 50mm KwK39 L/60 that had a far higher muzzle velocity. The J saw combat in North Africa and on the Eastern Front.

Between March 1941 and June 1942 a total of 1,549 Panzer III Ausf Js armed with the KwK38 L/42 were built. They were used to arm the 2nd and 5th Panzer Divisions plus an independent panzer regiment which were despatched to the Eastern Front as reinforcements in September 1941. The rest were issued as combat replacements for around 1,400 tanks lost during the first year of fighting in North Africa and the Soviet Union. By June 1942 the panzer divisions had about 500 Panzer IIIs armed with the 50mm KwK38 L/42 gun. By the time of the Battle of Kursk the following summer Army Groups Centre and South still had 141.

In August 1940 Hitler ordered the 50mm KwK39 L/60 gun be used to arm the Panzer III, but as the L/42 had been recently introduced with some success the Ordnance Department did not act on his instructions. It was on 18 April 1941 during an armoured equipment demonstration that Hitler witnessed the Ausf J without the long gun. Guderian was present and recalled:

> It was on this occasion that he noticed that the Panzer III had been re-equipped by the Army Ordnance Office with a 50mm L/42 cannon instead of with a 50mm L/60 as he had ordered. This independent act on the part of the Ordnance Office infuriated him all the more since it involved a weakening of his original intentions. The firm Alkett in Spandau was able by the end of April, to produce the guns Hitler wanted, which made the excuses of the Army Ordnance Office appear even more feeble.

Exactly the same problem was encountered with the Panzer IV. Albert Speer, Hitler's Armaments Minister, said:

> When the Russian T-34 appeared, Hitler was triumphant, for he could then point out that he had earlier demanded the kind of long-barrelled gun it had. Even before my appointment as Minister of Armaments, I heard Hitler in the Chancellery garden, after a demonstration of the Panzer IV, inveighing against the obstinacy of the Army Ordnance Office which had turned down his idea of increasing the velocity of the missile by lengthening the barrel.

Ironically events in the Soviet Union two months after Hitler's anger over the Panzer III were to demonstrate the urgent need for much more powerful anti-tank guns. The initial order for 900 Ausf Js was soon increased to 2,700.

The L/60 was introduced in 1941 to replace the 37mm anti-tank gun. It was developed by fitting a longer barrel in the 42-calibre weapon, so the breech rings and mountings were identical. This longer barrel with a lengthened chamber could take the 50mm PaK38 anti-tank gun round. Although almost identical to the PaK the muzzle brake on the tank gun was omitted and an electrical firing system installed. Also the gun carriage was modified for a tank mounting. Another version of the 50mm KwK39/I L/60 featuring a muzzle brake was used to arm the eight-wheeled Sd Kfz 234/3 Puma armoured car.

From December 1941 to July 1942 a total of 1,067 Ausf Js were built with the L/60. The only difference between the two versions was the length of the gun barrel and the reduced ammunition storage due to the increased length of the larger shell. They were easy to identify as the L/42 barrel did not extend beyond the glacis plate, whereas the L/60 did. In addition, the shorter weapon tapered out where it met the recoil mount.

These long-barrelled Ausf J were issued to the 3rd, 16th, 29th and 60th Motorized Infantry Divisions and the 5th SS Motorized Infantry Division Wiking in early 1942. The rest were used to replace the high losses sustained in North Africa and on the Eastern Front. Although the L/60 proved very useful against the British Grant and Valentine in North Africa, it could do little against the frontal armour of the Red Army's KV-1 and T-34 tanks.

After the sizeable production run of the Ausf J, the two subsequent models were built in relatively small numbers. This was a trend that continued up until Panzer III production came to an end. By early 1942 it had been decided to phase out the Panzer III and replace it with the proposed Panzer V known as the Panther. Delays with the latter until 1943 rather complicated things as the panzer divisions struggled to maintain their dwindling tank strength. Rather than waste the tried-and-tested Panzer III chassis it was agreed to eventually turn it over completely to assault gun production. The first version of the Sturmgeschütz III appeared in 1940 and was progressively improved and up-gunned with the 75mm L/43 or L/48 gun in March 1942.

Some 653 Panzer III Ausf Ls were produced from June to December 1942 and 250 Ausf Ms from October 1942 to February 1943. Improvements included doubling the armour on the turret and spaced armour on the superstructure. The only real difference between these two models was the M was fitted with fording equipment.

Despite arming the Panzer III with the 50mm L/60 gun, the tank still did not pack enough punch in the face of the fast-evolving armoured warfare on the Eastern Front and in North Africa. Work was carried out to see if the Panzer IV turret armed with the long 75mm gun could be installed on the Panzer III in March 1942. Due to excessive weight on the suspension plus the amount of modification work required these plans were quickly abandoned. The only option that remained on the table was the short 75mm gun.

By this stage the interim Panzer IV Ausf F2 armed with the powerful 75mm KwK40 L/43 gun was just going into production and the factories were gearing up to build the follow-on Panzer IV Ausf G with L/43 or L/48 guns. The Ausf G went into production in May 1942 and was followed by the Panzer IV Ausf H and Ausf J both with the L/48. The heavy Tiger I with an 88mm gun was also due to start production in July 1942. These developments made the Panzer III largely redundant as a gun tank, but poor overall tank production figures remained a problem.

Therefore, production of the Panzer III armed with the L/60 continued through 1942. The Ausf L had improved armour on the turret front with it increasing from 30mm to 57mm. Spaced 20mm armour was added to the superstructure front and many had spaced armour added to the gun mantlet. Not long into the production run, in order to simplify things the escape hatches on the hull side, the loader's vision port on the mantlet and the turret side ports were discontinued. The Ausf L also had the ability to transfer heated engine coolant from one vehicle to another. Other changes included replacing the coil spring for the main weapon with a torsion bar counterbalance. The hatches and air intake louvres on the rear deck were likewise changed.

At first 1,100 Ausf Ls were ordered but this was reduced when in June 1942 instructions were issued to mount the short-barrelled 75mm KwK37 L/24 gun (which had been used to arm the initial model Panzer IVs) in the Panzer III. Some Ausf Ls were diverted to this role and one was used for an experimental tapered-bore KwK0725 gun. Those armed with the L/24 were deemed to be a new model and became the Ausf N. The Ausf Ls were issued to the 1st SS, 2nd SS and 3rd SS Panzer Divisions and Panzergrenadier Division Grossdeutschland.

This tank was fitted with a modified exhaust valve high on the hull rear to facilitate fording rivers – always a useful ability in the Soviet Union. The hull air-inlets and the discharge louvres were fitted with sealing devices. Another visible difference was that three smoke dischargers were fitted forward on each side of the turret, replacing the rear-mounted smoke candle rack.

Production of the Panzer III Ausf M suffered from changing priorities which once again saw numbers cut and diverted to other uses. Now that the Panzer IV, Panther, StuG III and Panzer III Ausf N (armed with the L/24) were seen as greater priorities, the Ausf M became the last Panzer III armed with a 50mm gun. The order for 1,000 of the M model was reduced to 775 in July 1942.

Once the StuG III decision had been taken, 165 Ausf Ms were diverted for this purpose. Between February to November 1943 they were converted into StuG 40 Ausf Gs. Likewise the positive response to the Ausf N resulted in early November 1942 with instructions that Ausf M production be completed with the short 75mm gun. A further 100 Ausf Ms were diverted to be converted into flamethrower tanks and another 47 gun tanks were not completed. This meant that only 250 Ausf Ms were ever completed. These were used as frontline replacements. In 1944 a batch of battle-damaged Panzer IIIs sent back to the factory for overhaul were also converted into StuGs.

As well as the extra bolted-on armour and the spaced armour, in 1943 the Germans made it standard practice to attach Schürzen (skirts) to their panzers, assault guns and tank destroyers. These consisted of 5mm thick plates attached to the sides by brackets and 8mm plates attached to the sides and rear of the turret. The turret side doors could be accessed via hinged doors in the turret Schürzen. The Ausf M was regularly photographed on the Eastern Front with its Schürzen in varying states of disrepair.

The Schürzen, made of mild steel boiler plating, were intended to help defend the tank against attack from the new Soviet RPG-43 shaped-charge high explosive anti-tank (HEAT) hand grenade and later hollow-charge weapons such as the American Bazooka and the British PIAT (Portable Infantry Anti-Tank). The RPG-43 entered service in 1943 and could penetrated 75mm of armour at a 90° angle. Although it had to be thrown at close range it gave no warning like other anti-tank weapons.

The skirts would prematurely detonate an incoming projectile inches in front of the main armour and dissipate the force of the HEAT round. Although the plate would be destroyed, it saved the tank from direct impact. The hull Schürzen was fragile and easily damaged in combat or torn off whilst the tank was on the move. In consequence the additional turret skirts tended to last a lot longer.

By the summer of 1942 the Panzer III was increasingly ineffective against enemy tanks. In North Africa it was having to contend with the American built Grant and Sherman both armed with a 75mm gun. In some quarters it was felt that its future solely rested in being used as an assault gun. By March 1942 the StuG III assault gun and Panzer IV had stopped using the short-barrelled 75mm StuK37 L/24 and KwK37 L/24 respectively. At that point the StuG III Ausf F and Panzer IV Ausf F2 went into production with the long-barrelled 75mm anti-tank gun, giving Hitler the effective tank killers he desperately needed.

Although frustratingly for the Germans it had been found impractical to up-gun the Panzer III with the long-barrelled 75mm gun, the short version could be made to fit the existing turret. These guns were now available in abundance as they had been rendered surplus to requirements by the up-gunning of the Panzer IV. The 75mm KwK37 L/24 was better than the 50mm KwK39 L/60. The former not only delivered a much more effective Sprenggranate (high-explosive round), it also fired a Hohlladung (hollow charge) which had better armour-piercing capabilities at close range.

The Ausf N was largely the same as the J, L and M models from which it was derived except for the much shorter 75mm gun. Also the gun mantlet did not have the spaced armour because of the additional weight of the L/24. However, the spaced armour was fitted to the front of the superstructure. A new cupola with better armour and a single-piece hatch replacing the split hatch was installed on late production Ausf N. From March 1943 the Schürzen side armour was fitted during the production process.

The initial order for the Ausf N was 450 tanks using three Ausf Js and 447 Ausf Ls. Although these were considered support vehicles for larger tanks, the troops appreciated the extra firepower and in 1942 it was decided to complete the M series as Ausf Ns. Some 213 Ms were converted, as well as another 37 Panzer IIIs returned from the front for refurbishment. This meant that the N series amounted to around 700 tanks.

The Ausf N was never intended as a tank-to-tank weapon but rather as a Sicherheitspanzer (close support tank), taking over the duties of the earlier model Panzer IVs. Therefore, they were issued to the panzer divisions' tank regiments to be deployed in the same manner as the Panzer IV equipped with the short 75mm gun. For example, when the 6th Panzer Division was withdrawn from the Eastern Front to Paris in 1942 for refitting the three 'light' companies in each of the two tank battalions received the Panzer III Ausf J and a single platoon of Ausf Ns. The medium company was equipped with Panzer IV Ausf F2s or Gs. Organization of the heavy tank companies from September 1942 to May 1943 required ten Panzer III Ausf Ns to provide close support for nine Tiger tanks.

Some fought in Tunisia during the closing stages of the fighting in North Africa. In July 1943 at the start of Hitler's Kursk offensive Army Groups Centre and South had 155 Ausf Ns available. In Italy a number of Ausf Ns were supplied to the Italian 1st Armoured Division Camicie Nere. After the Italian armistice the unit reformed on the Allied side as the Armoured Legion Division and then as the 134th Armoured Division Centauro II. In 1943 German armoured vehicle deliveries to Mussolini included twelve Panzer IIIs and these were all probably the N model. Some also ended up on garrison duties in Norway.

The Panzer III hull and chassis, as well as being diverted for assault gun production, was employed in a wide range of other roles including artillery observation, command, flamethrower, recovery and swimming variants – none of which were built in particularly large numbers. In total some 350 command tanks, 260 observation tanks, 100 flamethrowers, 150 Bergepanzer III and 168 submersible Panzer IIIs were produced. This though represented the loss of about 1,000 gun tanks.

Chapter 4

A Blind Alley

The more powerful Panther and Tiger tanks have always eclipsed the Panzer IV but it played a far more pivotal role throughout the entire course of the Second World War. It outshone its stablemate the Panzer III, which was eventually abandoned as a gun tank. The Panzer IV, as well as providing a well-rounded tank, also provided a highly versatile platform for a whole family of self-propelled guns and tank destroyers.

These different types of Panzer IV saw combat with both the German Army and the Waffen-SS in all the major theatres of operations. The Panzer IV was also widely deployed by Hitler's Axis allies. It was supplied in limited quantities to Bulgaria, Croatia, Finland, Hungary, Italy and Romania, as well as Spain and Turkey. In some case it was subsequently turned against the Germans.

The British Army first encountered the Panzer IV in France in 1940, where its low-velocity gun was not a great threat to the very heavily armoured but cripplingly slow Matilda II tank. Rommel lost a number of Panzer IVs at Arras in the face of a valiant but doomed British counter-attack. However, in the deserts of North Africa the greater range of the early Panzer IV's high-explosive shells gave it a distinct advantage before British tanks could close.

Once it was up-gunned it enjoyed an even greater advantage and came into its own as a gun tank. Luckily for the British they were never deployed in great numbers in Libya and Tunisia. In Russia and Normandy, it was a different matter and the Panzer IV became the workhorse of the panzer divisions. On the Eastern Front the Panzer IV ultimately proved a worthy adversary of the highly respected T-34 medium tank.

Although the Panzer IV went into production in the late 1930s there were 50 per cent less than Russia's brand new T-34 by 1941. Nor was it produced in significant quantities until late 1942. Despite going on to form the backbone of Hitler's panzer divisions the Panzer IV actually started life as an infantry support tank and was not intended as battle tank. Its low-velocity gun, also fitted to the Sturmgeschütz III, was designed to fire high-explosive rounds and not armour-piercing ones. Nonetheless, Hitler's early Panzer IVs initially proved useful during his Blitzkrieg into the West and Russia.

While the Panzer III was a good design at the start of the war it became rapidly clear that its 50mm anti-tank gun was inadequate against the newer Soviet tanks armed with a 76.2mm gun. This 50mm gun had a much higher velocity than the weapon on the Panzer IV. Therefore, it became abundantly clear soon after the invasion of the Soviet Union that the T-34 outmatched both the Panzer III and IV. This inevitably led to an arms race as both sides sought to produce a more effective tank killer. In addition to up-gunning the Panzer IV, to counter the T-34 the Germans came up with the Tiger and the Panther but these were never built in decisive numbers.

While the Panzer III was completely given over to assault gun production the up-gunned Panzer IV was kept in production as a gun tank, seeing combat in one form or another throughout the whole of the Second World War. The Panzer IV had an ardent supporter in Guderian in his role as Inspector-General of Armoured Troops. It was he who lobbied to keep it in service even when newer types of panzer were being put into the field. Guderian never saw the over-engineered Panther and Tiger as viable solutions to the panzer divisions problem warding off ever-growing numbers of enemy tanks.

In fact, despite Nazi engineering ingenuity. they were never able to dispense with the Panzer IV, which became the equivalent of the Russian T-34 and American M4 Sherman. However, although it appeared in a number of successful guises the Panzer IV was never up-gunned to the extent that it became a decisive weapon in the same manner that the later T-34/85 tank did.

There were ten different production models of the Panzer IV – essentially they all looked the same though the last four types sported a very distinctive long-barrelled anti-tank gun. It was these later models that were the real tank killers. Otherwise ongoing changes mainly related to improving the powerpack and enhancing the armour. In all some 8,500 Panzer IVs were built from 1937 to 1945.

Throughout the war older models of the Panzer IV were progressively upgraded. This meant that they often had a mix and match of different parts making it on occasions difficult to precisely identify photographs of retrofitted models. Furthermore, there were three types of Panzer IV tank destroyer and a self-propelled anti-tank gun. These and other various specialized tracked armoured fighting vehicles, including self-propelled anti-aircraft guns, accounted for another 4,900 Panzer IV chassis.

As a good all-rounder the Panzer IV was a greatly respected adversary on both the Eastern and Western Fronts. It was on the battlefields of North Africa's deserts, Russia's steppe and Normandy's hedgerows that the Panzer IV gained its tough reputation for reliability and hitting power. Such was the bravery and tenacity of the crews that Panzer IVs were even known to tackle the mighty Joseph Stalin heavy tank. Ultimately the Panzer IV proved vastly more reliable and numerous than the Tiger and the Panther. In this respect it proved to be the better of the three and therefore was arguably the best panzer of the Second World War.

Development of Hitler's Panzer IV medium support tank commenced in the mid-1930s at the same time as that of the Panzer III medium tank. The latter was codenamed the Zugführerwagen (platoon commander's vehicle) and the former the Bataillonsführerwagen (battalion commander's vehicle), so were dubbed the ZW and BW series respectively. Each was assigned differing roles. As early as 1930 the German Army High Command through the Heereswaffenamt Wa Prüf VI (Army Ordnance Department VI) had requested that Krupp and Rheinmetall-Borsig each produce a support tank prototype. This had to be done secretly, along with all other tank development, because of the restrictions on German rearmament following the First World War.

The first prototype was dubbed the Vollkettenkraftfahrzeug 2001, which translates as fully-tracked experimental vehicle. Built in 1935, the Rheinmetall-Borsig Rh-B BW VK 2001 with four pairs of road wheels, three return rollers, front drive sprocket and rear idler, was powered by a 300PS motor giving a speed of 35km/hr. This 18-ton prototype utilized the Wilson-type steering and many of the design features were later incorporated into the development of the Krupp BW.

That same year Krupp-Gruson and Maschinenfabrik & Augsburg-Nurnberg also produced competing prototypes. A Daimler design never got much further than the drawing board. Interestingly all the initial drawings for the Daimler, Krupp and MAN plans had large interleaved road wheels, a feature that was later incorporated in the Panther and Tiger tanks. Following trials at the Kümmersdorf and Ulm testing grounds in southern Germany the Krupp model was selected as the most promising. The MAN prototype was too high and the Rheinmetall-Borsig pilot model had a vulnerable external suspension mechanism for the road wheels.

While the first Panzer III built by Daimler-Benz, armed with a 37mm gun, was initially intended to be in the 15-ton category, the Panzer IV armed with a 75mm gun was supposed to be five tons heavier. In reality wartime requirements meant that both tanks ended up over 20 tons with the final production models being 23 and 25 tons respectively. Both looked very similar and required a five-man crew, but the Panzer III ultimately proved problematic as it was very difficult to up-gun the turret.

Krupp was issued the development contract for the 7.5cm Geschütz-Panzerwagen (Vs Kfz 618) or the experimental 75mm gun armoured vehicle No.618. Rather confusingly the Panzer III was designated the 37mm gun armoured vehicle N.619. Geschütz-Panzerwagen was altered to PanzerKampfwagen (armoured fighting vehicle) or PzKpfw for short in 1937. The Panzer IV was re-designated the Vs Kfz 622 which was originally assigned to the Panzer II armed with a 20mm gun.

What gave the Panzer IV a better punch from the infantry's point of view than the Mk III was its short-barrelled low-velocity 75mm KwK37 L/24 gun. This was as discussed primarily a close-support weapon designed mainly for firing high explosives. Ammunition comprised 65 per cent HE shells, 25 per cent armour-piercing and 10 per cent smoke rounds. Its armour-piercing capability was relatively poor due to its low muzzle velocity. Nonetheless, it had a much greater range. As a result the Panzer III was later up-gunned with a more effective 50mm gun.

The 37mm KwK L/46.5 on the first five models of Panzer III depending on ammunition had a muzzle velocity of 745m/s and at 100m could penetrate 34mm of armour or at 500m some 29mm. The 75mm L/24 could manage less than 400m/s so was a lot slower. It was electrically fired with a semi-automatic breech action. The inner main gun mantlet on the Panzer IV featured a right-hand coaxial MG34 machine gun (fitted on the A, B and C models), with a second one in a ball mount on the right-hand side of the superstructure on the Ausf A. The KwK37 was also used on the early model Sturmgeschütz III which had the same role as the initial Panzer IV.

The Panzer IV consisted of four major sub-assemblies – the hull, front and rear superstructure and the turret. These were all bolted together in the final assembly stage. The hull itself was divided into three by two bulkheads. The engine was positioned in the ear with the drive shaft powering the front sprockets running forward to the driving compartment under the fighting compartment floor. The gearbox was located in the middle of the front compartment, with the driver to the left and the radio operator to the right. The superstructure over-hung the hull sides allowing good internal storage.

Visibility was provided for the tank commander by a prominent vertical drum cupola with a total of eight vision slits. This was the same type as that used on the Panzer III Ausf B and had a similar overhang on the rear turret plate. The turret's power traverse was driven by a 500cc two-stroke petrol engine located to the left of the main engine. A number of pistol ports and vision slits were installed throughout the turret and hull.

Whereas the driver and hull gunner's front plate was flat on the Panzer III, on the early IVs the driver's section was stepped forward of the rest of the super-structure. This feature permitted the driver to see to his right as well as giving more ammunition storage space. The hull machine gun was ball-mounted on the right of the superstructure. The driver also had a forward-facing vision port and binocular episcope. Roof hatches served both the driver and radio operator. Hinged flaps on the glacis plate gave access to the steering mechanism and gearbox.

The initial Panzer IV was powered by a V-12 cylinder 230hp Maybach engine (first the HL 108TR and then the HL 120TRM – also used in the Panzer III), which gave a speed of 31km/hr and a range of 150km. Subsequent improvements to the engine would provide later models a speed of 40km/hr and arrange of 200km. The drive was powered by the gasoline engine via a five-speed transmission with an epicyclic clutch and brake steering system.

Each side of the hull had four pairs of rubber-tyred road wheels with a front drive sprocket and adjustable rear idler, plus four upper return rollers. This immediately made the Panzer IV easy to distinguish from the Panzer III, which only had three pairs of road wheels and three return rollers. On the Panzer IV the rear roller was set slightly lower than the others in order to run the track down onto the idler which was set lower than the sprocket.

The suspension consisted of the leaf-spring design rather than the much newer torsion-bar system. This was in part as a result of Krupp-Gruson drawing on its experience with the Panzer I. The mounting bracket for the bogies and suspension was bolted to the side and base of the hull. Under the leading axle of each bogie were quarter-elliptic leaf springs, with the tail of the spring resting under a trailing axle on a roller.

Up to the Ausf E the Panzer IV idler wheel was fabricated from steel plate. The metal tracks were the single pin skeleton type utilizing a central triple guide horn to slot the links together. This meant they could be manufactured lighter than other tracks and were suitable for almost all terrain types. The first tracks consisted of 101 links either side, were 38cm wide and cast from manganese steel. From the Ausf F onwards the tracks were widened by a modest 2cm.

Production of the Panzer IV Ausf A commenced in the autumn of 1937, with a total of just thirty-five completed by Krupp-Gruson by March 1938. This small number rather suggested that it was just another developmental prototype undergoing extensive trials. However, all of them were accepted for service by the army with the first three being issued to the panzertruppen in January 1938. The numbers actually reflected their support role and there was a greater requirement for the Panzer III. By April that year thirty were in service and the Ausf A went on to see combat in the campaigns fought in Poland, Norway and France.

The main drawback with the Ausf A was that its very thin armour, just 15mm, was no better than the initial Panzer III's and it was slower than the latter. Access for the driver and radio operator was not ideal as they both had two-piece hatches that opened backward and forward. The rear section could catch on the main gun barrel and the mantlet. In consequence it was withdrawn before the spring campaigns of 1941.

The frontal armour on the next three models, Ausf B–D, was doubled to 30mm. Krupp-Gruson were instructed to produce forty-five improved Ausf Bs in April 1938 but only forty-two were finished due to problems with parts. Key changes from the A model included the doubling of the frontal armour and a more powerful 300hp Maybach HL120 TR engine and a six-speed SSG 76 transmission. This boosted the speed from 31km/hr to 40km/hr.

The Ausf B also had a new type of stepped cupola offering better protection for the commander. Other differences involved the installation of single-piece hatches over the driver and radio operator that only opened forward. The superstructure front was also one straight piece, thereby losing the A model's step, with the hull MG34 replaced by a visor and pistol port. Limited numbers of Ausf Bs saw combat in Poland, France, the Balkans and Russia. They were phased out through attrition by late 1943.

Just as the limited production run of the Ausf B was coming to an end work started on the 3rd series BW or Ausf C. This proved to be the most numerous of the first three models with 134 built between September 1938 and August 1939. The Inspectorate for Engineers was also provided with six chassis for bridge-laying tanks. The initial Ausf C order had been for 300 tanks, but this was cut by 160 before production even started. Changes on the Ausf C were largely internal with an improved turret race (or fitting), engine mount, redesigned gun mantlet housing and armoured sleeve to protect the coaxial machine gun. The engine was uprated to the Maybach HL 120TRM. Like its predecessor the Ausf C was progressively up-armoured with bolt-on armoured plates and remained in service until 1943.

A few of the early model Panzer IVs continued in service well into 1944, which were not upgraded. For example, the 21st Panzer Division had half a dozen Ausf B or Cs still with the short 75mm gun and the 116th Panzer Division had three on its books. They should have been brought up to G and H standard by this stage of the war. These outdated models were presumably employed for training or as observations tanks (in the case of one its crew were photographed shopping for cheese!). Nonetheless they ended up being sent into action in France. At the end of August 1944 one of the Ausf B/Cs belonging to 21st Panzer that had clearly not been up-gunned or up-armoured was photographed abandoned in Normandy. It was still armed with the 24-calibre 75mm gun, had a pistol port instead of a hull machine gun and featured the narrow tracks. It looked undamaged and one of the glacis access hatches was missing, indicating it had broken down rather than been knocked out.

Improvements to the Panzer IV were largely driven by the regular need to enhance the armour. The problem with this was that the Panzerwaffe were issued with a constantly changing tank, which was a mixed blessing as they did not have the same capabilities – the Panzerwaffe faced exactly the same problem with the similarly-evolving Panzer III.

Confusingly the Ausf D was known as the 4th and 5th series Panzer IV. Krupp was instructed to build 200 in the 4th Series BW and 48 in the 5th Series BW in January 1938. In the event just 229 were finished as gun tanks, the remaining 19 chassis were used for 16 bridgelaying tanks, two self-propelled gun mounts and a munitionsschlepper (ammunition carrier) for the super-heavy Karl mortar. Also as part of the experiments to up-gun the Panzer IV an Ausf D was fitted with a 50mm KwK39 L/60, which had double the muzzle velocity of the 75mm KwK37 L/24 and therefore vastly better penetration capabilities.

The Ausf D had the side and rear armour of its predecessors enhanced from 15mm to 20mm, and the main gun was fitted with an external mantlet. The front of the superstructure was once more stepped with the driver forward of the radio operator. The driver was provided with a pistol port to his right and the hull machine gun was reinstated for the radio operator. Ausf Ds at the tail end of the production run had 30mm plates bolted and welded to the hull front and superstructure front and an extra 20mm on the sides in 1943. A few Ausf D were armed with the long-barrelled 75mm KwK40 L/48 gun and deployed with training and replacement units. This gun was installed in late Ausf G and the subsequent H and J models.

Production of the Panzer IV support tank was such that by May 1940 every tank unit with a medium tank company could deploy six to eleven of them. At the start of the invasion of France on 10 May 1940 Hitler's panzer divisions were able to field a total of 280 Ausf A, B, C and Ds. Before it was phased out in 1944, the Ausf D saw action in France, the Balkans, Africa and Russia.

The 6th Series Ausf E went into production in September 1940. It had a new cupola design, other modifications to the turret and increased armour. The turret rear now had a single bent plate, which eliminated the cupola overhang. The turret roof was fitted with an exhaust fan to remove noxious gun fumes from the fighting compartment. The front of the Ausf E hull had 50mm of armour, with 20mm plate bolted on the hull and superstructure sides. Other modifications included countersinking the glacis hatches level with the surface of the glacis, a new driver's visor that pivoted and a simplified drive sprocket. In total 40 Ausf Ds and Es were shipped to North Africa while some 438 B–Fs were committed to the assault on the Soviet Union. Like its predecessor the Ausf E was phased out in 1944.

Whereas the Ausf A, B, C, D and E Panzer IVs had all been produced by Krupp-Gruson, construction of the Ausf F, or Ausf F1 as it became known, was extended to the manufacturers Nibelungenwerke and Vomag. Krupp was initially instructed to build 500 of the Panzer IV 7th series, but Vomag then received an order for 100 and Nibelungenwerke for 25. However, the German Army wanted the Panzer IV up-gunned with the long-barrelled 75mm KwK40 L/43 anti-tank gun as soon as possible to produce the F2. The result was that 25 of the F1 were converted before they were ever issued to the panzertruppen.

Once again the main improvement on the Ausf F1 was an increase in armour, which meant that it was a ton heavier than the Ausf E. The change in the armour also required modifications to the driver's visor (with installation of the Fahrersehklappe 50), vision ports, pistol ports, turret doors and the hull machine-gun fitting (the Kugelblende 50 ball mount replacing the Kugelblende 30 gimbal mount). The turret side door in previous models comprised a single hatch either side, but on the F double doors replaced these to make access easier. The glacis hatches also featured raised air-intake cowls to cool the steering brakes.

From the Ausf F1 onward the rear idler wheel was simplified and fabricated from tubular steel with plate reinforcing webs. This had seven rather than the previous eight spokes. Likewise, the tracks were modified on the F1 with a reduction of links from 101 to 99. Also the track width increased from 38cm to 40cm to help spread the ground weight of the tank.

F1s were mainly used as combat replacements, but several new units were equipped with them and they refitted the 2nd and 5th Panzer Divisions. Some 208 Ausf B–F1s were in the field when Hitler commenced Operation Blue, his summer offensive on the Eastern Front, in June 1942. By the time of the Kursk offensive the following summer these had been reduced to just sixty tanks.

Chapter 5

Tank Killer Par Excellence

By late 1941 it was very apparent that the 76.2mm gun mounted in the Soviet KV-1 heavy and T-34 medium tanks was superior to the Panzer IV's short 75mm gun. This meant it was imperative to install the much more powerful long-barrelled 75mm KwK40 L/43 anti-tank gun as quickly as possible. This process had started in the winter of 1941 and the intention was that this it would commence with the Ausf G in May 1942. However, to speed things up it was decided to co-opt Ausf F production first.

A month's worth of production of the Ausf F was disrupted in March 1942 in order to create the F2. The introduction of this model saw the length of the 75mm gun increased from 24 to 43 calibres. To compensate for the long barrel a coil-spring counter-balance was installed. It was designed to act as both an anti-tank and a high explosive firing weapon. None of its parts were interchangeable with the earlier gun, but like the 75mm KwK37 L/24 it was electrically fired and had a semi-automatic breech action. The barrel was fitted with a muzzle brake of which there were about four different types.

Initially the KwK40 was fitted with a very distinctive globular single-baffle muzzle brake, which was followed by a series of double-baffle designs. As there was a two or three-month overlap in production of both the F2 and the subsequent Ausf G, which came out of the same Krupp, Nibelungenwerke and Vomag factories, there was inevitably some overlap in appearance and design modifications. Essentially they were the same tank with the F2 being the interim version.

In the summer of 1942 the Ausf G went over to the double-baffle muzzle brake and it is quite possible some of the later F2 featured this. Similarly, some up-gunned Panzer IVs sent to the Eastern Front while they had the single-baffle muzzle brake, also had the newer-style Ausf G turret that eliminated the side vision ports.

The L/43 was a fundamental upgrade because it changed the Panzer IV's primary role from being a support weapon to a tank-to-tank weapon. It also meant it firmly superseded the Panzer III on the battlefield. From the F2 onwards the Panzer IV went from being a medium support tank to a medium battle tank. The StuG III assault gun went through exactly the same evolution when its close support weapon was upgraded to create the StuG Ausf F.

The earlier L/24 gun had a muzzle velocity of 385m/s and could penetrate 41mm of armour at 100m, 41mm at 400m and 35mm at 1,000m. This degraded to

33mm and 30mm at 1,500m and 2,000m respectively but at such ranges accuracy was a problem. In contrast the much more powerful long barrel L/43 had a muzzle velocity of 740m/s and could cut through almost 100mm of armour at 100m, 90mm at 500m and 80mm at 1,000m.

This was exactly what the Panzerwaffe needed at a crucial moment in the war. It was only now that the Panzer IV truly came into its own and it was to remain the backbone of the Panzerwaffe for the rest of the war despite the appearance of the Tiger and Panther. From mid-1942 onwards the Panzer IV began to take over the role of the Panzer III. Shortly after the chassis of the latter was given over to assault gun production.

Provision for full indirect fire was never made on German tanks. On the Panzer IV targeting of the main gun was achieved using a fixed eyepiece telescope type sight, known as the TZF5b manufactured by E. Leitz of Wetzlar. This had compound object glass and moving graticules giving magnification of about 2.5 times for the main gun and the coaxial machine gun. In the Ausf F2 and G a clinometer was fitted to measure the angle of elevation.

The main differences between the F1 and F2, other than the barrel length, involved the ammunition storage which had to be modified to allow for the larger rounds. The commander and gunner's seats were altered to allow more ammunition to be carried. An auxiliary hand traverse was fitted for use by the loader and the elevation mechanism was modified. The commander's cupola was also moved slightly forward.

When the F2 pitched up in North Africa the British dubbed it the 'Mk IV Special' with good reason. The heaviest British anti-tank gun could not compete. The 75mm gun on the American-supplied M3 Grant tank was inferior to the F2's because it could only penetrate 45mm of armour at 1,000 yards. German designers looked at ways of up-gunning the Ausf F even further. An experimental mock-up was produced of a Panzer IV F2 armed with a 75mm KwK42 L/70. Although this weapon did not feature a muzzle brake the barrel length made the tank very nose-heavy and unwieldy. The L/70 was at least twice as long as the L/43 and on the Ausf F was not really practical. While this up-gunned variant of the F2 did not go into production, the gun with muzzle brake was later employed on the Panther, which appeared in 1943. Similarly, it was used the following summer to arm the Panzer IV/70 tank destroyer but without a muzzle brake. This Panzer IV variant again proved nose-heavy which resulted in excessive wear on the front road wheels.

The Ausf F was similarly used as an experimental mount for a weapon using the Gerlich principle. The Panzer IV F with Waffe 0725 featured a gun using a tapered-bore barrel of 75/55mm. This fired a skirted round that was compressed as it travelled along the bore of the barrel, which greatly increased the velocity of the projectile. The round had added punch thanks to a core of tungsten carbide.

However, a shortage of the latter meant that the project was not viable and this F2 variant was also abandoned. Instead it was decided the best way to improve the armament of the Ausf F was to install the larger-calibre KwK40 L/48 which led to the Ausf G.

Between March and July 1942 some 200 interim Ausf F2s were produced including the 25 converted from F1. By the summer of 1942 there were 135 Panzer IVs with the L/43 gun on the Eastern Front. This could penetrate the T-34 out to a range of 1,600m. Although the Tiger armed with an 88mm gun appeared late that year it was not available in any great numbers, leaving the Panzer IV to do all the work. The Panther armed with a 75mm gun that was more powerful than the Ausf F2/G/H did not appear until the summer of 1943.

The next two production models, the Ausf G and H also armed with the KwK40, formed the bulk of the Mk IV panzer force, with 1,687 Gs and 3,774 Hs built during 1942 to 1944. From 1943 panzer divisions were meant to have one battalion equipped with Panzer IVs and one with Panthers, but due to problems with the latter this often did not happen. The net result was that there were always more Panzer IV than Panthers. Most of the Ausf Gs went to Russia while in 1944 most of the Panzer IVs in France were Ausf Hs supplemented by Ausf Js.

The Panzer IV Ausf G first went into production in May 1942 and was initially armed with the same tank gun as the interim F2. Visually there was very little to distinguish the two. Notably on the G model the vision ports on the sides of the turret were dispensed with as well as the one serving the loader's position on the front of the turret. By the summer of 1942 other alterations included a new muzzle brake and a system that permitted siphoning coolant from one panzer to another to help cold-weather starting. The smoke dispensers were also moved from the rear of the hull to the turret sides.

It was very quickly decided to up-armour some of the G model. From 20 June 1942 deliveries included additional 30mm armour plate bolted or welded to the front of the hull and superstructure. This gave the tank a total of 80mm on the front. It had been hoped to boost it to 100mm, but trials showed the Ausf G became too nose-heavy and difficult to steer. From July to November 1942 every month some sixteen production tanks were fitted with the additional protection. From December 1942 the number went up to 50 per cent of all production tanks which resulted in about 700 Ausf Gs having the extra armour.

At the beginning of 1943 the driver's KFF2 episcope on the Ausf G was removed. Also that year spaced armour consisting of thin steel plates or panels hung from steel brackets, known as Schürzen or skirts, were added to the sides of the hull and the sides and rear of the turret in response to a fresh Soviet threat. Hence the removal of the turret's side vision ports. To allow the turret side access doors to open hinged double doors were fitted to either side of the 8mm turret skirts. Despite these it was possible to escape via the turret without using the doors in the spaced plates.

On the Panzer IV the hull Schürzen consisted of six plates either side with the front two and the rear one tapered. The forward most was the smallest and created a greater taper than at the back, but this was easily damaged and often absent. These skirts covered the hull and superstructure, the return rollers and a quarter of the drive sprocket and idler. The eight road wheels were left exposed. Panzer IVs were regularly photographed with plate sections missing.

Another form of protection was added from early 1943. This was a light grey paste known as Zimmerit, which was applied to the vertical surfaces of the hulls and turrets of most tanks and assault guns. Panzer IVs were coated in the factory before painting and the paste was raked with a spreader, creating ridged and criss-cross patterns to increase the depth. The paste was then hardened off and spray painted. This prevented the attaching of magnetic anti-tank hollow charges. On occasion the Schürzen were also coated in it. The Zimmerit patterns varied from factory to factory.

Final production Ausf Gs were fitted with a new type of drive sprocket and the radio antenna was moved from the right of the hull rear to the left. The later alteration made it impossible to distinguish late Ausf Gs from early Ausf Hs. The new design sprocket wheel was intended to improve traction with the tracks. Mid model Ausf Gs were fitted with a double-baffle muzzle brake on the main gun used on the subsequent H and J models.

A total of 1,275 Ausf Gs were armed with the KwK40 L/43 gun. Then from late March 1943 the Ausf G followed by the H and J were armed with a gun with an even longer barrel, the 75mm KwK40 L/48. Although this fired the same ammunition as the 43-calibre gun, it had a barrel five calibres longer. The breech mechanism was also simplified to help with production. Nonetheless, apart from a few components, the barrel and breech rings of the 43 and 48-calibre guns were interchangeable.

Production of the Ausf G ended in June 1943. In total ten separate orders with Krupp-Gruson, Nibelungenwerke and Vomag amounted to 1,750, but only 1,687 were built as Ausf Gs. The rest were employed as prototypes for the Hummel (Bumblebee) self-propelled gun and Brummbär (Grizzly Bear) assault gun consisting of ten and fifty-three chassis respectively. When Hitler's summer offensive commenced on the Eastern Front in June 1942 he had about 170 F2 and Gs available. By the start of the Kursk offensive the following summer Army Groups Centre and South had 841 long-barrel Panzer IVs.

In early 1943 Guderian was appointed Inspector-General of Armoured Troops. He was not impressed with the new Panzer V, dubbed the Panther, which was having unending 'teething' problems. He recalled, 'In the tank production field it was decided during April, in accordance with my suggestion, that the Panzer

IV should continue to be built until such time as a high level of mass-production was absolutely assured for the Panther.' Later in the year Guderian was very displeased to learn that Panzer IV production was to be partially diverted to the construction of assault guns and tank destroyers.

The Ausf H went into production in April 1943 and was by far the most numerous type of Panzer IV ever built. Once more changes from its predecessor were fairly minimal and were alterations one would expect. On the front of the H model the armour evolved from the 50mm basic plus additional 30mm to 80mm basic – inevitably this meant a sizeable weight increase by one and a half tons bringing the tank's overall weight to 25 tons. It also meant that the tank's armour had increased fourfold over that of the original version – the Ausf A.

The turret featured a better-armoured cupola, a single-piece cupola hatch hinged to the left (all the previous models had a two-piece hatch that opened in opposite directions) and a cupola mount for an anti-aircraft machine gun. On the hull other changes involved deletion of the driver and radio operator's side vision ports to give the armour better integrity, new-style drive sprockets and idler wheels, all steel return rollers and external air filters.

In order to give the Panzer IV better ground clearance, in 1943 designers and engineers tried to alter the suspension, which had remained largely unchanged since 1937. These experiments were not fruitful and the Panzer IV retained the same basic suspension until the end of the war.

A total of 3,935 Ausf H chassis were built, and of these 3,744 were gun tanks, while 130 were diverted to Brummbär construction by Deutsche Eisenwerke. Nibelungenwerke diverted another thirty to Krupp for the initial Sturmgeschütz IV production. By June 1944 some two-thirds of the Panzer IVs deployed in France were the H model the rest being the new Ausf J.

As the war progressed most of the older models of Panzer IV were recalled for upgrading. For example, the Tank Museum at Bovington has an Ausf D that was factory-modified to Ausf H specifications. This principally included installing the long-barrel KwK40 L/43 gun. The driver and hull machine-gunner's positions were up-armoured using bolt-on armour plate. The bow plate armour was increased and extra armour was bolted to the front plate. The turret was fitted with spaced armour and wider tracks were fitted. From a distance it looked like any other late model Panzer IV but up close the forward driver's compartment of the Ausf D is clearly visible.

The last model of the Panzer IV had many features dropped in order to simplify and speed up construction. Notably one of the four return rollers was dispensed with as well as the pistol ports; some of the vision ports and the electric turret traverse plus the exhaust system were simplified. In the name of further expediency wire mesh screens were mounted on the sides of the hull instead of the normal armour plate Schürzen. It also had steel-rimmed road wheels due to the shortage of rubber. Some 1,758 of this type were built from June 1944 to March 1945. The Ausf J saw combat in the battles for France, the Ardennes, Rhineland and on the Eastern Front.

In light of problems refuelling and re-equipping in the field, German tank designers in their infinite wisdom decided to increase the Panzer IV's range by 110km. For Operation Barbarossa tanks, including the Panzer IV, had been furnished with a field-manufactured fuel trailer. This could carry two extra 200-litre petrol tanks. The 20-litre 'Jerricans' (or jerrycans) were also strapped to the turret. However, both measures were largely temporary fixes, especially as the trailers were easily damaged.

The designers boosted the 210km range of the Ausf G and H to 320km. This was achieved by increasing the 470-litre fuel capacity of the Ausf H to 680 litres. This came at a price because the extra space needed meant removing the auxiliary engine that powered the electric turret traverse on the Ausf J. On previous models this was positioned at the rear of the hull to the left of the large exhaust outlet. A dual gear-ratio hand traverse was installed instead. This was clearly a retrograde step and slowed firing response times. On late Ausf J the bulky engine silencer and exhaust outlet was replaced by two simple vertical exhaust mufflers.

There had been some hope of installing the Panther tank turret armed with the KwK42 L/70 gun on the Panzer IV chassis, but the turret proved much too heavy and overloaded the chassis and transmission. Instead the thickness of the turret roof armour on the Ausf J was increased and for close defence a Nähverteidigungs-waffe smoke projector was fitted. This final model also used at least two different types of the modified 'East Tracks', which gave a better overall performance. As the name suggests these were developed as a result of battlefield experience on the Eastern Front.

In North Africa the Sherman was able to hold its own against the early model Panzer IVs. In Normandy the frontal 80mm hull and superstructure armour of the Ausf H and J easily resisted the Sherman's 75mm gun. Only the turret remained vulnerable. Limited numbers of Shermans were up-gunned with 17-pounder or 76mm guns but these were not up-armoured, leaving them at a real disadvantage.

The first Ausf J deployed to Normandy were fitted with standard Schürzen and coated in Zimmerit. While the hull Schürzen on the Ausf Gs and initial Ausf Js consisted of six adjoining steel plates, on later production Ausf Js they were replaced by simple wire-mesh. These screens consisted of only three sections but covered the same area. Also by this stage the use of Zimmerit had been discontinued and was not applied to the final batches of Ausf J. Both types of Schürzen were fitted to the Panzer IV/70 tank destroyer – photographic evidence shows a Panzer IV/70(A) with wire-mesh skirts.

By late 1943 production of the Panzer IV was increasingly under pressure. Although Guderian, in his role as Inspector of Hitler's armoured forces, supported the factories being switched solely to the Panther, retooling would simply have been too disruptive. Panther manufacture was lagging behind and by this stage Germany was increasingly on the defensive on the Eastern Front. The result of this was that the Panzer IV was kept in production and was increasingly diverted to making assault guns and tank destroyers. This was exactly the same fate that had befallen the Panzer III.

In December 1943 Krupp-Gruson finally stopped building the Panzer IV gun tank and in the New Year switched production to the StuG IV. Likewise, in January 1944 Vomag began producing the Jagdpanzer IV alongside its Panzer IV. This continued until May when tank production was abandoned in favour of the Jagdpanzer IV and then the Panzer IV/70. In August 1944 Nibelungenwerke started building its own version of the Panzer IV/70. The result of this was that Nibelungenwerke was the only company to produce the Ausf J. As well as the 1,758 gun tanks some 278 Ausf J chassis were diverted to Panzer IV/70 production from August 1944. Another 142 chassis were converted to Brummbärs.

Production was concentrated with Nibelungenwerke for a reason – the Allied air war. The original Panzer IV prototypes had been built by Krupp-Gruson at Magdeburg. Upon series production the Krupp factories in Essen and Eisen un Huettenwerke had built the hulls and turrets. Subcomponents had come from other companies. It was only with the Ausf F/G that production needed to be shared. At this point Vomag and Nibelungenwerke became involved. In the face of escalating Allied bombing of Germany's industrial centres the main production was then relocated to Nibelungenwerke which was out of range of the bombers.

Chapter 6

Bring Me a Tiger

The evolution of the Tiger I is a story of lost opportunities, both in design terms and operationally. By the spring of 1941, following the Wehrmacht's experiences fighting the British Matilda and French Char B heavy tanks, Adolf Hitler was firmly of the view that he needed a tank heavier than his existing Panzer IV. Although work had been carried out in the late 1930s on producing a successor to the Panzer III and IV, the designs had come to nothing. The development of the Tiger I was tortuous, going through at least six different design stages.

In 1937 the German Ordnance Department or Waffenamt tasked Henschel with developing a heavy breakthrough tank that would be twice the weight of the Panzer IV. The first prototype, dubbed the DW I (Durchbruchwagen – breakthrough vehicle), was completed in September 1938 with five road wheels and was sprung by torsion bars. The side armour comprised two pieces joined at the back of the fighting compartment.

Despite the fact that war was looming over Europe the DW I trials were suspended to allow work on a huge 65-ton tank designated the VK 6501, short for 'Vollkettenkraftfahrzeug [fully tracked experimental vehicle] 65 tons, first design'. Two VK 6501 prototypes were built, only then to have work switched back onto the DW.

The follow-on DW II appeared in 1940, featuring one-piece side armour and different tracks. The engine, a Maybach HL 120 coupled to a Maybach Variorex eight-speed gearbox, gave a speed of 35km/hr. Weighing in at 32 tons it had a crew of five and was to have been armed with the short 75mm gun used on the Panzer IV. Lacking any apparent sense of urgency this work now lapsed though the hull arrangement would be used on the VK 3001(H).

The VK 3001 project was authorized by the Waffenamt on 9 September 1938. Henschel turned to the DW II but replaced the needle-bearing tracks with dry-pin tracks. However, trials did not take place until early 1940 when eight test vehicles were ordered. The first VK 3001 did not appear until March 1941 and two months later it was decided to go with the heavier 36-ton VK 3601 requirement. Subsequently two further VK 3001(H) were finished along with twelve turrets built by Krupp.

While Henschel was working on their VK 3001 design, the Porsche design bureau was conducting similar research. Although officially designated the VK 3001(P)

Porsche designers knew it as the Type 100 or the Leopard. For the suspension Dr Ferdinand Porsche employed longitudinal torsion bars mounted externally, while power was supplied by air-cooled engines and electric transmission. Two prototypes were produced between 1940 and 1941 but the engines proved a problem and they went the way of the Henschel prototypes.

These plans though had to be resurrected in the summer of 1941 when it was discovered that Soviet tank design had stolen a lead with the T-34 and KV-1, both in terms of armour and firepower. The initial remit was to procure a tank mounting a gun capable of piercing 100mm of armour at 1,500m or a mile. At the same time such a design had to be able to take similar punishment. Hitler turned to Henschel and Porsche once more. It is quite remarkable that Hitler, who had committed Nazi Germany to fight a two-front war, felt he had time to indulge in developing two competing designs. To complicate matters further Krupp was given the contract to produce the turrets for both the Henschel and Porsche designs. Henschel was requested to design a tank in the range of 36–40 tons armed with a tapered squeeze bore gun (designed Waffen 0725) produced under Project VK 3601. Under project VK 4501 Porsche was asked to come up with a 45-ton vehicle capable of taking an anti-tank gun version of the 88mm Flak gun.

Once again Henschel found themselves going down a dead end. Although drawing on the VK 3001(H), the VK 3601(H) had larger road wheels on eight axles. The lack of adequate foresight immediately stymied Waffen 0725, because of the war tungsten steel was in short supply, which meant ammunition for the tapered-bore guns could not be produced. Hitler cancelled Waffen 0725 and opted to use the VK 4501 turret on the 3601. This in turn caused further problems because the replacement turret had a larger diameter meaning the hull superstructure had to be widened to accommodate it. The knock-on effect of increasing the superstructure and the track width caused a weight increase that required an extra run of road wheels to decrease ground pressure. This became Project VK 4501(H).

Henschel was able to draw on the key features of their VK 3001(H) and VK 3601(H) programmes, though the company's designers must have wearied at the ever-changing goalposts each time the requirement was revised and the tank got heavier. They built two models, the H1 mounting an 88mm KwK36 L/56 gun and the H2 with a 75mm KwK42 L/70 gun in a Porsche turret. The latter though only got as far as a wooden mock-up. To try and avoid confusion the Porsche vehicle was re-designated the VK 4501 (P) and drew on the earlier VK 3001 (P) which had been cancelled. The Porsche air-cooled engines essentially did not work forcing Porsche to consider abandoning his electric transmission for a hydraulic one.

Both the Henschel and Porsche prototypes were put through their paces before Hitler at Rastenburg on his birthday on 20 April 1942. It soon became apparent that the Henschel design was much more ready for mass production with far fewer teething problems. Not only did the Porsche lose out, but also its name was appropriated by the Henschel vehicle and thus the PzKpfw VI Tiger was born. After being judged a far superior design by virtue of its conventional layout and construction methods, the Henschel tank was designated the Panzerkampfwagen VI Tiger Ausf H, its Sonderkraftfahrzeug or ordnance number was Sd Kfz 181. However, in February 1944 its designation was altered to PzKpfw Tiger Ausf E, Sd Kfz 181.

The Henschel Tiger had eight sets of triple overlapping and interleaved road wheels with a torsion bar suspension to give maximum weight distribution of the 57 tons. The superstructure and the hull were welded together, with the superstructure extending out over the tracks to allow for the wider turret. The 88mm KwK36 was fitted coaxially with an MG34 in the external gun mantlet.

Despite a lack of preliminary testing, Porsche Tiger production was instigated with delivery scheduled for July 1942. Problems with the V10 air-cooled engines and the suspension meant only five had been built when production came to a halt in August 1942. As the Porsche Tiger had air-cooled engines it had been planned to form two detachments for service in North Africa, instead the completed vehicles were sent to Döllersheim for training purposes. Production was officially abandoned because Porsche had been unable to resolve the technical difficulties.

Although only a single Henschel Tiger I model was produced there were a number of distinctive changes during the vehicle's production life. The initial Tiger Is are identifiable by their rubber-rimmed road wheels, the large Feifel air filters at the rear, the tall commander's cupola and dual headlights. While the mid production Tiger I retained the rubber-rimmed road wheels, it has a different turret that included a smaller cupola. Finally, the late production Tiger I from January 1944 is instantly recognizable by its all-steel disc wheels, which were internally sprung, and periscope-equipped cupola.

It was soon found that the selected engine in the shape of a Maybach V-12 petrol engine, the 21-litre HL 210 P45, was just too underpowered. From December 1943 it was replaced by the 24-litre HL 230 P45. The weight of the Tiger made the use of the earlier clutch-and-brake type of steering unpractical. Instead Henschel produced something similar to the British Merritt-Brown steering unit that was regenerative and continuous. The gearbox provided eight forward gear ratios and allowed for a twin radius of turn in each gear. This and the pre-selector made the Tiger relatively easy to handle considering its size.

Nonetheless the Tiger's overall lack of mobility and relatively low speed meant it was vulnerable to flank attack. The Germans compensated for this by adding platoons of Panzer IIIs or IVs to the Tiger battalions that acted as flank guards. These flanking platoons usually had the thankless task of moving forward first, which inevitably meant they also acted as decoys drawing enemy fire that the Tiger using its longer-range gun could zero in on and then pick off. The Panzer III and IVs' other job was of course to cover the Tigers' withdrawal if they were forced to retreat.

To avoid joins and welds the Tiger I's turret was made from a single plate bent into a horseshoe shape. Initially this had a cylindrical cupola with visions slits and two machine pistol ports in the rear. An escape hatch replaced the right-hand pistol port in December 1942 and the cupola was replaced by a design incorporating periscopes in July 1943. While the specified weight of 45 tons was exceeded by up to 11 tons with the production models, when the Tiger entered the war in late 1942 it was the best armed and most heavily armoured tank in existence.

The Tiger's main armament was the 88mm KwK36 anti-tank gun that had ballistic qualities similar to the famous Flak 18 and Flak 36 88mm anti-aircraft guns from which it was derived. Modifications included a muzzle brake and electric firing by a trigger operated primer on the elevating hand wheel. A 7.92mm MG34 was coaxially mounted on the left side to the 88mm, which was fired by a foot pedal operated by the gunner.

The Tiger's 88mm gun could tear open 100mm of armour at over 1,000 yards (1,000m) and could easily defeat the T-34 Model 1943. The KwK36 had a breech of the semi-automatic falling wedge type scaled up. The weight of the barrel was counterbalanced through a large coil spring housed in a cylinder on the left front of the turret. The elevation and hand traverse were operated by the gunner by hand wheels to his right and left respectively. The commander also had an emergency traverse hand wheel.

The gunner also operated the hydraulic power traverse by rocking a right-hand footplate. Due to its weight the turret had to be rotated in low gear. To do this manually took the gunner 720 turns of the hand wheel to get a full 360 degrees rotation. Likewise, a power traverse through 180 degrees required a lot of foot-work and concentration. This delay often meant that Allied tanks were able to get off a first shot, though it was often their last.

The gunner was provided with a binocular telescope for sighting the 88mm gun and a clinometer for firing high explosive as well as a turret position indicator dial. As space was a premium, the main gun ammunition was stored either side of the fighting compartment and partly alongside the driver in storage bins as well as under the turret floor.

As the 56 tons of the production Tiger was simply too great for most bridges, it was decided to give it a wading and submersion capability. The first 495 tanks were equipped for snorkel breathing and could take depths of up to 13ft. This required all the doors and hatches be fitted with rubber seals, while the turret ring was water proofed using an inflatable rubber tube. Similarly, the gun mantlet was fitted with a sliding frame with a sealing ring, while the machine-gun ports were bunged using expanding rubber plugs once the machine guns had been removed. Air for the engine and the crew came in via a snorkel pipe. In theory the

Tiger could stay underwater for up to two and half hours, but all this was highly expensive and time-consuming to fit. Inevitably, as economies had to be made this was abandoned, leaving the Tiger capable of tackling depths of only 4ft.

Early Tigers were also equipped with a particularly ingenious, if gruesome, anti-personnel defence system. This was the 'S' mine, an anti-personnel bomb about 4in wide and 5in deep. This was fired up to 5ft in the air where it exploded showering the immediate area in ⅜ in steel balls thereby killing any enemy infantry threatening the tank. The mine dischargers were fitted to the superstructure with a total of five being mounted in various positions.

To try and simplify construction the Tiger's hull sections and superstructure were welded together rather than bolted. The front and rear of the superstructure was one unit and interlocking stepped joints, fixed by welding were used for both the superstructure and the lower hull. Side panniers were created by extending the superstructure out over the tracks and to the full length of the hull. The top front plate of the hull covered the full width of the tank and it was this width that allowed for an internal diameter turret ring of 6ft 1in that housed the breech and mounting of the 88mm gun. The breech mechanism almost reached the inside rear turret wall, effectively dividing the fighting compartment in two.

Inside, the hull was divided into four compartments, two forward housing the driver and bow gunner/wireless operator, a central fighting compartment and the rear engine compartment. The driver was to the left steering via a wheel that acted hydraulically on the tank's controlled differential steering unit. The driver's visor was opened and closed using a sliding shutter operated by a hand wheel on the front vertical plate. Periscopes were fitted on both the driver's and wireless operator's escape hatches.

It was the Tiger I's armour that made it a tough nut to crack. The contemporary model of the Panzer IV Ausf G and Panzer III Ausf L/M and N only had 50mm of armour on the front of the turret, superstructure and the hull (though they were given additional 20mm spaced armour) and 30mm on the sides. The Tiger I sported double this with 100mm on the front, 60mm on the sides and 80mm at the rear. The top and bottom armour was 25mm thick, with the turret roof thickened to 40mm in March 1944.

Initially production was planned to commence in July 1942 with 285 ready by May 1943 in time for Hitler's major summer offensive on the Eastern Front. Once the Porsche Tiger contract had been halted the Henschel order was increased by fifty to make up the shortfall. Production commenced in August 1942 at a rate of just twelve tanks per month. By November this had been increased to twenty-five per month. Maximum production was reached in April 1944 when 104 Tigers rolled off the assembly lines.

The Tiger I and the subsequent Tiger II were particularly vulnerable to the Allied bomber offensive as only one factory was involved in producing them.

Tiger I production ran from July 1942 until August 1944 and the Tiger II from January 1944 to March 1945. Henschel achieved a monthly rate of 106 Tigers in the summer of 1944, but this had dropped to just 36 by the autumn. By early December 1944 these attacks and the general disruption caused by the strategic bombing campaign had cost the Germans at least 200 Tigers.

Hitler's second heavy tank, the Tiger II, was one of the largest and most impressive panzers ever built. Armour and armament wise it was a formidable combination, this and its distinctive appearance made it a particularly terrifying tank to come up against. However, its weight and mobility was another matter and like the Tiger I, these handicaps and the small production run proved to be its undoing.

Although dubbed the Tiger II, this subsequent heavy tank was in fact a new design that certainly in appearance had more in common with the Panther than the first Tiger. This last German heavy tank became known variously as the Tiger Ausf B, Tiger II or King Tiger (Königstiger), while the Western Allies dubbed it rather grandly the Royal Tiger. Its ordnance inventory number was Sd Kfz 182. For the purposes of this book and for the sake of consistency we will use the term Tiger II.

The requirement for the Tiger II originated in the summer of 1942 when the German Ordnance Department issued specifications for a Tiger I replacement that would be superior to the T-34 both in terms of firepower and armour. Both Henschel and MAN, who built the Panther, were requested to design second-generation vehicles for the Tiger and the Panther respectively. Porsche was also asked to meet the replacement Tiger requirement with VK 4502. Rather than start from scratch, Porsche adapted his earlier unsuccessful Tiger designs.

The Porsche design offered two different layouts with the turret mounted at the front or back of the hull. The latter had slopped armour similar to that of the Panther. Like the previous Porsche projects, the suspension had paired bogies with longitudinal torsion bars. Wegman deigned the turret to take the 88mm KwK43 L/71 gun and fifty were ordered but VK 4502 (P) was abandoned. Porsche's final submission was hampered by the retention of the ill-fated petrol-electric drive plus the copper needed for the transmission was in short supply.

VK 4502(H) was also rejected, so Henschel submitted the revised VK 4503(H). This design, although based on the original Tiger concept, had to be considerably modified at the Ordnance Department's insistence that it incorporate most of the features included in the Panther II programme. Not unreasonable the Ordnance Department was trying to achieve commonality in spare parts for these projected new tanks. While this was accepted the design work was not completed until 1943. The MAN project VK 5402 (MAN) was accepted, but the war ended before the Panther II could go into production.

Any attempts to enhance the Tiger I by replacing the 88mm KwK36 L/56 anti-tank gun with the improved KwK43 L/71 were thwarted by the lack of space in

Heinz Guderian who, along with Oswald Lutz and Wilhelm von Thoma, was one of the founding fathers of Germany's panzer divisions. (all images via author)

When Adolf Hitler came to power he tore up the Versailles Treaty, ending the restrictions on Germany possessing tanks.

When Hitler saw Guderian's early tanks on exercise he immediately became a supporter of Germany's panzer programme.

The tank that started it all: the small two-man Panzer I Ausf A.

Panzer I Ausf As on exercise – the sight of these convinced Hitler he must have a dedicated panzer force.

The second model Panzer I known as the Ausf B.

Panzer I and Panzer II.

Panzer IIs on the Eastern Front, where they were used in a reconnaissance role.

Panzer II captured in North Africa.

The Panzer III Ausf E was initially armed with a 37mm gun but this was replaced by the 50mm KwK38 L/42.

Panzer III Ausf G and crew taking a break from the fighting in Libya.

Panzer III Ausf H or J serving on the Eastern Front.

Russian troops with a captured Panzer III and StuG III assault guns.

This Panzer III Ausf J armed with the 50mm KwK39 L/60 was lost at Tobruk in Libya.

Panzer III Ausf L belonging to the 2nd SS Panzer Division.

The distinctive Panzer III Ausf N armed with the 75mm KwK37 L/24 close-support gun.

Abandoned Panzer III in the midst of the Russian winter.

Not a tank but an early model turretless assault gun based on the Panzer III known as the Sturmgeschütz III Ausf B armed with the 75mm StuK37 L/24 gun.

the turret. In January 1943 Hitler ordered the new Tiger must have a turret large enough to mount the L/71. Also frontal armour was to increase to 150mm, though the sides were to remain at 80mm. To this end Henschel displayed an enormous wooden mock-up on 20 October 1943 to give Hitler some idea of the size of the new vehicle. Initially the VK 4502(P) turret, with a distinctive curved front and curved mantlet, was selected to house the L/71, though in reality this turret was designed with both prototypes in mind.

By November 1943 the Henschel Tiger II pilot model was ready and production commenced at the Henschel factory in Kassel in December 1943 with the first models completed by February 1944. In total only about 500 Tiger IIs were built by the end of the war. Under the rationalization programme of autumn 1944 according to which only two tanks with traversing turrets would be produced in 1945, the Panther Ausf G and Tiger II were chosen. However, two Panthers could be produced for every Tiger. Production of the Tiger II was scheduled at 20 a month, ramping up to 145. In reality the highest it got was eighty-four in the summer of 1944 with the number falling to just twenty-five in March 1945.

There were grandiose plans to build 1,500 Tiger IIs, but the Allied bomber offensive put paid to that. Between 22 September and 7 October 1944 five raids took out 95 per cent of the Henschel factory floor at Kassel. This cost the loss of production of almost 660 Tiger IIs. As a result one was produced in 1943, 379 in 1944 and 112 in 1945, giving a total of 492 tanks. By that stage the Tiger II was the best protected mass-produced tank. Its hull armour was up to 150mm thick on the glacis plate at 40 degrees, while the nose was shielded by 100mm at 55 degrees. The turret and hull had armour of 80mm, while the top and belly plates were 42mm thick.

The first fifty Tiger IIs were fitted with the Wegmann turrets that had been built for the abandoned VK 4502(P). The curved front to the turret was soon found to create an unwelcome shot trap, and on 6 December 1943 this feature was ordered to be removed and Henschel quickly redesigned the gun mantlet and the front of the turret to eliminate the curve. They did this by decreasing the frontal area of the turret and installing a bell-shaped mantlet.

Internally the Tiger II layout was almost the same as the Panther, though there was no turret basket. While externally the Tiger II shared some of the heritage of the Panther's sloping body work, some of its design features came from the Tiger I. For example, the engine, engine covers and cupola were common to the Tiger I as well as the later Panther. The all-steel resilient wheels were common to the late production Tiger I and the very late production Panther Ausf G.

The massive suspension was by torsion bars with nine sets of overlapped wheels, rather than interleaved as on the Tiger I and Panther. This cut down on clogging and made wheels changes easier. While the wheels were all steel, they had rubber resilient cushions and this cut down on tyre rubber. The tracks came in narrow and wide versions the same as the Tiger I.

The Tiger II was armed with the massive 88mm KwK43 L/71, an improved and longer version of the gun used in the Tiger I. To allow for rapid firing twenty-two rounds were stored in racks in the rear of the turret with the tips of the rounds facing the breech mechanism. The gun had a monocular sight while the commander had the advantage of a vision cupola the same as that used in the later model Panther.

The Tiger II could kill all Allied tanks head-on at over 2.5km, easily outranging Allied tank guns. Indeed until the arrival of the American M26 Pershing armed with a 90mm gun in February 1945 neither the British or Americans had any heavy tanks. The only Allied gun capable of tackling the Tiger at around 1,100m was the British 17-pounder installed in the Sherman Firefly.

The Tiger II's Achilles heel, like all panzers, was its underpowered gasoline engine. Bearing in mind the Tiger II weighed 70 tones it had the same engine as the much lighter Tiger I and Panther, namely the V12 Maybach HL 230 P30. There were plans to upgrade the engine with the inclusion of fuel injection and an uprated drive train, but this never happened. Likewise, there was talk of replacing the main gun with a 105mm KwK L/68.

Initially the Tiger II suffered from an overburdened drive train, the double-radius steering gear had a nasty habit of failing and the gaskets and seals leaked. The Tiger IIs delivered to Heavy Panzer Battalion 501 nearly all suffered from drive train failures, which meant when the unit arrived on the Eastern Front only eight of its forty-five tanks were operational. Similarly, the first five Tiger IIs sent to the Panzer Lehr Division broke down and had to be destroyed to prevent capture before they had even seen any action. Modifications to the Tiger II greatly improved its reliability but by that stage the war was coming to a close.

Despite the tank's massive size, good vision was provided. The driver was equipped with a periscope in the roof of the hull and he could raise the seat if he was driving with his hatch open. Also, an episcope provided vision for the hull machine-gunner while there was another one in the turret roof for the gunner.

The Tiger II was issued to the training units in February and May 1944, but they did not reach the first combat units until June, some five months after production had commenced. They were all issued to the independent heavy panzer battalions except for five which were sent to the Feldherrnhalle Division in March 1945.

In a face-to-face shootout the Tiger II outranged almost all Allied tanks and was almost impervious to all Allied armour-piercing rounds. However, like the Tiger I there were simply too few Tiger IIs. Also while it was well armoured and armed it was still an unwieldy tank. Like its predecessor its weight and size made it a tactical liability. It was simply too heavy for most road bridges and it offered a large target for enemy gunners and fighter-bombers. The Tiger II's finest moment came during Hitler's Ardennes offensive when it was partnered with the Panther.

Its subsequent role in Hitler's counter-offensive in Hungary though only proved what a liability it was.

Like all panzers manufactured in the later part of the war the Tiger II suffered from quality control problems. Inevitably the lack of alloys impacted on the steel. This meant that when the armour was hit, even if the round did not penetrate, the welds quite often cracked and there was extensive spalling. The latter could be dangerous to the crews if this occurred on the inside.

In the summer of 1944 the Red Army fighting at Sandomierz captured a number of Tiger IIs. These were whisked off to the Soviet tank testing ground at Kubinka. The Soviets were not impressed with what they found. The underpowered engine overheated and packed up, and the transmission and suspension regularly gave out. Their anti-tank gun tests showed how shoddy the armour was. The quality of the welding was found to be very bad and tended to crack after repeated battering by anti-tank shells.

Chapter 7

I Want a T-34

The Panther tank represented Hitler's 'great white hope', born out of necessity in the harsh Russian winter of 1941. Hitler's key panzer expert Heinz Guderian had swiftly identified the danger facing the German Army; it needed an answer to Mikhail Koshkin's utilitarian T-34 tank. While most of the Red Army's tank designs had been easily overcome in the summer of 1941, it was the T-34 that represented the biggest long-term threat to Hitler's panzer forces.

Although the T-34 was almost strangled at birth by competing interests amongst the Soviet defence industries and when it first deployed was less than successful, Guderian appreciated Hitler needed to counter this revolutionary tank and quickly. Crucially though it took German industry a year and a half to produce the Panther and then it fell afoul of unending teething problems. Damningly, Guderian was to dub it our 'problem child'. Despite his best efforts to get the crews fully proficient with their new panzer and solve the snags Hitler insisted the Panther be thrown into battle immediately.

This decision was foolhardy as there were insufficient numbers to make a decisive impact at the Battle of Kursk. The decision to commit both the Panther and its heavier cousin the Tiger in penny packets was a tactical and strategic disaster. The Panther did not cover itself in glory at Kursk, instead continually breaking down, while its inexperienced crews were repeatedly ambushed in the opening days of the battle. Nonetheless once fine-tuned it proved a worthy adversary on the Eastern Front, Italy and in Normandy.

In his memoirs *Panzer Leader*, Guderian recalled how he set off the chain of events that led to the Panther:

> Numerous Russian T-34s went into action and inflicted heavy losses on the German tanks at Mzensk in 1941. Up to this time we had enjoyed tank superiority, but from now on the situation was reversed. The prospect of rapid decisive victories was fading in consequence. I made a report on this situation, which was for us a new one, and sent it to the Army Group; in this report I described in plain terms the marked superiority of the T-34 to our PzKpfw IV and drew the relevant conclusion as that must affect our future tank production.

This abrupt and unwelcome reversal of the panzers' superiority, thanks to the unexpected appearance of the T-34, forced the German Army Staff out of its complacency resulting from the performance of the Panzer IV. Although the panzers had come up against the T-34 during the summer, it had suffered severe transmission problems, carried insufficient ammunition and had poorly trained crews who simply panicked. By the winter these shortcomings had been largely overcome.

It soon became apparent that the panzers were unable to cope with the mud, snow and ice. The panzers had quite narrow tracks that struggled with adverse conditions, while the T-34's tracks were much wider spreading the weight of the tank giving it much better cross-country performance especially in bad weather. Guderian took immediate action:

> I concluded by urging a commission to be sent immediately to my sector of the front . . . it could not only examine the destroyed tanks on the battlefield, but could also be advised by the men who had used them as to what should be included in the design for our new tanks. I also requested the rapid production of a heavy anti-tank gun with sufficient penetrating power to knock out the T-34. The commission appeared on the Second Panzer Army's front on 20 November 1941.

It worked quickly, investigating the key design features of the 30-ton T-34. These in fact were blatantly obvious; namely the sloping armour that gave greater shot deflection thereby greatly enhancing protection; the large simple road wheels and broad tracks which gave a stable and steady ride for the crew; and the overhanging gun where the recoil mechanism was partially outside the turret, which the Germans had always considered impractical for their panzers. Of the three, the sloping armour was the most revolutionary.

The German Armaments Ministry was quick to act and on 25 November 1941 instructed the companies of Daimler-Benz and MAN to produce two competing designs for a new medium tank in the 30–35-ton category under the ordnance designation of VK 3002. This required 60mm of frontal armour and 40mm of side armour, with the front and sides sloped in the same manner as the T-34's hull. Top speed was to be 55km/hr (35mph). The assumption that the tank would not exceed 35 tons was to prove to be optimistic.

This insistence that two competing companies produce different designs showed a complete lack of focus or urgency. This was a luxury that could be ill afforded in light of the titanic struggle being waged on the Eastern Front. Time was of the essence and yet Hitler, as with the development of the Tiger tank, seemed happy to waste precious resources instead of insisting the panzer manufacturers coordinate their efforts.

The two designs were submitted to Heinrich Ernst Kniepkampf and the Waffenprüfungsamt (ordnance test department) in April 1942. Kniepkampf was one of Koshkin's German counterparts; he had been with the Waffenprüfamt 6 section since 1936 and had worked his way up to chief engineer and designer. Most notably he had previously worked as a designer at MAN, casting doubts over his impartiality.

Kniepkampf was principally responsible for German half-track development and the introduction of interleaved road wheels, torsion bar suspension and the Maybach-Olvar gearbox in the panzers. All of which, while excellently designed, were ultimately over-engineered when it came to the requirements of mass production and the realities of the battlefield. Such was Kniepkampf's influence that he remained in post almost until the end of the war in 1945. This inevitably meant that he played a key role in the development of the Panther.

The two designs were deeply contrasting. Daimler-Benz gave Guderian exactly what he wanted, which was a shameless copy of the T-34. It had the hull shape of the T-34, with the turret so far forward that the driver had to sit within the turret cage. It also featured jettisonable external rear fuel tanks replicating the T-34 and side hull escape hatches. It also had a rear sprocket drive driven by a MB507 diesel engine duplicating the T-34 drive and transmission layout. Dual steel road wheels were suspended by leaf springs (a departure from Christie suspension, but simpler and cheaper).

Like the T-34, the Daimler-Benz design meant that the compact engine and transmission sited at the rear ensured the all-important fighting compartment was relatively uncluttered, allowing for structural change or up-gunning. Likewise, a diesel engine would help reduce the dangers of fire and compensate for inevitable petrol shortages. Leaf springs were easier to produce than complicated space consuming torsion bars and the use of all-steel wheels would help if there were rubber shortages. From the start Hitler was impressed by the VK 3002 (DB) 'T-34 type' design though pressed for the gun to be improved from the 75mm KwK40 L/48 model to the more powerful KwK42 L/70.

MAN went the other direction, with an original German design that was sophisticated rather than simple. Some might argue that it was over-designed. Notably it had a much wider and higher hull than the VK 3002 (DB) or the T-34. The turret was set much further back to allow for the overhang created by the long 75mm gun. A torsion bar suspension was employed with interleaved road wheels and it was this that gave rise to the hull's much higher profile. In contrast to the Daimler-Benz design, MAN proposed employing a gasoline or petrol Maybach HL. 210 V-12 engine with front drive sprockets.

Due to Hitler's personnel preference an initial order for 200 VK 3002 (DB) was placed and prototypes went into production. However, the Waffenprufamt 6 'Panther Committee' led by Kniepkampf preferred to play safe with the

VK 3002 (MAN) design as it was far more conventional by German engineering standards and in terms of internal layout. It is also likely that there was an element of national pride at stake – in some quarters copying an enemy tank may have been seen as an admission of design failure and indeed quite frankly embarrassing.

This presented Hitler with a dilemma as he had instructed that when it came to military equipment under no circumstances were two different designs to be produced at the same time. Karl-Otto Saur, deputy to Armaments Industry Minister Albert Speer, argued a diesel engine would not be ready in time and that the MAN design should be reconsidered. Aluminium shortages certainly posed problems with the development of a diesel engine. Hitler on 14 May 1942, after comparing the statistics of the MAN and Daimler-Benz designs decided that in hindsight the MAN version was the superior and would go into production instead. Arguable Hitler and Kniepkampf did the Panzerwaffe a great disservice.

MAN's proposal was accepted six months after the T-34 first showed its true potential on the battlefield. The company was instructed to produce a mild steel prototype as quickly as possible and the order for the 200 DB vehicles was quietly dropped. It was at this point that Kniepkampf took charge of the detailed design work on the MAN vehicle. The first pilot model of the VK 3002 (MAN) was not completed until September 1942 and tested at Nuremburg in the MAN factory grounds. A second test model was sent to the Heereswaffenamt testing grounds at Kummersdorf for official army trials.

By this time the Panther's rival the Tiger had just come into production, but its shortcomings in terms of excessive weight, low speed and poor ballistic deflection would soon become apparent following its combat debut in North Africa and on the Eastern Front. The Tiger's slow production rate was a real cause for concern leaving the Army reliant on the tried and tested Panzer IV. Consequently the VK 3002 (MAN) was ordered into immediate production as the PzKpfw V Panther with the German ordnance designation of SdKfz 171 (sonderkraftfahrzeug – special purpose vehicle).

Hitler though stipulated the glacis plate armour be increased from 60mm to 80mm, raising the Panther's weight to 45 tons. In contrast the Panzer IV was only around 25 tons. He also instructed that an air-cooled diesel tank engine be given priority but Speer and Kniepkampf chose to ignore him. The first production Panther rolled out of MAN in November 1942 exactly a year after the fateful clashes with the T-34 at Mzensk. It was intended to produce 250 a month, but at the end of 1942 this was increased to 600. MAN was simply unable to do this alone, so a Panther production group was formed with the other tank manufacturers. Daimler-Benz was instructed to abandon its almost completed prototypes and switch to the MAN design. They began retooling to build the Panther, with the first DB produced vehicle appearing in early 1943. In the meantime, the German

Army suffered a catastrophic defeat at Stalingrad. This left Hitler's aspirations on the Eastern Front hanging in the balance.

In January 1943 Hanover-based Marienfelde Maschinenfabrik Niedersachsen (MNH) and Tiger manufacturer Henschel in Kassel were instructed to start tooling for Panther production. Likewise, numerous subcontractors were involved making the Panther one of the most concentrated German armament programmes of the Second World War. Even the Luftwaffe felt the squeeze as aircraft production was cut back to free up manufacturing facilities for Panther engines and subcomponents and to conserve fuel for use in the panzers. Next stop for the Panther was Kursk and controversy.

The first model of the Panther, known as the PzKpfw V Ausf D (Sd Kfz 171), went into full-scale production in January 1943. Initially though the first twenty pre-production models to come off the MAN factory line from November 1942 were designated in the normal German manner as the Ausf A, but this was later changed to D1.

It was planned that the ZF type AK7-200 gearbox would be replaced by the Maybach Olvar eight-speed gearbox to create the Ausf B. This though proved unsatisfactory so the Ausf B designation was skipped, as was the Ausf C, which seems to have remained on the drawing board. Therefore, the first full production model became the Ausf D, hence the initial Ausf A being designated D1 with the D sometimes being referred to as the D2. The upshot of this was that the three Panther models in order of manufacture were designated the Ausf D, A and G respectively.

The Ausf D required five crew, comprising the commander, gunner, loader, driver and wireless operator. On first inspection it looked to be a formidable panzer. Developed by Rheinmetall-Borsig, the Panther's 75mm KwK42 L/70 anti-tank gun was designed as a high-velocity weapon capable of cutting through 140mm of plate armour at 1,000m. This was mounted in an external, curved gun mantlet that included a coaxial machine gun. All but the earliest models had the L/70 gun with the double-baffle muzzle brake. In a stand-off fight this weapon was easily able to tackle the armour of the T-34.

The gunner sat in the turret on the left-hand side and was initially provided with an articulated binocular sight (this was later replaced by a monocular sight). He fired the main gun electrically by a trigger fitted on the elevating hand wheel; the gunner also operated the coaxial machine gun using a foot switch. Either side of the mantlet exposed on the external sides of the turret were three smoke dischargers.

The turret had very distinctive sloped sides and a rounded front covered by a curved cast mantlet. The interior turret cage had a full floor that rotated with the turret. The drive for the hydraulic traverse was taken through the centre of the floor to a gearbox and then to a motor. The commander's station was located to the left rear of the turret, the offset position being due to the length of the gun's breech that all but divided the turret in two. The loader occupied the right hand side of the turret.

The Ausf D's superstructure and hull comprised a single built-up unit of machineable-quality homogeneous armour plate of welded construction. All the main edges of the hull were strengthened by mortised interlocking joints. The front glacis plate, which was angled at 33 degrees to the horizontal to deflect shells upwards clear of the turret mantlet, was 80mm thick on the upper plate and 60mm on the lower. On the initial Ausf D1 this was 60mm and 40mm respectively.

The massive Maybach HL 230 P30 V-12 23 litre engine producing 700hp at 3000rpm was located in the rear compartment. This provided a top speed of 46km/hr with a range of 200km. Access to the engine was via a large inspection hatch in the centre of the rear decking. The cooling grilles and fans took up most the remaining rear decking space. The engine on the Ausf D was uprated from the HL 210 P30 installed in the initial D1.

The hydraulic power take-off for the turret and gun was connected to the engine by a propeller shaft. This was also connected to the gearbox and the brake/transmission unit in the front of the tank. Because it was heavier and bulkier than previous panzers, the Panther needed a a beefed-up gearbox (the Panzer IV, which the Panther was meant to eventually replace, was over 20 tons lighter). Designated the AK 7-200 this was an all-synchromesh unit with seven forward gears and one reverse. Argus hydraulic disc brakes provided the steering by braking the tracks. The epicyclic gears could in addition help steering the Panther through driving one of the sprockets against the main drive, this retarded the track and permitted sharper radius turns.

German engineers usually paid attention to detail but the warning signs were already there, confirming that the Ausf D was a rushed job. Despite its radical departure in hull shape compared to the previous family of panzers a number of weaknesses were instantly apparent with both the sloped hull and turret design. Notably there were openings in the turret that reduced the overall integrity of the armour. On the left-hand side was a small ammunition-loading hatch while at the rear was a crew-access hatch, both of which presented stress points. Similarly, the front glacis plate had two openings, on the left-hand side the driver was served by an armoured flap with a vision port fitted with a laminated glass screen. Under combat conditions this flap was kept shut and the driver had to rely on two fixed periscopes on the hull roof; one faced directly forward and one half left – as they were fixed this greatly limited driver visibility. The wireless operator who also served as hull machine gunner was provided with a primitive vertical opening flap in the glacis plate on the right, through which he could fire the standard MG34 machine gun. Understandably the lack of a ball mount for the machine gun greatly restricted its utility when engaging the enemy.

While the Panther turret was well armoured and angled to deflect shot, its size and height presented a welcome target for enemy gunners. In addition, the front mantlet was found to deflect shot into the thinly-armoured hull roof. The latter problem was not fully addressed until the third model Panther tank. On the T-34 the turret's rear overhand created a shot trap that caused a similar problem.

Access to the turret could also be made via the cupola hatch that pivoted to the side. Due to its prominent vertical shape it was known as the 'dustbin' cupola and feature six vision slits that offered poor visibility. The pivoting driver and radio operator hatches were far from ideal and it was soon discovered that they jammed easily if debris caught in the hinges.

The Panther's suspension comprised eight pairs of large interleaved dished discs with solid rubber tyre road wheels sprung on torsion bars, a front drive sprocket and rear idler. The first, third, fifth and seventh road wheels from the front were double with the intervening axles carrying the spaced wheels overlapping the others on the inside and outside. Each bogie axle was joined by a radius arm to a torsion bar coupled in series to a second bar laying parallel to it. While technically advanced and giving excellent floatation, it was hellishly difficult to maintain because of the size of the wheels and inaccessibility of the axles and torsion bars. Replacing the heavy road wheels was a time-consuming task and the number of wheel rim bolts proved insufficient and led to failures. The lack of track covers also left the tracks vulnerable to anti-tank weapons.

In summary the key distinctive characteristics of the Panther Ausf D were the 'dustbin' cupola, the vision port and machine-gun port on the glacis, smoke dischargers on the turret sides, plus a straight edge to the lower sponson sides with separate storage bins fabricated beneath the rear ends. Towards the end of the Ausf D production run an improved cupola was installed and the smoke dischargers dispensed with and replaced by an anti-personnel bomb thrower fitted in the turret roof and operated by the loader. Some later D models were fitted with side skirt armour to protect the upper track run. Textured Zimmerit anti-magnetic mine paste was also applied.

From January to September 1943 MAN, Daimler-Benz, MNH and Henschel built a total of 850 Ausf Ds. At an average of about 100 a month this was a pitifully low rate of production. The first vehicles were sent to their units in February, but in April the process was halted after those issued were recalled for major modifications. During the summer and following the Panther's performance at Kursk it was evident that a new production model was required to remedy the Panther's existing shortcomings.

Just as the Panther was making its appearance Guderian was appointed Inspector-General reporting directly to Adolf Hitler. He found himself with responsibility for almost all armoured units in the German Army, Waffen-SS and the Luftwaffe – the artillery though would not relinquish control of their assault guns thanks to the wording of Guderian's terms of reference.

Guderian was not happy with the Panther Ausf D and indeed tried to delay it being sent to the Eastern Front. As he recalled:

> I spent June 15th [1943] worrying about our problem child, the Panther, the track suspension and drive were not right and the optics were also not yet satisfactory. On the next day I told Hitler of my reasons for not wishing to see the Panthers sent into action in the East. They were simply not yet ready to go to the front.

Hitler though would not listen and the 'problem child' was sent to a place called Kursk and suffered as a result. The very hard won lessons involving the Ausf D at the Battle of Kursk were soon put into practice. Confusingly the second production model of the Panther, which appeared in August 1943, was designated the Ausf A rather than the Ausf E as might have been expected. While the basic design remained the same as the initial Ausf D it featured a series of detailed modifications in an attempt to improve the Panther's troublesome performance.

The Ausf A was fractionally larger than the D, the hull armour was unchanged but the turret was up-armoured at the front by an extra 10mm giving it 110mm, while the sides and rear remained 40mm and the roof just 16mm. Although the hull was the same, a new ball machine-gun mount was installed to replace the clumsy letterbox port. The latter proved far from ideal to use in the heat of battle and could allow enemy infantry to fire into the interior of the tank. The upgrade was not immediate as the ball mounts were initially only fitted to a proportion of Ausf As, though were eventually installed in all of them from the close of the year. Likewise, the gunner's TZF12 binocular sighting telescope was gradually replaced by the improved monocular TZF12A.

The turret received many minor modifications that included a new cupola with seven equally-spaced armoured periscopes and a semi-circular rail to mount an MG34 machine gun for air defence, a tacit acknowledgement following Kursk that perhaps the Red Air Force had not been defeated after all. The later type cupola fitted to the Ausf A (and subsequent Ausf G) was machined from a homogeneous armour casting. The mountings for the episcope blocks were welded onto the casting. The new cupola hatch opened vertically. To simplify turret production and strengthen the armour the side pistol ports and small loading hatch of the Ausf D were dispensed with, leaving just the big round escape/loading hatch in the turret rear. This also served to improve the integrity of the turret armour.

As long as the turret could rotate the coaxial machine gun was normally the best method for keeping enemy infantry at bay along with the hull-mounted machine gun. While turret pistol ports were a common feature, they were a crude expedient for coping with close-quarters fighting in the event of enemy infantry clambering over a tank's hull. On the Ausf D these consisted of an opening on either side of the turret that could be sealed by a steel bung held in place by a chain (a similar arrangement was used on the later T-34). The crew could fire handguns or machine pistols out the port either blind or using the vision blocks in the cupola.

Clearly the pistol ports were rather hit and miss when it came to defending the tank. On the Ausf A the pistol ports were swapped in favour of the much more effective Nahverteidigungswaffe or close-in defence weapon mounted in the roof. This was designed to dispense smoke and allowed the crew to fire a flare pistol through it. The pistol could discharge smoke rounds, flares and small-calibre fragmentation grenades. The latter had the advantage of keeping enemy infantry away from the tank before they could close in.

A number of modifications were made to the drive train and engine cooling to improve reliability and the number of wheel-rim bolts was doubled. On the Ausf D the heads had a habit of shearing off when placed under excessive stress. Side skirts of 5mm armour and the Zimmerit paste coating were standardized. However, the skirt fittings were not terribly robust and tended to get torn off in combat or simply removed by the crews. These changes caused a slight increase in weight, whereas the Ausf D came in at about 43 tons the Ausf A increased to almost 45 tons, though this made no real discernible difference to its performance.

The Ausf A proved far more successful than the initial model, with double the production. From August 1943 to May 1944 Hitler's panzer factories run by Daimler-Benz, Henschel, MAN and MNH produced 2,000. These saw action on the Eastern Front and in Italy. The Panther Ausf A was the principal type of Panther deployed to counter the Allied invasion of Normandy. Unfortunately for the Panther in many instances geographical conditions did not favour its key asset.

The Ausf G was the third in the Panther series drawing on recommendations from the panzer crews in the field who had fought with the Ausf D and A. Not surprisingly the panzertruppen had been quick to identify the earlier models shortcomings. The main difference with the G model was a redesigned hull, which featured an increase in the side armour on the upper hull side and the side was formed from a single plate. Soviet tank crews had swiftly learned at Kursk that the best way to kill a Panther was from the side and preferably from a hull-down position. Penetrating the Panther's glacis plate was almost impossible except at short range.

Visually the most obvious change was the removal of the driver's vision port from the glacis plate to improve the integrity of the armour. The driver now steered either with his head poking out of the hatch courtesy of a seat that could be raised, or if closed up employing a rotating periscope. The driver and radio operator's pivoting access hatches were replaced by hinged ones to improve reliability. If the crew had to bail out in a hurry the last thing they wanted was a hatch that jammed at the critical moment.

Efforts were made once again to tackle the vexed issue of reliability, most notably with the overstressed drive train. An oil cooler was also installed with the gearbox to improve performance. The suspension remained the same though in some later production vehicles the rearmost hydraulic dampers were deleted. In September 1944 a trial production series were fitted with steel rimmed 'silent bloc' wheels that were also to be standard on the aborted Panther Ausf F.

At the same time some turrets were fitted with a new gun mantlet that had the under curve eliminated to stop hits being deflected into the thin hull roof armour. This improvement showed the problem was commonplace enough to need remedying. Again at Kursk Soviet anti-tank gunners had been able to get above the Ausf D and shoot down into the upper hull. The cupola on the late Ausf G, as on the Ausf A, had Ersatzgläser blocks held in place by a simple spring-lock mechanism. This permitted any blocks damaged by shell splinters to be quickly replaced.

As with the Ausf A, the G was equipped with the TZF12a monocular sight marked with range scales for all types of ammunition carried, with the high explosive scale also being used for aiming the machine gun. A total of seventy-nine main armament rounds were carried in the Ausf A and D. This increased to eighty-two in the G which were stowed in racks and lockers in the lower half of the fighting compartment, with 5,100 rounds of MG34 ammunition carried in the first two models and 4,800 in the Ausf G.

Also, in the name of crew comfort, from October 1944 the fighting compartment was belatedly fitted with a dedicated heating system that drew warm air from a tower-like device installed over the left-hand side engine fan. On the Eastern Front such a mechanism was vital during the bitter winters. These various improvements to the Ausf G again meant an inevitable slight increase in weight over the Ausf D with the new Panther weighing in at 45.5 tons.

Although the introduction of the Ausf G did fix many of the persistent problems that had beset the early Ausf D and A, such as the engine fires and weak drives, the Panther remained a gas-guzzler and by mid-1944 was increasingly vulnerable to Soviet 85mm and 122mm tank guns. Nonetheless the Ausf G proved to be the most numerous Panther with 3,126 built from March 1944 to April 1945. This type served on both the Eastern and Western Fronts and saw combat with Hitler's last offensives in East Prussia, Hungary and Belgium. Ultimately though the Ausf G proved too few too late by this stage of the conflict.

Panther construction continued until the end of the war and was expanded beyond the initial Panther group of MAN, Daimler-Benz, Henschel and MNH, incorporating Demag and MIAG (the main gun was built by Rheinmetall-Borsig of Berlin-Tegel). Use was also made of three key steelworks in Polish Upper Silesia; Bankhütte was involved in engineering and hull/superstructure fabrication and Bismarckhütte and Konigshütte produced electric steel. Although the MNH Panther factory at Hanover was severely damaged several times by Allied bombing, quantities of Ausf G and Jagdpanthers components including turrets, hulls and superstructures were found to be largely intact when it was finally captured.

Construction of the Panther highlighted a problem that plagued German armoured fighting vehicle production. Hitler employed numerous companies to build his panzers, assault guns and tank destroyers and this inevitably caused coordination headaches for Armaments Minister Speer. It also meant that the process was never really centralized out of harm's way.

Daimler-Benz, Krupp and Rheinmetall-Borsig had first been given a taste of things in the late 1920s and early 1930s. They were involved with the Grosstraktor and then the Panzer I but from that point on at least a dozen other major manufacturers became involved at different locations. For example, building the Panzer IV involved at least three different companies and the Panther involved over half a dozen. In the end the Panzer IV was rationalized to just one as the rest were diverted to building assault guns and tank destroyers. Some of the companies, such as Henschel, were involved with nearly all the panzer types, which meant constant re-tooling.

At the same time at least a dozen other companies were employed producing armoured cars, armoured personnel carriers, half-tracks and self-propelled guns. Inevitably there was some overlap between them and the tank, gun and engine manufacturers. All this required considerable coordination bringing the various sub-assemblies together. As the Second World War progressed moving things around by railway became increasingly hazardous. Getting the panzers to the troops became almost harder than actually building them.

PART II

OFF TO WAR

Chapter 8

Blitzkrieg Babies

By the 1930s Guderian and his colleagues were firmly convinced that the infantry should support the tanks and not the other way round. For tanks to fight to their strengths they should be grouped into armoured divisions with their own supporting mobile infantry and artillery units. Mobility was the key. Tanks were not a decisive weapon fighting on their own or fighting alongside infantry divisions. Britain, France and the Soviet Union were too slow in coming to the same conclusion. Initially their tanks would fight in support of their infantry and this was to cost them dearly.

'Only movement brings victory' became the German philosophy. German strategy and tactics revolved around the schwerpunkt or centre of gravity. This essentially meant where should the main military effort be focused to gain the maximum effect. Guderian paraphrased it as 'Klotzen, nicht kleckern'. This crudely translates as 'Thump 'em, don't pepper 'em'. General Hans von Seeckt, former commander of the Reichswehr, wrote in 1928 'the whole future of warfare appears to me to lie in the employment of mobile armies, relatively small but of high quality and rendered distinctly more effective by the addition of aircraft . . .'. This sounded very much like Blitzkrieg.

German armoured warfare tactics evolved around the creation of the panzer division. The key was the panzer regiment supported by motorized infantry in lorries or panzergrenadiers in armoured personnel carriers. These in turn were supported by dedicated reconnaissance, artillery, anti-tank and engineer units. The concept for Blitzkrieg in phase one or the advance to contact centred on reconnaissance units supported by artillery and dive-bombers detecting weaknesses in enemy lines. In their wake would come the fast light tanks followed by the medium tanks and mobile infantry. Phase two was contact when the reconnaissance units would race behind enemy lines creating chaos and isolating the enemy ready for the German main force. At the same time the Luftwaffe would be destroying enemy aircraft, lines of communication, troop concentrations and industrial centres. The idea was that once surrounded, an enemy ground force would become so bewildered that they would quickly surrender.

For the panzer crew suppression of enemy fire was a priority. Usually this meant the destruction of enemy tanks and anti-tank guns as they posed the most immediate threat. It also required an efficient system of fire control. Each tank

commander was responsible for providing his gunner with accurate target information as well as selecting what type of ammunition to employ. At platoon and
company level the tanks had to be mutually supporting. For the tanks to operate
at a battalion, regimental and divisional level required a very effective chain of
command and extensive training.

As the war progressed German tank tactics evolved as did the organization of
the panzer divisions. Typically, the panzer regiments went from three battalions
down to one. The number of tank companies within the battalions varied enormously.
Officially each tank company normally had four platoons each with five tanks, but
shortages resulted in just four per platoon. In addition, the fourth platoon was also
dispensed with. Major reorganizations were conducted in 1940 after the French
campaign and again in 1944. Although Hitler created numerous panzer divisions,
they became weaker and weaker. Likewise, training became increasingly shorter,
with recruits often being sent to new formations rather than being used as combat
replacements.

Austria, Czechoslovakia and Poland were to become the testing grounds for
Germany's cutting edge theories. Hitler's visit to the ordnance testing ground at
Kümmersdorf in early 1935 is cited as clear evidence of his belligerent attitude
towards Germany's neighbours. Guderian was given 30 minutes to show off his
motorized troops:

> I was able to demonstrate a motorcycle platoon, an anti-tank platoon,
> a platoon of Panzer Is in the experimental form of the time, and one
> platoon of light and one of heavy armoured reconnaissance cars. Hitler
> was much impressed by the speed and precision of movement of our units,
> and said repeatedly: 'That's what I need! That's what I want to have!'

One suspects Hitler was referring to everything on display, rather than just the
tanks. To the initiated the Panzer I looked little better than a glorified lawnmower
when compared to what the French and Soviets were producing. Guderian
in his memoirs *Panzer Leader* implies the visit was in 1933. This cannot be
correct because no Panzer Is were built until the following year. His use of the
term 'experimental form' could suggest the turretless training version, but it is
more likely he would have wanted to show Hitler the Panzer I Ausf A – both were
available in 1934. However, the consensus is that Hitler's visit took place in
February 1935.

Nonetheless it was evident that Hitler was a keen supporter of Guderian's
new mobile forces. That summer they held a training exercise at Munsterlager
involving an improvised panzer division. 'The attendance of Hitler, whom General
Lutz had also invited to be present,' observed Guderian with some annoyance 'was

prevented by the passive resistance of his military adjutant.' Despite this, within a matter of a few years the Panzer I and II were used in operations to incorporate Austria and Czechoslovakia in a greater Germany.

When Austria was incorporated into the Reich in 1938 Guderian avoided commenting on the performance of the Panzer I and II other than to say 'The majority of the tanks arrived safely in Vienna'. This was not entirely true and once again he was putting a brave face on things. The 420-mile journey from Würzburg via Passau to the Austrian capital achieved in 48 hours caused major problems for his armoured columns. This was a severe embarrassment to Guderian who had been appointed commander of the world's first armoured corps.

His panzer crews were inexperienced and many were still undergoing training. The mechanics did not have the ability to carry out anything more than the most basic maintenance. For any major repairs the tanks had to be sent back to the factory. Some 30 per cent of the tanks reportedly broke down, though the true figure was almost certainly higher. After the war during the Nuremburg trials General Jodl stated that it was actually 70 per cent. The lack of supporting fuel supplies meant that the tanks were forced to use roadside petrol stations and trucks had to be commandeered in Passau. Even a military fuel depot lacking prior orders refused to cooperate until Guderian threatened to use force.

Guderian's invasion force consisted of the 2nd Panzer Division, the 27th Infantry Division and Hitler's bodyguard regiment Leibstandarte SS Adolf Hitler under Sepp Dietrich. The latter had served with Germany's rudimentary tank force during the First World War and both men seem to have taken an immediate liking to each other. On hearing that Dietrich had an audience with Hitler just before the operation, Guderian requested Dietrich suggest to Hitler that their tanks be covered with flags and greenery to show to the Austrians there was no hostile intent. Hitler approved this immediately.

Despite the setbacks Guderian received a warm welcome 'The flags and decorations on the tanks proved highly successful. The populace saw that we came as friends, and we were everywhere joyfully received. . . . At every halt the tanks were decked with flowers and food was pressed on the soldiers.' He was lucky the Austrians embraced Anschluss: if they had resisted the whole operation could have ended in disaster.

Afterwards Guderian wrote defensively 'It was alleged that tanks were now proved incapable of performing any lengthy and sustained advance. In fact, the proper targets for criticism were quite different.' The real culprit was the complete lack of logistical support and valuable lessons were learned in peacetime conditions. Guderian was understandably annoyed that his previous recommendations had been not acted upon and that the same mistakes were made 'in the full glare of publicity during the spring of 1938'.

To be fair to Guderian and his tanks, Hitler had only decided at the last minute that unification with Austria should be backed by a show of force. The planning for the drive to Vienna had been a rushed job. 'This mistake was never made again', said Guderian with an air of 'I told you so'. The subsequent operations against the Sudetenland and Czechoslovakia were much slicker. When the German Army mobilized in 1939 it had five panzer divisions and four light divisions (which only had a single tank battalion).

The Panzer I and II saw combat during the invasions of Poland, France, the Low Countries and Scandinavia during 1939–40. The outgunned Panzer I was then phased out of service with just around seventy-five remaining with the panzer regiments at the time of the invasion of Russia in mid-1941, although some of the self-propelled variants continued to see combat well into 1943. The Panzer II was also phased out with the panzer regiments in late 1943, although it remained on secondary fronts until the end of the war. However, the successful self-propelled Marder II anti-tank gun and Wespe artillery variants saw active service with the panzer and panzergrenadier divisions until the very end of the war.

The Panzer IA, IB and the command vehicle variant were first tested in combat in the Spanish Civil War in 1936. To support the Luftwaffe's Condor Legion sent to aid Franco, under the codename Imker, the German Army also provided a ground component. This included Panzergruppe Drohne (or Imker Drohne) technically a training unit which by late 1936 had forty-one Ausf As and twenty-one Ausf Bs. Including those supplied directly to Franco's nationalist forces a total of 122 Panzer Is served in Spain. These were never enough to conduct a massed armoured attack.

The German panzer instructors handed the tanks over to the Spanish crews as soon as they were competent, and mainly restricted themselves to an advisory role in the latter part of the conflict. The Panzer Is were supplied in dark panzer grey with earth-brown shadow camouflage. This colour scheme was used by the German Army for a period during the mid-1930s.

The Republicans were equipped with significant numbers of the much more powerful Soviet BT-5 and T-26 tanks armed with a 45mm gun. Fortunately for the panzergruppe the Germans brought with them their 37mm anti-tank gun. Also the Republicans did not adapt well to tank warfare and they lost many of their Soviet tanks and anti-tank guns intact, which were subsequently turned against them.

Notably the Germans viewed their experiences in Spain as being of technical rather than tactical value. Panzergruppe Drohne discovered that the Panzer I was woefully inadequate even by the standards of the day. Their experience showed up the shortcomings of the two-man crew and the lack of an anti-tank gun. Its hull was lightly armoured and its crevices and joins made it vulnerable. The engine, particularly in the IA, was underpowered and gave the tank a poor performance. Likewise, there was little crew comfort. Vision was restricted when closed down, so the commander tended to operate standing up with his upper body extremely exposed. It was not until the Panzer III and IV that adequate cupolas were fitted for the commander to provide some protection.

By 1939 sufficient tanks of a more powerful type in the shape of the Panzer III and IV had not been built to replace their predecessors. As a result, the light tanks had to be deployed both against Poland and against France the following year. There were still 1,445 Panzer Is in service when Poland was invaded on 1 September 1939. Against the disorganized Polish Army they proved quite useful. Ironically it had never been the German High Command's intention to use them in such major campaigns in this way. In total the Poles had some 660 tanks, though other than the Polish 7-TP and British-supplied Vickers 6-tonner, none of them could be classed as anything other than light tanks.

For the attack on Poland the Germans had available forty infantry, six panzer, four light and four motorized divisions. Two panzer and two motorized divisions were assigned to Army Group North; all of them apart from one panzer division were under the direction of Guderian's XIX Corps. Despite the presence of the panzers and the motorized infantry the German Army was still far from mechanized. The Polish Army comprised thirty infantry divisions, eleven cavalry brigades, two motorized brigades and a single armoured brigade.

Interestingly the Polish motorized brigades consisted of two motorized cavalry regiments riding in lorries and motorized artillery battalions with 37mm anti-tank guns. They were supported by one company of Vickers 6-ton tanks and two companies of tankettes, which were versions of the British Carden-Loyd Mark VI. The armoured brigade fielded two battalions of 7-TP tanks, an improved Polish version of the Vickers 6-tonner, which had thicker armour and a 37mm gun, plus one battalion of French-built Renault 35s also armed with 37mm guns. The infantry divisions were supported by eighteen independent companies, each with thirteen tankettes. The cavalry brigades had a reconnaissance squadron of thirteen tankettes and eight armoured cars.

Strategically the Polish Army was in an impossible position. After Hitler's occupation of Czechoslovakia, it found itself defending a 1,450-mile common frontier with Germany. Its flanks were terribly exposed to attack from Czechoslovakia in the south and Pomerania and East Prussia in the north. The massed ranks of panzers were awe inspiring. One young German soldier wrote on the eve of the invasion of Poland 'It is a wonderful feeling, now, to be a German. . . . The row of tanks has no end. A quarter of an hour, tanks, tanks, tanks.'

The panzers' mobility offered great advantages in Poland as General von Thoma observed when turning the Poles' flank at the Jublenka Pass:

> I carried out with my tank brigade a flanking move – through thick
> woods and over the ridge. On descending into the valley I arrived in a

village to find the people all going to church. How astonished they were to see my tanks appearing! I had turned the enemy's defences without losing a single tank – after a night approach march of fifty miles.

The issue of reliability once again reared its ugly head. At the start of the Polish campaign mechanical failure in 25 per cent of the tanks was considered acceptable. By the end, thanks to the combat conditions and mileage travelled, every vehicle required maintenance, echoing their experiences in Austria.

The Germans also learned of the perils of using tanks in urban areas. The 4th Panzer Division fighting in the suburbs of Warsaw found themselves sitting ducks for Polish gunners and lost 57 of their 120 tanks. Nonetheless they had covered 140 miles in the space of a week having exploited a gap in the Polish defences. In total the Germans suffered 217 tanks casualties during the invasion. This was in part due to a lack of armoured cross-country vehicles to carry the panzergrenadiers. This meant that the tanks often lacked infantry support and suffered as a consequence.

Over 520 Panzer I Ausf Bs and earlier Ausf As took part in the campaign in the West in 1940, along with almost 100 of the command variant. During the Allies' retreat to Dunkirk many Panzer Is were knocked out by the British 2-pounder anti-tank gun. Panzer Is were also used in the Balkans, Greece and North Africa in 1941. A Panzer I Ausf B was photographed approaching El Aghelia in Libya early in the North African campaign and another was recorded parked next to a captured British Matilda tank. A few also saw service during the opening stages of the campaign in Russia. Despite the tank's inadequate armour protection and firepower, in July 1941 there were still over 800 in service. Shortly after they were redeployed for training or converted to self-propelled gun carriages. The self-propelled gun variants of the Panzer I, armed with a 47mm anti-tank gun or a 150mm infantry gun, were not a great success as the chassis was overloaded, although these two types were in service for the battle of France in May 1940 and despite its shortcomings the Panzerjäger I provided useful support in North Africa.

The Panzer II, like the Panzer I, was employed in Poland in 1939 and in France in 1940, when the Ausf c formed an important part of the force. Some 955 Panzer IIs were in service at the start of the Western campaign. They formed the backbone of the panzer divisions because they represented the highest number of any one type out of 2,500 German tanks deployed for the invasion. The number had risen to 1,067 Panzer IIs by the following year.

In the accounts of his exploits in France and North Africa Erwin Rommel rarely referenced light tanks. His main preoccupation was the performance of the Panzer III and IV. When he did write about them it was because they were causing him problems. For instance, during the attack on France he recorded when crossing the Andelle river on 8 June 1940:

> Although there was over three feet of water near the eastern bank the first tanks crossed without any trouble and soon overtook the infantry. However, when the first Panzer II attempted it, its engine cut out in midstream, leaving the crossing barred to all other vehicles. . . . One of the Panzer IIIs which had already crossed was brought back to tow out the Panzer II.

On another occasion Rommel was infuriated when his light tanks did not return fire when shelled by an enemy anti-tank gun. With his column pinned down he recalled:

> I jumped down from my vehicle and ran to the Panzer II standing on the embankment left of the road, where I also found the commander of the leading tank. I told him what I thought of him . . . Then I ordered the Panzer II to open fire at once . . . the Panzer II's 20mm shells and tracer ammunition caused such a firework display that the enemy ceased fire, as I had expected.

During the invasion of Poland, it was found the Polish Army anti-tank rifle could penetrate the hull of the Panzer II Ausf A, B and C. In response to this additional 20mm armour plates were bolted onto the front of the hull, superstructure and turret on 70 per cent of the tanks by May 1940. The rest were completed by the time of the attack on the Soviet Union. This meant that the front of the Panzer II lost its rounded shape and became angular.

Likewise, during the Polish campaign tank commanders grumbled about the Panzer II's limited vision. This proved a problem during the invasion of the Low Countries and France. It was solved by installing a commander's cupola with eight periscopes from October 1940, that was supplied as a kit to those units with the A–C models.

By the time of the Polish campaign the German Army had just under 100 Panzer IIIs. The appearance of the Ausf E enabled the 1st platoon of the light tank companies to be boosted from three to five Panzer IIIs. Nevertheless, the requirement for Panzer IIIs to be available for training units, such as the Panzer Lehr Armoured Training Detachment, resulted in some panzer divisions having to fight in Poland without any Panzer IIIs. By this stage the German Army was increasingly clamouring for a fully massed-produced version of the Panzer III.

The Ausf F was rapidly issued to the panzer regiments from late 1939 and early 1940. By 10 May 1940 there were 348 Panzer IIIs (mainly Ausf Es and Fs but also a few Ausf Gs) with Hitler's seven panzer divisions on the Western Front. Some Ausf Fs were known to have still been in service with the 116th Panzer Division as late as June 1944.

A few Panzer IIIs, largely the early models though including some Ausf Es, had their baptism of fire in Poland in 1939. 'In this campaign the quality of our materiel left much to be desired,' wrote Major-General Friedrich von Mellenthin. 'We only had a few Mark IVs with low velocity 75mm guns, some Mark IIIs carrying the unsatisfactory 37mm, and the bulk of our armoured strength was made up of Mark IIs carrying only a heavy machine gun.'

Guderian, by now a corps commander, insisted the Panzer Lehr Battalion that had the new Panzer III and IV be included in his XIX Corps for the invasion of Poland. This was a training unit but he was determined that they test out their panzers and tactical theories under combat conditions. Because both tanks were armed with short-barrelled guns they offered an indifferent anti-tank capability. Fortunately for the Germans the Polish Army own tanks were little more than reconnaissance vehicles making the panzers shortcomings of little significance.

Hitler visited Guderian in Poland to find out how the new panzers had performed. Guderian informed the Führer that their speed was fine but they needed better armour and guns. 'I told him,' wrote Guderian 'that the most important thing now was to hasten the delivery of the Panzer III and IV to the fighting troops and to increase production of these tanks.' Points which Hitler took on board. It was shortly after the Polish campaign came to an end that the Panzer III and IV were accepted as the standard equipment of all the tank battalions.

At the start of the campaign in the West in May 1940 a total of 349 Panzer IIIs and 278 Panzer IVs formed the core of the attack. There were also thirty-nine Panzer III command vehicles supporting them. Hitler fielded an overall force of 2,574 tanks. In France the Panzer III proved inadequate against the heavier British and French tanks. The Germans ready solution to this was using their flak guns in an anti-tank role and calling on their heavy artillery and dive bombers to deliver high explosives. Rommel was to repeat this highly successful tactic in North Africa.

In contrast some 3,200 panzers were ready for the invasion of the Soviet Union in the summer of 1941 with a high proportion of this number being Panzer IIIs. By this point the 50mm gun had been introduced on the Panzer III, with the progressive replacement of the 37mm gun in existing vehicles, and as the standard weapon of the new ones being built from the latter part of 1940 onwards.

During the invasion of France, whilst commanding the 7th Panzer Division, Rommel became only too familiar with the capabilities of the Panzer III and IV. He almost lost his life in one of the former. For the breakthrough on the River Meuse he directed operations from inside one. He does not relate whether he replaced the tank commander or whether he and the five crew were all squeezed into the tank. Once on the move his tank was hit twice, once on the upper edge of the turret and once in the periscope. A splinter from the shell that hit the periscope wounded Rommel in the right cheek and he bled profusely. He could have lost an eye or even been killed. The driver trying to evade French artillery and anti-tank fire accidently slid the tank down a steep bank, where it became stuck on its side and dangerously exposed. Unable to rotate the turret Rommel and the crew bailed out and only just made it to safety.

Rommel also briefly employed a Panzer III as an escort for his command vehicle at Le Câteau until it suffered mechanical problems. At Arras his tanks received a nasty surprise at the hands of the British Matilda. Rommel lost six Panzer IIIs and three Panzer IVs, but quickly restored the situation by deploying his artillery to support his tanks.

Had Operation Sealion, the invasion of England, taken place the Panzer III would have played a prominent role. Ultimately though getting the panzers ashore was an insurmountable problem at the time. War correspondent and historian Chester Wilmot observed 'the Germans would not have been able to land tanks in large numbers until they had captured and opened ports on the south-east coast. At the end of August [1940] the Wehrmacht had available for landing from the sea only 42 Mark IVs and 168 Mark IIIs.' It was simply not enough.

Hitler massed seventeen panzer divisions on the border with the Soviet Union ready for Operation Barbarossa in June 1941. Eleven of these were issued with the Panzer III and six with the Czech-built Panzer 38(t). Despite the previous production problems every light armoured company had its full complement of 17 Panzer IIIs. This meant that including regimental and detachment level headquarters Hitler had a total of 960 Panzer III Ausf Es to Js (he also had 438 Panzer IVs).

The Panzer III and IV could only fight the new Soviet T-34 and KV-1 tanks at very close range, but the latter were initially available in just limited numbers. In contrast the more numerous obsolete Soviet light tanks proved a different matter and were destroyed wholesale. During the winter of 1941 as the T-34 became more abundant the Soviet 76.2mm tank gun showed just how inadequate the main armament was on both the Panzer III and IV. This and experiences in North Africa made it imperative to up-gun both tanks.

By late June 1942, at the start of his summer offensive on the Eastern Front, Hitler had about 600 Panzer IIIs with the 50mm L/60 gun. At the end of the year the Panzer III played a prominent part in the failure to rescue the German Sixth Army trapped at Stalingrad. When the LVII Panzer Corps launched its attack on 12 December 1942 to try and relieve Stalingrad, the weak 6th Panzer Division had sixty-three Panzer IIIs, twenty-three Panzer IVs and seven command vehicles, whilst elements of the 23rd Panzer Division had forty-six Panzer IIIs and eleven Panzer IVs. They were unable to cut their way through the Red Army.

The following summer, although the Panzer III had lost its effectiveness as a tank-versus-tank weapon, there were still 432 with the 50mm L/60, 155 with the 75mm L/24 and 41 Panzer III flamethrowers with Army Groups Centre and South at the start of the Kursk offensive. Therefore, all the Army's panzer and panzergrenadier divisions as well as the Waffen-SS panzergrenadier divisions fielded quite large numbers of Panzer IIIs. For example, 4th Panzer Division with Army Group Centre had forty while the 11th Panzergrenadier Division with Army Group South had fifty.

The Battle of Kursk marked the swan-song of the Panzer III. Predictably losses were high and production of the Panzer III as a gun tank was subsequently stopped. In Sicily, to try and fend off Operation Husky, Panzer Division Hermann Göring and 15th Panzergrenadier Division mustered forty-nine Panzer IIIs. They constituted about a third of the German tank forces on the island. Although superseded by the Panzer IV and Panther, remarkably some Panzer IIIs were encountered by the Allies in Normandy in 1944. In particular, the Panzerbefehlswagen radio command vehicles continued to be of service with the panzer divisions. The headquarters units of the 21st Panzer Division's 22nd Panzer Regiment had two Panzer III command vehicles and four gun tanks.

When the 116th Panzer Division Windhund deployed to Normandy in July 1944 its armoured units included about ten Panzer IIIs (consisting of seven tanks with the long-barrelled 50mm L/60 and three with the short-barrelled version – the latter were Fs) and six StuG IIIs. Some of these vehicles were largely considered cast offs and were due to be reissued to other units. The Waffen-SS also still retained some Panzer IIIs in Normandy. The 10th SS Panzer Division Frundsberg had three Panzer III command vehicles on its books. Only a very few Bergepanzer IIIs served with some of the panzer regiments in Normandy. These included the 9th SS Panzer Division as well as the 2nd and 116th Panzer Divisions.

Chapter 9

Panzers in North Africa

Although the Panzer II was really obsolete by 1941 it provided valuable service in North Africa. As it could manage over 20mph in most conditions and had a range of 125 miles it was well suited to a scouting role and for reconnaissance duties Rommel deployed a mix of Panzer IIs and four- or eight-wheeled armoured cars.

When Rommel's 5th Light Division (later renamed 21st Panzer Division) began to arrive in Tripoli during early 1941, its 5th Panzer Regiment was equipped with 165 tanks, of which 25 were Panzer Is and 45 Panzer IIs, the rest being Panzer IIIs and IVs. The 15th Panzer Division also arrived in Libya with a complement of forty-five Panzer IIs. General von Mellenthin who was on Rommel's staff in North Africa had little to say about Hitler's early panzers stating 'Of the German tanks, 70 were Mark IIs, which only mounted a heavy machine gun, and could therefore play no part in a tank battle, except as reconnaissance vehicles.'

The Panzer Is and IIs, like their heavier cousins, arrived in Tripoli still in their panzer grey. All four panzer types were sent to the front in this colour – with the crews having to wait for the belated provision of sand-coloured paint. Photographic evidence depicting a newly-arrived column of four Panzer IIs clearly shows that although they are covered in dust and sand their base colour is very dark. Another shot of two Panzer IIs gathering British prisoners during Operation Crusader shows they are still in panzer grey.

Alexander Clifford, who reported on the fighting in the region throughout 1941, was full of grudging praise for the Panzer III and IV but saw fit not to mention the earlier models. He had regular discussions with British tank crews and it would seem that the Panzer I and II were not a topic of conversation. The balance of German light and medium tanks understandably shifted as the fighting in Libya progressed. The Panzer IIs were replaced by Panzer IIIs and IVs whenever possible. It was the Panzer III that became the workhorse in North Africa. Nonetheless, by November 1941 Rommel's tank forces still included fifteen Panzer Is and forty Panzer IIs. Examples of the latter were photographed outside Tobruk's defensive perimeter the following month and they continued to serve through much of the campaign.

By April 1942 the German Army still had a total of 860 Panzer IIs on its overall tank strength. Some of the panzer divisions were still fielding Panzer IIs in Tunisia in early 1943. It was at this point that Panzer II production was diverted to self-propelled gun manufacture, in particular the Wespe. Nonetheless, the Panzer II saw combat during the battle of Kursk in the summer of 1943, one of its main roles being as an armoured artillery observation post.

The Panzer III spearheaded Rommel's operations in North Africa, outnumbering the Panzer IIs and IVs by two to one. Until early 1942 the most potent versions available were the Ausf F, G and H with the 50mm L/42 gun. This was capable of penetrating 45mm of homogeneous armour plate sloped at 60 degrees at its effective range of 750 yards.

The 5th Light Division (later 21st Panzer) arrived in Tripoli with seventy-five Panzer IIIs and twenty Panzer IVs. Beforehand the division suffered a mishap in Naples where a cargo ship caught fire and sank with the loss of ten Panzer IIIs and three Panzer IVs. Rommel was fortunate to get the rest ashore unscathed as shortly after the RAF bombed Tripoli. In one attack on the harbour an ammunition ship was hit and exploded, destroying an entire block of buildings. This good fortune was of Rommel's own making as he had insisted the tanks be unloaded during the night. Replacements for the 5th Panzer Regiment did not reach them until the end of April. The 15th Panzer Division's 8th Panzer Regiment was shipped to Libya in three convoys between 25 April and 6 May 1941. This unit initially fielded 146 tanks, including 71 Panzer IIIs, 20 Panzer IVs and 10 command tanks.

The Panzer IIIs' first role in Tripoli was to take part in a show of force and an act of duplicity on 15 March 1941. Rommel instructed:

> The moment every panzer is unloaded, the German 5th Panzer Regiment and the tanks of the Italian Ariete Division will parade in a fashion that will not escape the attention of, first the Italian civil population, and second the enemy's spies. . . . On completion of the paraded the regiment will immediately proceed to the front . . .

When the parade commenced, having rolled down the main street they turned into a side street and circled back to create the impression that there were more panzers than there really were. Lieutenant Heinz Schmidt, who was on Rommel's staff, was highly amused by the subterfuge when he realized one of the tanks 'somehow looked familiar to me although I had not previously seen its driver. Only then did the penny drop, as the Tommies say, and I could not help grinning. Still more panzers passed, squeaking and creaking round that bend.'

German observers were disappointed by the Italian crowd's complete lack of enthusiasm and utter silence. Tripoli's officials cannot have been pleased that the panzers' tracks were chewing up the road surface. It was only when the slower moving Ariete Division appeared that they began to cheer. The British on the other hand were suitably alarmed by the news of Rommel's arrival.

Initially the Panzer III's chief opponent in North Africa was the British Cruiser Mk IV (A13 Mk II), armed with the 2-pounder (40mm) gun capable of piercing 40mm of armour at the same range as the L/42. As neither tank had armour in excess of 30mm and as both had comparable speeds they were largely evenly matched. Rommel was impressed by the Cruiser Mk VI Crusader which appeared in June 1941 as it was better armoured and much faster. Once again though it was only armed with the 2-pounder gun and at first proved mechanically very unreliable. It was later up-gunned with a 6-pounder (57mm) gun.

Rommel's Panzer III crews were photographed in the desert wearing a tropical sun helmet, called the Tropische Kopfbedeckung, which was issued to the Afrika Korps in early 1941. This was stowed on the outside of the turret because it was simply not practical to wear it inside the tank. Not surprisingly the crews soon abandoned them in favour of the more comfortable field cap and even captured South African Army sun helmets that were smaller (though they still ended up hung on the outside of the turret).

To fend off the British summer offensive in 1941 Rommel only had ninety-five Panzer IIIs and IVs. By the time of Operation Crusader, launched by the British on 18 November 1941, he could muster about 139 Panzer IIIs, but half of them were still armed with the 37mm gun, and just 35 Panzer IVs.

Views on the Panzer III's performance differed greatly on either side. Mellenthin who served as a staff officer with the Afrika Korps recalled:

The Mark III used by the Panzergruppe in the Crusader battle only mounted a low-velocity 50mm gun, which British experts now admit had no advantage over their 2-pounder gun. Nor did we have any advantage in the thickness of armour. The British heavy infantry tanks – Matilda and Valentine – completely outclassed us in that respect, and even the Crusaders and Stuarts were better protected than our Mark III. For example the maximum basic armour of the Mark III in the Crusader battle was 30mm, while the Crusader nose and hull fronts were protected by 47mm, and the Stuart had 44mm protection there.

Interestingly, war correspondent Alexander Clifford, after talking to a British tank commander, took a much different view:

The Mark IIIs and Mark IVs both had more fire-power than anything we had got. We found ourselves up against the Mark IIIs' 50mm guns firing four-and-a-half-pound shells and the Mark IVs' definitely heavier type. It was like pitting destroyers against cruisers. It meant that the British had to start every battle with a sprint of half a mile under fire before they could fire back.

He calculated that 100 panzers could claim 30 British tanks before they could even get in range to engage. 'It was absurd to pit British and American tanks with their 37mm guns against the Mark IIIs with their 50mm and the Mark IVs with their 75mm weapons and pretend that the terms were equal,' concluded Clifford. 'To do so was grossly unfair to our armoured brigades.'

From the end of 1941 the next generation of Panzer III began entering service in North Africa. This was the improved Ausf J, dubbed the 'Mk III Special' by the British. It was armed with the 50mm L/60 which could penetrate almost 54mm of armour at 900 yards; it could achieve a velocity of up to 3,930ft/s that enabled it to engage most British tanks with success beyond 1,000 yards. This made it considerably superior to the British 2-pounder. From April 1942 spaced armour 20mm thick was also fitted to the gun mantlet and hull front of the Panzer III including those deployed to North Africa. This advantage was then nullified by the 75mm gun on the American-supplied Grant and Sherman tanks.

German intelligence on the arrival of the Grant prior to the Gazala battles was good. Mellenthin recalled that in May 1942:

> Moreover the [British] 8th Army now had about 200 American Grant tanks, mounting the 75mm gun. These outclassed the 220 Mark IIIs which made up the bulk of our armoured strength, and the only tanks we had to compete with them were 19 Mark III Specials with high velocity 50mm guns. . . . The Panzerarmee also had four Mark IV Specials but these had no ammunition at the beginning of the battle.

Before the Shermans arrived General Brian Horrocks recalled how grateful they were for the Grant. 'These were the only tanks which could compete with the German Mk IIIs and IVs; they were known, in fact, as the ELH. Egypt's Last Hope . . .'

Not surprisingly British tank crews found it difficult to tell the Panzer III and IV apart at any distance due to their similar appear in terms of shape and general layout. The only giveaway was the Panzer IV's stubby 75mm gun but by the time that was visible a tank commander was in trouble. For example, tanker B.H. Milner who was a 75mm gunner recalled in late October 1942: 'I scored one direct hit on a Mk III or Mk IV and put it out of action and put down some very near shots on other tanks and transport. I had a shot at an 88 at long range, but didn't wait to see if I was successful.'

In terms of firepower Rommel had to rely on his towed and self-propelled anti-tank guns plus the up-gunned Panzer IV F2. Even after his defeat at El Alamein and long retreat the Panzer III continued to support Rommel's operations. During the Battle of Tebourba fought in Tunisia at the beginning of December 1942 Captain Helmut Hudel commanded a battlegroup of forty tanks. During the same engagement Group Djedeida included two Tigers supported by three

Panzer IIIs. An abandoned Panzer III Ausf L belonging to the 15th Panzer Division was photographed with a dead crew member at Mareth in Tunisia, following the fighting there in late March 1943 just before the German surrender. By this point the division had only ten tanks left.

Significantly the most common Panzer IVs were the Ausf D, E and F1 which made up around 25 per cent of Rommel's armoured formations. Armed with the short 75mm KwK37 L/24 gun, they were inferior to the later 50mm-armed Panzer III. Prior to the Crusader battles in November 1941 the British were able to field 748 tanks armed with 40mm or 37mm high–velocity guns against 248 panzers, of which 174 were Panzer IIIs and IVs, the rest being Panzer IIs carrying a 20mm gun. The Italians supported Rommel with 146 inferior tanks that were armed with a low–velocity 47mm gun. What really gave Rommel an advantage was his superior tactics.

In the summer of 1942 he began to receive the up-gunned F2 armed with the long-barrelled 75mm KwK40 L/43 gun. This vastly was superior to the British 2-pounder (40mm) and 6-pounder (57mm) and the American-supplied M3 Grant's 75mm gun. Luckily for the British the Germans had only received twenty-seven Panzer IV F2s by August 1942, which they employed to spearhead Rommel's counteroffensive. Despite their presence Rommel's attack at Alam Halfa was held.

Crucially the F2 was never available in sufficient numbers, with around thirty with each of the Afrika Korp's panzer divisions at any one time compared to 100 Panzer IIIs. While its gun could penetrate all British and American armour at a distance and more arrived between August and October 1942 they were nothing like the quantities of tanks reaching the British Eighth Army prior to El Alamein. Some Ausf Gs also fought with the Germans in Tunisia.

British armour could cope with the Panzer I and II but not the subsequent two models. The Panzer III armed with a 50mm gun was superior to any Allied armour until 1942 and the arrival of the M3 Grant. The early Mk IV with its short 75mm gun was able to fire armour-piercing, high explosive and smoke so could outshoot very vulnerable British cruiser tanks and shell exposed 25-pounder gun crews. British cruiser tanks as well as the Matilda and Valentine infantry support tanks armed with the 2-pounder gun could only fire armour-piercing rounds. Initially the 6-pounder installed on the Crusader and the Churchill was also only intended to fire armour-piercing. While the Panzer IV could fire from 3,000 yards with HE, British tanks had to wait for them to close to within 1,000–500 yards to engage with their solid shot AP, and in the meantime their exposed artillery would have to retreat.

The Panzer IIIs and Panzer IV F2s therefore had little trouble dealing with their opponents. British cruiser tanks such as the Mk II and IV had a maximum of 30mm of armour, while the Mk I and III were even more lightly armoured at just 14mm. The Mk VI Crusader was little better – with the final production version, the Crusader III, sporting 51mm of armour. It was also up-gunned to the 6-pounder. The Matilda and Valentine had a respectable maximum of 78mm and 65mm respectively but like all British tanks were slower than the panzers and under-gunned. The Grant and Sherman had 37mm and 75mm armour.

Against the F2 the Grant was not only disadvantaged by its gun, but also by mounting the weapon in the hull instead of a fully revolving turret. This meant it could not fight dug in from a 'hull-down' position when on the defensive. Likewise, the Grant's high silhouette exposed the top of the tank to enemy fire when on the offensive. The Panzer IV also proved more than a match for the Sherman in North Africa.

Ultimately though the Panzer III and IV were overwhelmed by superior numbers and air power. Hitler never adequately bolstered his forces in North Africa until it was way too late and they were trapped. Despite the effectiveness of the Panzer IV F2 and the introduction of a few Tigers, particularly against the inexperienced American army, capitulation was inevitable. The very last of the Panzer IVs were disabled by Allied bombers – one of which was photographed on 10 May 1943 just two days before the Axis surrendered in Tunisia.

While Hitler deluded himself that the Henschel Tiger I was a war-winner, he simply could not wait until it was fully ready for combat and available in numbers that would make its presence truly decisive. There was no escaping its poor debut on the Eastern Front and it was to compound this by a poor showing in North Africa. Heavy Panzer Battalion 501 was formed in Erfurt in May 1942 and intended for duty in Africa.

During the summer of that year Hitler, floundering around trying to find a use for the rejected Porsche Tigers, pressed for them to be used in North Africa. Guderian was quick to dismiss such ideas as nonsense.

> During the discussion on the Porsche Tiger, Hitler expressed his opinion that this tank, being electrically powered and air cooled, would be particularly suitable for employment in the African theatre, but that its operational range of only 30 miles was quite unsatisfactory and must be increased to 90 miles. This was undoubtedly correct; only it should have been stated when the first designs were submitted.

Hitler's senior commanders, including Guderian, tried to stop him despatching the Tiger I to Tunisia in the closing months of 1942 but with no success. The situation for the surrounded German forces there was at best precarious and few could understand the rationale for sending their latest and best tank to an uncertain fate. Guderian wrote in his memoirs, 'Units were still being sent over to Africa and there committed to the flames, among others our newest Tiger Battalion. All argument against such a policy was quite ineffective.'

The 501 had to wait three months before it received its first Tigers. It then moved to southern France in October 1942 with twenty Tigers and sixteen Panzer IIIs. The following month the battalion travelled by rail down through Italy and the first three Tigers of 1st Company arrived in Bizerte in Tunisia on 23 November 1942. Any illusions that the panzertruppen may have had about enjoying warmer climes in Italy, Sicily and Tunisia were soon dispelled by the winter weather. They deployed from Germany via Italy to the port of Reggio. Those involved in the move were keen to avoid the mishaps that had beset the panzers when they had first deployed to Libya with Rommel (see above).

Once they were in Sicily the Tiger crews cannot have been immune to the rumours that the war was not going well across the Mediterranean following the British victory at El Alamein and the American landings in French North Africa. German troops had been successfully rushed to Tunisia to protect Rommel's rear. Nonetheless, the Luftwaffe flights bringing back a steady stream of wounded did little to help morale and there was unease amongst the Italian garrison on Sicily. Convoys had to hug the coast. The Mediterranean was not safe with the Allied air forces escalating their attacks on Rommel's maritime supply lines. Long-range Allied fighter-bombers and submarines operating from Malta were a particular menace. Axis shipping losses in the Mediterranean were heavy, but luckily for the Germans the Tigers made the crossing unscathed.

The Tiger battalion found the docks at Bizerte and the outlying airfields hives of activity as the Germans sought to expand and defend their bridgehead in Tunisia. This time, instead of being met by mud and forests, the Tigers were confronted by mud, rain and mountains. The nights were also bitterly cold and the mountains were capped by snow and frost. They first went into action in early December and throughout the month more tanks were shipped across to Africa.

The Tigers did not get off to a good start. The first tank to arrive seized up on the dock in Bizerte; the second then broke down on the road west. Four others made for Djedeida under Captain Nikolai Baron von Nolde, who eccentrically insisted on wearing gym shoes into battle. On the morning of 2 December 1942 they smashed into the positions of the British Royal Hampshire Regiment. Although the British were overrun, the Germans got a hot reception. Nolde foolishly clambered from his tank to give an order to another officer. He was killed instantly when both his legs were blown away by an anti-tank shell. A sniper killed the second exposed officer. The German attack rolled on into Tebourba and Allied losses included 55 tanks, 53 field guns and 300 other vehicles.

On 6 December 1942 Major Leuder with the 501 noted:

Fleeing enemy columns and tanks were observed as soon as the Tigers appeared. These fleeing enemy infantry could only be engaged with difficulty, because the hilly terrain constantly provided cover for the opponent. . . .

One Tiger was hit in the idler wheel and the road wheels by self-propelled 75mm gun. However it remained driveable. From covered positions on the heights north-west of Medjerda, medium enemy batteries fired at the Tigers without success.

The US 1st Armored's 2nd Battalion lost forty-two M3 General Grant tanks around Djedeida and Tebourba by 10 December 1942 when it was pulled out of the line. By this stage the Tiger crews had learned that they were impervious to the 75mm gun on the M3 General Grant/Lee medium tank, whereas surprisingly the 37mm gun on the M3 Stuart light tank was more of a nuisance. Accurate fire at the Tiger driver's visor, commander's cupola and the gap between the turret proved a problem. In one instant a shell fragment jammed a Tiger's turret, putting the panzer temporarily out of action. The solution was a deflector channel similar to that on the Panzer II and III. Land mines also proved a threat to the Tiger's running gear. At 600m Allied 37mm and 40mm anti-tank guns were only a threat to the Tiger's road wheels and tracks. Artillery only tended to cause minor damage to the road wheels. In contrast the Tiger's 88mm gun easily dealt with the Lee and Stuart tanks.

The panzertruppen of the 501 were not long in making field modifications to their tanks, which included altering the mudguards to cope with the dust and sand and lowering the headlights to make them less conspicuous. The Tiger deployed to Tunisia and southern Russia was a tropical version known as the Tiger (Tp). It was fitted with the Feifel air filter system attached to the back of the tank and linked to the engine via the engine cover plate. This was a luxury that could well be dispensed with and it was discontinued on all production vehicles from early 1943 onwards.

The British Army claimed several of the 501's Tigers in early 1943, when they destroyed one and captured another. The British first came up against the Tiger I near Pont du Fahs when 6-pounder anti-tank guns took on nine Panzer IIIs and two Tigers. The British had been forewarned of the attack and concealed their guns with orders to hold their fire until signalled to open up at very close range. Both the Tigers were knocked out at 300–500 yards.

The British soon found that their best weapon for countering the Tiger was the 17-pounder (76.2mm) anti-tank gun. This had similar hitting power to the German 88mm gun and had been first issued to the British Army in the summer of 1942. Hurriedly mounted on a 25-pounder gun carriage, they were ordered to supplement the 6-pounders in Africa. Under the codename 'Pheasant' 100 of these prototype 17/25-pounders were rushed to North Africa and first saw action in February 1943. As a towed gun it proved to be the best anti-tank weapon in the Allies armoury. However, installing it into a tank was to prove to be an altogether different matter.

Tigers of the 501 were involved in the attack on the US 1st Armored Division between the Faid Pass and Djebel Lessouda on 14 February 1943. On St Valentine's Day the 1st Armored was deployed around the Djebel Lessouda while on top of these features an American observation post was keeping watch on the Faid Pass. Reports of firing on the road from Faid began to filter in to the commander of the 1st Battalion. The distant roar of artillery seemed to indicate some sort of firefight was going on in the direction of Lessouda.

The wind coming in over the mountains and the blinding sand masked the advance of two battlegroups from the 10th Panzer Division that numbered about sixty panzers. The Tigers spearheading the attack rumbled through the pass with impunity. 'The Tigers are coming!' went up the cry and the lightly-equipped Americans abandoned their positions in terror.

In response the 1st Armored sent forward fifteen Stuart light tanks to try and delay the attack. Armed with just a 37mm gun there was nothing they could do against the Tiger's 88mm gun and the 75mm gun of the Panzer IV. One after another they were destroyed, their puny rounds simply bouncing off the advancing German armour. The Shermans of the US division's inexperienced 1st Battalion were then committed to the battle, but they made little impression either and many of these tanks were soon blazing wrecks. The experiences of the US 1st Armored Division provided a stark lesson in just how foolhardy it was to pitch light tanks against German heavy and medium tanks. The net result was a major reduction in the number of light tanks deployed in American armoured divisions with them being replaced by mediums – namely the Sherman.

Deployment of the Tigers in Tunisia soon proved to be a cause of friction between Rommel and his subordinate General Hans-Jürgen von Arnim. Rommel was irritated that these new weapons had been assigned to von Arnim's Fifth Panzer Army and not placed directly under his Army Group Afrika. Even if it meant lying to Rommel, von Arnim had no intention of giving up his powerful new panzers.

For his Kasserine counter-attack on 19 February 1943 Rommel wanted the Tigers to support the 10th Panzer Division's push on Thala. He later recalled:

> Before the start of the operation, we had asked von Arnim to send us the 19 Tiger tanks which were with 5th Panzer Army. If we had these tanks at Thala, we might have been able to push on farther. But von Arnim had refused our request, saying that all the tanks were under repair, a statement which we later discovered to have been untrue. He had wanted to hold on to the detachment of Tigers for his own offensive.

In the event 10th Panzer were forced from Thala thanks to the arrival of the British 6th Armoured Division and other units. Rommel noted on 22 February, 'I drove up to Thala again, where I was forced to the conclusion that the enemy had grown too strong for our attack to be maintained'. Rommel clearly held von Arnim responsible adding, 'The stubborn American defence of the Kasserine Pass and the delayed arrival of the Fifth Army's forces prevented us from making a surprise break in to the enemy hinterland.'

The tired and weary Rommel argued that if von Arnim had sent him the Tigers and more infantry he may well have succeeded. 'That may be true,' responded Field Marshal Kesselring, 'but you had the authority to overrule von Arnim. Why didn't you?'

Four days later Fifth Panzer Army, employing the Tigers, opened its own attack at Medjez el Bab 40 miles west of Tunis. The initial breakthrough was soon met with heavy counter-attacks. Rommel was furious:

> It made me particularly angry to see how few Tigers we had in Africa, which had been denied us for our offensive in the south, were thrown in to attack through a marshy valley, where their principal advantage – the long range of their heavy guns – was completely ineffective. The heavy tanks either stuck fast in the mud, or were pounded into immobility by the enemy. Of the 19 Tigers which went into action, 15 were lost.

While the German High Command was filled with optimism following the mauling of the Americans at Kasserine, Rommel knew that the presence of a few Tigers was not ultimately going to affect the final outcome of the battle for North Africa. Commenting on the Americans' resources he observed, 'their armament in anti-tank weapons and armoured vehicles was so enormous that we could look forward with but small hope of success to the coming mobile battles'. Rommel was also dismayed at the weight of American airpower, which came into play once the bad weather that had masked his attack lifted.

By the end of February Heavy Panzer Battalion 501 could muster eighteen Tigers but on 1 March seven were destroyed by their crews, then on the 17 March the survivors were attached to Heavy Tank Battalion 504. This was the second Tiger unit to be despatched to North Africa. It was formed from two companies of men from Panzer Regiment 4 in mid-January 1943 at Fallingbostel. The battalion was issued with two command Tigers, eighteen Tiger Is and twenty-five Panzer IIIs.

They arrived in Italy in early March and the first three Tigers serving with the 1st Company reached Tunisia on 12 March. Shortly after eleven Tigers of Heavy Panzer Battalion 501 joined them. The 2nd Company remained on Sicily. During late March and early April Tigers continued to be delivered to Bizerta with the last one arriving on 16 April 1943. During a three-day period four Tigers were lost in action, including the one now preserved at Bovington Tank Museum.

Hitler soon lost interest in the fate of his Tiger tanks and indeed the rest of the Afrika Korps. By mid-April 1943 Guderian was reporting:

> The situation in Africa had become hapless, and I asked [General] Schmundt to help me arrange that the many superfluous tank crews – particularly the irreplaceable commanders and technicians with years of experience behind them – be now flown out. Either I failed to convince Schmundt or else he did not press my arguments with sufficient energy to Hitler, for when I next saw the Führer and personally mentioned the matter I met with no success. The question of prestige – as so often – proved more powerful than common sense.

The Americans found their treatment by the Tiger in Tunisia very sobering. One American colonel reporting on its qualities in 1943 noted:

> I have inspected the battlefield at Faid Pass in Tunisia, being with the force which retook it. Inspection of our tanks destroyed there indicated that the 88mm gun penetrated into the turret from the front and out again in the rear. Few gouges were found indicating that all strikes had made penetrations.

Yank, the US Army Weekly, could not help striking a triumphant note when it featured a knocked-out Tiger on its cover:

> This vicious-looking machine, photographed by *Yank's* Sgt. George Aarons during the Tunisian campaign, is a PzKW VI (*Panzer Kampfwagen*) which translates literally as armoured battlewagon. More often it was called the Tiger, but here with the sleeve knocked off its 88mm cannon and resting against the muzzle brake, it is definitely a tamed one.

Understandably both the British and US Armies were keen to evaluate the 'tamed' Tigers captured in Tunisia as quickly as possible. The US Army shipped a captured Tiger tank back to the Aberdeen Ordnance Research Center's proving grounds in America and *Yank* reported in late January 1944:

> Specially assigned recovery crews, ordnance men trained to know and work with enemy material, roam the battlefields of the world to collect the captured rolling stock, which is being accumulated here. It arrives with the dust of its respective theater still on it, plus the names and

addresses of GIs who scratch *Bizerte* or *Attu* or *Buna* Mission in big letters on the paint.

The famous Tiger, the largest and heaviest German tank. Weighing 61½ tons, it is propelled at a speed of from 15 to 18 miles an hour by a 600-to-650 horsepower Maybach V-12 cylinder engine. Maybach engines are used in many of the Nazi *panzer wagonen* and in submarines. The PzKW VI has an armor thickness which ranges from 3¼ to 4 inches. An additional slab of steel mounted in conjunction with its 88-mm forms frontal armor for the turret. Besides the long-barreled 88, it carries two MG34 (Model 1934) machine guns. Largest tank used in combat by any nation today, the Tiger is more than 20 feet long, about 11¾ feet wide and 9¾ feet high. It has a crew of five.

The engineers, who judge by the mass of detail employed in all German-built machines, are convinced that the Nazi idea has been to sacrifice speed for over-all performance and manoeuvrability. The German equipment, from the sleek motorcycle to the massive PzKW VI, is rugged.

Along with the rest of the German and Italian armies, both Tiger units surrendered in Tunisia on 12 May 1943. Afterwards Guderian argued there was no point in leaving the survivors in Sicily in the face of an impending Allied invasion. Recalling how the Tigers had been needlessly wasted in North Africa he recorded with some bitterness that:

> the same thing was to happen in the defence of Sicily. On this occasion, when I urged that the Tigers be withdrawn to the main land, Göring [commander of the Luftwaffe] joined in the argument with the remark: 'But Tigers can't pole-vault across the Straits of Messina. You must realize that, Colonel-General Guderian!' I replied: 'If you have really won air supremacy over the Straits of Messina the Tigers can come back from Sicily the same way they went out'. The air expert fell silent; the Tigers remained in Sicily.

Predictably the remaining seventeen Tigers serving with the 2nd Company, Heavy Panzer Battalion 504 were lost on Sicily following the American and British landings on the island. The survivors then regrouped in Italy and continued to fight there until the end of the war equipped with Tiger Is.

Probably the most famous Tiger I in the world came from Tunisia. It belongs to the British Tank Museum and is the only example restored to full working order. Tiger 131, selected to be sent back to Britain, immediately acquired celebrity status in light of the VIPs that came to see it. The tank had been knocked out during an engagement at Medjez-el-Bab on 21 April 1943 with British Churchill tanks of No.4 Troop, A Squadron, 48th Royal Tank Regiment.

Royal Electrical & Mechanical Engineers recovered the Tiger using a bulldozer and it arrived in Tunis on 24 May 1943. The following month it was examined by no less than King George VI, Winston Churchill and Anthony Eden. Afterwards it was moved to La Goulette and from there to Bizerte by landing craft. It was subsequently shipped to Glasgow where it arrived on 8 October 1943 and sent to the Department of Tank Design in Surrey. Displayed as a war trophy on Horse Guards Parade in London, Londoners were able to gawp at Hitler's latest panzer. It was dismantled at the end of the year for technical assessment. Tiger 131 was given to the Tank Museum at Bovington in 1951 where it has been ever since.

In the meantime, thanks to Hitler's haste, not only had the Russians got hold of the Tiger, so had the Americans and British before it had even been deployed in any significant numbers. This was to have serious ramifications for its subsequent performance in Russia and Normandy.

Chapter 10

Panzers on the Steppe

The short-barrel Panzer IVs lost during the invasion of the Soviet Union in the summer of 1941 were replaced by the spring of 1942, but crucially there was no increase in overall numbers. However, the Red Army's T-34 tank with a maximum of 70mm frontal armour was now vulnerable to the recently introduced Panzer IV Ausf F2 and the subsequent Panzer IV Ausf G and H which were both armed with the more powerful Kwk40 L/48.

They finally gave the Panzerwaffe parity. However, in terms of tank production the Germans could not compete; in November 1942 they managed just 100 Panzer IVs compared to 1,000 Soviet T-34s. The following month, rather than retool for the Panzer IV, the Panzer III assembly lines were turned over to StuG III assault gun production.

The Tigers' crews must have been impressed. This new heavy tank was clearly very different to its predecessors. The Panzer I through to the Panzer IV had a clear lineage and shared very common design features. The Tiger was something else. The first thing that must have struck the panzertruppen was the size of the gun, followed by the horseshoe shape of the turret.

While the Tiger crews would have heard the tales from the instructors of how Hitler's Blitzkrieg the previous summer had smashed Stalin's tank fleet, there was no escaping a sense the war was bogging down especially in the face of the bitter Russian winter. The men must have wondered if the Tiger was the weapon with which Hitler hoped to break the deadlock. Army Group Centre could have done with it on the road to Moscow.

Guderian recalled the fateful decision:

> It was, therefore decided that the following solution be adopted: the construction of the Tiger tank, a panzer of some 60 tons, which had recently been started would continue: meanwhile, a light tank, called the Panther, weighing 35 and 45 tons, was to be designed.

However, Hitler had seriously miscalculated the importance of his panzers. At the start of the war in May 1940 German industry was only producing 125 panzers a month, and it was another two years before Hitler ordered production to increase to 600 a month. To make matters worse the Tiger took twice as long to build as previous panzers. Any dreams that Hitler and his generals may have had about deploying large numbers of Tigers on the Eastern Front to deliver a bloody nose to the Red Army were soon dashed.

Guderian recorded:

> On 19 March 1942 [Albert] Speer [Minister for Armaments and War Production] informed the Führer that by October, 1942, there would be 60 Porsche Tigers and 25 Henschel Tigers available, and that by March, 1943, a further 135 would be produced, bringing the total by that time to 220 – assuming that they were all employable.

On the basis of these figures it is hard to credit that a major war in Europe was even underway. Also of course the Porsche design was found wanting and would end up being converted into the Ferdinand tank destroyer.

With the Tiger I rolling off the production line Hitler was desperate to get his new heavy tank into action as quickly as possible. Logically the crews should have been given plenty of time to practise their gunnery and offensive and defensive tactics, while the mechanics and technicians ironed out the inevitable design problems on the proving ground – but there was a war on. In this respect Hitler was just like the British Prime Minister Winston Churchill: he was impatient to see results. Churchill had insisted that when the Crusader, Grant and Sherman tanks arrived in North Africa they be rushed to the front as quickly as possible. This had dire consequences for the ill-prepared Operation Crusader.

Hitler chose to ignore the warnings from his staff that his Tigers and their crews were not yet ready. Guderian lamented that the Führer would not see sense:

> A lesson learned from the First World War had taught us that it is necessary to be patient about committing new weapons and that they must be held back until they are being produced in such quantities as to allow their employment in mass. In the First World War the French and British used their tanks prematurely, in small numbers, and thereby failed to win the great victory which they were entitled to expect. . . . Hitler was well aware of the facts. But he was consumed by his desire to try his new weapon.

To make matters worse, Hitler chose to despatch the Tigers to a part of the Eastern Front that was simply not suited to their capabilities. Army Group Centre might have appreciated them on the vast open Russian Steppe where their range would have given them a decided edge; instead Hitler decided that the troublesome city of Leningrad was a greater priority. This area was covered in heavy forests, lakes and swamps, none of which were ideal for armoured warfare. The Tiger would not be at its best in the close confines of such a landscape. Also this geography favoured the defenders, which was partly why the Red Army had been able to cling on to Leningrad in the face of determined German attacks.

The German High Command should have known better. The ease with which German artillery destroyed Soviet tanks near the front lines at Leningrad once the surrounding forests had been flattened should have served as a warning. Once caught on narrow tracks and in the open the outcome was always the same and the crews were lucky if they managed to escape. The terrain around Leningrad was simply not suited for armoured operations.

Very briefly it seemed as if Hitler had seen sense and he changed his mind. His dithering over where to commit the Tigers perplexed senior German commanders including Guderian who grumbled:

> On 8 July 1942, he [Hitler] ordered the first Tiger Companies were to be made ready with all speed for operations against Leningrad. By 23 July, that is to say fifteen days later, Hitler had changed his mind; he now demanded that the Tigers be ready for operations in France by September at the latest. It would thus appear that he was already expecting a large scale Allied landing.

At the same time Hitler was pressing to get any technical problems resolved as quickly as possible. 'In August 1942 Hitler ordered an inquiry to be made as to how quickly the 88mm cannon could be installed in the Tiger Tank,' noted Guderian, 'This gun was to be capable of firing a shell that could penetrate 200mm of armour'. He went on to add:

> Hitler insisted quite correctly that the Tiger be armed with the long 88mm flat trajectory gun, preferring this weapon to one of the heavier calibre but lesser muzzle velocity. The primary purpose of the tank gun must be to fight enemy tanks, and to this all other considerations must be made subordinate.

Hitler was to change his mind again and insisted on sending a few Tigers to the Leningrad Front with predictable results. The 1st Company of the Heavy Panzer Battalion 502 was the first unit to receive the band new Henschel Tigers. The first four were delivered on 19 and 20 August 1942. The crews were very impressed; this was a tank that you could go to war in with confidence. They marvelled at the armour and the gun.

In preparation for an anticipated Soviet attack, General Georg von Kuechler, commander of Army Group North, was ordered by the German High Command to move the 170th Infantry Division northwards from Mga, which lay south-east of Leningrad. It also sent him several Tigers that were en route from Pskov by train. Suspecting that the Soviets were driving on the Neva River via Siniavino, Kuechler ordered his 5th Mountain and 28th Jäger Divisions earmarked for Operation Northern Light to move from their staging areas to Maga. He also moved the 12th Panzer Division to protect the Neva and hastened the 170th Infantry's move on Siniavino.

Supported by four Panzer IIIs, the Tigers were shipped to the Leningrad front and arrived at Mga on 29 August. Kuechler committed his four Tigers to combat south of Siniavino Heights. The crews, while confident in their new tanks' capabilities, were uncomfortable trundling round the Russian forests. The rudimentary roads and tracks were not intended to take the weight of a Tiger and when the drivers tried to go cross country they found the going even more unforgiving. Getting to the jump-off point for the attack was a struggle. The transmissions quickly packed up on three of the Tigers and two of them broke down almost immediately. By the end of the day only half were still operational and the other two had to be recovered. While the Soviet penetration was contained, the Tigers played no part in it.

Three more Tigers arrived during 16–18 September. The unit was sent back into action on 21 September, this time one Tiger and three Panzer IIIs were lost. The Tiger became stuck after it bogged down, the net result was that one of Hitler's brand-new tanks had to be destroyed. The Soviets immediately went to work trying to find ways to overcome this new Nazi war machine.

Guderian held Hitler personally responsible for the Tigers failure saying:

> He therefore ordered the Tigers be committed in a quite secondary operation, in a limited attack carried out in terrain that was utterly unsuitable; for in the swampy forests near Leningrad heavy tanks could only move in single file along the forest tracks, which of course, was exactly where the enemy anti-tank guns were posted, waiting for them. The results were not only heavy, unnecessary, casualties, but also the loss of secrecy and of the element of surprise for future operations. Disappointment was all the greater since the attack bogged down in the unsuitable terrain.

In the meantime, the rest of 1st Company, Heavy Panzer Battalion 502, did not arrive at the front until 25 November 1942, equipped with five Tigers and fourteen Panzer IIIs. Battlefield loss replacements in the shape an additional seven Tigers were delivered in February 1943. By mid-year the company had fourteen Tigers on its strength. The battalion did not get its 2nd Company as this was reassigned to Heavy Panzer Battalion 503. Reinforcements in the shape of a new 2nd and 3rd Company did not reach the 502 until the summer of 1943, by which time the Tiger's element of surprise had been completely lost.

The Tiger I came with two types of track, a wide one measuring 28½in for combat and a narrower one of 20½in for travel and transportation. In order to fit the narrow tracks the outer wheels were removed from each suspension unit. While the triple-wheel suspension gave a smoother ride, it also meant the interleaved wheels were susceptible to becoming fouled with mud and snow. On the Eastern Front, if this clogging was allowed to freeze it could set like concrete and jammed up the wheels, leaving the Tiger completely immobile. The Soviets soon discovered that the Tiger was vulnerable to the Russian winter and timed their attacks for the early hours when they knew that enemy vehicles had been frozen solid during the night.

Evgeni Bessonov, who served as a lieutenant in the Red Army, later observed first hand that mud could be a significant problem for the Tiger when his unit was attacked by eight of them. 'The tanks were some 50 metres from us, when all of a sudden a miracle happened,' recalled Bessonov 'the Tigers skidded on the wet soil and stopped. The tanks were stuck on one spot, their tracks spinning, but the tanks could not move. We were lucky that because of the Tiger's weight it tracks did not have good cohesion in the mud.' Luckily for him and his men the Tigers, lacking infantry support, withdrew.

After this very inauspicious debut the Tigers found themselves resisting Soviet attempts to lift the siege of Leningrad when the Second Shock Army tried to cut its way to Schlüsselburg on the south side of Lake Ladoga. Operation Iskra or 'Spark' was a Soviet offensive launched on 11 January 1943 to reopen a land corridor to the besieged city which had been cut off since 15 September 1941 with the arrival of the German Eighteenth Army at Schlüsselburg. After the failure of the similar offensive at the end of September 1942 the Red Army had massed much larger forces on a smaller front to ensure they overwhelmed all before them. Overall the Tigers were unable to make much difference to the fighting. On 12 January 1943 they knocked out twelve T-34/76 tanks. The Red Army got its hands on a Tiger on 14 January 1943 after they managed to disable one. A second vehicle was taken a few days later.

The post-mortem of what went wrong at Leningrad did not seem to dissuade Hitler from wasting his Tigers by deploying them the minute they came off the factory floor. The Tiger had good armour and standoff capabilities that could outshoot any tank in a face-to-face battle, so it needed to fight in open tank country where the enemy could be picked off. Deployed in sufficient numbers it would simply overwhelm all before it. Instead thinking of ways of helping Generals Rommel and von Arnim fighting in North Africa, Hitler now began to look at the hills and mountains of Tunisia.

To compound his dismay at the Tigers' lost opportunities Guderian recalled:

> At the beginning of December there were renewed discussions concerning the correct employment of tanks. It was then pointed out to Hitler that

the commitment of the Tigers piecemeal was highly disadvantageous. He now expressed the opinion that commitment in detail was suitable for the requirements of the Eastern theatre, but that in Africa employment in mass would be more rewarding. Unfortunately I do not know on what grounds this incomprehensible statement was based.

For better or worse Hitler was set on sending the Tiger to face the British and Americans in North Africa.

Following Hitler's major summer offensive in 1942 by early 1943 the eighteen panzer divisions on the Eastern Front had less than 600 tanks. This did not bode well for his Kursk offensive. However, Hitler managed to gather 1,850 panzers supported by 200 obsolete tanks and over 530 assault guns. Along with the Panzer IV, the Panzer III provided the bulk of Hitler's armour employed during Operation Citadel. The Panther, making its debut, was in short supply, as was the Tiger.

Also making their debut at Kursk in July 1943 were the Panzer IV-based Hummel self-propelled gun and the Hornisse tank destroyer. While the latter had a very effective anti-tank gun it was really a defensive rather than offensive armoured fighting vehicle. The numbers available though were once again a problem. Both had only gone into production in early 1943, with about 100 of each type ready for the summer. The Hummel units were supported by obsolete Panzer IIs equipped with radios to act as command and observation tanks. Also to help smash Soviet fortifications were sixty-six newly-built Brummbär comprising a short 150mm howitzer mounted on a Panzer IV chassis.

Despite their best efforts the Panzer IVs, and the newly-introduced Panthers and Tigers, were simply swamped at Kursk by a well-prepared and superior enemy. Hitler had been warned he was outnumbered but refused to give ground or let the initiative pass to the Red Army so had chosen to attack first with dire results. The panzers were crushed in a massive tank battle at Prokhorovka. Hitler lost many panzers of which 300 were irreparable losses.

Although the Panzer IV remained the German workhorse on the Eastern Front, the earlier Ausf D, E and F armed with the short 75mm gun were completely phased out through attrition in early 1944. The panzer divisions were equipped with the newer F2, G and H variants although they were in danger of being outclassed by some of the newer heavily-armed Soviet armour.

In the summer of 1944 Hitler had too few Panzer IVs supporting Army Group Centre that was holding the exposed front line in Byelorussia. The army group under Field Marshal Ernst Busch was predominantly equipped with assault guns. Busch's only unit with Panzer IVs, that constituted his solitary reserve, was the 20th Panzer Division. Army Group North was little better off with just the 12th Panzer Division equipped with Panzer IVs. The two Army Groups in Ukraine were much stronger, with fourteen panzer divisions, but this was where Hitler was anticipating Stalin would strike.

Stalin conducted a major offensive to liberate Minsk and Byelorussia in late June 1944. General Jordan, commanding the German Ninth Army, sought and received Busch's permission to commit the 20th Panzer Division to try and stem the Soviet tide. The division could muster seventy-one Panzer IVs, its other panzer regiment being busy re-equipping with Panthers. At that very moment General Batov's Sixty-Fifth Army broke through on the southern approaches to Bobruisk and General Rokossovsky committed the I Guards Tank Corps to exploit the breach. A dithering Jordan ordered 20th Panzer to retrace its tracks and head south, bumping into the Soviets near Slobodka south of Bobruisk.

It rapidly became apparent that not only was German-held Bobruisk under threat but also those German divisions still east of the Berezina River. By 26 June the battered 20th Panzer had been driven back to the city with the Soviet IX Tank Corps bearing down on it from the east and the Soviet I Guards Tank Corps from the south. The I Guards Tank Corps cut the roads from Bobruisk to the north and north-west on the night of 26/27 June, closing the trap.

The 5th Panzer Division was moved up from Kovel to defensive positions east of Borisov with a view to covering those troops withdrawing from Mogilev, which had been overrun late on the 27th. Under General Karl Decker, 5th Panzer began to arrive in Minsk on 26 June with the all but impossible task of holding the Moscow-Minsk Highway. The division was equipped with just fifty-five Panzer IVs and seventy Panthers, supported by Captain von Beschwitz's twenty-nine Tiger Is of Heavy Panzer Battalion 505. Their first mission was to put a stop line in place north-east of Borisov but like 20th Panzer they failed to stem the Red Army's tidal wave.

The year was a complete disaster for Hitler and those regiments equipped with the Panzer IV. Throughout 1944 Hitler lost several thousand Panzer IVs on the Eastern Front. This was more than could be replaced. The previous year he had suffered similar losses with some divisions down to as few as twelve tanks; such destruction was increasingly difficult to replace. The no-frills Panzer IV Ausf J which appeared in mid-1944 was the final production model and was greatly simplified to speed construction. However, the manual turret traverse was not greatly liked by the crews. Production ran until March 1945 by which time less than 2,000 had been produced. It was not enough.

Chapter 11 .

Failure at Kursk

In the months preceding the summer of 1943 General Kurt Zeitzler, German Army Chief of Staff, was preoccupied with preparations for Operation Citadel. This was a massive and desperate effort to wrest back the strategic initiative on the Eastern Front following the catastrophic defeat at Stalingrad during the winter of 1942–3. Red Army operations had left them in possession of a vast salient around Kursk, flanked by German re-entrants centred in the south on Kharkov and in the north on Orel. Hitler's intention was to snip off the Soviet salient, trapping the Red Army using all available means. This meant deploying the brand-new Panther.

After his appointment as Inspector General, Guderian visited the Henschel tank works at Kassel, which was producing Tigers and Panthers. He also inspected the Nibelungen works at Linz that were likewise producing Panthers. Whilst impressed by these new panzers he was clearly not impressed by the rate of production, noting 'we can reckon to equipping a limited number of battalions with Panthers and Tigers during 1943, but the Panther battalions at any rate will not be ready for action before July or August'. Such a view was at odds with Hitler's scheduling for Citadel.

At the beginning of the year the very first Panther battalions were established at Grafenwöhr consisting of the 51st Panzer Battalion, based on the 2nd Company, 33rd Panzer Regiment from the 9th Panzer Division and the 52nd Battalion based on the 1st Panzer Company, 15th Panzer Regiment, 11th Panzer Division. Panther training was undertaken at Erlangen near Grafenwöhr and this was up and running by May 1943. The intention was that it would turn out one trained Panther battalion every month.

The initial training did not go at all well and set the tone for the Panther's future shambolic performance. Whilst some of the tank gunners were sent to the Putlos gunnery school, training at Erlangen never got above platoon level. This was to have very serious consequences when the Panthers were shipped east to Kursk. The battalions' mechanics spent much of their time liaising with MAN engineers trying to iron out the 'problem child's' persistent 'teething troubles'. By April everyone admitted defeat and the Ausf Ds were unceremoniously returned to the manufacturers for modification.

The Panther crews now found themselves without tanks, so for some reason it was decided to despatch them to the panzer base at Mailly le Camp in France.

They suffered yet more misfortune when the RAF caught them en route at Mannheim, killing four panzertruppen. They did not return to Grafenwöhr until June to be reissued with their Panthers. Nevertheless, problems remained with the steering and transmission (both originally intended for a much lighter tank). The engine remained overloaded, which once overheated could and did catch fire. This problem was aggravated by the waterproof rubber engine compartment lining, which while intended to keep water out also kept in a great degree of heat.

On his way to see Hitler, Guderian flew to Grafenwöhr on 18 June 1943 to assess the problems being experienced by the 51st and 52nd Panzer Battalions. He found not only were the Panthers still suffering from technical problems, but also the crews had not really got to grips with handling their new panzers. The weight and size of the Panther made it a challenge to manoeuvre even for former Panzer IV crews. To make matters worse half of the panzertruppen lacked combat experience, which in light of them transitioning to a brand-new tank type seemed a recipe for disaster. Guderian wrote:

> New equipment must be held back (that is to say, for the time being, Tigers, Panthers and heavy assault guns [Elefant]), until the new weapon is available in sufficient quantity to ensure a decisive surprise success.
>
> Premature commitment of new equipment simply invites the enemy to produce an effective defence against it by next year, which we shall not be able to cope with in the short time available.

To his dismay the new Panther units were under orders to load their tanks onto railcars ready for deployment to the Eastern Front. It would take almost a week for them to reach their disembarkation point at Borisovka. In Guderian's eyes Kursk was a premature debut for the unreliable Panther.

By this stage the German Army was hoping optimistically to equip all the panzer divisions on the Eastern Front with a Panther battalion in the next six months. However, it was decided to keep the 51st and 52nd Panzer Battalions together to create the 39th Panzer Regiment under Colonel Meinrad von Lauchert. Fittingly he had been with the 4th Panzer Division when it had come up against the T-34 at Mzensk in October 1941.

After its disappointing showing in Tunisia and at Leningrad, Guderian remained determined to get the most out of the Tiger. In late March 1943 he visited General von Mellenthin's XLVIII Panzer Corps. Von Mellenthin later recalled that:

> Guderian particularly wanted to discuss the experiences of the Tiger battalion of the 'Gross Deutschland' Division in the recent offensive, and Count Strachwitz, the very dashing commander of their panzer regiment, was able to give him many interesting details regarding the performance

and limitations of the new tank. As a result of his visit Guderian ordered a speed-up in the production of Tigers and Panthers.

Grossdeutschland received the Tiger before many other units, forming a heavy panzer battalion from the summer of 1943. As early as January 1943 the Grossdeutschland Panzer Regiment had formed a heavy tank company that consisted of nine Tiger Is and ten Panzer IIIs. These were shipped to the Eastern Front the following month, arriving at Poltava for the offensive to retake Kharkov. By the time of the Kursk offensive the unit had been officially dubbed the 9th Company and was equipped with about a dozen Tigers.

In addition, the 505th Heavy Panzer Battalion was created in early 1943 and by May had twenty Tigers and twenty-five Panzer IIIs. At the end of April it was assigned to Army Group Centre and shipped to the Eastern Front. During 8 to 10 June it received eleven more Tigers. Therefore, at the start of Operation Citadel the battalion had thirty-one Tigers, plus supporting Panzer IIIs, and four days into the fighting on 9 July was joined by the 3rd Company.

At the time of Kursk Army Group South had a total of 102 Tigers deployed with the II, III and XLVIII Panzer Corps. The 503rd Heavy Panzer Battalion had been earmarked to join Rommel in North Africa but instead found itself in southern Russia during the Don campaign and the retreat from Stalingrad. It had anticipated receiving the Porsche-designed Tiger, but with the cancellation of this programme the unit was equipped with twenty Henschel Tigers and twenty-five Panzer IIIs in late 1942. By April of the following year it had forty-five Tigers on its strength. The battalion was able to muster forty-two operational Tigers in time for the Kursk offensive, but these were divided up between three panzer divisions.

Other panzer units serving with Army Group South were also equipped with Tigers these included the 9th Company Panzer Regiment Grossdeutschland, part of Grossdeutschland Panzergrenadier Division which had twelve operational Tigers at the start of Kursk; 13th Company 1st SS Panzer Regiment, 8th Company 2nd SS Panzer Regiment and 9th Company 3rd SS Panzer Regiment which also had twelve each, that were serving with the 1st, 2nd and 3rd SS Panzer Divisions respectively.

By 1943 the German High Command knew that despite whatever was said publicly it was simply not in a position to win on the Eastern Front. At best it could bleed the Red Army to such an extent that Stalin would be forced to the negotiating table. Hitler's generals though were hoping newly-deployed quality would help them counter the Red Army's superior numbers. Indeed, for the first time since Barbarossa the German Army was fielding tanks and self-propelled guns that had a distinctive qualitative edge. Guderian recalled that the Army was pinning great hopes on Hitler's new panzers, 'the Chief of the General Staff [General Zeitzler] believed that by employing the new Tigers and Panthers, from which he expected decisive successes, he could regain the initiative'.

For his summer Kursk offensive, dubbed Operation Citadel, Hitler was placing great faith in his 'zoo' of tanks and armoured fighting vehicles names after wild animals, notably the Tiger, Panther, Elefant, Rhinoceros, Bison and Grizzly Bear. It was hoped that these would tear great holes in the ranks of the Soviet tank corps. The intention was that the Tiger, Panther and Ferdinand would be able to stand off and destroy Soviet armour at great ranges. If there was a chance to keep the Soviet tank numbers at arm's length and stop them closing, this would prevent the panzers from being overwhelmed.

Most, if not all, the Tiger's teething problems had been ironed out following its performance at Leningrad the previous summer. By contrast the new Panther was undeniably a rushed job, and sorting out ongoing technical problems in the heat of the battle was not a recipe for success. Nonetheless, its 75mm KwK42 L/70 anti-tank gun was a great weapon. Well-trained and experienced crews were capable of knocking out tanks at ranges in excess of 1,000m. This stand-off capability meant it was fatal for Soviet tanks to engage the Tiger and the Panther in the open. The T-34's 76.2mm gun could penetrate the Panther's side armour out to 1,000m, but could only penetrate the glacis armour at 300m and could not overcome the turret frontal armour. An improved armour-piercing round was not introduced until October 1943. Although the Panther's frontal armour was on par with the Tiger's, its side armour was little better that the Panzer IV.

The cumbersome Ferdinand self-propelled anti-tank gun constructed on the chassis of the failed Porsche design for the Tiger I, armed with an 88mm PaK 43(L/71), was able to penetrate Soviet tanks at extreme range. Unfortunately, in the haste to build the Ferdinand the designers saw fit not include any machine guns, which had inevitable consequences in the heat of battle. While the Ferdinand's 200mm of armour meant it was impervious to most Soviet guns, its 65 tonnes of weight meant it could only manage a grindingly slow 10km/hr off road. The thought of being under intense enemy fire while travelling at such speed cannot have been very encouraging for the crew. While the Tiger had an undeniable air of menace and the Panther a certain deadly grace thanks to its sloping armour, the crews must have looked at the Ferdinand with a sense of despair. It was little more than a lumbering mobile pillbox, which while packing a powerful anti-tank gun had very limited traverse. Anyone could see that it was an ill-conceived venture, like the newly commissioned Nashorn it was essentially a defensive weapon that was not suited to offensive warfare. Crucially none of these new armoured vehicles were available in decisive numbers. Notably there were just 100 Tigers, about 200 Panthers and 90 Ferdinands; over 1,000 older Panzer IIIs and IVs formed the backbone of the panzer forces. The Tiger and all the other panzers had their work cut out for them.

During a conference in May 1943 Guderian had noted that General Model had good intelligence,

> which showed that the Russians were preparing deep and very strong defensive positions in exactly those areas where the attack by the two army groups was to go in. The Russians had already withdrawn the mass of their mobile formations from the forward area of their salient; in anticipation of a pincer attack, as proposed in this plan of ours, they had strengthened the localities of our possible break-throughs with unusually strong artillery and anti-tank forces.

General von Mellenthin, with XLVIII Panzer Corps, which included the Grossdeutschland Tigers, recalled:

> The ground rose slightly to the north, thus favouring the defender. Roads consisted of tracks through the sand and became impassable for all motor transport during rain. Large cornfields covered the landscape and made visibility difficult. All in all, it was not 'good tank country', but it was by no means 'tank proof'.

Soviet defences in the Kursk salient were formidable. By June 1943 300,000 civilians had been marshalled to dig a series of in-depth defensive lines stretching back almost 110 miles. Using brute strength, picks and shovels they had carved almost 3,100 miles of trenches across the landscape. Minefields sealed off the trenches and fire support positions.

The fields of wheat and corn ripening in the summer sun concealed a deadly threat. In the killing grounds between the strongpoints the sappers meticulously concealed about 2,400 anti-tank mines and a further 2,700 anti-personnel mines per mile. Initially as the panzers and supporting infantry struggled through the minefields they would be deluged by artillery and mortar fire.

Once through this the Tigers would encounter Soviet anti-tank defences or 'pakfronts' consisting of emplaced 76.2mm anti-tank guns supported by anti-tank rifles, machine guns and mortars. The plan was that along expected axis of attack the German armour would meet clusters of anti-tank guns whose job it was to funnel the panzers into yet more minefields.

Citadel was doomed from the start. It got underway on 4 July 1943, making little headway before being checked by the Soviet defences. The Tigers charged forward. Many troop commanders must have been torn between standing off and destroying as many Soviets as possible and closing to escape the anti-tank mines, anti-tanks guns and heavy artillery (especially the heavy howitzers) that were quickly turning the Kursk steppe into a panzer graveyard.

The need to clear the Soviet minefields and the front-echelon weapons positions meant that only the 20th Panzer Division was involved in the initial assault. They scored some success pushing through the Soviet 15th Rifle Division's front-line trenches at 09.00 and fighting their way between Bobrik and Gnilets. The Soviet 321st Rifle Regiment was barged out of the way and Bobrik secured three miles behind Soviet lines.

On 20th Panzer's left the 6th Infantry Division thrust down the Oka Valley supported by Tigers of 505th Heavy Panzer Battalion. The Soviet T-34s and anti-tank guns were unable to stop them taking the village of Butyrki. This exposed the Soviet 81st Rifle Division, which was busy trying to fend off the 292nd Infantry Division. The heavy Ferdinands initially ploughed through the Soviet lines with impunity, reaching Alexsandrovka, but they soon found they could not deal with the swarms of Soviet infantry. The German 86th Infantry Division reached Ponyri late that afternoon, while the 78th and 216th Infantry Divisions fought their way through the Soviet defences toward the road junction at Malaorkhangelsk with the support of Ferdinands.

Individually the Tigers worked wonders. On 6th July the Tigers led the charge of the 1st and 2nd SS Panzer Divisions up the Belgorod-Oboyan road. The Soviet 51st Rifle Division was barged out of the way as the Tigers came face to face with the T-34 tanks of the V Guards Tank Corps south of Iakovlevo. A German witness recalled:

> On separate slopes, some 1,000m (1,094 yards) apart the forces face one another like figures in a chessboard, trying to influence fate, move by move, in their own favour. All the Tigers fired. The combat escalated into an ecstasy of roaring engines. The humans who directed and serviced them had to be calm; very calm, they aimed rapidly, they loaded rapidly, they gave orders quickly. They rolled ahead a few metres, pulled right, manoeuvred to escape the enemy crosshairs and bring the enemy into their own fire. We counted the torches of the enemy dead which would never again fire on German soldiers. After one hour 12 T-34s were in flames. The other 30 curved wildly back and forth, firing as rapidly as their barrels would deliver. They aimed well but our armour was very strong.

One of the most fiercely contested points in the Kursk salient was the village of Ponyri. Trying to ease the pressure, the Germans launched the Tigers of the 505th Heavy Panzer Battalion and the 2nd and 20th Panzer Divisions between Samodurovka and Ollkhovatka. However, those forces that broke through were surrounded by a Soviet counter-attack. After an attack at Ponyri and at the 1st May State Farm by a Soviet rifle division on 8 July the Soviets claimed to have knocked out sixteen Tigers and twenty-four medium tanks.

Several German tanks aces stood out during the Kursk offensive. Notably Sergeant Franz Staudegger on 8 July was getting his Tiger repaired at Teterevino when a report came in that up to sixty Soviet tanks were heading his way. Hurriedly fixing their tank, he and his crew spent two hours knocking out seventeen enemy tanks. When the Soviets finally withdrew he gave chase and caught them hiding in a gully and knocked out another five T-34s. Two days later he became the first Waffen-SS Tiger commander to be awarded the Knight's Cross.

Similarly, Second Lieutenant Michael Wittmann who was commanding a troop of Tigers with the 1st SS Panzer Division achieved great success. On the first day of Operation Citadel he claimed eight enemy tanks. It was his troop who broke the attack of the Soviet 181st Tank Brigade at Prokhorovka on 12 July. During Kursk he and his crew claimed thirty enemy tanks and twenty-eight anti-tank guns.

The 505th Heavy Panzer Battalion lost three Tigers on 7 July and three days later still had twenty-six Tigers and five Panzer IIIs operational. On the 17th another two Tigers were lost in action with a third lost three days later. In total it lost four Tigers during Kursk itself and another six by the end of July. During August twelve Tigers were lost. Afterwards the unit moved to the Smolensk area and was subsequently issued with new-production Tigers that featured steel-rimmed wheels, cast cupolas and Zimmerit anti-magnetic mine coating. It later fought with the 24th and 25th Panzer Divisions in East Prussia. The 503rd Heavy Panzer Battalion lost four Tigers during the Kursk offensive and another four during its withdrawal. It received twelve replacements during August 1943.

While the Tigers proved a great success at Kursk, inflicting staggering losses on the Soviet tanks, there were simply too few of them. The 1st SS Panzer Regiment destroyed ninety tanks in the space of three hours on one day alone but still the enemy kept coming. While the crews now knew how to get the most out of the Tiger, this did not make up for their limited numbers. Once the Soviet tankers had closed in on them the Tigers advantage of long range and thick armour was lost.

By late June 1943 around 200 rebuilt Panthers had been issued to Panther Regiment von Lauchert and the 1st Panzer Battalion of Grossdeutschland to create the 10th Panzer Brigade. This was assigned to Fourth Panzer Army's XLVIII Panzer Corps. On paper the Panthers of this brigade formed the single most powerful armoured unit of all the panzer forces committed at Kursk. On unloading from the trains at Borisovka two Panthers immediately suffered engine fires and were write-offs. This was a warning of things to come. By 5 July, when Operation Citadel commenced, there were 184 operational Panthers but within two days this had fallen to just 40.

Major General von Mellenthin, Chief of Staff of XLVIII Panzer Corps, which had over 300 panzers and 60 assault guns, noted:

'Grossdeutschland' was a very strong [panzergrenadier] division with a special organization. It mustered about 180 tanks, of which 80 were part of a 'Panther Detachment' commanded by Lieutenant Colonel von Lauchert, and the remainder were in the panzer regiment.

Panzer Regiment 39 only reached Grossdeutschland's assembly area north of Moshchenoye late on 4 July. This meant that it missed the division's opening attack at 04.00 the following day. Frustratingly, at 08.15 von Lauchert's Panthers lurched forward only to lose at least four tanks to fuel leak fires. By this stage there must have been much swearing and cursing from the crews. Nonetheless when 51st Battalion, under Captain Heinrich Meyer and 52nd, under Major Gerhard Tebe, finally deployed they covered an area some 500m wide and around 3km long.

Thanks to Soviet artillery, which had set fire to the rolling cornfields, Grossdeutschland's engineers were slow in breaching the Red Army's extensive and clearly deadly defences. As a result, when the Panthers reached the 80m-wide Berezovyi Ravine they were immediately held up. A number rumbled down to follow a cleared path only to have their drives fail trying to get out the other side. Once again reliability was causing operational problems.

In total about twenty-five Panthers found themselves immobilized in the ravine due to breakdowns, mines and the mud. As the tension rose so did the stress levels of the beleaguered crews whose sense of annoyance was escalating. Desperately the drivers tried to back up but the Panthers did not want to reverse up the muddy banks. Engines began to overhead and drive sprocket teeth were damaged. When some of the Panthers attempted to shift westward they promptly ran into a Soviet minefield causing yet more delay.

It was not until early afternoon that a better crossing had been established 1.5km to the west and thirty Panthers, fifteen Panzer IVs and four battalions of infantry traversed Berezovyi Ravine. At Cherkasskoye the Panthers helped mop up Soviet resistance and thwarted a counter-attack. The Ausf D, lacking a ball-mounted hull machine gun (though a crude weapon port was provided), in the heat of battle had to rely on the coaxial machine gun mounted in the turret next to the main 75mm armament for defence against infantry attack. The Panther's performance on that opening day of the Battle of Kursk had been extremely disappointing. It showed up the lack of battalion level training and highlighted poor communication with the chain of command. On 6 July, performance was little better, with the regiment getting lost.

Near Alekseyevka Grossdeutschland ran into a T-34 tank regiment that was well dug in thereby presenting a very low profile. Some 2km east of Cherkasskoye the Panthers blundered into Soviet mines and T-34s of the 14th Tank Regiment opened up on the Panthers' flanks at ranges of 1,000–1,200m. A platoon leader in 5th Company, 52nd Panzer Battalion by the name of Sergeant Gerhard Brehme had the dubious honour of commanding one of the very first Panthers to be knocked out by a T-34. Eventually the Panther's superior firepower and gunnery enabled von Lauchert to extract his forces from the ambush. Once more though this episode highlighted a complete lack of experience.

By the end of 6 July Panzer Regiment 39 had lost nineteen tanks, having claimed only around a dozen T-34s. All in all, it was not an auspicious start to the Panther's combat career. The following day while trying to take Dubrova the Panthers once again presented their side armour to the enemy, this time to dug-in T-34s of the 16th Tank Regiment and 85mm anti-tank guns of the 756th Anti-tank Battalion. When they ran into a minefield east of Syrtsev some fifteen Panthers were hit. Once more the Panther's L/70 gun got the better of the T-34s but at a cost of twenty-seven Panthers knocked out that day. The battlefield became known as the 'Panther cemetery at Dubrova'.

Guderian wanted to see first-hand how the Panther was performing and his worst fears were soon realized:

> I visited both the attacking fronts during the time between 10th and 15th of July; I went first to the southern and then the northern area, and talked to the tank commanders on the spot. I there gained an insight into the course that events were taking, the lack of our men's experience in the attack and the weakness of our equipment. My fears concerning the premature commitment of the Panthers were justified.

He reported the following regarding the Panther's disappointing performance:

> Due to enemy action and mechanical breakdowns, the combat strength sank rapidly during the first few days. By the evening of 10 July there were only 10 operational Panthers in the front line. 25 Panthers had been lost as total write-offs (23 were hit and burnt and two had caught fire during the approach march). 100 Panthers were in need of repair (56 were damaged by hits and mines and 44 by mechanical breakdown). 60 percent of the mechanical breakdowns could be easily repaired. Approximately 40 Panthers had already been repaired and were on the way to the front. About 25 still had not been recovered by the repair service . . . On the evening of 11 July, 38 Panthers were operational, 31 were total write-offs and 131 were in need of repair. A slow increase in the combat strength is observable. The large number of losses by hits (81 Panthers up to 10 July) attests to the heavy fighting.

Guderian must have been deeply vexed at the breakdown rate, especially when the faults were only minor things. Combat losses were one thing but constant breakdowns were clearly unacceptable.

Extravagantly von Lauchert claimed his Panthers destroyed 263 Soviet tanks from 5–14 July at ranges of 1,500 to 3,000m. In reality Panzer Regiment 39 was ambushed three times by dug-in T-34s, often on the flanks, at ranges of less than 1,200m, which casts serious doubt on the veracity of such claims. Although Hitler had categorically instructed that no Panthers were to fall into the Red Army's hands, seven were captured on 19 July and Guderian's fears came to fruition.

Following the Soviet counteroffensive at Belgorod the 52nd Panzer Battalion, with only 27 operational Panthers and 109 under repair, was obliged to blow up 72 at Tomarovka and retreat. By the time they reached Akhtyrka just nine Panthers remained operational. A subsequent report on 20 July 1943 indicated forty-one Panthers were operational, eighty-five repairable, sixteen severely damaged and needing repair in Germany, fifty-six burnt out due to enemy action, and two that had been destroyed by engine fires. By 11 August 1943 the numbers of total write-offs had risen to 156, with only nine operational.

It is self-evident that the Panther's baptism of fire at Kursk, against Guderian's wishes, had been a complete and utter disaster. General von Mellenthin summed up Guderian's disappointment after Kursk, saying, 'the Panthers were still in their infancy and were a failure'. Clearly the crews needed more time to learn how to handle the Panther effectively, but Hitler did not have time. As a result, the crews paid the price as they blundered inexpertly around the battlefield. The very mistakes that had been made with Panzer Regiment 39 were to be repeated on a much bigger scale the following year during the Battle of Arracourt in France.

Perhaps inevitably, the haste with which the Panther had been designed and the speed with which it had been put into mass production resulted in the numerous teething problems. The engine suffered cooling issues that resulted in very unwelcome engine fires. The complicated suspension and tracks also gave the crews trouble with frequent breakages. The reality was in the first few months of the Panther's entry into service there were far greater losses thanks to breakdowns than enemy action. It was not an auspicious start for Hitler's T-34 killer.

Chapter 12

An Italian Sideshow

Significant numbers of Panzer IVs were never available in Italy. German panzer divisions were always thin on the ground during the Italian campaign. Generally German infantry divisions relied on the support of panzergrenadier units, which had fewer armoured fighting vehicles than the regular panzer divisions and mostly had assault guns not tanks.

The key tank unit was the 26th Panzer Division, which transferred to Italy in 1943 and remained there for the rest of the war until its surrender near Bologna in May 1945. The 16th Panzer Division only fought in Italy for six months between June and November 1943, seeing action at Salerno and Naples before being sent to the Eastern Front. These divisions were equipped with the Panzer IV Ausf G, H and J.

The Luftwaffe also fielded the Panzer IV in Italy. The Hermann Göring Panzer Division, destroyed in Tunisia, was reformed in southern Italy and Sicily and played a key role in the Sicilian campaign in July and August 1943. Escaping to the Italian mainland following the Allied landings on the island, it was given the title Fallschirm Panzer Division Hermann Göring, although the Fallschirm (Parachute) designation was purely honorary. The Parachute Panzer Regiment Hermann Göring included a panzer and assault gun battalion.

There was no hiding Guderian's bitter disappointment over the performance of the Panther at Kursk. Reliability was to remain a bugbear throughout 1943. After the formation of the ill-fated 39th Panzer Regiment, subsequent Ausf Ds were issued to the 23rd and 26th Independent Panzer Regiments. The 1st SS, 3rd SS and 5th SS Panzer Divisions were also supplied with a limited number of Ausf Ds in late July 1943. The 2nd SS Panzer Division, which had been training in Germany, returned to the Eastern Front equipped with the Ausf D the following month.

The Panther did not get off to an exceptional start when it first deployed to Italy. After the 1st SS Panzer Division, on occupation duties, was issued with their first batch of Panther Ausf As in September 1943 they proved so unreliable the panzertruppen rejected all of them out of hand. Once again the Panthers were sent back to the manufacturers.

The Panther did not make its presence felt in Italy again until the spring of 1944, just in time to help counter the Allies' Operation Diadem. After urgent appeals from General von Vietinghoff a company of Panther Ausf As deployed to Melfa in May 1944 where they arrived just in time to confront the Canadian Army.

In the face of stiff German resistance French forces succeed in breaching the Gustav Line on 13 May 1944 at one of its deepest points at Monte Majo. The fall of Majo unhinged the XIV Panzer Corps' left wing greatly contributing to the Allies' success. On 23 May General B.M. Hoffmeister, commanding the Canadian 5th Armoured Division, felt a large enough breach had been achieved to commit his tanks. It was now that the Allies first came up against the Panther in Italy the next day.

Shortly after midday the tanks of the Canadian Army's Vokes Force (British Columbia Dragoons) and supporting infantry reached their objective about two miles north-west of Aquino and Griffin Force (Lord Strathcona's Horse and the Westminster Regiment) was ordered forward.

Lieutenant Edward J. Perkins with the Reconnaissance Troop of Lord Strathcona's Horse, racing ahead of the main body of Vokes Force, had a near miss with a Panther. His unit were equipped with turretless M3 light tanks armed only with machine guns. He spotted an enemy half-track parked by a farmhouse and recalled:

> My troop opened fire, and the crew tried to escape. Five enemy soldiers were hit, two got away. Next we encountered a Panther tank, the first that we had seen in Italy. It suddenly appeared on my right front about 300 yards away. The crew commander was standing up in the turret. I fired at him with the .50 heavy machine gun and saw him slump over. With its commander hit the Panther kept going and made no attempt to retaliate. We kept going as fast as we could.

At 15.00 Perkins' troop crossed the Melfa. Having secured a bridgehead he sent for the infantry of the Westminster's 'A' Company and the Shermans of the Strathcona's 'A' Squadron. The Shermans had to first clear the south bank of enemy tanks and self-propelled guns before they could help. To the south progress was slow and 30 minutes later two Panthers and a self-propelled 88mm gun appeared and began to shell Perkins' position as well the Strathcona tanks on the far bank. Perkins, reinforced by Major J.K. Mahoney's Westminsters, knew the enemy armour on the north bank had to be pushed away from their bridgehead and a nearby house held by enemy troops cleared. Perkins recounts:

> The SP [self-propelled] 88mm on our left was still firing at A Sqdn's tanks, and Tpr J.K. Funk of my troop offered to volunteer to destroy it with a PIAT [hand-held anti-tank weapon], covered by two Bren gunners

of the Westminster's A Coy. He crept to within 100 yd of the SP gun and hit it with his fourth shot. The Bren gunners shot one of the SP crew and the rest were captured. The two Panther tanks withdrew to positions about 800 yd from the house, which Maj Mahoney now occupied as his Company HQ.

Vokes Force had brushed with the Panthers early on 24 May and remarkably had managed to account for three Panthers for the loss of just four Shermans.

However, while 'A' and 'C' Squadrons of the Strathcona's were trying to cross the Melfa and drive the Panthers to the far bank, they lost seventeen Shermans, claiming just five panzers and not all these were Panthers. An infantry officer spoke of the Canadian tank crews with amazement, 'I'll never forget the way the tanks would keep coming and then one would get knocked out and then another and still they'd keep coming.'

Meantime the Canadians were unable to get any anti-tank weapons over to the Strathcona/Westminster bridgehead and the Germans launched three counter-attacks with using Panthers. Just before dusk three Panthers almost overran the Canadians' positions. The advancing Panzertruppen fired high explosive but their aim was high and they caused no casualties. PIAT fire made the panzers lose their nerve and they wheeled away. Fortunately, by 21.00 some 6-pounder anti-tank guns had got over the river and during the night artillery fire kept the Panthers at bay.

The following day the Canadians counter-attacked, finally driving the Germans away from their tenuous foothold. By the end of the two-day battle for the Melfa River bridgehead the Canadians had accounted for seven Panthers, four Panzer Mk IVs and nine self-propelled guns for the loss of seventeen Shermans. The hesitancy with which the Panthers had pressed home their attacks indicated a lack of experience and training – not to mention poor intelligence regarding the strength of the Canadian bridgehead.

The Canadians were impressed by the performance and qualitative edge of the Panther and appreciated that it could only be tackled by weight of numbers. Summing up the Melfa battles a staff officer with the Canadian 5th Armoured wrote,

As for the main obstacle of the German tanks... the only reason why it was possible to make headway against their qualitative superiority was by weight of numbers . . . General Leese [Commanding Eighth Army] was prepared to lose 1,000 tanks. As he had 1,900 at his disposal, the Panther stood a fair chance of becoming an extinct species among the fauna of S. Italy.

Fortunately for the Allies in Italy the Panther (and the Tiger for that matter) was never encountered in significant numbers. In fact, the two German armies fighting in the Italian campaign largely had to rely on assault guns rather than panzers to form the heart of their armoured units. The Germans fought a defensive war in Italy so relied heavily on fixed defences rather than mobile units. As a result of this strategy surplus Ausf D turrets known as Pantherturm were used to provide defensive strongpoints in Italy. They comprised a turret fitted to a fabricated steel box; this provided a fighting compartment and living space for the crew. These boxes could be entrenched, or were stabilized on a bed of logs or rocks with earth banked up around the edges. Some were also embedded in concrete. They were used in the Hitler and Gothic Lines in Italy (and were also used on the Western and Eastern Fronts). At ground level the turrets presented a low silhouette and were often well concealed which meant the 75mm gun took a heavy toll on advancing Allied tanks.

Manned by Field Marshal Kesselring's Tenth and Fourteenth Armies the Gothic Line was the final major obstacle between the Allies and the Alps. This proved to be probably the best of all the German defences. As it was the very last line the Germans had much greater time to prepare it and with the assistance of conscripted Italian labourers. Although the Gothic Line was never finished it still presented a formidable barrier. The positions included these Panther tank turrets set in steel and concrete. Kesselring no doubt though would have preferred Panther gun tanks but the turrets were better than nothing.

Assault guns provided the backbone of the German armoured forces in Italy during 1943-45. German panzer divisions were always thin on the ground as they were needed elsewhere. Once the Allies had broken out of their various bridgeheads the low-profile assault gun proved to be an ideal weapon for the Germans' defensive war in the mountains of Italy.

Five panzergrenadier divisions saw long-term action in Italy: the 3rd, 15th, 16th SS, 29th and 90th. The 15th Panzer Division, having been lost in Tunisia, was reconstituted in Sicily as the 15th Panzergrenadiers and served there and on the mainland. Most of these units started life as motorized infantry divisions and were converted in 1943. On the whole they were all equipped with assault guns not panzers, though in the case of the Parachute Panzer Regiment Hermann Göring this included a panzer and assault gun battalion. Jagdpanzer IVs were issued to the tank hunter detachments of the panzer divisions from March 1944. They first went into action in Italy with the Hermann Göring Division.

Sturmgeschütz III Ausf F armed with the more powerful 75mm StuK40 L/43 or L/48 gun somewhere in Russia.

StuG III lost in Italy. Guderian viewed the assault gun, intended to support the infantry, as a defensive weapon that dissipated the offensive capabilities of his panzers.

GIs posing with a StuG III Ausf G captured during the fighting in Normandy.

More StuG III Ausf Gs, this time serving in Italy. Panzers were in very short supply during the Italian campaign.

The howitzer version of the StuG III known as the StuH42

The Panzer IV Ausf A, developed at the same time as the Panzer III, was intended as a support tank. However, its larger turret meant it could be upgraded with a larger gun for tank-to-tank combat.

Panzer IV Ausf D destroyed in Libya.

Panzer IV Ausf Es on the way to the Eastern Front and an uncertain fate.

British soldier examining a Panzer IV Ausf H captured in Italy.

Factory–fresh Panzer IVs.

Panzer IV Ausf J in Poland fitted with Schürzen side plates designed to ward off bazooka fire.

This derelict Panzer IV was a casualty of the fighting in Normandy.

The StuG IV was very similar to the StuG III.

The Hummel 150mm self-propelled gun used a hybrid Panzer III/IV chassis.

The second version of the Panzer V, confusingly known as the Panther Ausf A.

The third and final model Panther, designated the Ausf G.

Panther Ausf A captured in Normandy.

Another Panther Ausf A knocked out in Normandy.

Chapter 13

Panzers in Normandy

The Panzer IV played a significant part in the battle for Normandy. The most common types of panzer resisting the Allies in occupied France in 1944 were the Panzer IV Ausf H and Ausf J, totalling around 750 tanks. Around two-thirds of the Panzer IV battalions were armed with the Ausf H and the rest with the newer Ausf J. With frontal armour of 80mm and the 75mm KwK40 L/48 anti-tank gun, the Mk IV provided the fighting mainstay of the ten panzer divisions deployed to France (in all five Army and five Waffen-SS divisions fielded the Panzer IV in Normandy).

Along with the Panther and Tiger tanks, it gave the Germans a distinct advantage in tank-to-tank engagements during the battles in the Normandy bocage. Notably its gun had a 20 per cent greater muzzle velocity than that of the ubiquitous American-built M4 Sherman's 75mm gun, meaning it could punch through 92mm of armour at 500 yards, while the Sherman could only manage 68mm. Furthermore, the Mk IV proved remarkably reliable, maintaining consistently good operational rates.

Normally the Panzer IV was allocated to the II Abteilung or 2nd Battalion of a panzer regiment, while the 1st was equipped with the Panther, although there were a number of exceptions in France. In the case of the 9th Panzer Division the 1st Battalion of its 33rd Panzer Regiment was equipped with Panzer IVs and both battalions of 21st Panzer's 22nd Panzer Regiment were equipped with them.

At the beginning of June 1944 the 2nd Panzer Division, deployed east of the Seine at the start of the campaign, had a total of ninety-eight Panzer IVs on its strength. By early July the division still had eighty-five Panzer IVs in the field with another eleven in the workshop. The 9th Panzer Division, based in the south of France, arrived in Normandy in early August with a total of eighty-two Panzer IVs.

The 21st Panzer Division, already in Normandy from the start, had a total of 104 Panzer IVs, including six old Ausf Gs and six even older Ausf Bs or Cs with the short 75mm gun. None of the latter seems to have been upgraded and lacked Zimmerit and Schürzen. Before D-Day one of the Ausf B/Cs, dubbed 'Heidi', was photographed in St Martin de Fresnay, south-east of St Pierre-sur-Dives, where its crew were happily shopping for Camembert cheese. It is not clear if this was an authorized use of official military equipment or simply a PR exercise. On 24 May 1944 another fourteen Panzer IVs were despatched to 21st Panzer, but it is unlikely that they had arrived by early June. During the battle for Normandy another thirty Panzer IVs were sent to the division including three command tanks. The final ten gun tanks probably did not arrive in time to take part in the fighting.

Panzer Lehr Division, initially north-west of Orleans, had ninety-nine Panzer IVs. It was sent another eleven as replacements on 8 July 1944. Following heavy fighting with the Americans by 22 August the division had just ten remaining. When the 116th Panzer Division Windhund, north of Paris, was committed to the battle for Normandy in late July it had eighty-six Panzer IVs. Its other armoured fighting vehicles include three older Panzer IVs with the short-barrelled 75mm main gun. Following the German retreat and the fighting at St Lambert the division was only able to retrieve four Panzer IVs from the battlefield.

The Waffen-SS panzer divisions committed to Normandy were also equipped with the Panzer IV. The 1st SS Panzer Division Leibstandarte Adolf Hitler, east of Brussels, mustered forty-two Panzer IVs in its 1st Battalion. A further eight were in for repair. Deliveries during June amounted to another fifty-three tanks. After being sent to Normandy by late July the division was able to field sixty-one Panzer IVs. The 2nd SS Panzer Division Das Reich had fifty-four Panzer IVs by the beginning of June, of which ten were in the workshops. Further deliveries of armour meant that the division was to field a total of eighty-three Panzer IVs, which included the newer Ausf J. Many of these were lost in the Roncey pocket at the end of July, though a battalion of Panzer IVs managed to escape. The 9th SS Panzer Division Hohenstaufen had forty-eight Panzer IVs at the start of the campaign, but seven of these were in the shop. Its sister division 10th SS Frundsberg was able to deploy thirty-nine and by mid-August had only lost twelve. However, just eight Panzer IVs were available to hold the Americans at bay. The formidable 12th SS Panzer Division Hitlerjugend had an authorized strength of 101 Panzer IVs though only 91 were combat ready. By 10 August, after much heavy fighting, the division had just fifteen remaining.

By 1944 the panzer divisions were largely relying on flak guns mounted on half-tracks for air defence, including the SdKfz 10/4 and SdKfz 7/1. In Normandy the Flakpanzer 38(t) using Czech-built chassis was in service instead of the Flakpanzer IV with the 2nd, 9th, Panzer Lehr and 1st SS Panzer Divisions. In theory eight Flakpanzer IV Möbelwagen were allocated to the anti-aircraft section of a panzer regiment's headquarters company. In July 1944, on paper at least Möbelwagens, were assigned to the 12th SS Panzer and 116th Panzer Divisions. Very limited numbers of Wirbelwind also saw combat in Normandy.

The lack of infantry divisions, which were held north of the Seine, meant the panzers bore the brunt of the fighting. By the beginning of July 1944 the unrelenting operational commitment of the panzers had taken its toll: 42 per cent of the Panzer IVs and 58 per cent of the Panthers were in the maintenance depots. Prior to Montgomery's Goodwood offensive on 18 July Panzer IVs of 21st Panzer along with Tiger tanks from Heavy Panzer Battalion 503 were caught in the Allied saturation bombing near Château de Manneville 10km east of Caen. The effects were devastating, with tanks simply tossed upside down like they were toys. From a force of about fifty panzers over half were lost, many others suffering mechanical damage.

Although Operation Goodwood failed to break through the incredibly tough German defences, it contributed further to the attrition of the Panzer IVs in Normandy and helped pin them in the British sector. In August for the renewed counter-attack at Mortain against the Americans the Germans could only gather seventy-seven Panzer IVs and forty-seven Panthers, roughly the same inadequate number that had been launched in the initial attack, which involved fifty-seven Panzer IVs and seventy Panthers.

A few weeks later, unable to contain the American breakout, the German army was in headlong flight and then trapped at Falaise and defeated. After the battle for Normandy, despite the presence of surviving panzers belonging to the SS at Arnhem, Montgomery was not put off launching Operation Market-Garden that resulted in the disastrous battle for the Rhine crossing.

In the summer of 1944 the main models of Panther deployed in Normandy were the Ausf A and Ausf G. Following the D-Day landings on 6 June 1944 these were very quickly in the thick of it and were committed to the battle for Normandy. When the invasion commenced there were 156 Panthers deployed on the Western Front, but by the end of July this had risen to 432.

In theory the 1st Battalion of each panzer regiment was equipped with the Panther, but this was not always the case. The 21st Panzer Division's organization was unique in Normandy; unlike the other panzer divisions (with the exception of 10th SS) it had no Panther battalion and and an anti-tank battalion with towed 88mm guns. The Jagdpanther, based on the Panther chassis armed with the 8.8cm Pak43/3, was very scarce in Normandy, about a dozen at most, so had little bearing on the fighting.

On arriving in Normandy Sherman crews quickly learned that their short 75mm gun could not overcome the Panther's frontal armour. Their only hope was to get a shot at the Panther's turret, which might cause some damage. Otherwise they had to slip round the sides or the rear of the Panther to strike the thinner armour. Such a manoeuvre often entailed the Sherman exposing its own sides. The Panther could easily overcome the Sherman's frontal armour.

Two-thirds of the tanks used by British, Canadian and Polish armoured units in Normandy were Shermans, the rest being mainly British-built Cromwell plus the Churchill tanks assigned to the infantry divisions. The Cromwell cruiser tank was numerically and qualitatively the most significant British tank and along with the

Sherman formed the main strength of the British armoured divisions. However, even armed with a 75mm gun it was inferior to the late model Panzer IVs and the Panther. Similarly, the British Churchill infantry tank, though heavily armoured, could not take any gun larger than the 75mm. The British Sherman Firefly was the only Allied tank capable of taking on the Panther and the Tiger on equal terms in Normandy. The British-built 17-pounder (76.2mm) anti-tank gun could penetrate 120mm of armour at 500 yards and was either towed or mounted in limited numbers of Shermans designated the Firefly VC. Due to a shortage of 17-pounders the Fireflies were only issued one per troop.

The most powerful armoured unit deployed to Normandy, the Panzer Lehr Division under General Fritz Bayerlein, had ninety-nine Panzer IVs, eighty-nine Panthers, thirty-one Jagdpanzer IVs, ten Sturmgeschütz IIIs and eight Tigers I/IIs, giving an impressive total of 237 panzers and assault guns. Initially Panzer Lehr was stationed in the Chartes-Le Mans-Orléans area. Fate partly favoured the Allies when it was decided to ship the Panthers of the 1st Battalion, 6th Panzer Regiment, which was on loan from the 3rd Panzer Division, to the Eastern Front. On 5 June 1944 the very day before D-Day the first train carrying this unit reached Magdeburg in Germany, whilst the last was loitering in Paris. Once the Allied landings were underway the battalion was ordered to retrace its steps. As a result, the Panthers did not arrive until 10 June.

The second most powerful armoured division was the 1st SS that fielded 103 Panzer IVs, seventy-two Panthers and forty-five StuG IIIs during the fighting in Normandy. The 9th SS Panzer Division's Panther battalion was at Mailly-le-Camp undergoing training, which was hampered by the slow rate of new tank deliveries. Its full complement of seventy-nine tanks was not received until mid to late June.

The 12th SS arrived in Normandy with 12th SS-Panzer Regiment, under SS-Lieutenant Colonel Max Wünche, that had an authorized strength of seventy-nine Panthers. Its actual strength was close to this with sixty-six Panthers and two undergoing maintenance at the beginning of June. A further thirteen Panthers were despatched to the division on 7 June.

The Panther was soon in action. On 8 June 1944 the 12th SS Panthers found Carpiquet airfield deserted by the Luftwaffe and unoccupied by the advancing Canadians. They turned on the Canadian 7th Brigade, part of the Canadian 3rd Division driving it from Bretteville l'Orgueilleuse and Putot-en-Bessin, though the Canadians in turn recaptured Putot claiming six Panthers. Around 22.00 the 25th SS-Panzergrenadier Regiment supported by the Panthers struck toward Bretteville from three directions.

The attack from the south resulted in the platoon commander's tank being immobilized in the town and surrounded. The attack from the south-west was ordered to rescue him, but the lead tank was knocked out and driven off. In the attack from the west three Panthers were hit simultaneously by concealed Canadian anti-tank guns. Two managed to withdraw, but the other burned like a torch though its crew managed to escape. The following morning the attack was broken off.

On 9 June Panthers of 3rd Company, 12th SS-Panzer Regiment, under SS-Lieutenant Rudolf von Ribbentrop, having missed the attack on Bretteville, moved on Norrey with the Caen-Cherbourg railway embankment protecting its right flank. Von Ribbentrop had been wounded so Hauptmann Lüdman led his twelve Panthers. However, once beyond the cover of the railway bank well-concealed anti-tank guns knocked out seven tanks and the advance was halted. Crew losses were also heavy, with eighteen of the thirty-five men involved killed.

At the village of Buron north-west of Caen elements of the 25th SS-Panzer-grenadier Regiment were surrounded and on the verge of being overrun by Canadian tanks. Kurt Meyer, commanding the 12th SS, was at the Ardenne monastery. He recalled the dramatically unfolding events:

> The tank company of von Ribbentrop with its fifteen Panthers deployed against this mass of enemy tanks and they shot up the enemy armour halting its advance. The last enemy tank was destroyed only 100 metres west of Ardenne but von Ribbentrop had saved the command post. His initial instructions had been to relieve the panzergrenadiers and clear the Canadians from Buron, however he was distracted by the Canadian armour to the left of the village and had to send a platoon of Panthers to deal with them. Reaching Buron von Ribbentrop's Panthers knocked out several Canadian tanks.

Loathe to enter the village without infantry support, von Ribbentrop quickly found the tables turning, as he noted:

> Just then a well-camouflaged Canadian anti-tank gun must have opened fire, because two or three tanks to my right went up in flames one after another. There was nothing left to do but pull back to our starting position and support the hard-pressed infantry from there.

SS-Sergeant Freiberg, serving with von Ribbentrop, found himself in one of the three Panthers knocked out:

> We crossed the open field to the wall around the village of Buron at high speed. As we moved past an opening in the wall, there were suddenly two explosions. Sepp Trattnick's tank and another tank burst into flames. We immediately opened fire with both machine guns on the opening of

the wall. I saw some movement there and then a flash from the muzzle of an anti-tank gun. The round struck our gun mantlet and the solid projectile ended up in the fighting compartment. Our sight was smashed, and the gunner was wounded in the face. I received several fragments in my left arm.

After fighting on the Eastern Front the 2nd Panzer Division made the most of its well-earned rest in France and by late May/early June 1944 the 3rd Panzer Regiment had seventy-nine Panthers. Frustratingly the Panther battalion with fifty-two operational tanks did not arrive until 19 June; twenty were damaged in transit. For the rest of June, the division fought in the Caumont area, although the Panthers were despatched to resist the British Epsom offensive.

When the British broke through east of Tilly-sur-Seulles on the front held by Panzer Lehr on 25 and 26 June, the 12th SS supported by the 1st Battalion, 3rd Panzer Regiment counter-attacked on the right. On the 28th the Panthers destroyed fifty-three British tanks and fifteen anti-tank guns. By 1 July they had claimed eighty-nine enemy tanks, thirteen Bren carriers and nineteen anti-tank guns for the loss of twenty panzers. By early July the division still had and twenty-one operational Panthers and thirty-eight undergoing maintenance.

The 9th SS counter-attacked on 29 June at 07.00 on the left of the Odon. SS-Lieutenant Colonel Walter Harzer, Chief Operations Staff Officer of the 9th SS, observed:

As it was, our counter-offensive broke down under air attack and artillery fire, particularly the heavy guns of the battleships. They were devastating. When one of those shells dropped near a Panther, the 56-ton tank was blown over on its side, just from the blast. It was these broadsides from the warships, more than the defensive fighting of the enemy's troops, which halted our division's Panzer Regiment.

During the fighting against the Epsom salient the 9th SS lost sixteen Panzer IVs, six Panthers and ten StuG IIIs. By at this stage the 12th SS had lost fifty-one Panzer IVs and thirty-two Panthers. By the evening of 25 July the 9th SS was able to muster eighteen Panzer IVs, eighteen Panthers and eleven assault guns, but with their maintenance teams working full out three days later the total stood at twenty-two Panzer IVs, twenty Panthers and twenty-two assault guns.

On 11 July Panzer Lehr counter-attacked the Americans at Le Désert and made some ground. The attack launched in the early hours caused the American 30th Infantry Division problems, though the initial success of the panzers was due to a gap between the American 39th and 47th Infantry Divisions south-west of Le Désert. The Americans rushed in reinforcements, but to the west a column of ten panzers reached south of la Scellerie before losing three Panthers and being driven off.

On 18 July Montgomery threw three armoured divisions down a narrow corridor to the east of Caen and through the German defences on the Bourguébus ridge. The Panther tank played a key part in halting this armoured charge. The Panthers of the 1st SS stormed down from the ridge forcing back the British. In the process of trying drive them back to Caen-Troarn the 1st SS and 21st Panzer Divisions lost 109 tanks, while by the end of the first day the British had suffered 1,500 casualties and 200 tanks destroyed for the gain of just six miles (10km) beyond the Orne.

However, the north-south line from Frénouville to Emiéville held and with the commitment of the 1st SS Operation Goodwood came to a grinding halt over the next few days. The 1st SS, 12th SS and 21st Panzer effectively hemmed in the British armour. By this point, west of Bourguébus at Verrières on the far side of the Caen-Falaise road, the 1st SS had gathered seventy Panzer IVs and Panthers.

Just prior to Operation Cobra Panzer Lehr had eighty tanks, of which only fifteen Panzer IVs and sixteen Panthers were operational and rated suitable for only for defensive missions. When the Americans launched Cobra on 25 July it was the Panther tanks that were at the front. Luckily Fritz Bayerlein's Panzer IVs had been withdrawn to form a reserve and in fact only a few Panthers and tank destroyers were lost to the preliminary bombing.

Panzer Lehr weathered the first attack on the 24th, losing just 350 men and ten vehicles. The following day the bombing cost the division 1,000 men and numerous vehicles caught near the Periers-St Lô road, in particular a number of Panther tanks were lost. By the end of the month the Panthers had not been able to stop the Americans breaking out of the Normandy bridgehead and coherent German resistance collapsed.

Fritz Bayerlein was not a big fan of the Panther in Normandy. Highlighting its shortcomings, he noted:

> While the PzKpfw IV could still be used to advantage, the PzKpfw V proved ill adapted to the terrain. The Sherman because of its manoeuvrability and height was good . . . [the Panther was] poorly suited for hedgerow terrain because of its width. Long gun barrel and width of tank reduced manoeuvrability in village and forest fighting.

The Panther was to suffer from exactly the same problems during Hitler's Ardennes offensive.

In southern France the performance of the Panther was to be equally disappointing. During September 1944 half-a-dozen newly-raised Panther brigades failed to secure victory for Hitler's counteroffensive against Patton's US 3rd Army at Arracourt in Lorraine. These brigades, which included Panzer Mk IVs, were poorly organized and lacked vital supporting units. Predominantly made up of armour, they operated without reconnaissance troops so had to go into battle largely blind. The crews were poorly trained and poorly led. This lack of preparedness echoed the experiences of Panzer Regiment 39 at Kursk.

These new Panther brigades were intended for the Eastern Front where they could have acted as a powerful mobile reserve. The Red Army often lacked tactical support and could not always call on adequate anti-tank weapons, artillery or close air-support. In contrast in Lorraine the Panthers were thrown against American and French tanks, which were well supported by anti-tank guns, artillery and dive-bombers. US tankers had by this stage developed innovative tactics against the panzers. On encountering enemy armour, American Shermans and supporting tank destroyers would open fire with everything they had. Experienced US tank battalions when running into Panthers often fired phosphorous smoke rounds. The acrid smoke drawn into the Panther's ventilator could cause their crews to bail out in panic. Likewise, the use of high-explosive rounds sometimes had the same result. Even if the panzertruppen stayed with their tank the smoke obscured their sights.

The inexperienced Panther crews became the victims of a turkey shoot. They exposed their weak side armour and failed to press home their attacks when the going got tough – even though they could have easily overpowered their weaker opponents. By the time the Lorraine counteroffensive came to a halt the Germans had lost 118 Panthers and a similar number of Panzer IVs.

PART III

STURMGESCHÜTZ
NOT PANZERS

Chapter 14

Fiddling While Rome Burns

Following Hitler's invasion of the Soviet Union it rapidly became apparent that the Red Army was deploying newer and superior tank types to those in its existing inventory. Specifically, the appearance of the KV-1 heavy tank and the T-34 medium tank was a worrying development that did not bode well for the future. During the summer of 1941 the Red Army had insufficient numbers of these tanks and those that it did have suffered as a result of poor training. By the winter Soviet crews had realized that the T-34 had the makings of a first-class tank and its performance began to improve.

In response Oberkommando der Wehrmacht (German Armed Forces High Command) instructed the army that Hitler wanted the StuG III to be up-armoured and up-gunned with the long-barrel 75mm StuK40 gun as soon as possible. At the same time the Panzer IV, armed with the short 75mm KwK37 gun, was rearmed with the much more powerful long KwK40. This seemed to offer the best quick fix. The StuG Ausf F constituted the sixth in series from March to July 1942 and the seventh from July to September 1942.

There was little to distinguish the Ausf F from the previous model's superstructure except for the addition of a prominent circular exhaust fan to the right of the commander's hatch on the roof to remove gun fumes. Although the StuK40 gun was installed in the same place as the StuK37, it had a completely new bolted box-like gun mantlet that was vertical rather than horizontal and tapered in toward the gun. This was needed to contain the larger recoil of the much bigger gun. It also meant that the upper front of the superstructure was slightly enlarged to accommodate the mantlet and improve crew protection – this gave it a height of 2.15m compared to the previous 1.98m. Some of the early models lacked muzzle brakes.

The bulk of the F model was armed with the StuK40 L/43 but thirty-one were fitted with the later, slightly more powerful L/48 gun. They both provided the front-line troops with a much-needed antidote to the KV-1 and T-34. This weapon upgrade meant that the StuG Ausf F changed from an artillery support role to a predominantly anti-tank role. Some Ausf Fs were fitted with additional armour (Zusatz Panzerung) from June 1942. Inevitably this led to a slight increase in weight from around 20 tons of the previous models to 21.6 tons. This caused a slight reduction in range from 160km to 140km. From a total of 359 Ausf Fs built, 182 had the additional armour.

The follow-on F/8 appeared in September 1942 and production ran until December that year. The main change with this model was the introduction of an improved hull design that drew on the Panzer III Ausf J and L. At the front the side plates extended beyond the front plate and had holes drilled to create towing brackets. The superstructure and the front of the hull was up-armoured with an additional 30mm of bolted-on armour. Also the thickness of the rear hull armour was boosted from 30mm to 50mm. The rear deck was extended further back and the air louvers were changed to increase engine ventilation.

In light of the inadequate gun in the Panzer III (which had been progressively upgraded from a 37mm, then a 50mm and finally the short 75mm) in 1942 Alkett was ordered to cease production of this tank and build only StuGs. As a gun tank the Panzer III would continue to be built until the summer of 1943 by Hitler's other panzer manufacturers. Alkett used a number of existing Panzer III hulls for assault gun production and these could be identified by a distinctive single-piece forward opening hatch over the final drive. Some 334 Ausf F/8s were built; four were converted to Sturmhaubitze 42 (StuH42) heavy assault guns and another twelve chassis were used for the Sturminfanteriegeschütz 33B (StuIG33B) self-propelled infantry gun. Although the number of assault gun units continued to increase, the F/8 was largely issued as a combat replacement for battle-damaged Ausf Es and Ausf Fs. In addition, some of the Waffen-SS panzer divisions received a Sturmgeschütz detachment equipped with Ausf Fs and Ausf F/8s in 1942.

The Ausf G was the last production Sturmgeschütz based on the Panzer III and proved to be by far the most numerous and therefore the most common. It is certainly the most photographed StuG variant. In total 7,720 were built from December 1942 to March 1945, in addition 173 were converted from Panzer III gun tanks in 1944. This large production run was due to the StuG III absorbing the Panzer III manufacturing facilities once the latter was completely phased out. Although the Ausf G went into production in 1942 and remained so until early 1945, by the end of the war there had been no major visual design changes except for the gun mantlet.

By the time the Ausf G began to roll off the assembly lines it had been decided to phase out the Panzer III altogether and replace it with the Panzer V Panther. This naturally caused complications with existing plans and was not a straightforward process. It was not simply a case of shutting down production and switching immediately over to a new vehicle.

The hull of the StuG Ausf G was the same as that used on the F/8. The main changes were due to differences in the superstructure. The sides were slanted and slanted plates were included to protect the front of both the side panniers. A simple commander's cupola with periscopes was installed as well as a much-needed shield for the machine gun in front of the gunner's hatch.

Photographic evidence shows that there were at least two types of cupola, one with vertical sides and another with a cast sloping front rising up from the superstructure roof. The latter was undoubtedly an improvement to counter the cupola front being a potential shot trap. Likewise, photographic evidence of StuGs in Italy and Normandy shows that not all Ausf Gs were fitted with the cupola, instead retaining the same hatch arrangement as the earlier Ausf F.

The fabricated box-like mantlet used on the Ausf F and initial Ausf G was supplemented in 1943 by an improved single piece cast one known as the Topfblende (pot mantlet) or Saukopfblende (sow or pig's head mantlet). This was a smooth conical casting that had much better shot deflection qualities. The previous one tended to trap enemy rounds under the barrel, while the top of the mantlet could flick rounds onto the barrel or nose plates. Photographic evidence shows that the front of the box was vulnerable and could come off when struck with sufficient force to cut the retaining bolts.

Also in 1943 a coat of textured anti-magnetic mine paste was added to the hull and superstructure. Similarly, in an act of desperation or simply wartime expediency some vehicles had the front armour enhanced by a layer of concrete up to 6in deep on the armoured roof of the driver's compartment. The close-in defence of the Ausf G was enhanced with the installation of a coaxial machine gun, remote-controlled machine gun on the superstructure roof and the Nahverteidigungswaffe (close-in defence weapon). Those vehicles used to equip the remote-control companies were fitted with an additional radio aerial on the left front of the fighting compartment.

At the start of Hitler's ill-fated Kursk offensive against the Red Army in the summer of 1943 there were twenty-eight independent Sturmgeschütz detachments, four divisional StuG detachments, two remote control companies and twelve StuG platoons with the weak Luftwaffe field divisions.

Guderian was far from a fan of the StuG Ausf G or the howitzer-armed StuH42. At the end of 1942 he observed:

> The construction of the Panzer III was now entirely discontinued, the industrial capacity thus freed being given over to the building of assault guns. The production figure for assault guns was to reach 220 per month by June 1943, of which 24 were to be armed with light field howitzers. This gun, with its low muzzle velocity and its very high trajectory, was undoubtedly well suited to the requirements of the infantry, but its production resulted in a fresh weakening of our defensive power against hostile tanks.

By 1944–5 the StuG Ausf G crews found themselves acting and looking increasingly like panzertruppen. The reality is that by this point in the war the distinction between the role of the Sturmgeschütz, Panzerjäger, Jagdpanzer and other self-propelled guns had become largely blurred. Increasingly they were called upon to fulfil the role traditionally carried out by the panzers, with many so-called panzer battalions being equipped with assault guns.

The assault gun crews were a breed apart and belonged to the artillery and not the Panzerwaffe. To emphasise this fact the assault gun brigades were renamed assault artillery brigades. This meant they were not permitted to wear the black panzertruppen uniform (though in practice many did).

The artillery vehicle crews wore a field grey version; the collar patches were the same shape as the panzer crews' but field grey piped with artillery red Waffen-farbe with metal skulls. They also initially wore a field grey version of the Shutzmütze padded black panzer beret, this was then replaced by a field grey Feldmütze (side cap) or Einheitsmütze (field cap).

In the case of the Panzerjäger units they also initially wore the field grey uniform, but from 1944 those serving with panzer and panzergrenadier divisions were instructed to wear black. Those serving with infantry and mountain divisions kept the grey uniform. A third style of uniform was introduced in mid-1942 with the reed-green panzer denim suit issued to Army armoured formations as working attire. This was worn over the black panzertruppen uniform or as a uniform in its own right.

As the Wehrmacht was driven back, the crews could only wear what was available from the quartermaster and they often did not have a choice in the matter. Toward the end of the war Sturmartillerie crews were known to wear the black panzer uniform or a combination of black and grey. It is quite possible that they also ended up with the panzer denims as well.

The Sturmhaubitze 42 was a heavy assault StuG variant armed with a 105mm howitzer. This armoured fighting vehicle was developed because the StuG units realized they needed heavier fire support when fighting alongside infantry. Despite an initial shaky start over 1,200 of these were built from October 1942 to February 1945. As early as 1941 there had been moves to produce a heavy fire support assault gun. Initial attempts involved marrying the 150mm Stu I G L/11 gun to the Panzer III chassis. The resulting Sturminfanteriegeschütz 33B (assault infantry gun, StuIG33B or sIG33B for short) was the third installation of the sIG33 on a panzer chassis. However, those fitted to the Panzer I and II chassis had open fighting compartments and like the sIG33B were only ever built in very small numbers.

Alkett was instructed in July 1941 to provide twelve Panzer III chassis to take the 150mm gun, which were to be completed by mid-September. Whilst the sIG33B utilized the StuG Ausf E and F/8 hull, the superstructure had to be completely redesigned to create a very boxy fully-enclosed fighting compartment for the much larger gun. The main armament was mounted in a sliding gun mantlet offset to the right. The secondary armament was supplied by a MG34 mounted in the right-hand side of the superstructure's front.

Delays resulted in the initial version being finished in late 1941 and early 1942. Then on 20 September 1942 another order for twelve assault vehicles, capable of smashing houses, to be completed in two weeks was placed. The original batch of sIG33B were rebuilt and twelve new ones were constructed in October 1942 bringing the total number built to just twenty-four.

In November 1942 a heavy StuG company was deployed to Stalingrad to add punch to the panzer and panzergrenadier divisions. A second company was formed as part of the 201st Panzer Regiment serving with the 23rd Panzer Division. This formation was sent to try and break the Red Army's stranglehold on the German Sixth Army trapped at Stalingrad in the winter of 1942–3.

Another attempt to design a heavily-armed assault gun involved mounting the leFH18 105mm light field howitzer in a trial series of twelve StuGs to run from January to March 1942. This gun was the German Army's standard towed divisional field piece, but, it was rather heavy and not as mobile as the gunners would have liked. Due to a number of setbacks just a single prototype was completed in March 1942, with five Sturmhaubitze (StuH) built on StuG Ausf F and another four on StuG F/8 chassis finished in October 1942.

Delivery of the first production series of the StuH42 did not commence until the following year in March 1943, with the highest monthly output being reached in September 1944 with 199 vehicles. These were armed with the StuH42 L/28 105mm gun fitted with a muzzle brake, similar to the leFH18(M), to allow it to fire more powerful ammunition giving it greater range.

The Ausf F, F/8 and G were used to produce the StuH42, so the hull and superstructure was the same. The only real difference was the altered gun mount in order to take the bigger weapon, similarly the internal storage had to be changed to take the larger rounds. Like the Ausf G, late production models of the StuH42 also included a coaxial mount for a machine gun. Some late production StuH42 lacked a muzzle brake like the leFH18 and were fitted with a remote-controlled machine gun. Those based on the StuG Ausf G had the Saukopf gun mantlet.

When the Battle of Kursk started the German Army Groups Centre and South had sixty-eight StuH42. From 1943 the StuH were issued to the StuG detachments that became full brigades. Each unit was supplied with nine StuH42 to support the Ausf F and G by providing heavier firepower and supplementing close range anti-tank defence.

A final armed support variant in the assault gun family was the Sturmgeschütz (Fl) flamethrower. These were extremely limited in number with just ten converted in May and June 1943. The ending of Panzer III production resulted in just 100 tanks being available for the Flammpanzer (flamethrowing tank) programme. To compensate for this, it was proposed that ten of the 220 StuGs due for delivery in June 1943 would be armed with the 14mm Flammenwerfer, which was also installed in the Panzer III (Fl). Photographic evidence shows that the Ausf F/8 was used as the base vehicle. The Flammenwerfer replaced the 75mm sturmkanone and flame fuel tanks were installed, otherwise the appearance was that of a standard StuG. The range of the flamethrower was 55–60m.

In light of the slow rate of production for the Tiger heavy tank and the unwelcome teething problems experienced with the Panther medium tank, Guderian, as Inspector General of Armoured Troops appreciated that the Panzerwaffe remained very reliant on the Panzer IV. During the summer of 1943 following a visit to the Eastern Front he became ill with dysentery. Guderian recalled:

> Meanwhile during my absence an attempt had been made to stop producing Panzer IVs and to build assault guns in their place. The Todt Organization, which was building the Atlantic Wall and other fortifications, proposed that tank turrets be built into pillboxes; in view of our limited production this would undoubtedly be a serious blow to our mobile tank forces and showed a complete lack of comprehension of the real situation.

Hitler's armoured vehicle designers were looking at ways to improve and ultimately replaced the tried and tested StuG III. Events soon forced his hand. Fortunately for Hitler, but much to Guderian's displeasure, trials had already been conducted into the feasibility of marrying the StuG III superstructure to the Panzer IV chassis. Guderian was of the view that the StuG III was more than adequate and did not need replacing. He could understand the utility of employing the Panzer III factories to build StuGs, though would have rather they had been converted to Panzer IV production.

Guderian was understandably annoyed because in April 1943 he had won agreement that Panzer IV production would continue and be expanded during 1943–4 until mass production of the Panther could be assured. He was therefore far from happy about the development of the forthcoming StuG IV and Jagdpanzer IV, as he saw them as an unwanted distraction. He recorded:

> In October [1943] tank production suffered further in favour of the production of assault guns: Panzer IVs were diverted to carrying the 75mm L/70 cannon and Panthers [Jagdpanthers] the long 88mm L/71. . . . the actual result was simply a decrease in the production of the only useful combat tank available to us at the time, the Panzer IV;

and furthermore it was only in this month that the production figures for that tank reached the really very modest total of 100.

Allied bombers played a part in Hitler's decision to press ahead with the StuG IV. The Alkett factory building the StuG III was bombed in late November 1943, severely disrupting output. Hitler wanted the shortfall remedied as quickly as possible, which meant that part of the Krupp works at Magdeburg was instructed to manufacture the StuG IV. Hitler was shown a StuG IV on 16 December 1943 and he insisted it go into production immediately. Hitler and his staff were in part swayed by combat reports that showed the Panzer IV was struggling to hold its own. Furthermore, it was imperative that losses suffered at Kursk be made good, as assault guns were easier to build it seemed a preferable and swifter solution.

The vital Krupp tank plant halted Panzer IV production in early December 1943 and in the New Year went over completely to manufacturing the StuG IV. The first thirty was produced from chassis supplied by the Nibelungenwerke from their regular tank production line.

Utilizing the battle-proven Panzer IV chassis, the StuG IV assault gun was armed with the 75mm StuK40 L/48 gun and the Jagdpanzer IV tank destroyer with the 75mm Pak39 L/48. The 75mm L/70 gun noted by Guderian was actually fitted to the Panzer IV/70 designed as the Jagdpanzer IV's eventual replacement. Almost 1,140 StuG IVs were built between December 1943 and March 1945 and 769 Jagdpanzer IVs from January to November 1944. The latter first went into action in Italy with the Hermann Göring Division.

The Panzer IV-based assault guns and tank destroyers were easily recognizable as they had eight road wheels and four return rollers, whereas the Panzer III had six and three respectively. On the StuG IV the driver's position was relocated to an armoured cab equipped with two periscopes, but no vision port and with an access hatch in the roof rather than the glacis. It was up-armoured from its predecessor by the application of 6in concrete slabs fitted to the front of the superstructure and the driver's cab, hence the loss of the vision port.

In early 1944 the cast Saukopfblende was introduced and in the summer the external machine-gun shield, used by the loader, was upgraded to a remote-controlled machine-gun mount and a Nähverteidigungswaffe close-defence weapon installed on the roof. The StuG IV was issued to the artillery's StuG brigades, plus the panzerjäger detachments of the panzer and infantry divisions.

Built by Vomag, the Jagdpanzer IV first appeared in early 1944 and had been developed as a specific replacement for the StuG III. Hitler had been shown a soft steel model in October 1943 and a final prototype at the end of the year. Initially until May 1944 Vomag produced the Jadgpanzer IV and the Panzer IV side-by-side until the factory went completely over to Jagdpanzer IV production.

Whilst the Jagdpanzer had the same basic chassis, suspension and drive train as the gun tank from which it was derived, the hull front was redesigned. Two plates forming a sharp-nosed front replaced the vertical front plate and the superstructure had sloping sides. The upper hull front and superstructure front armour was increased to 80mm and the sides increased to 40mm in May 1944. The main armament was flanked by two machine-gun ports.

From March 1944 the Jagdpanzer IV was issued to the panzerjäger units of the panzer divisions. They first saw combat in Italy and then with the 4th and 5th Panzer Divisions on the Eastern Front and with Panzer Lehr, 9th Panzer and the 12th SS in Normandy. Despite Guderian's concerns over the German Army dwindling tank fleet, Panzer IV production was also given over to the Panzer IV/70 tank destroyer in the summer of 1944. This was at the very point that Army Group Centre was collapsing on the Eastern Front and Army Group B was being defeated in France.

The Panzer IV/70(V) tank destroyer went into production in August 1944, in parallel with the StuG IV and Jagdpanzer IV and ran until the end of the war, by which time 930 had been produced. Its key combat role was supporting Hitler's Ardennes offensive in December 1944. Some 278 Panzer IV/70(A) models were also built during the same period and fought on the Eastern Front. While similar in appearance to the StuG IV and especially the Jagdpanzer IV, the Panzer IV/70 variants lacked a muzzle brake on their main gun.

The Panzer IV/70(V) was Vomag's improved version of its Jagdpanzer IV, with the 75mm PaK42 L/70 gun replacing the Pak39 L/48 of its predecessor. It went into production in the summer of 1944 alongside the Vomag Jagdpanzer until the latter was completely replaced in December 1944. The Panzer IV/70(V)'s longer gun and 80mm frontal armour made it quite nose heavy, which meant that the rubber-tyred road wheels suffered excessive wear. To remedy this problem on later production models the first two wheel stations were fitted with all steel rimmed wheels. Also the later models only had three return rollers in keeping with the savings made on the Panzer IV Ausf J – the final production model of the Panzer IV.

The Panzer IV/70(V) was issued to the 105th and 106th Independent Panzer Brigades in the summer of 1944. Other tank brigades along with independent panzerjäger units and those assigned to the panzer divisions were likewise equipped with this new tank destroyer. In the winter of 1944 a total of 137 Panzer IV/70(V)s were available for Hitler's surprise Ardennes offensive against the American Army.

While pressing on with StuG III and StuH42 production, Alkett also became involved in Guderian's unwanted tank-building distraction. The Panzer IV/70(A) was the Alkett variant of the Panzer IV tank destroyer and was produced at the Nibelungenwerke alongside the Panzer IV Ausf J. Like the Vomag version it was armed with the 75mm PaK42 gun and both variants were built simultaneously until the end of the war.

The Panzer IV/70(A) utilized the Panzer IV chassis and was very similar in appearance to the Panzer IV/70(V) – with both using the same type of gun mount and mantlet. However, the superstructure was stepped where it was fitted to the hull with vertical edges to the lower front and sides. While the Panzer IV/70(V) was the same height as the Jagdpanzer IV at 1.85m, the Alkett version was considerably higher at 2.35m. This also made the Panzer IV(A) higher than the StuG III and StuG IV.

Alkett's tank destroyer also suffered with nose-weight problems, which again necessitated using steel-rimmed road wheels at the front. Most of the Panzer IV/70(A) were deployed to the Eastern Front; a few though were encountered by the Western Allies, with the French Army capturing at least one example. Tellingly its' frontal armour had been penetrated in the upper part of the raised superstructure.

In late 1944 the Panzer IV/70 was used to equip the tank destroyer unit of each panzer division, which normally comprised twenty-one vehicles. On the eve of the Ardennes offensive the 1st SS Panzer Division's SS-Panzerjäger Abteilung I only had half its complement. These supported Kampfgruppe Hansen in the fighting at Poteau and then moved to assist Kampfgruppe Peiper.

At Petit-Spai some of 1st SS's Panzer IV/70s reached the southern bank of the Amblève River, but the bridge there was not capable of taking the vehicle's 25 tons. Despite SS-Hauptsturmführer Otto Holt's objections his Panzer IV/70 company was ordered to cross. As a result his lead vehicle crashed through the bridge and into the river. The end of the shattered bridge created a vertical barrier in front of Holt. His Panzer IV/70 flooded and remained trapped in the water until captured by the Americans. Clearly Guderian was not a fan of the StuG IV, Jagdpanzer IV or the Panzer IV/70. In his view vital tank output diverted to numerous types of assault gun and tank destroyer production wasted over 3,100 Panzer IVs that would been better employed issued to the panzer divisions.

By March 1943 it was very apparent that the open fighting compartment on the various panzerjäger based on the highly-reliable Panzer 38(t) chassis left the crew simply too vulnerable to both direct and indirect enemy fire. Guderian in his role as Inspector of the Armoured Units called for a light tank destroyer with a lower profile, better armour and crucially overhead protection. This finally led to the design of the Jagdpanzer 38(t) Hetzer für 7.5cm PaK39 which featured a wide hull and angled armour. Guderian recalled:

> On 7 December [1943] it was decided that the full production capacity
> of the old Czech 38-ton tank be switched to tank destroyers, these, to
> be built on Czech tank chassis, and protected by sloping armour plate,

were to mount a recoilless gun and a machine-gun with a curved barrel. They passed their tests very satisfactorily. This tank destroyer was intended to be the basic weapon for the anti-tank battalions of the infantry divisions, and thus the belated answer to my proposals made on March the 9th.

Guderian can only have fumed that nine long months had been wasted while a series of unsatisfactory stopgaps had been rushed to the troops at the front instead of an adequately armoured light tank destroyer. The Hetzer was a completely new and dedicated design employing the 38(t) chassis that created an armoured vehicle, which was unlike any of the previous bodged stopgaps.

This included a much wider hull that took the angled superstructure armour over the top of the tracks and the nose plates forward of the drive sprockets. This made it over a metre longer than the Marder III Ausf M and almost half a metre wider. The Hetzer had a slightly lower profile and most importantly an armoured roof. It was over five tons heavier than the Marder III, so to take the extra weight the eight rubber-tyred road wheels were slightly larger.

The frontal armour on the superstructure, gun mantlet and hull was 60mm while the sides were protected by 20mm. This was a vast improvement on its predecessors but not on the StuG and Jagdpanzer, which enjoyed up to 80mm of armour. However, the Hetzer's armour was much enhanced by its 60–degree angle on the front and 40 degrees on the sides. This meant that it enjoyed the equivalent protection of 120mm of armour on the front. The vehicle also featured a roof-mounted remote-controlled machine gun for close protection. Essentially the infantry was provided with a much-needed miniature version of the Jagdpanther.

Initially the decision to proceed with the vehicle was on the basis that it would have a novel fixed non-recoiling mount for the 75mm PaK39 gun. This was known as the Jagdpanzer 38(t) Starr (inflexible – after the gun mounting). The plan was it would speed up production and recoil would simply be passed through the hull and chassis. Such an innovation would undoubtedly not have added to crew comfort. The practicalities of implementing the design proved a headache and just ten pre-production Starrs were ever built. The installation of the troubled rigid mounting for the PaK39 and the StuH42 was progressively deferred and was overtaken by the end of the war.

In the event the Hetzer went into production with a recoiling gun. Nine of the pre-production Starrs were converted into Hetzers. To overcome the space limitations, the 75mm PaK39 L/48 gun was installed in a compact mounting and offset to the right. This greatly restricted the traverse, permitting just 5 degrees to the left and 11 degrees to the right. It also made the vehicle nose heavy and put extra weight on the right hand suspension. The PaK39 was not fitted with a muzzle brake but firing a solid 6.8kg projectile could cut through 82mm of armour at 1,000m.

BMM commenced initial production of the Hetzer and Skoda took also took it up in July 1944. From April 1944 until the end of the war in May 1945 some 2,584 Hetzers rolled off the production line in Prague. In light of Nazi Germany's failing fortunes this was a quite an achievement. Output was to be ramped up in 1945 with a 1,000 Hetzers every month by mid-year. The compact Hetzer proved ideal for Germany's defensive battles, but the limited traverse on the 75mm gun and the extremely cramped fighting compartment were major drawbacks for the four-man crew.

There were three Hetzer non-anti-tank variants but these were never built in any great quantity. To support the Hetzer units in the field about 170 Bergepanzer 38(t) Hetzer armoured recovery vehicles were constructed. Production in the summer of 1944 was so slow that sixty-four regular Hetzers were converted to a recovery role. Dedicated production was then resumed at the end of the year. The Bergepanzer 38(t) had no gun, a lower superstructure and was open-topped. A tubular crane derrick and a winch were carried in the open fighting compartment. These recovery vehicles were underpowered and therefore struggled with their allotted role.

Two combat variants of the Hetzer were produced at the end of 1944. One consisted of just thirty self-propelled heavy infantry guns known as the 150mm Schweres Infanteriegeschütz 33/2 (sf) au Jagdpanzer 38(t) Hetzer. This used the Bergepanzer 38(t) superstructure, which was raised around the sIG33 150mm gun. These were employed to supplement the exiting Grille 38(t) self-propelled guns.

To support the Ardennes offensive twenty Flammpanzer 38(t) flamethrowers were hastily converted from existing Hetzers. These were created by replacing the 75mm gun with a 14mm Flammenwerfer 41 that had a range of up to 60m. Some 700 litres of fuel were carried internally that provided 87.5 seconds of fire. From a distance the flammpanzer looked like a regular Hetzer as a dummy funnel-shaped barrel was installed over the flame thrower. During the Ardennes offensive Flammpanzer 38(t) served with the 352nd and 353rd Panzer Flamm Companies attached to Army Group G. Most of them subsequently ended up with the XIII SS Corps and were lost in the fighting for the Lower Vosges mountains.

As noted above, the Jagdpanzer 38(t) was not used to equip the panzer battalions, but instead was deployed with the infantry divisions' sturmgeschütz companies that had not been equipped with the ubiquitous StuG assault gun. It served on the Eastern Front and in the West, particularly during the Ardennes offensive. The first combat units equipped with the Hetzer were Panzerjäger Battalions 731 and 743 along with the 15th and 76th Infantry Divisions. After that they were widely distributed. The Hetzer first entered service in the Waffen-SS with the assault gun battalion of the 8th SS Kavallerie Division Florian Geyer, though the deployment of this tank destroyer did little to save the division. It was annihilated in Budapest in February 1945 by the Red Army along with its sister division 22nd Freiwilligen Kavallerie Division der SS Maria Theresa.

In February 1945, just three months before the end of the war, plans were drawn up for the Panzerjäger 38(d) series. This was to have provided a short-term light tank replacement until the E-10 was ready with tank destroyer, anti-aircraft, reconnaissance, armoured personnel and armoured weapons carrier variants. Development of a 75mm-armed self-propelled version was given priority in 1944–5, presumably as a replacement for the Hetzer. The Germans were planning to turn production of the Panzerjäger 38(d) over to the German factories that had produced the Panzer III and IV. The aim was to produce 2,000 a month but with the end of the war the project was abandon.

The Czech-built chassis was deemed so successful that the Germans were planning to continue using it once they had won the war! Plans had been afoot for a new design of 10.5-ton light reconnaissance tank dubbed the T-15 and a 22-ton medium tank known as the T-25. Both were to use a lengthened and widened version of the Skoda 38(t) chassis with sloping armour, thought to have been influenced by the T-34. In light of Germany's crumbling defences neither tank got much beyond the design stage. In late 1944–early 1945 the Wehrmacht were also planning a tracked troop carrier using a stretched 38(t) chassis, but this project was abandoned as well. Once the Red Army had captured Prague production of the Hetzer came to a halt.

One new successor Czech vehicle that almost got off the ground was the Waffentrager self-propelled gun that was to use 38(t) components. Development of this gun carriage with two variants began in 1943 with armament ranging from an 88mm gun to a 150mm howitzer. The drawings for both were ready by March 1945 and moves toward production were being made. It was intended that this would commence in the spring of 1945 with an output of up to 350 vehicles a month. Components were to come from both the 38(t) and 38(d) programmes and once again production would have been turned over to German firms such as Ardelt in Eberswalde.

Chapter 15

Firmly on the Defensive

Whilst the Western Allies dabbled with the tank destroyer concept utilizing the Sherman tank, it was the Soviets who were most impressed by the sturmgeschütz. Employing the T-34 tank chassis the Soviets produced the SU-122 (which was a self-propelled howitzer rather than a true anti-tank weapon), SU-85 and the SU-100 tank destroyers followed by the ISU-122 and ISU-152 on the modified KV tank chassis. In the assault gun role, the Soviets created the SU-76 which married a 76.2mm gun to the chassis of the T-70 light tank. Production of this compact self-propelled gun was only surpassed by the T-34.

The German assault gun requirement arose from a need to provide infantry with an armoured vehicle that could serve as both a mobile artillery support weapon and an anti-tank gun. Increasingly the tank destroyer role took over, especially on the Eastern Front where the German Army had to contend with ever growing numbers of Soviet tanks. On the whole the main task of the StuG was to arm the sturmgeschütz brigades. Not surprisingly most of these were deployed on the Eastern Front. Between 1942 and 1945 there were up to thirty independent assault gun units fighting the Red Army in what became a war of attrition.

In the summer of 1944 Army Group Centre's armoured forces on the Eastern Front included eight independent sturmgeschütz brigades that had recently been upgraded from battalion strength. These were spread out through the component armies. The 3rd Panzer Army had two assault gun formations; the 28th and 245th Sturmgeschütz Brigades assigned to VI and IX Corps respectively. The Fourth Army also had two assault gun brigades; the 185th deployed with the XXXIX Corps and the 190th Light Brigade. Under Second Army's direction was the 237th and 904th Sturmgeschütz Brigades serving with VIII Corps.

Army Group Centre lay directly in the path of Stalin's Operation Bagration, his version of D-Day. It was entirely a defensive formation formed largely from infantry divisions; although it included a panzer army and two panzer corps, it had no whole panzer divisions so crucially lacked tanks. The panzerjäger battalions of the infantry divisions were armed with self-propelled anti-tank guns, all of which were designed for defensive not offensive operations. Army Group Centre mustered just three panzergrenadier divisions and their panzer battalions were equipped with assault guns not tanks. A typical panzergrenadier division consisted of two panzergrenadier regiments, a tank battalion with three batteries of StuGs and a panzerjäger battalion with three companies of self-propelled anti-tank guns and a company of self-propelled anti-aircraft or flak guns. A StuG battery numbered up to fourteen vehicles. An artillery regiment with about four batteries of guns provided fire support.

The 18th Panzergrenadier Division's principal units consisted of the 30th and 51st Panzergrenadier Regiments, 118th Panzer Battalion equipped with sturmgeschütz, 118th Panzerjäger Battalion equipped with self-propelled anti-guns and the 18th Artillery Regiment. Likewise, the 25th Panzergrenadier Division consisted of the 8th Panzer Battalion, 125th Panzerjäger Battalion, 25th Artillery Regiment and 35th and 119th Panzergrenadier Regiments. Panzergrenadier Division Feldherrnhalle with a similar organization had started out as the 60th Motorized Infantry Division; the latter under Generalmajor Hans-Adolf von Arenstorff had been destroyed at Stalingrad.

The veteran 20th Panzer Division was reassigned to Army Group Centre in mid-June 1944 with just a single battalion of panzers. The division comprised a weak panzer regiment, two panzergrenadier regiments, an artillery regiment and a panzerjäger battalion armed with self-propelled guns. At best it could muster two kampfgruppen or battle groups organized around the armoured and infantry formations. As a fighting reserve it was wholly inadequate and could only respond to a single breakthrough or be fatally weakened by being committed piecemeal to various sectors. When the time came Army Group Centre's StuGs and panzerjäger were unable to stop the Red Army breaking through en mass.

In Normandy the StuG equipped many of the tank destroyer battalions of the panzer divisions. This was the case with the 1st and 2nd SS Panzer Divisions. All the other divisions (apart from the 9th and 10th SS which did not have tank destroyer battalions in Normandy) employed the StuG to bolster their obsolete Marders and limited numbers of Jagdpanzer IVs. When the Battle for Normandy commenced the StuG III and the rarer StuG IV were standing in for the Panzer IV in two companies of the 2nd SS, 9th SS and 10th SS Panzer Divisions. These units were mainly equipped with the StuG III Ausf G.

In the case of the 17th SS Panzergrenadier Division, its panzer battalion was equipped with forty-two StuG IIIs while the panzerjäger battalion had a dozen Marder self-propelled anti-tank guns. Initially the independent 902nd Sturmgeschütz Battalion with another thirty-one StuG III was assigned to the 17th SS, but it ended up in southern France with the German Nineteenth Army. Confusingly the numbers for Panzergruppe West controlling German armour in Normandy included tanks, assault guns and tank destroyers, but not light tanks, self-propelled guns or armoured cars.

In Normandy the German infantry divisions' anti-tank battalions largely consisted of towed weapons, but at least six Army panzerjäger battalions were also each equipped with fourteen Marder self-propelled and ten Sturmgeschütz assault guns (these served with the 243rd, 326th 331st, 346th, 352nd and 353rd Infantry Divisions).

The battle for Normandy also involved three independent StuG brigades (12th, 341st and 394th) and two independent StuG battalions (902nd and 1348th). These units were not very strong and only fielded a total of 148 assault guns between them. There were also three independent panzerjäger battalions but one of them only had towed guns. Of the remaining two one was a heavy tank hunter battalion (654th) equipped with limited numbers of the Jagdpanther.

The Jagdpanzer IV developed to replace the StuG only started entering service at the beginning of 1944 and was in the process of replacing the Marder in the tank destroyer battalions. It was rare in Normandy with only about sixty available, these were spread across five panzer divisions meaning each battalion had on average about a dozen.

In the South of France Army Group G lost all its armoured units (with the exception of 11th Panzer Division) including the 341st Sturmgeschütz Brigade. It began as a battalion in December 1943, but was reorganized to brigade strength the following February. By May 1944 it was deployed in southern France near Narbonne. By June it had nineteen StuG III and nine Sturmhaubitze 42s. It remained in southern France for the rest of the month and much of July having been issued a total of thirty-three StuG IIIs and twelve StuH42s. It was despatched to Normandy on 25 July 1944 and was first committed to combat in the Brécey-Avranches area six days later. By the end of August, it had been reduced to just twelve assault guns.

The other independent assault gun units in Normandy did not fair terribly well. For example, 12th Fallschirm Sturmgeschütz Brigade was still forming and undergoing training at the time of D–Day. It appears that it never received its full authorized strength of thirty-one assault guns. By late June 1944 it had just eleven combat ready StuGs and by the end of July could muster seven StuG IIIs and three StuH42s. It is unclear how many of these escaped over the Seine. Brigade 394 had thirty-one StuG IIIs by early August but after seeing combat in the Vire area only managed to save a single StuG from the Falaise pocket.

The 902nd Sturmgeschütz Battalion was fighting in support of the 91st Infantry Division in the Cotentin Peninsula in June 1944 with twenty-one combat-ready StuG IIIs. It escaped encirclement but by early August only had one StuG III and three StuH42s available. In September it was reassigned to Nineteenth Army with ten assault guns. Sturmgeschütz Battalion 1348 went into action with just five assault guns with another five due for delivery. It arrived in Normandy on 6 August 1944 but nothing further is known about its performance.

After Normandy assault guns were involved in Hitler's Ardennes offensive in the winter of 1944–5. While his forces included two whole panzer armies, the German Seventh Army lacked armour except for the 5th Parachute Division's

11th Sturmgeschütz Brigade and the panzer units of the 15th Panzergrenadier Division. Two Normandy veterans that took part in the Ardennes offensive were the 341st and 394th StuG Brigades assigned to Fifteenth Army's LXXX1 and LXXIV Corps respectively. The 394th StuG Brigade was reassigned to Fifth Panzer Army's XLIX Panzer Corps in the New Year.

Like the panzertruppen the sturmartillerie crews produced a number of aces such as Sergeant Richard Schramm of the 202nd Sturmgeschütz Brigade. He was awarded the Knight's Cross in December 1942 for destroying forty-four Soviet armoured fighting vehicles. He was later posted missing presumed dead. Schramm's assault gun was dubbed 'Sea Devil' by its crew. In March 1943 when Guderian requested the 'subordination of all assault artillery to the Inspector General', this was opposed, he recalled, on the grounds 'that the assault artillery was the only weapon which nowadays enabled gunners to win the Knight's Cross'.

Platoon leader Lieutenant Walther Oberloskamp with the 667th Sturmgeschütz Brigade earned the Knight's Cross on 10 May 1943 after scoring forty kills. The Waffen-SS also produced a number of StuG aces. SS–Major Walter Kniep commanded the 2nd StuG Battalion of the 2nd SS Panzer Division, which from 5 July 1943 to 17 January 1944 claimed a total of 129 Soviet tanks. Kniep was also awarded the Knight's Cross.

Sturmartillerie crews had their own battle badges. The General Assault Badge or Allgemeines Sturmabzeichen was instigated in June 1940 and was frequently awarded to self-propelled artillery and anti-tank units. Specifically, it was awarded to personnel involved in three attacks on three different days but did not qualify for the Infantry Assault or Panzer Battle (Panzerkampfabzeichen) badges, i.e. artillery, anti-tank, anti-aircraft, and engineer personnel. The General Assault Badge was a silver oval made in both cast and stamped versions and was very similar in appearance to the Panzer Assault Badge. This was edged by an oak wreath surrounding a crossed bayonet and stick grenade (rather than a panzer) topped by the folded-wing eagle and swastika. After June 1943, along with the Panzer Battle Badge, the General Assault Badge was divided into higher grades with two and three signifying the number of attacks with '25' and '50' cartouches at the bottom of the badge wreath, larger, black eagles and emblems on sliver wreaths. The grade four equated to '75' and '100' larger still with gold wreaths. Other awards were worn in the same manner as the panzer crews, so the Knight's Cross was worn at the throat, the Iron Cross 1st Class pinned to the chest on the left, and the ribbon of the Iron Cross 2nd Class either in the buttonhole, or a ribbon bar on the left breast.

Regardless of Guderian's reservations about the development of the sturmgeschütz and panzerjäger they played a major role in the armoured battles fought by Hitler's Wehrmacht. His perceptions were clouded by inter-service rivalry and the fact that 90 per cent of the assault guns were initially outside his terms of reference due to an undoubtedly deliberate clerical error. Nonetheless, Guderian also appreciated that the infantry should be provided with their own dedicated mobile anti-tank weapons and not have to rely on the panzers to fend off enemy tanks.

The lack of mobility with the infantry's towed anti-tank guns and the inadequacy of the initial top-heavy self-propelled anti-tank guns were only ever partially overcome by the StuG and Jagdpanzer. By the time the Hetzer appeared the tide had already turned against Nazi Germany. Guderian favoured the panzers because he did not want to face the reality that strategically the Panzerwaffe had gone from being a highly decisive offensive arm to a defensive one. In Italy, France and on the Eastern Front the assault gun constituted a major proportion of Hitler's armoured forces.

The Sturmartillerie crews considered themselves the elite of the artillery and by 1944 claimed to have knocked out 20,000 enemy tanks. The surviving number of StuGs by the end of the war showed that they had borne the brunt of the fighting as much as Guderian's panzers. On 10 April 1945 just 1,053 StuG IIIs and 277 StuH 42s were listed as operational.

PART IV

WASTED OPPORTUNITES

Chapter 16

The Last Hurrah

Following the Panzerwaffe's mauling in Normandy, by late 1944 the Panzer IV was in very short supply. As a result of continual battlefield attrition and the disruption caused by Allied bombing, the panzer divisions struggled to field both a battalion of Panzer IVs and a battalion of Panthers. The 2nd and 11th Panzer Divisions and the 2nd SS and 9th SS Panzer Divisions each had two companies of StuG assault guns instead of Panzer IVs; the 9th and 116th Panzer Divisions had no Panzer IVs at all, instead three companies of StuGs. Other divisions had a single battalion of mixed Panzer IVs and Panthers. The second battalion had to be substituted by panzerjäger and sturmgeschütz units.

Prior to Hitler's winter Ardennes offensive, to make up for such shortfalls the 1st SS was supplemented by a battalion of heavy Tiger IIs, while the other divisions had to be brought up to some semblance of strength using StuGs and Jagdpanthers. The 1st SS ended up with a panzer regiment consisting of one battalion of mixed Panzer IVs and Panthers and one of Tigers. The division should also have had twenty-one Panzer IV/70 tank destroyers but its panzerjäger battalion only had ten on the eve of the battle. Nonetheless, a total of almost 140 Panzer IV/70s were available for the Ardennes offensive. The panzer divisions had Jagdpanzer IV and Panzer IV/70 tank destroyers equipping two companies of their panzerjäger battalion, the third company being equipped with towed anti-tank guns.

The 1st SS and 12th SS Panzer Divisions' Ardennes spearhead included 100 Panzer IVs. Two tank companies from 1st SS Panzer consisting of thirty-four Panzer IVs formed Kampfgruppe Peiper that led the daring attack toward Antwerp. The 1st SS also had a number of Flakpanzer IVs, which included Ostwind and Wirbelwind. Some of the latter were involved in the fighting at Stoumont where they acted in support of the infantry.

One knocked-out Panzer IV was photographed north-west of Bastogne. A massive explosion had shattered the glacis plate tearing out the gearbox and differential assembly. The turret had also been blown off and rested on its side vertical to the hull. After the war this much-published image came to epitomise the Battle of the Bulge and the defeat of the panzers in North-west Europe.

In the winter of 1944 Hitler massed the greatest concentration of Panthers for his Ardennes offensive through Belgium. Army Group B had approximately 450 available, likewise the largest concentration of Jagdpanthers was also gathered to take part in the battle for the Ardennes. Fortunately for the Allies the Panther's standoff capability was nullified by the close-quarters combat in the Ardennes. As a result, the Panthers fell victim to bazookas as well as 37mm, 57mm and 75mm anti-tank guns. American artillery fire was also to take its toll. Nonetheless, American Sherman crews had legitimate concerns about the superiority of enemy armour. Opposing the Panther, Panzer Mk IV, Tiger I and Tiger II was the standard American 33-ton M4 Sherman still equipped with the short-barrelled 75mm gun. While the Sherman could fight the Mk IV on roughly equal terms it could only kill a Panther with a shot to the rear or side armour.

The Sherman's only advantages were a greater rate of fire thanks to gyrosta-bilization and power traverse and its slightly better mobility due to its lighter weight. Some Shermans were up-gunned with an improved long-barrelled 76mm high-velocity gun, but these were not available in any great quantities. The Sherman's 75mm gun and the 76mm towed anti-tank guns and those on the tank destroyers were normally ineffective against the Panther's frontal armour. However, experi-enced American crews knew that side or rear shots would deliver a deathblow and that a shot to the Panther's drive sprocket would immobilize it. This though normally involved lying in ambush and needed nerves of steel.

German artillery heralded Hitler's surprise offensive on Saturday, 16 Decem-ber 1944 and for the next five weeks his panzers fought to reach Brussels and Antwerp. This became known as the Battle of the Bulge. While the Panther helped form the backbone of the panzer forces committed to the battle it was also given a very unusual deception role. Five days into the offensive special operations commander SS-Lieutenant Colonel Otto Skorzeny, watching from a hill overlooking the battlefield, witnessed ten Panthers crudely disguised as American tanks from his Panzer Brigade 150 attack along the Warche Valley as part of Operation Griffon. Skorzeny had been personally appointed by Hitler to command Panzer Brigade 150 tasked with capturing the vital Meuse bridges at Amay, Andenne or Huy.

Skorzeny had been summoned to Hitler's Rastenburg HQ on 22 October 1944 and instructed to lead an armoured force of 3,300 men. This was to be no ordinary outfit for they were to pass themselves off as withdrawing American troops fully kitted out with American uniforms, weapons and vehicles. To create an affective illusion that his command was indeed American he needed 15 Sherman tanks, 29 self-propelled guns, 20 armoured cars, 120 trucks, 100 jeeps and 40 motorcycles. Despite the vast numbers of American military vehicles captured by the Germans in the preceding months, Skorzeny found the hard-pressed front-line commands reluctant to give up their precious booty.

Under Operation Rabenhügel, Oberkommando West divided the requisition of equipment for Skorzeny's mission between the three Army Groups in the West. Army Group G was ordered to provide eight American tanks and twenty trucks; Army

Group H was to provide two tanks and fifty jeeps and Army Group B five tanks and thirty jeeps, which were to be delivered to Skorzeny's training area at Grafenwöhr. In the event only seventy-four trucks and fifty-seven jeeps arrived, along with just two Shermans and two American armoured cars. Skorzeny discovered he was the recipient of much worn-out rubbish, as 30 per cent of the vehicles needed repairs and both the Shermans were inoperable. Initially his unit was equipped with five Panthers, five Sturmgeschütz assault guns, six German armoured cars and six armoured personnel carriers. When they finally went into battle they only deployed ten Panthers and five StuGs. There was simply no way to make a Panther look like a Sherman, so Skorzeny's men ingeniously opted to make then look like the Sherman's tank destroyer cousin, the M10 Wolverine, based on a Sherman chassis but with a much more angular hull and turret. To do this the Panthers were disguised with sheet metal, painted olive green and given prominent white five-pointed American recognition stars.

Kampfgruppe Peiper, drawn from 1st SS Panzer Division, consisted of seventy-two Panzer Mk IV and Panthers, about twenty Tiger IIs and twenty-five assault guns. 1st and 2nd Companies of SS-Panzer Regiment 1 forming part of Kampfgruppe Peiper fielded thirty-seven Panthers, largely Ausf Gs, at the beginning of the offensive. It was almost four in the morning on 17 December when the Kampfgruppe advance guard comprising two Panthers and three half-tracks began the advance on Honsfeld, their initial objective. These were followed by four Mk IV flakpanzers armed with 37mm cannon and two other flak vehicles with 20mm quads. The two leading Panthers entered Honsfeld and shot up the equipment of an American unit stationed there. It was not until they emerged the other side that American anti-tank guns engaged them.

Panzer Brigade 150's three battlegroups or Kampfgruppen were assigned to the 1st SS and 12th SS Panzer Divisions and the 12th Volksgrenadier Division. The 1st SS and 12th SS launched the 6th SS Panzer Army's main thrusts. Skorzeny cynically noted that his fake M10s were sufficient to 'deceive very young American troops seeing them at night from very far away'. One, coded B4, under the command of Lieutenant Peter Mandt, led the attack in the direction of Malmédy and hit a mine in front of the railway overpass to the south-west of the town. B5 was disabled at Malmédy by a US bazooka team and another, B10, crashed into the café at La Falize. B7 commanded by Senior Staff Sergeant Bachmann was the only Panther to get as far as the northern bank of the Ambléve. It was brought to a halt by US bazooka fire 50m from the Warche bridge at Malmédy.

Fritz Bayerlein's Panzer Lehr Division was short of tanks and on the night of 15 December he could only muster fifty-seven Panthers and Panzer IVs. To bolster these, he received an assault gun brigade and two battalions of self-propelled tank destroyers. He cobbled together an advanced guard led by a company of Panthers that were to exploit any gains made by the 26th Volksgrenadier Division.

Crossing the Our River posed a problem because of the weight of the Panther. The proposed bridging sites were in a deep river gorge that meant heavy equipment could not be brought up to help the German engineers. Therefore all the bridging equipment had to be manhandled into place which was a slow process. Even when a bridge was completed at Dasburg the approaching panzers found it hard to negotiate the very narrow hairpin turns. Just ten tanks had got over before a tank took the final turn too short, crashed into the bridge and into the river. While most of the crew escaped the unfortunate driver drowned. It would take two hours to repair the damage.

On the morning of 18 December 2nd Panzer's reconnaissance battalion probed the positions of Task Force Rose at Antoniushof, in the early afternoon the Panthers and Panzer IVs supported by panzergrenadiers attacked. The American infantry and artillery were put to flight but the Shermans stayed to fight. Seven Shermans were knocked out and when Captain Lawrence Rose and the survivors attempted to escape they ran into the 116th Panzer Division near Houffalize, ten miles north of Bastogne. Panthers and Panzer IVs equipped with new infra-red night fighting devices overwhelmed Task Force Harper at Fe'itsch.

In the early hours of the 20th eight Panthers led the attack toward Dom Bütgenbach. They were greeted by American artillery. The company commander's Panther was hit and caught fire and three more succumbed to the barrage. When several Panthers broke into the American positions they were illuminated by flares and a 57mm anti-tank gun crew poured four rounds into a Panther causing it to burn; a second Panther received the same treatment. Only a jam on the 57mm prevented the gunners from engaging a third tank, which after losing its commander withdrew.

The day before Christmas at 22.00 Panthers and Panzer IVs led by a captured Sherman from 2nd SS Panzer ran into American tanks on the road to Manhay. The Americans hesitated because elements of the US 3rd and 7th Armored Divisions were holding the line Trois Points–Manhay–Hotton so there were concerns about friendly fire. Panzergrenadiers armed with Panzerfausts swiftly destroyed four Shermans and severely damaged two others. Two Panthers received direct hits but the rest of the column sped through the broken American positions.

At this point panzer ace SS-Sergeant Ernst Barkmann commanding Panther 401 got lost and drove alone onto Highway N15. The highly decorated Barkmann was a veteran of the Eastern Front and Normandy, who along with his unit SS Panzer Regiment 2 had re-equipped with the Panther in early 1944. The experiences of Barkmann and his crew in the Ardennes were typical of the confused and chaotic nature of the fighting there. While experience was invaluable, luck also played its part.

In the darkness Barkmann, assuming his comrades were in front of him, pressed on. Some 50m ahead and to the right he saw a tank with its commander standing in the turret. Assuming it was from the 2nd SS Barkmann drew up to the left-hand side of the tank. Instructing his driver to kill the engine he removed his radio headset. At that point the other commander dropped into his tank and slammed the hatch shut. Then the driver's hatch popped open on the other tank and Barkmann noticed the instrument panel light was not the same as a Panther's (wine red rather than green).

Realizing it was an American-crewed Sherman he ordered his gunner to fire. The gunner traversed only to catch the L/70 gun barrel on the enemy's turret. The impact jammed the Panther's turret. The quick-thinking driver started the engine and backed up a few yards and the gunner slammed a round into the rear of the Sherman. Rumbling past the burning enemy tank Barkmann spotted two more Shermans coming from the forest on the right of the road. These were also dealt with in quick succession. Then rounding a large S-bend Barkmann ran into nine partially dug-in American tanks. He ordered his driver to press through them and for some reason the enemy tanks did not engage. Instead the American crews bailed out.

Barkmann's Panther reached Manhay only to be confronted by three Shermans coming from the direction it needed to take toward Grandmenil and Erezee. Heading north-west he rumbled past yet more enemy tanks that were parked with their crews dismounted. The Americans watched as a Panther roared by, then waking to the danger leapt into their tanks, but as they were nose to tail they could not target Barkmann. The Panther's crew hastily threw out a smoke bomb to cover their escape. Barkmann estimated they passed more than eighty enemy tanks having stumbled into the assembly area for the US 7th Armored Division, as well as the US 82nd Airborne and 75th Infantry Divisions.

The chaos did not end there. An American jeep promptly ran headlong into the Panther which crushed it, but in doing so crashed into a stationary Sherman. The Panther's drive sprocket became entangled in the Sherman's tracks and its engine stalled. The driver restarted the engine and backed up, successfully freeing the Panther. It rolled on past more American vehicles and equipment, but now with growing numbers of Shermans giving chase. Barkmann coolly traversed his turret and knocked out the lead tank; doing this several times he closed off the road behind him. Barkmann and his men finally took shelter in the forest and calmly dismounted to take the morning air and marvel at their luck. At such close quarters Panther 401 could have been destroyed numerous times. As they stood about they could hear Panthers firing from the direction of Manhay. Retracing his path to rejoin their company Barkmann counted twenty American tanks that had surrendered.

After Christmas Hitler's Ardennes offensive very quickly lost momentum especially once the weather cleared and Allied fighter-bombers set about the panzers. In addition, a shortage of fuel proved to be the panzers' Achilles heel.

After the withdrawal of Kampfgruppe Peiper at least fifteen Panthers were left in La Gleize and Stoumont. One of those abandoned in La Gleize was a rare Ausf G produced as a trial vehicle for the new suspension, with the steel-rimmed 'silent-block' wheels that were to be standardized on the Ausf F.

By mid-January 1945 reportedly 282 Panthers had survived the Battle of the Bulge, of which just 97 were listed as operational. When the Allies crossed the Rhine in early 1945 very few Panthers remained in the West, most had already been sent east to take part in Hitler's doomed counteroffensive against the Red Army in Hungary.

About 150 Tiger Is and IIs fought in the Ardennes, deployed in their individual heavy tank battalions supporting the panzer and SS panzer divisions. They were unable to achieve much during the hard fought Battle of the Bulge. Key amongst them was the Tiger II unit Heavy SS-Panzer Battalion 501 assigned to Kampfgruppe Peiper leading the attack in the north. Five Ferdinands also fought to the south of Bastogne, which arrived in time to help cover the German withdrawal.

The battalion was filmed passing through Tondorf on their way to Kampfgruppe Peiper's assembly area and the Tiger IIs certainly looked an imposing and formidable fighting force. Even so, the tanks were still dwarfed by the surrounding houses that lined the narrow streets. They were clear of external storage, though the turrets had been reinforced with the addition of spare track links. The crews looked quietly confident, but then they were posing for the camera.

The Tigers were later photographed at Deidenberg and Kaiserbarracke carrying German paratroops and these images came to epitomise Hitler's powerful Ardennes thrust. They were a symbol of his revived military power with elite troops borne by his very latest panzers; the reality of the battle was to prove somewhat different. They were not to be assigned the Durchbruchwagen role originally envisaged for the Tiger.

As the offensive was essentially a race against time Peiper saw his battalion of cumbersome Tiger IIs as much less value than his Panzer IVs and Panthers. He deployed them at the rear of his attack column, ready to be called forward once they reached the open countryside near the River Meuse. He was being wildly optimistic if he really thought they were ever going to get that far. The road from Ligneuville to Stavlot was, in Peiper's words, suitable for little more than bicycles. Getting them all over the Amblève and Salm proved to be a major problem after the Americans blew up several bridges.

During the early hours of 19 December, masked by dense fog, Peiper's forces pressed on Stoumont west of La Gleize, which was defended by American infantry supported by towed anti-tank guns. They also had two 90mm anti-aircraft guns, which had only just arrived from America. Unfortunately, one gun ended up stuck in a ditch.

Under the covering fog and early morning darkness two Tigers and two Panthers approached the town. Half the panzers were immediately caught in the rear by American bazooka fire and began to burn. One of the remaining Tigers then ran into the remaining 90mm gun, the first round hit its front left sprocket and the second took off most of the gun barrel. Its crew fled. Later in the day American reinforcements including Shermans and a M36 tank destroyer armed with a 90mm gun blocked Peiper's advance at Stoumont Station. The latter had only entered service in late 1944 and proved very successful against the Tiger at long range.

Thwarted at Trois-Ponts, by 21 December Peiper was holding a defensive position around La Gleize. The half-dozen Tiger IIs with his force were deployed on the south-eastern and north-eastern approaches where they had good fields of fire. However, they soon succumbed to heavy bombardment from American artillery and counter-attacks by the US 3rd Armored Division. By the end of the day half the Tigers were out of action. Although another half-dozen operational Tiger IIs were east of Peiper at Stavelot they were unable to get to him as the bridge over the Amblève was down. Tiger 222 was hit by the Americans and abandoned on the southern end of Stavelot Bridge on the 19th. Two more were hit in the rear in the narrow streets.

By 24 December Peiper's battle group had ceased to exist. Tiger 008 had the dubious accolade of being the last operational panzer still on the northern bank of the Amblève between Stavelot and Trois-Ponts. Although the tank carried on fighting it had been immobilized by mechanical trouble. Its crew set it on fire east of Petit-Spai near La Ferme Antoine on Christmas day.

Peiper left seven Tiger IIs in or near La Gleize. Amongst them was Tiger 204, which the Americans tried to drive to the railway station at Spa. Sporting a precautionary white flag it got as far as Ruy before breaking down. Tiger 213 was found in a field near Wérimont Farm at La Gleize and after being restored was eventually placed outside La Gleize Museum.

On Christmas Day Tiger 332 heading for Peiper's abandoned positions was caught by a Sherman firing phosphorus. The crew, thinking they were on fire, bailed out. Tiger 332 was eventually shipped to America. Another three Tigers were left at Stavelot. So ended the Tiger II's less-than-glorious role in the Ardennes offensive. In unfavourable conditions its role as a breakthrough tank had ended in failure.

Chapter 17

To the Bitter End

The Soviets did all they could to counter the Tiger I and II. As General von Mellenthin recalled, they

> produced an improved model of the T-34, and finally in 1944 the massive Stalin tank which gave our Tigers plenty of trouble. The Russian tank designers understand their job thoroughly; they cut out refinements and concentrated on essentials – gun power, armour, and cross-country performance.

In response to the Tiger the Red Army also produced the SU-152. Redesigning the KV-1 chassis, it was armed with a massive 152mm howitzer that could be used in an anti-tank role. Fortunately for the Germans only twelve were available for Kursk though they accounted for twelve Tigers and seven Ferdinands. As a result it gained the reputation as a 'Beast' killer. The mighty ISU-152 appeared in late 1943 as a successor to the SU-152, which also gained the nickname 'Animal' or 'Beast' killer. Likewise armed with a powerful 152mm howitzer they were grouped into independent heavy assault gun regiments and brigades, which were attached to the tank corps in a support role. By the time of Operation Bagration in the summer of 1944 the Red Army had 295 ISU-152s and ISU-122s.

Heavy SS-Panzer Battalion 502 was refitted at Sennelager, while the 503's 1st Company moved to Bentfeld, the 2nd at Eilsen and the 3rd to Hovelhof. The Panzer Training and Replacement Battalion 500 at Paderborn provided much need crews and between 19–22 September 1944 503 received forty-five new Tiger IIs. The following month it was shipped to Hungary and subordinated to the Feldherrnhalle Panzer Corps and assisted in the futile defence of Budapest.

The Tiger II's debut on the Eastern Front did not go terribly well. Elements of Heavy SS-Panzer Battalion 501 first went into battle with the Tiger II on 12 August 1944 in the face of the Soviet Lvov-Sandomierz offensive near Baranów. In this action under Guards Lieutenant Os'kin, a single Soviet T-34/85 from the 53rd Guards Tank Brigade knocked out three Tiger IIs by hitting their side armour from an ambush position. In addition, eleven IS-2 heavy tanks of the Soviet 71st Heavy Tank Regiment, took on fourteen Tiger IIs, knocking out four and damaging another seven, for the loss of three IS-2s.

Those Tiger IIs captured near Sandomierz were soon tested by the Soviets at Kubinka. The range trials revealed that they were less of a threat than the much lighter and cheaper Tiger I, and the Soviets were puzzled at the German decision to produce them. Tests showed that the transmission and suspension broke down regularly and the engine was likely to overheat. They also discovered surprising deficiencies in the Tiger II's armour: not only was the metal poor quality, so was the welding. As a result, even when shells did not penetrate the armour, there was a large amount of spalling, and when struck by heavier shells the armour plating cracked at the welds.

Two months later, on 15 October 1944, Tiger IIs of Heavy Panzer Battalion 503 were involved in Operation Panzerfaust, during which Otto Skorzeny seized Budapest to stop Hungary defecting to the Soviet camp. In subsequent fighting in Hungary the battalion accounted for 121 Soviet tanks, 244 anti-tank guns and artillery pieces, five aircraft and a train! The 503 lost twenty-five Tiger IIs; ten were knocked out and caught fire, thirteen were destroyed by their own crews to prevent them from falling into enemy hands and two were sent back to Vienna to be overhauled.

After taking part in Hitler's ill-fated Ardennes offensive that winter, the mighty Tiger II or Königstiger was also involved in the last major offensive of the war on the Eastern Front. Heavy Panzer Battalion 503, having refitted with Tiger IIs in France and after fighting in Normandy, moved into Hungary. Similarly, the 509 refitted with Tiger IIs in Germany in late 1944 and moved into Hungary in January 1945.

Reportedly 287 Panzer IVs were lost on the Eastern Front during January 1945. Within months the Red Army was poised before the very gates of Berlin and victory. By this stage the German armies tasked with protecting the capital had very few panzers left. In total it is estimated that the Red Army accounted for 6,150 Panzer IVs or about 75 per cent of all Panzer IV losses during the war.

By January 1945 Heavy Panzer Battalion 503 was back in Germany to take part in one of Hitler's last ill-fated counter-attacks. Split in two, one group was sent to the Arnswalde-Pomerania area and the other to the Landsberg-Kustrin area. The first group under Lieutenant Colonel Fritz Herzig, along with a panzer support battalion, were trapped in Arnswalde on 4 February. Herzig's Tiger II could easily have broken out but that would have meant abandoning everyone else to their fate at the hands of the Russians. Three days later Second Lieutenant Fritz Kauerauf with three Tiger IIs set out from Stargard for Arsnwalde via Reetz. Instead he became involved with the 11th SS trying to stop the Russian advance to the Baltic.

Initially they made good progress on the first day of the attack, penetrating the Soviet envelopment of Arnswalde and rescuing the German garrison. The 503's Tiger IIs were instrumental in holding the corridor open as the wounded and civilians were evacuated and fresh troops sent in. During the fighting in the Danzig-Gotenhafen area Tigers of the 503 destroyed sixty-four Soviet tanks. The 10th SS and 503's short-lived success was to swiftly come to halt. The Tigers could do little once the 2nd Soviet Guards Tank Army brought up heavy Joseph Stalin tanks.

The 60th Panzergrenadier Division Feldherrnhalle with a handful of Tiger IIs, 13th Panzer Division and the IX SS Corps (8th SS and 22nd SS Kavallerie Divisions) were trapped in the Hungarian capital Budapest, while the 18th SS Panzergrenadier Division was forced to retreat. In the bitter fighting for the city the Tiger IIs were to become little more than glorified pillboxes.

Hitler wanted to strike between Lake Balaton and Lake Velencze south-west of Budapest. Dubbed Operation Spring Awakening, Hitler believed if the Soviets were caught by surprise he could throw them back. The 6th SS Panzer Army fielded two heavy tank battalions equipped with about sixty Tiger IIs. On the morning of 6 March 1945, after a 30-minute artillery bombardment supported by air attacks, the Germans crashed into the Soviet defences. The deployment of the mighty Tiger IIs proved a disaster: there was no frost and the mud immediately claimed fifteen tanks that sank up to their turrets. Wherever the remaining Tiger IIs went they dealt with their opponents with impunity, but they were heavy, mechanically unreliable and never available in sufficient numbers.

Heavy Panzer Battalion 503 had been issued with thirty-six Tiger IIs in February 1945, but by mid-March it had just ten, which were moved to defend the Oder. Six Tiger IIs of the 503 were involved in the final death throes of Berlin. During January to April 1945 the 503 claimed 500 enemy tanks for the loss of 45 Tiger IIs, most of which were abandoned after they broke down. On 18 April they knocked out sixty-four Russian tanks for the loss of one tank, before withdrawing on the German capital. Five were still operational by 1 May and they attempted to breakout during the night, but did not get far. After destroying thirty-nine Russian tanks on the streets of Berlin, the last Tiger II was blown up by its crew.

Heavy Panzer Battalion 502 fared little better. On 5 January 1945 it was renumbered 511, and on 31 March 1945 the crews of 3rd Company Battalions 510 and 511 collected the last thirteen Tiger IIs directly from the Henschel factory. They also received three second-hand Tiger IIs from the Waffenamt at Senneläger and one from Northeim. The delay in the delivery of Tiger IIs to Battalion 502 due to heavy air attacks on the Henschel plant in Kassel meant that the battalion did not move to the Oder between Frankfurt and Kustrin until early March and then only with twenty-nine tanks. Thrown into an attack near Sachsenheim, the Russians fell back and the Tigers soon outstripped the other panzers. On 26–27 March the battalion was involved in an attempt to break through to Kustrin, and it ended its days with the Ninth Army in the Halbe Pocket.

Panzer driver Lance Corporal Lothar Tiby witnessed the end of the Tigers on 2 May 1945:

> The heavy fighting against a vastly superior force lasted all day. There were very high losses of vehicles, infantry, and civilians on our side and very high losses of personnel carriers and infantry on the Russian side due to the action of the two Panzers. During a renewed attempt to break through, Schafer's Panzer took a direct hit, two men dead, the rest seriously wounded. A further attempt to break out was no longer possible. Our vehicle, the last Panzer of the battalion, was destroyed.

Chapter 18

No Wonder Weapon

In November 1940 the production target for the Panzer III was set at 108 per month. After the attack on the Soviet Union and the decision to increase the Panzerwaffe to thirty-six panzer divisions, it was decided that 7,992 Panzer IIIs were required. This target was never met, with around 6,100 produced, compared to 8,500 Panzer IVs, almost 6,000 Panzer Vs (Panther) and 1,800 Panzer VIs (Tiger I and II). However, about 10,300 Panzer III chassis were given over to assault gun production. This means well over 16,400 Panzer IIIs and variants were built compared to 13,400 Panzer IVs and variants. This clearly made the Panzer III Hitler's most numerous tank type, even if the Panzer IV did prove to be the best German gun tank of the Second World War.

On closer inspection it soon becomes apparent that the Tiger's reputation is built upon its quite remarkable tactical success and no more. There can be no denying that there were simply too few Tiger Is and even fewer Tiger IIs to make a difference to the outcome of the war. Furthermore, the Tiger was designed as a heavy breakthrough tank and yet ended up being used in environments that did not play to its strengths and increasingly in a defensive role. All the Tiger did was help slow down what after the summer of 1944 became inevitable defeat for Nazi Germany. If Hitler's factories had had the wherewithal to gear up to produce just Tiger tanks, then the Second World War might have gone very differently. The reality is that they were never in a position to do so.

For a long time, the Panther was described as the best tank of the Second World War. Certainly it was a vast improvement on the Tiger I which although a tank killer par excellence was costly, time-consuming to build and ultimately very unwieldy on the battlefield. Most notably the Panther's 75mm gun was much better than the one installed in the Panzer IV. Also the Panther's gun had better penetrating power than the Tiger's 88mm KwK36 L/56 gun because of its higher muzzle velocity.

While the Panther had a huge advantage thanks to its excellent main armament, in comparison to the T-34 in terms of reliability, armour protection and mobility it was found wanting. It was the T-34 that helped Stalin seize the operational initiative in Ukraine and Byelorussia, whereas the Panther singularly failed Hitler. Mikhail Koshkin ensured that the Red Army had a tank that by 1943 was easy to produce, and had better mobility and crucially was reliable in all conditions.

In contrast the heavy Tiger and medium Panther had to move up to their operational areas by train or face continual mechanical breakdowns. Trains were always vulnerable to air attack and sabotage. From 1941 Guderian had wanted a panzer with superior mobility to the T-34 but he did not get it. MAN's engineers had designed the chassis and running gear for a 24-ton tank which ended up weighing 45 tons, with predictable results. The severely strained engine and transmission kept failing. The Panther units at Kursk were beset with what were called 'teething troubles' but in reality these actually afflicted the Panther throughout much of its operational life.

The 75mm KwK40 L/43 gun on the Panzer IV Ausf F2 could easily kill the T-34. The Panther's 75mm KwK42 L/70 anti-tank gun was an even more formidable weapon and firing standard armour-piercing could penetrate 111mm of armour at 1,000m, i.e. far thicker armour than on any Soviet tank. The improved tungsten-cored Panzergranate 40/42 round could penetrate 150mm of armour at 1,000m. This meant that the Panther was easily capable of killing a T-34 at 800m while from the side it could manage this at three times the range.

Well-trained and experienced crews were capable of knocking out tanks at even greater ranges, though commanders usually forbade engaging to avoid wasting ammunition. Both the L/70 and L/56 could penetrate targets out to 2,000m, but at such distances accuracy became a problem. While the L/70 ensured the Panther could kill enemy tanks at far greater distances and easily outgunned the T-34, this sole advantage came at a price that was reflected in the Panther's overall performance. The larger L/70 compared to the L/43 meant a bigger turret, which needed a wider hull that was heavier and reduced mobility, thereby straining the drive train.

This stand-off capability meant it was fatal for Soviet tanks to engage the Tiger and the Panther in the open. The T-34's 76.2mm gun could penetrate the Panther's side armour out to 1,000m but could only penetrate the glacis armour at 300m and could not overcome the turret frontal armour. An improved Soviet armour-piercing round was not introduced until October 1943, but then it could only damage the Panther's frontal armour at ranges under 100m. Although the Panther's frontal armour was on par with the Tiger's, its side armour was little better than that of the Panzer IV.

The T-34's TMFD gunner's sight was inferior to the Panther's TFZ12 sight, as it had a narrower field of view and poorer magnification. However, the T-34 had quicker reaction times thanks to its turret traverse. The T-34/76 could rotate at 30 degrees per second, giving it a full rotation in 12 seconds which crucially was five times faster than the Panther Ausf D and 50 per cent faster that the Ausf A. This meant once the T-34 had closed on the Panther its gunner could redirect fire much faster. Likewise, the turret on the M4 Sherman could be fully rotated in 15 seconds, giving it the same advantage over the Panther in close-quarters fighting.

For both the T-34 and Sherman it was imperative they closed with the Panther as quickly as possible.

Soviet gunners tended to be trigger-happy and often with good reason. The net result was that they regularly fired half their ammunition in a single action whereas their German counterparts had to be more conservative as they could not guarantee timely reloads. The T-34/76 Model 1943 typically carried seventy-five high explosive-fragmentation and twenty-five high explosive-armour-piercing rounds (this included four tungsten-cored rounds after October 1943). The Panther normally carried an even mix of AP and HE.

In armoured warfare mobility is as important as firepower. Thanks to their rivalry, German panzer designers at Daimler-Benz and MAN had chosen to ignore the T-34's fundamental design attributes. Whereas the T-34 was a 30-ton tank with a less flammable diesel engine and rear-wheel drive, the Panther weighed in at 45 tons with a highly-flammable petrol engine and vulnerable front wheel drive. In the Ausf D the two fuel pumps were prone to leaks that caused serious engine fires. The T-34's uncomplicated Christie suspension was also ignored in favour of the complex interleaved road wheel running gear that was easily fouled on the Eastern Front.

Although the Panther had lower ground pressure and a better road speed, especially once the T-34/85 appeared with the much heavier turret, the Panther could only move faster once it was in seventh gear – a difficult task in combat conditions. In third gear the T-34 could rumble along at 29km/hr (18mph) while the Panther could only manage 13km/hr (8mph). Added to this the Ausf D and A required almost four times as much fuel as a T-34 to cover 1km. Such poor fuel efficiency was clearly a major problem as Germany began to feel the squeeze on its oil supplies and the Allies enjoyed ever growing air superiority. Such shortages proved fatal in the Ardennes.

Guderian knew that the Panther and Tiger were too little, too late and were simply not good enough. After the war he said:

> Thus the T-34 tank was superior to the German tanks in tracks, in motors, in armour and in gun, but inferior in optics and radio and it had no turret [cupola] for the tank commander with all-round sight. When – in 1943 – the German Panther and Tiger tanks appeared on the battlefields, the superiority passed again to the Germans, but it applied only to a single tank, and not to the quantity. The Russians produced their T-34 tanks without modifications in great series, while Hitler could not be prevented from perpetually changing the types, thus causing repeated reductions of the series.

The final model Panther designed by Daimler-Benz never went into production, though at least one prototype was completed along with eight hulls in 1945. In an attempt to counter shot penetration under the wide gun mantlet, it was decided to reduce the turret's frontal area while still having the same size turret ring. Daimler-Benz was instructed to produce a 'Schmal' or narrow Panther turret that could be installed on the proposed Ausf F and the Panther II. This move belatedly acknowledged the superiority of the narrow-fronted T-34 turret.

It also indicates that the modifications to the curved lower edge of the mantlet on the Ausf G were not entirely successful. In fact, the flat front may have aggravated the problem. The Panther's turret front presented a large target and numerous Panthers were photographed with shot damage and penetration holes on the mantlet. Even if the enemy rounds did not penetrate the armour plate the resulting shrapnel could damage the turret traverse, the barrel and the hull hatches.

Dr Wunderlich, assisted by a Waffenprufamt 6 gunnery expert Colonel Henrici, directed the new turret development. This proved to be successful, although it had the same ring diameter as the old turret, it had 30 per cent more armour plate and took 30 per cent less time to build. A single prototype turret armed with the KwK42/1 L/70 was produced and there were plans to develop mounts that could take a proposed lengthened L/100 version of the same weapon and the powerful 88mm KwK with a stabilized sight. The gun mantlet was conical (known as Saukopf or pig's head) with rangefinder bulges in the turret sides.

Other changes included increasing the hull roof armour from 16mm to 25mm. This was a shortcoming with all three models of Panther. For reasons that are not entirely clear the hull machine-gun mount was designed to take the MP44 assault rifle rather than the normal machine gun. The Ausf F was also designed so that it could be easily converted to a command tank whilst in the field. Despite these alterations the tank weighed 45 tons.

Indications are that this was a finally-perfected version of the original Ausf D. Certainly it would have provided a better weapon of war than the bulky 68-ton Tiger II. In the event the Ausf F was never mass-produced as conditions were such that Hitler's panzer factories had to press on producing already-proven tanks such as the Panzer IV. In addition, it was probably felt there was little point in continuing with the Ausf F when the successor Panther II was already on the drawing board.

Once the Tiger and Panther tanks were in production German designers began to plan for a new generation of panzers that could draw on lessons from all the existing designs. In light of the heavy fighting on the Eastern Front, reducing maintenance, economizing on materials and simplifying production became paramount. In addition a key request from the Panzertruppen and their mechanics was that components be standardized as much as possible, which would reduce the need for large stocks of differing spare parts and would greatly speed up getting repaired panzers back into the field.

Waffenprufamt 6 instructed MAN and Henschel in February 1943 to come up with improvements for the Panther and the Tiger ensuring interchangeability of parts. At the time the main priority was coming up with a replacement for the less than perfect and very expensive Tiger, so Henschel pushed ahead with the Tiger II that went into production at the end of 1943. Kniepkampf was in overall charge of both the Tiger II and improved Panther projects.

In the meantime, the enhanced Panther or Panther II was to have a similar hull to the existing Panther, but using the same interleaved all-steel resilient wheels as the Tiger II. It was to feature an improved gearbox and transmission, the AK7-400 and mechanical parts including brakes identical to those of the Tiger II. The hull top armour was doubled to 25mm and the ball mount was altered to take the MG42.

Plans for the Panther's successor envisaged an up-armoured 47-ton variant with 100mm frontal armour and 60mm side armour. The Panther II design was conducted alongside the Tiger II, which led to unwelcome delays with the latter. The need to produce as many Panther Ausf G as possible meant that the Panther II was not seen as a priority, but two prototypes were ordered in 1944 and one featuring a Panther I turret was delivered by MAN in 1945. At 55 tons its running gear utilized the steel-rimmed wheels, drive and idler sprockets of the Tiger II. It featured only seven wheel stations either side. However, by the time the war ended the Panther II design had already been superseded by the E-50 and E-75 tank projects.

For the Panther II chassis a panzerjäger self-propelled variant was proposed using a massive 128mm gun, the largest possible weapon that could be installed on it. Gerät 5-12 was Krupp's design for a 128mm K43 on the Panther chassis, while Gerät 5-1213 was Rheinmetall's design for the same weapon on the Panther. None of these got beyond the drawing-board and are again indicative of how Hitler was happy to let his designers waste time and resources dreaming up new flights of fancy.

With the advent of the Tiger I Hitler allowed his designers to abandon the balance of firepower, armour and mobility by placing greater emphasis on firepower and armour. Certainly the armour and the gun were first class. While the Tiger's speed was not a real problem its weight certainly was, as it put a strain on the drive train, gearbox and engine. It also meant that if it got bogged down or if it was flipped over it was very difficult to recover. Bridges struggled to withstand the burden of it and while the Tiger could physically demolish a house unscratched it could easily drop through the floor. Tiger tanks were regularly captured because they were too heavy to recover from the battlefield.

In North Africa the British Army had marvelled at Rommel's tank recovery capabilities and his supporting field maintenance depots. Time and time again he was able to rescue damaged and stranded tanks and get them back into action. This could make all the difference between winning and losing a tank battle. During the initial stages of the Normandy campaign and the fighting on the Eastern Front German recovery rates were still good, but the Tiger had practically no dedicated recovery infrastructure or specialized vehicles to help. The German armed forces lacked heavy tank transporters, which meant the Tiger had to get to the front under its own power and often broke down before it ever got there. Due to the lack of purpose-built recovery vehicles three heavy-duty half-tracks were needed to budge an immobilized Tiger. Using another Tiger inevitably led to its engine overheating. If the tank's tracks overrode the sprockets and jammed it took two Tigers to tow the disabled one. Getting the broken track off was also a major headache for the crews and their mechanics. None of these time-consuming activities were really possible while under fire. All the crew could do if their Tiger was disabled and they survived was bale out.

The Tiger II suffered the same problems, especially where the drive train was concerned. Nonetheless, strenuous efforts were made to address many of the Tiger II's problems. Notably its availability became almost as good as that of the Panzer IV and for its size its agility was also quite good. In contrast the Jagdtiger proved to be pretty much an unmitigated disaster. At almost 72 tons it was the heaviest armoured fighting vehicle of the Second World War. It was too immobile and was simply abandoned by its poorly-trained crews at the roadside. To be fair, although dubbed a hunting tank, it was not a tank at all but a tank destroyer in the same mould as the German Army dedicated anti-tank assault guns and self-propelled guns. The French tank museum at Saumur has the only running Tiger II and the Tank Museum at Bovington has one of the few remaining Jagdtigers.

The 60-ton Tiger I and 70-ton Tiger II were not to have been the end of the heavy tank story. Up until the summer of 1944 Hitler had plans for a successor tank that would have been at least twice the weight and with a gun twice as big. While the Tiger series set the trend for tanks sporting ever larger anti-tank weapons and thicker armour, their legacy was actually quite short-lived. Ultimately there is a limit in the weight to armament ratio that can be achieved with tanks. Certainly the Tiger I and II were great successes compared to Hitler's more hare-brained schemes. No other armies ever followed up on his flirtation with super-heavy tanks such as the proposed Panzer VII Löwe and Panzer VIII Maus.

The Löwe never got any further than a single prototype chassis and in the case of the enormous Maus its ridiculous weight of almost 200 tons ensured it never went into production. Hitler had wanted 150 of the things. Likewise, the 140-ton E-100 never came to fruition. The latter drawing on the Tiger series would have essentially looked like a scaled-up Tiger II. The plan was that the Maus would be armed with a 128mm gun and the E100 with a 150mm gun. Similarly plans for a Tiger II self-propelled gun got no further than a prototype chassis at the very end of the war.

Where the Maus was concerned Hitler had completely lost the plot, as it would have fallen through almost every single bridge it tried to cross. Making it submersible is unlikely to have solved the problem. Europe's mighty rivers would have made short work of it. Had it seen the light of day its fate on the battlefield would have been similar to that of the Soviet KV and T-35. Wasting design and production effort on the Maus and E-100, two separate and competing heavy tanks, at such a crucial stage of the war was inexcusable – but that was Hitler's way of doing things, as witnessed during his development of the Tiger I, with both Henschel and Porsche vying for the contract. It is likely that these super-heavy tanks would have been just as burdensome to build as the Tiger I and II. At a time when he was losing the tank production war even he came to his senses.

These projects are quite remarkable when you consider that German tank development and theories for their use were so radical in 1940–1. Yet between 1942–5, despite their wealth of experience, it seemed as if panzer development was going backwards, mobility having increasingly been sacrificed for firepower. If Hitler had had his way, the Tiger series would have been just the tip of the proverbial iceberg. To what end is difficult to fathom, but of course by 1944 Hitler was increasingly desperate to fend off the encroaching Red Army and its proven T-34. Hitler was largely on his own in his conviction that heavy tanks were a good thing. The Soviets initially abandoned heavy tanks after their unsuccessful T-35 and KV proved to be lumbering liabilities in the face of the Nazi Blitzkrieg. The British TOG, A33 and Tortoise and American M6 and T-28 also proved to be developmental dead ends. They were all deemed to be of extremely limited tactical value. Even Hitler finally called a halt to the development of his super-heavy tanks in 1944, though his designers continued to tinker with them until the very end of the war. The two Maus prototypes were unceremoniously blown up at Kummersdorf. The only heavy tanks to appear in the closing days of the Second World War were the American M26 Pershing and Soviet Joseph Stalin and both proved equal to the Tiger. However, their post-war service was very limited.

Even if the design limitations could have been overcome the concept of a Durchbruchwagen or heavy breakthrough tank was a luxury that armies could ill-afford. Only the Soviet IS-2, which went into action in 1944 armed with a 122mm gun and was lighter than the Tiger, was employed in a breakthrough role. Most modern armies settled for a main battle tank in the 60-ton range with a gun of around 125mm calibre.

Modern tanks are very costly to build and few nations have the desire or need to deploy more than one tank type. What is needed is a good all-rounder. Nonetheless, the public myth that the Tiger was some sort of super tank remains undiminished. Such is the enduring fascination with it that in 2011 a Russian movie production company built an exact replica of a Tiger I from scratch – clearly cost was no object. In the UK the imposing presence of the restored Tiger 131 and the Tiger II at the British Tank Museum as always remain major crowd-pleasers.

The Panzer IV proved to be the one constant in the Panzerwaffe's armoury during the Second World War. Like the T-34 it served throughout the conflict, although it was not built in sufficient numbers and up-gunned until late 1942 and early 1943 by which time it was too late. Hitler's hopes that he could step up production of the technically superior Panther and Tiger tanks never came to fruition because they were over engineered and therefore difficult to mass-produce.

The Panzer IV appeared in ten different models (with three different guns) as well as a dozen different armoured fighting vehicles, whereas the T-34 essentially comprised two – the T-34/76 and T-34/85 (though to be fair there were five and three production models respectively of each as well as half a dozen AFV variants). To put the Panzer IVs contribution in perspective, 8,500 were built compared with 55,000 T-34s. Nonetheless it proved to be one of the key, if not best, panzers of the Second World War and was Hitler's rock.

The Panzer IV proved to be quite a remarkable weapon. The Panzerwaffe recognized it for what it was – a robust and durable design. As a result, it was the only German tank to remain in continuous production throughout the war, and was in production longer than any Allied tank. It was only rivalled by the Soviet T-34, which also stayed in production throughout. However, T-34 mass production did not commence until mid-1940 giving the Panzer IV a slight lead. In its favour the T-34 was almost impervious to the standard German 37mm and 50mm anti-tank guns, and of the Panzer III and IV, it outclassed the former in all respects and the latter in all except gun power where the up-gunned variants equalled it.

Due to the urgent need to find a counter to Soviet tank designs, production of the Panzer IV was in part marred by wasteful experimentation. This was because of Hitler's inability to standardize his tank force and settle on a single utilitarian design. He struggled with quality over quantity. For example, in October 1942 just 100 Mk IVs were built against about 900 T-34s. From spring 1942 to the summer just over 1,800 of the vastly-improved Ausf F2 and G were built. It was not enough and many of them were swallowed up as combat replacements. In a similar timeframe from spring 1943 to the summer of 1944 production was finally ramped up, with almost 3,800 Ausf H, but after that production declined as the chassis was diverted to tank destroyers. The Panzer IV and indeed the Panther and Tiger simply could not compete with the vast numbers of T-34s coming out of Stalin's factories.

Nonetheless, the Panzer IV accounted for over a third of German wartime tank production, making it the most widely-used tank of the war. It saw combat with the panzer divisions in all theatres of operation including Poland, France, the Balkans, North Africa, Russia, Italy and North-west Europe. Manufacture of the

Panzer IV easily outstripped that of the overrated Tiger and Panther combined. These totalled around 1,800 and 6,000 respectively.

Hitler had to maintain Panzer IV production because of the German Army constant urgent need for serviceable tanks. This prevented him from switching solely to the Panther and Tiger; however, this is certainly no reflection on the excellent and basic design of the Panzer IV. Both the Panther and Tiger were labour intensive and while they had exceedingly good anti-tank guns were often mechanically unreliable. Their weight strained the transmission and drive train and made them very difficult to recover. Once swamped by enemy tanks, the Panther and Tiger's long-range stand-off kill capability was completely nullified. Crucially the Panzer IV was much more reliable than both of them and at half their weight was easier to recover and repair. Like its key adversary the T-34, the Panzer IV's design ensured that it could be regularly upgraded. American and British tanks did not offer such flexibility – the Sherman and Cromwell are prime examples of this very serious shortcoming.

Likewise, the size of the Panther and the Tiger proved a problem, making them easier targets. General von Manteuffel said the Panther 'would have been close to ideal' but for its high and bulky silhouette. The Tiger was almost 4m wide and 3m high, the Panther 3.5m wide and 3m high. The Panzer IV measured in at 2.8m and 2.7m (which included a bulkier cupola) respectively. All these faults it might be argued permit the Panzer IV to steal the laurels as the best German tank of the Second World War.

APPENDICES

APPENDICES

Panzer, Assault Gun and Tank Destroyer Production

Panzers	No.	Manufactured
Panzerkampfwagen I	1,563	1938–42
Panzerkampfwagen II	1,814	1938–42
Panzerkampfwagen III	6,157	1938–43
Panzerkampfwagen IV	8,544	1938–45
Panzerkampfwagen V Panther	5,976	1943–5
Panzerkampfwagen VI Ausf E Tiger I	1,354	1942–4
Panzerkampfwagen VI Ausf B Tiger II	489	1944–5
Total:	**25,897**	1938–45

Assault Guns	No.	Manufactured
Sturmgeschütz III 7.5cm L/24	822	1940–2
Sturmgeschütz III 7.5cm L/43 & L/48	8,587	1942–5
Sturmgeschütz IV	1,108	1943–5
Total:	**10,517**	1940–5

Assault Artillery	No.	Manufactured
Sturminfanteriegeschütz 33B	24	1941–2
10.5cm Sturmhaubitze	1,212	1942–5
Sturmpanzer IV	298	1943–5
Total:	**1,534**	1941–5

Tank Destroyers	No.	Manufactured
Pz Jag Ferdinand	90	1943
Jagdpanzer IV	769	1944
Panzer IV/70(V)	930	1944–5
Panzer IV/70(A)	278	1944–5
Jagdpanther	392	1944–5
Jagdtiger	77	1944–5
Total:	**2,536**	1943–5

Appendix B

Panzer and Panzergrenadier Divisions

Panzer Divisions

Division	Formed
1st Panzer Division	Weimar 15 October 1935 from 1st Kavallerie Division
2nd Panzer Division	Wurzburg 15 October 1935
3rd Panzer Division	Wunsdorf, Berlin 15 October 1935
4th Panzer Division	Wurzburg 10 November 1938
5th Panzer Division	Opplen 24 November 1938
6th Panzer Division	Wuppertal 18 October 1939 from 1st Light Division
7th Panzer Division	Gera 18 October 1939 from 2nd Light Division
8th Panzer Division	Cottbus 16 October 1939 from 3rd Light Division
9th Panzer Division	3 January 1940 from 4th Light Division
10th Panzer Division	Czechoslovakia April 1939
11th Panzer Division	1 August 1940
12th Panzer Division	Stettin 5 October 1940 from 2nd Infantry Division
13th Panzer Division	Austria 11 October 1940 from 13th Infantry Division
14th Panzer Division	15 August 1940 from 4th Infantry Division
15th Panzer Division	1 November 1940 from 33rd Infantry Division
16th Panzer Division	1 November 1940 from 16th Infantry Division
17th Panzer Division	1 November 1940 from 27th Infantry Division
18th Panzer Division	26 October 1940 from 4th & 14th Infantry Divisions

19th Panzer Division	1 November 1940 from 19th Infantry Division
20th Panzer Division	15 October 1940 from 19th Infantry Division
21st Panzer Division	1 August 1941 from 5th Light & 3rd Panzer Divisions
22nd Panzer Division	France 25 September 1941
23rd Panzer Division	France September 1941
24th Panzer Division	Stablack 28 November 1941 from 1st Kavallerie Division
25th Panzer Division	Eberswalde 25 February 1942
26th Panzer Division	Belgium 14 September 1942 from 23rd Infantry Division
27th Panzer Division	France/Russia 1 October 1942 from 22nd Panzer Division
116th Panzer Division	France 28 March 1944 from 116th Panzergrenadier Division
Panzer Lehr Division	Potsdam November 1943
Panzer Division Grossdeutschland	Formed as a panzergrenadier division in May 1942
Führer-Begleit Division	Upgraded from brigade strength January 1945
Führer Grenadier Division	Upgraded from brigade strength January 1945
Fallschirm Panzer Division Hermann Göring	Luftwaffe unit that came under Army control in 1943

Reserve Panzer Divisions

Division	Formed
155th Reserve Panzer Division	Absorbed by 9th Panzer Division April 1944
179th Reserve Panzer Division	Absorbed by 116th Panzer Division May 1944
233rd Reserve Panzer Division	Re-designated 233rd Panzer Division April 1945
273rd Reserve Panzer Division	Absorbed by 10th Panzergrenadier Division and 11th Panzer Division in March and May 1944 respectively

Other Panzer Divisions

Various ad hoc divisions were formed in early 1945 from training and reserve units:

Division	Formed
Panzer Division Clausewitz	Elements of Panzer Division Grossdeutschland, Putlos Panzer School & other units
Panzer Division Courland	Elements of 14th Panzer Division
Panzer Division Donau	Training units
Panzer Division Feldherrnhalle 2	Elements of 13th Panzer Division & 60th Panzergrenadier Division Feldherrnhalle
Panzer Division Holstein	Elements of 233rd Reserve Panzer Division, used to reform 18th Panzergrenadier Division
Panzer Division Juterborg	Absorbed by 16th Panzer Division in March 1945
Panzer Division Kurland	Elements of 14th Panzer Division
Panzer Division Kurmark	From Kampfgruppe Langkeit January 1945
Panzer Division Munchenberg	Elements of 1st SS Panzer Division
Panzer Division Nibelungen	Elements of 38th SS Grenadier Division
Panzer Division Norwegen	Formed August 1943 from elements of 25th Panzer Division, absorbed by parent unit in June 1944
Panzer Division Schlesien	Absorbed by 18th Panzergrenadier Division in March 1945
232nd Panzer Division	Formerly Panzer Ausbildungs Division Tatra, re-designated 21 February 1945
Panzer Division Thuringen	Training units
Panzer Division Westfalen	Training units

Panzergrenadier Divisions

Most of these units started life as motorized infantry divisions and were converted in 1943 with the inclusion of an assault gun battalion:

Division	Formed
3rd Panzergrenadier Division	
10th Panzergrenadier Division	
14th Panzergrenadier Division	Re-designated the 14th Infantry Division June 1943
15th Panzergrenadier Division	

16th Panzergrenadier Division	November 1942, re-designated the 116th Panzer Division March 1944
18th Panzergrenadier Division	
20th Panzergrenadier Division	
25th Panzergrenadier Division	
29th Panzergrenadier Division	
60th Panzergrenadier Division	Re-designated Panzer Division Feldherrnhalle November 1944
233rd Panzergrenadier Division	Re-designated the 233rd Panzer Division April 1943
Panzergrenadier Division Brandenburg	September 1944
Panzergrenadier Division Grossdeutschland	See panzer divisions

SS Panzer Divisions

These units initially started out as SS Panzergrenadier Divisions but were re-designated Panzer Divisions in October 1943:

Division
1st SS Panzer Division Leibstandarte Adolf Hitler
2nd SS Panzer Division Das Reich
3rd SS Panzer Division Totenkopf
5th SS Panzer Division Wiking
9th SS Panzer Division Hohenstaufen
10th SS Panzer Division Frundsberg
12th SS Panzer Division Hitlerjugend

SS Panzergrenadier Divisions

These lacked a second tank battalion so did not qualify as a panzer division:

Division
4th SS Polizei Panzergrenadier Division
7th SS Freiwilligen Gebirgs Division Prinz Eugen (mountain division equipped with tanks)
11th SS Freiwilligen Panzergrenadier Division Nordland
16th SS Panzergrenadier Division Reichsführer-SS
17th SS Panzergrenadier Division Gotz von Berlichingen
18th SS Freiwilligen Panzergrenadier Division Horst Wessel
23rd SS Freiwilligen Panzergrenadier Division Nederland
28th SS Panzergrenadier Division Wallonien

Appendix C

Panzer I Variants

Limited numbers of Panzer I variants included self-propelled guns, bridgelayers, command vehicles, ammunition carriers, flamethrowers and repair and maintenance vehicles. The most notable was the Panzerjäger I designed as a mobile anti-tank gun platform, which saw action in France, North Africa and Russia. This made the best use of the Ausf B chassis and because of its widespread deployment it was extensively photographed.

Self-propelled Guns

150mm sIG33(Sf) auf Panzer I Ausf B

The most interesting of the Panzer I variants are undoubtedly the self-propelled guns which utilized the Ausf B chassis. The first, also known as the Bison, was armed with the 150mm sIG33 L/11 heavy infantry gun. It was designed to provide mobile close fire support for mechanized infantry. The conversion work was conducted by Alkett at Berlin-Spandau in February 1940.

This was the very first German self-propelled gun of its kind (though many more were to follow) and was very much an experimental project. Notably only thirty-eight were converted. The modification involved removing the turret and superstructure and replacing them with a large box-shaped gun shield that was open at the rear and the top. The gun, still on its field carriage, was fitted in the fighting compartment.

Two narrow vertical doors were fitted on the rear of the fighting compartment, but these did not meet, leaving the crew exposed. They are often shown swung forward either side of the box superstructure so their exact function is not entirely clear. It may be that they were intended to provide the crew with some protection when dismounting.

The conversion work increased the vehicle's weight to 8.5 tons which put a great strain on the Maybach engine. It was also a metre higher than the Panzer I at just under 3m tall. The bulky profile inevitably made it a tempting target for enemy gunners.

The vehicle required four crew, consisting of the commander, gunner, loader and the driver. They were issued to the 701st–706th Heavy Infantry Gun, Self-Propelled, Companies and assigned to six panzer divisions before the operations against Belgium, the Netherlands and France in May–June 1940. Despite their faults these self-propelled guns remained in service until 1943. This was when the last unit, the 704th Company serving with the 5th Panzer Division was finally refitted. A subsequent version mounting the sIG33 on a Panzer 38(t) light tank chassis was known as the Grille or Cricket.

47mm PaK(t) auf Panzer I Ausf B

The Panzerjäger I variant proved much more successful. It was the very first German self-propelled anti-tank gun, comprising a captured Czech 47mm gun in a limited-traverse field mounting on the Ausf B chassis. The conversion work was likewise conducted by Alkett from March 1940 to February 1941 with just over 200 produced.

The modification was fairly simple, involving the removal of the turret and the superstructure roof and replacing it with the anti-tank gun protected by a three-sided shield open at the rear and the top. The gun was mounted within the shield using a pivoting mount supported by girders. There was space for eighty-six rounds for the gun. The armour on both these types of self-propelled gun was just 13mm at the front, sides and rear.

The Panzerjäger I was issued to five tank hunter battalions. It first saw action in Belgium and France in 1940. Subsequently it was employed in the infantry anti-tank units with the Afrika Korps in 1941 and in the opening stages of the invasion of the Soviet Union. From May to October 1941 the 47mm gun continued to be fitted for a panzerjäger role, but instead of the Panzer I was mounted on the converted chassis of captured French Renault R35 light tanks. These though were mainly used for security duties in France.

Flakpanzer I Ausf A

A very limited number of Ausf A were converted in early 1941 to carry the 20mm FlaK 38 anti-aircraft gun. These were used to equip three batteries of the 614th Flak Battalion and sent to Russia.

Command and Maintenance Vehicles

Kleiner Panzerbefehlswagen I

Following early exercises with the Panzer I it was apparent that commanders of the tank units, at least up to battalion and regimental level, needed to keep in close contact with their tanks in order to exert effective control. The Panzer I only carried a single receiver so space was required to install a transmitter as well. Initially the existing gun tank was modified for this role until a dedicated command tank could be developed.

The resulting Kleiner Panzerbefehlswagen I, or small armoured command vehicle, was based on the lengthened chassis and running gear also used on the Ausf B, although the latter had in fact been designed for the command vehicle first. To allow for a crew of three, plus two radio sets and a map table, the turret was eliminated and the superstructure raised in height. An elevated observation cupola was also fitted for the commander on the roof on some of the later versions. To keep the radio batteries charged the only change to the automotive specification was to increase the dynamo capacity.

Armament consisted of one machine gun in a ball mounting on the front of the superstructure. The armour was increased to 17mm. Two radio sets, the FuG2 and FuG6, permitted unit commanders to maintain communication with their sub units and higher formation headquarters. From 1935 to 1937 some 184 command vehicles were built plus another six based on the Ausf A.

This command vehicle was issued to company, battalion, regimental and brigade headquarters in the panzer divisions from 1935 to 1940. It was also issued to the signals and observation battalions of the panzer divisions' artillery regiments. They played a valuable role on the Polish campaign when they were first operationally deployed. At the beginning of the 1940 campaign in the West some ninety-six Kl Pz Befs Wg I were employed. By early 1941 they had been withdrawn from company level and from late 1942 were withdrawn from higher levels. Some were converted to an ambulance role.

Panzer I Ausf B Ohne Aufbau

The Ohne Aufbau was built to supply a fully-tracked repair and maintenance support vehicle for each tank company. It comprised the Ausf B chassis without the superstructure and turret, although the rear deck remained unchanged. This support vehicle had the standard-model engine, namely the Maybach NL38TR. The Ohne Aufbau only required a two-man crew, but could also carry mechanics as required.

From 1936 until the end of 1938 a total of 164 maintenance vehicles were built. These served with the repair and recovery units of the armoured companies until 1941. However, from mid-1940 it was mainly used as a training vehicle and it was too lightweight to act as a true recovery vehicle.

Support Vehicles

Brückenleger auf Panzerkampfwagen I Ausf A

Using the Panzer I as an armoured bridgelayer was never really a practical option. Nonetheless a number of Brückenleger auf Fgst Panzer I were built using the shorter Ausf A chassis. Trails were conducted as photographs exist of a Panzer II crossing the bridging of two such vehicles. Ironically the bridges were subsequently used for similar projects using the Panzer II.

Fahrerschulewagen I

After their withdrawal from service many old Panzer Is had their turret and superstructure removed for use by the Army tank schools or the National Socialist Motor Corps as driver training vehicles. This meant they essentially looked like the original Krupp Tractor LaS.

Flammenwerfer auf Panzerkampfwagen I Ausf A

The Panzer I flamethrower was a field conversion. In 1941 when Rommel was about to assault Tobruk in North Africa a number of the 5th Light Division's Panzer I Ausf A were modified as flamethrower tanks. A portable flamethrower was installed in the turret, replacing the right-hand machine gun. Its range extended to 25m and the fuel permitted up to twelve one-second bursts. Such a conversion had been carried out before using an Ausf B during the Spanish Civil War.

Ladungsleger auf Panzerkampfwagen I Ausf B

This was a demolition charge-laying vehicle. The Ladungsleger device was installed on the rear deck of the Panzer I. This could then be used to place a 50kg explosive charge onto enemy defences or obstacles to clear a path for other tanks. The simplest version simply dropped the charge behind the tank via a rectangular steel slide mounted on the engine deck. A second type utilized a cable-operated twin arm that pivoted above the vehicle to deliver the charge to the rear. The arm gave the tank a slightly better reach when depositing the explosives. Demolition devices were installed on ten Panzer I Ausf Bs with the 3rd Armoured Engineers Company of each pioneer battalion serving with the panzer divisions.

Munitionsschlepper auf Panzerkampfwagen I Ausf A

This was the very first tracked ammunition carrier, using the Panzer I Ausf A. The idea was that it could ferry ammunition to the panzer regiments when they were on the front line. It simply consisted of removing the turret and covering the opening with a two-piece circular hatch. This provided some protection for the driver and the ammunition he was carrying. Around fifty tanks were converted in September 1939 and saw action in Poland and France.

Munitionsschlepper auf Panzerkampfwagen Ia und Ib

By the spring of 1942 the Panzer I was completely obsolete, so a number were converted into ammunition carriers by removing the turret and installing a large steel box. Early the following year it was ordered that all remaining tanks be converted to Munitionsschlepper Ohne Aufbau. Also, by 1944 over 1,120 surplus Panzer I turrets had been made available for use on static fortifications.

Fighting in Poland, this Panther served with the 5th SS Panzer Division in the summer of 1944.

Another Panther serving with the 5th SS Panzer Division.

Two snow-covered Panthers lost during the Battle of the Bulge.

Panther Ausf Gs in Alsace in the winter of 1944–5.

The Panzer VI or Tiger I made its debut at Leningrad in the winter of 1942, much against Guderian's wishes.

The Tiger I was never available in sufficient numbers in Russia or Normandy.

Early production Tiger I captured by the British in Tunisia. Guderian despaired at Hitler's desire to commit the Tiger piecemeal.

Mid-production model Tiger I serving with the 1st SS Panzer Division in Russia. Its long-range 88mm made it deadly on the open steppe.

Tiger I on the streets in Normandy.

Heavily-camouflaged Tiger I in Normandy.

Mid-production Tiger I abandoned in Normandy.

The close confines of Normandy's streets and the rural hedgerows did not favour the Tiger I's capabilities.

The strange-looking Sturmtiger was armed with a massive 380mm mortar.

The mighty Tiger II on the streets of Budapest in October 1944.

This Tiger II was knocked out during the Battle of the Bulge. Intended as a heavy breakthrough panzer, it ended up being deployed in a defensive role.

The compact Hetzer tank destroyer was based on a Czech tank chassis and remained in production until the very end of the war. It was designed as an infantry support weapon.

The final resting place for a Panther at Houffalize in Belgium.

Despite being a fine tank, ultimately the Panther was eclipsed by the Panzer IV.

American GIs inspect captured Panzer IIIs at the end of the war.

Ultimately Guderian despaired of Hitler's inability to centralize tank production with a single design. Instead the German army ended up with a plethora of different tanks, tank destroyers, assault guns and self-propelled guns.

Appendix D

Panzer II Variants

The Panzer II was used for a variety of different tasks, which included flame-throwers and self-propelled guns, such as the very successful Marder II and Wespe armed with a 76.2mm anti-tank gun and 105mm light howitzer respectively. Over 850 Marders, 675 Wespes and some 150 flamethrowers were produced. Other specialized variants were produced in much smaller quantities and many got little further than the drawing board.

Self-propelled Guns

150mm sIG33 auf Fahrgestell Panzer II

Following the problems with the Panzer I self-propelled gun armed with the 150mm sIG33 it was decided to mount this weapon on a better chassis (Fahrgestell). It would spread the weight, lower the height and improve mobility, or so it was hoped. In February 1941 a prototype was produced utilizing a standard Panzer II Ausf B, but it was quickly discovered that the chassis was not long enough.

To resolve this, it was decided to lengthen the chassis by 60cm and widen it by 32cm. This was simply achieved by adding a sixth road wheel either side and no other modifications to the suspension were needed. A fighting compartment was created using 15mm plates at the front and on the sides. The side armour was not very high and this left the upper half of the gunners' bodies dangerously exposed. The rear and top were open again exposing the crew.

This heavy infantry gun carrier was a much better vehicle than the version cobbled together using an Ausf D and a captured Russian gun. The 15cm sIG33 auf Sf II was low and inconspicuous and the additional road wheel on either side helped space the weight and gave more room for the crew and ammunition. It required four crew and weighed just over 11 tons. Powered by the Maybach HL62TRM engine it could manage a respectable 40km/hr. Large hatches were fitted on the rear deck that could be propped open to improve engine cooling.

Although a sound concept, due to design problems only a dozen of these self-propelled guns were delivered in late 1941. These were sent to support Rommel in North Africa in early 1942, being issued to the 707th and 708th Heavy Infantry Gun Companies. The took part in the spring offensive at Gazala and continued to be used by the Afrika Korps until the last were destroyed in the spring of 1943. No further 15cm sIG33 auf Sf II were built and the Panzer II chassis was subsequently used for the much more successful Wespe self-propelled howitzer.

7.62cm PaK36(r) auf Fahrgestell Panzer II Ausf D

In early 1942 the Germans began to examine the possibility of using the Panzer II as a self-propelled anti-tank gun in a light panzerjäger role, as it was no longer viable as a gun tank. Initially the weapon selected was the 50mm PaK38. Two Ausf G prototypes were produced and sent to the front for trials, but by this stage the 50mm gun was simply not powerful enough. At least one was also built using the Ausf A, B or C which looked very similar to the Marder II.

Instead, as a stopgap it was decided to make use of captured Russian 76.2mm guns that were available in abundance. Initially the Ausf D and E chassis was used as a mount with just over 200 converted from April 1942 to June 1943. The hull and superstructure was that of the Ausf D, E and the Flamingo (see below), but was heightened to create a fighting compartment for the gunners. The gun was mounted on a modified field carriage with a gunshield which angled back either side. There appear to have been a number of different versions that varied slightly in superstructure and gunshield design.

This was one of the crudest of the improvised self-propelled mountings produced by the Germans during the Second World War. However, it served its purpose by getting the largest number possible of self-propelled anti-tank guns into the field as quickly as possible. The gun, rechambered to take German ammunition, was protected by its own shield, mounted toward the rear of the vehicle on top of the armoured superstructure.

Alkett got the order on 20 December 1941 and the first batch of 150 were finished by 12 May 1942. An order for another sixty superstructures was placed for installation on Ausf F returned from the front for maintenance. By May 1944 a total of eighty-eight Ausf F turrets had been released for use with fixed fortifications. It is unclear if these models were armed with the Russian gun or were absorbed into the Marder II programme.

Although built to similar standards to the Marder II, it was never officially called the Marder I (this designation was used for the self-propelled gun cobbled together using a PaK 40 and French Lorraine carrier chassis). Instead it was designated the Panzer Selbstfahrlafette 1 für 7.62cm PaK36(r) auf Fahrgestell Panzer II Ausf D or LaS 762 for short. It was issued to the panzerjäger units of the panzer and panzergrenadier divisions from the spring of 1942 onwards and those that survived where not retired from frontline service until early 1944.

Marder II

From June 1942 the Germans also utilized the Ausf F to produce the Marder II. This was one of the earliest of the tank destroyer conversions, with a German

75mm PaK40 anti-tank gun mounted directly on top of the Panzer II chassis which was otherwise unmodified. The gun was installed in a raised fighting compartment and while the upper portion of the gun field carriage was kept it was modified with girders to support the weapon. From a distance the Marder II looked similar to the Wespe self-propelled field gun, but the PaK40 barrel was much longer, extending far beyond the front of the vehicle.

Initially it was planned to use half of the monthly production run of fifty Panzer II as Marders, this was then changed to three-quarters, with a view to converting all of them to this role if the Army wanted them. In the event 576 were built from mid-1942 to mid-1943. Another seventy-five were converted from existing Panzer II from July 1943 to March 1944. Production Marders were curtailed because instructions were issued that Panzer II factories switch over to the Wespe.

Wespe

This was one of the most successful and widely-deployed self-propelled gun conversions of the war and was certainly a good use of the Panzer II chassis. Nonetheless it was not greatly liked by its crews. It was designed by Alkett at the beginning of 1942 to take the 105mm leFH18M field howitzer. To accommodate the weapon, the turret was removed and a small fighting compartment was created at the rear using sloping plates.

The suspension was changed slightly, the most visible sign of this being the reduction of the four return rollers to three. Spring bumper stops were added to the first, second and fifth road wheels to help cope with the gun recoil. To make space for the gunners the engine had to be moved forward beneath the gun and the glacis lengthened. Two distinctive louvered air intakes for the engine were fitted either side of the fighting compartment.

The Wespe required a crew of five and was powered by the standard HL62TR engine. The driver was squeezed into a small compartment on the left next to the transmission. Initially the standard Panzer II chassis was used, resulting in a very cramped fighting compartment. To try an alleviate this the chassis was lengthened by 254mm (10in) by increasing the space between the road wheels and the idler. However, it made little difference to the crew who had nowhere to store their personal kit.

Although a compact and reasonably well-armed self-propelled gun, the Wespe was not without its problems. The commander and three gun crew had little room to manoeuvre in the tiny fighting compartment. Often the commander and another crewman would climb out to give the gunner and loader room to operate the weapon when firing. The latter would then fold down the rear flap of the fighting compartment and use it as a shelf for rounds to ease loading.

In addition, the Wespe was mechanically unreliable. The suspension did not like tight turns and the steering gear wore out. The final drive had a tendency to leak oil over the brakes. The narrow Panzer II tracks did not cope well with the mud on the Eastern Front during the spring and autumn. All these were mechanical problems that would have also affected the standard Panzer II.

The initial order was for 1,000 built by FAMO but this was reduced to 835 in late 1943 and included the munitions carrier variant. It was issued to the self-propelled detachments of the panzer artillery regiments serving with the panzer and panzergrenadier divisions.

Support Vehicles

Artillerie-Panzerbeobachtungswagen II

For Operation Citadel in 1943 obsolete Panzer IIs were converted into armoured artillery observation vehicles to support the new Hummel self-propelled gun batteries. This involved installing extra radio equipment and a large frame antenna on the rear deck. To make space inside the 20mm gun was removed and a dummy gun barrel fitted to give the illusion that it was still armed. The turret was fixed in place.

Bergepanzer II Ausf J

A solitary Ausf J model had its turret removed and replaced by a jib to make an armoured recovery vehicle. This was found in 1944 and it is not clear if it was a field modification. As the Ausf J was not very numerous there was no real call for such a vehicle.

Brükenleger auf Panzer II

Experiments using a turretless Ausf b as a bridgelayer involved a pivoting bridge. However, the production version which was in service in 1940 had a two-part sliding bridge that had previously been tried on the Panzer I. It is unclear how many were actually built but four are known to have deployed with the 7th Panzer Division during the 1940 campaign in the West.

Panzer II Flamm Ausf A & B – Flamingo

In early 1939 an order was placed for ninety pre-production flamethrowers based on the Panzer II. These were wanted for bunker-busting and dealing with other strongpoints. Ausf D chassis were made available for this purpose with a soft steel prototype ready in July 1939. Once the concept of a cavalry light tank had been dropped, manufacture of what was called the Panzer II Flam Ausf A Flamingo commenced in May 1940.

The most obvious external difference that the Flamingo had was its much smaller turret, which only carried a single machine gun. The two flame projectors were fitted on the front of the superstructure over each of the front track guards in what looked like mini turrets. Also on either side of the superstructure were added long armoured box compartments to house four tanks of compressed nitrogen. The vehicle could carry up to 320 litres of flamethrower fuel which was stored internally. This permitted eighty bursts of 2–3 seconds from the pump-operated projectors. The range of the flammenwerfer was about 40 yards.

The second series Flamingo known as the Ausf B had minor improvements to the suspension and a new sprocket design. It was also fitted with smoke dischargers mounted on the track guard either side of the engine compartment. Over 110 Flamingos were built direct from the production line and another 43 were converted from existing Ausf Ds and Es. Further production was disrupted by the Ausf D and E chassis being given over to the building of self-propelled anti-tank guns.

The Flamingo did not prove very successful. It first took part in combat during the invasion of the Soviet Union with dedicated panzer battalions designed for close support. These units were too large and the Flamingo's thin armour and flammable fuel resulted in heavy losses. This led to the units being reorganized as regular tank units and the Flamingos were recalled to be converted into self-propelled anti-tank guns.

Panzer II ohne Aufbau

The older Panzer IIs returned from the front for repair from 1942 were converted into tracked pioneer vehicles for use by engineer units. This consisted largely of just removing the turret. By May 1944 some 740 Panzer II turrets were available for use in fortifications, with 485 having already been issued for such purposes. However, it is unknown just how many of these pioneer vehicles were made and some would have been field conversions.

Panzer II Munitions Carrier

A munitions carrier was produced to support the Wespe. The 105mm howitzer and traverse mantlet were removed and the resulting gap plated over. This carrier could transport ninety rounds and required a crew of three. It was designed in such a way that field mechanics could still install the gun so that it could be used as Wespe combat replacements. A total of 159 Munitions-Sf auf Fahrgestell Panzer II (Ammunition SP on chassis AFV II) were built by FAMO as part of the Wespe production run.

Panzer II mit Schwimmkôrper

This swimming tank design resulted from plans to invade England in 1940. Trials involved attaching bulky pontoon like flotation devices to Ausf C tanks. Propulsion in the water was transferred from the drive sprocket and it could manage 10km/hr. These tanks were issued as standard Panzer IIs to the 18th Panzer Regiment and saw action in Russia in the summer of 1941.

Panzer III Variants

As well as being diverted for assault gun production, the Panzer III hull and chassis was employed in a wide range of other roles including artillery observation, command, flamethrower, recovery and swimming variants – none of which were built in particularly great numbers. In total some 350 command tanks, 260 observation tanks, 100 flamethrowers, 150 Bergepanzer IIIs and 168 submersible versions were produced. This though represented the loss of about 1,000 gun tanks.

Combat Variants

There were three main combat variants of the Panzer III besides the regular gun tank models. These comprised the assault gun, flamethrower and submersible tank, the most successful of which was the family of assault guns which utilized the Panzer III's proven chassis and hull.

Assault Guns

On 22 January 1943 the 11th Panzer Division submitted a report that was dismissive of the Panzer III's inadequate combat capabilities:

> The Panzer III is in no way equal to the demands of the war in the East[ern Front]. Its armour is too thin, and the calibre of its gun is inadequate. In contrast, the assault gun has proved an outstanding success in the Steppe war, even though it lacks a movable turret. The reason for this success lays in its considerably heavier armour and more powerful gun.

This succinctly summed up the problems faced by the Panzer III. The first Sturmgeschütz III variant appeared in 1940 using the same suspension, drive train and basic hull shape as the Panzer III Ausf F and subsequently appeared in eight different models. These were built by Alkett. The StuG III Ausf A–E versions were armed with the short-barrelled 75mm StuK37 L/24 while the subsequent models from early 1942 were up-gunned with the long-barrelled 75mm StuK40 L/43 or L/48.

By far the most numerous was the StuG 40 Ausf G (also known as the StuG III Ausf G) of which 7,720 were built from December 1942 to March 1945. Many of the remaining Panzer III gun tanks, totalling 173 vehicles, were rounded up in 1944 and converted into StuGs. A similar number were also relegated to armoured recovery vehicles. An assault howitzer known as the 105mm Sturmhaubitze 42 was also produced from October 1942 until the end of the war.

Flamethrower

In part driven by the appalling urban warfare fought in Stalingrad, in late 1942 it was suggested that the Panzer III could be used for close support by installing a flamethrower. The conversion work was supposed to have commenced in January 1943 but problems with the production of the Flammenwerfer pushed it back to February. MIAG supplied 100 Ausf M to Wegmann to produce the Panzer III (Fl).

The 50mm gun was replaced by the 14mm Flammenwerfer's 1.5m-long flame delivery tube. The latter had a range of up to 60m and the Fl carried 1,000 litres of Flammöl (flame fuel) in two tanks. Under ideal conditions it could fire up to eighty flame jets each lasting two or three seconds. Extra armour was added with 30mm plates welded to the front of the hull. The space taken up by the internal fuel tanks meant that the tank could only accommodate three crew, the commander who also operated the Flammenwerfer, radio operator/bow machine-gunner and driver.

The Panzer III Fls were completed by April 1943 – by which time the German forces trapped at Stalingrad had surrendered. Each panzer regiment was issued seven tanks for their flamethrower platoons. At the time of Kursk the 6th Panzer Division, 11th Panzer Division and Panzergrenadier Division Grossdeutschland were able to muster forty-one Panzer III flamethrowers for use against the Red Army. A few were also deployed to Italy.

Submersible Tank

The Panzer III als Tauchpanzer was developed in mid-1940 to support Hitler's proposed seaborne invasion of England. This consisted of fitting a submersion kit, with non-return valves installed on the exhausts and locking covers on the air-intakes. Waterproof fabric covers were fitted to the hull machine gun, gun mantlet and cupola. An inflatable rubber tube went around the turret ring to seal it.

The idea was that a landing vessel with a hinged ramp would disembark the Tauchpanzer some distance from the shore. In depths of up to 15m the tank received air via a flexible pipe attached to a snorkel and radio antenna kept on the surface by a towed float. This air pipe was either attached to the engine compartment or the turret roof. The crew of the Tauchpanzer navigated underwater using a gyrocompass.

From July to October 1940 some 168 Panzer III were converted to this role using Ausf Fs, Gs and Hs. A further forty-two were converted using Panzer IVs. Although the invasion of England was scrapped the Tauchpanzers did not go to waste. In the spring of 1941 they were sent to Czechoslovakia and modified for river crossing. This was achieved by installing a rigid vertical snorkel pipe to the commander's cupola that was designed for shallower water. Three sections of Tauchpanzer were serving with the 18th Panzer Division when Hitler's attack on the Soviet Union commenced.

Support Vehicles

Once the Panzer III's role as a battle tank had been superseded by the Panzer IV, Panther and Tiger tanks it was increasingly diverted for use in secondary support roles. In fact, most of the surviving Panzer III guns tanks not used as StuGs ended their days as armoured recovery vehicles.

Command Tank

The Panzer III was also used a Panzerbefehlswagen or command vehicle and the Panzerbeobachtungswagen or artillery observation post vehicle. Hundreds of these were produced but by 1944 they were increasingly in short supply due to the end of Panzer III gun tank production. To make up the shortfall the German Army had little choice but convert existing Panzer IVs to Panzerbefehlswagen mit 7.5cm KwK L/48.

Five different types of Panzerbefehlswagen were produced for the Panzerwaffe. About half the Panzer III command vehicles did not have a main gun in order to create additional interior space. None of the Panzer III observation vehicles had their tank gun. This meant they were reliant on a single machine gun for protection and were at risk if they got too close to the action. In contrast, the Panzer IV command vehicle retained its 75mm gun.

Panzerbefehlswagen Ausf D[1]

From the creation of Hitler's panzer regiments in the mid-1930s it was apparent that an armoured command vehicle was needed to exercise tactical control over the tanks. The very first was the Kleine Panzerbefehlswagen (light armoured command vehicle) based on the Panzer I chassis. This though did not provide enough work space so it was decided to create a grosse Panzerbefehlswagen (large armoured command vehicle) using the Panzer III as the basis. This was on the grounds that the Panzer II was likewise too small for the role. The Panzer I and II could only accommodate two and three crew respectively.

On the factory floor the Ausf D was adapted by simply omitting the 37mm gun and ammunition racks, then fixing the turret rigidly in place, to create extra radio and work space. The hull machine gun was also replaced by a pistol port. The vehicle took a crew of five like the regular gun tank, but comprising a commander, executive officer, two radio operators and the driver. The radio fit included the FuG6 (Funkgerät – radio equipment) tactical command set (replacing the FuG5), plus the Fug7 ground-to-air set with a range of 50km or the FuG8 the main divisional link set with a range of 40km. To help with visibility the superstructure sides were fitted with extra vision and pistol ports.

In an effort to avoid enemy fire the mantlet was fitted with a dummy 37mm gun barrel to give the impression from a distance at least that it was a regular gun tank. Nevertheless, the prominent square frame radio antenna fitted to the engine deck readily revealed its command role. The tank's only defence was a single machine gun in the mantlet and the 30mm armour was largely inadequate. Some thirty Panzer III Ausf D¹ command vehicles were completed by Daimler-Benz during June 1938 to March 1939.

The plan was that each panzer unit Stab (HQ) up to brigade level would be issued with a grosse Panzerbefehlswagen. Production levels though could not meet such demand. By 1 September 1939 just thirty-eight Pz Bef Wg Ausf D¹ and Ausf E were available which was not enough to go round. Although the Ausf D¹ continued in service during the Western campaign of 1940 it was retired the following year because of the troublesome suspension with its eight road wheels either side.

Panzerbefehlswagen Ausf E

The second Panzer III command vehicle was based on the improved Ausf E suspension. This time just forty-five were produced by Daimler-Benz from July 1939 to February 1940. The adaptation was the same as the Ausf D¹ except the radio fit differed slightly. It either comprised the FuG6 and FuG2 listening set (with a range of 4km this could receive only but allowed commanders to know what was going on), or the FuG6 and FuG7 or FuG6 and FuG8. Like its predecessor it only had 30mm of armour. By the start of the 1940 Western campaign the panzer divisions had sixty-four Pz Bef Wg Ausf D¹s and Ausf Es, with another eight supplied as combat replacements. The Panzerbefehlswagen Ausf Es were simply phased out by attrition.

Panzerbefehlswagen Ausf H

An order for the third in the series was placed in January 1939 for 145 grosse Panzerbefehlswagen. These were produced from November 1940 to September 1941, but were followed by a second batch of thirty from December 1941 to January 1942.

After experiences in Poland and France it was clear that the command vehicles needed much thicker armour, so the Ausf H was used with the 30mm basic armour boosted by the 30mm bolt-on plates. On the early versions the dummy gun again resembled the 37mm but on the later ones it was made to look like the larger 50mm KwK38 L/42.

In the beginning of the summer of 1941 Hitler's 17 panzer divisions had 120 gr Pz Bef Wg Ausf E and Ausf H. The second batch of Panzerbefehlswagen Ausf H were issued to new units such as the 2nd SS Panzergrenadier Division Das Reich, 25th Panzer Division and Panzergrenadier Division Grossdeutschland. By late June 1942 there were seventy-five gr Pz Bef Wg operational on the front.

Panzerbefehlswagen with 50mm KwK38 L/42

From August to November 1942 Daimler-Benz produced 81 command vehicles which retained their 50mm KwK38 L/42 guns. Then in January 1943 it was ordered that there would be no further specially-adapted Pz Bef Wg coming out the factory as they were a low priority. All future command vehicles would have to be built using the standard Panzer III gun tank. Consequently a further 104 Panzer III Ausf J with the L/42 gun were converted from March to September 1943 simply by removing an ammunition rack and adding a long-range radio.

For the Panzerwaffe this was a relief as they had long argued that a single machine gun was insufficient to protect the command vehicles and their staff officers. Now in emergencies they could fight as a regular tank. The Panzerbefehlswagen with 50mm KwK38 L/42 lost the front superstructure machine gun, but this was compensated for by the coaxial machine gun. The loss of the ammunition rack meant a reduction of ninety-nine rounds to seventy-five, but this was a small price to pay for the retention of the 50mm gun. An observational periscope was also mounted in the roof.

Panzerbefehlswagen with 50mm KwK39 L/60

The decision to retain the 50mm KwK39 L/60 in Panzer III command tanks had been taken as early as October 1941. The intention was to provide the panzer divisions with 200 of them, but this was derailed by production practicalities. The order was postponed firstly because of the second batch of Pz Bef Wg Ausf H and again due to the construction of the first batch of Pz Bef Wg mit 5cm KwK L/42 converted from Ausf J production.

The order was finally green-lighted in October 1942 with the plan of building the Pz Bef Wg mit 5cm KwK L/60 Schmal (small gun mantlet), also dubbed the Pz Bef Wg Ausf K, alongside the Panzer III Ausf M. By this stage though the decision had been taken to terminate Panzer III production in favour of the StuG III, plus shortly remaining gun tanks would be converted to the role. As a result, Daimler-Benz only built fifty Pz Bef Wg Ausf Ks from December 1942 to February 1943.

In appearance the Ausf K was essential the same as the Panzer III Ausf M except it had extra vision and pistol ports on the sides of the superstructure. The main armament had a shortened gun mantlet and the coaxial machine gun was omitted and replaced with a visor that was very similar to the driver's visor. The Ausf K's function was less obvious as the large tale-tell frame antenna was replaced by a star antenna. The Ausf K continued to serve right up until mid-1944 with units equipped with the Panzer IV.

Observation Tank

Once the German Army began to field increasing amounts of self-propelled artillery it was obvious that they needed to be served by a fully-tracked armoured observation vehicle. This would act to coordinate battery fire onto targets. In light of the Panzer III Ausf E–H lacking punch they offered the readiest interim solution until a specially-designed Artillerie-Panzerbeobachtungswagen could be built.

The main way to identify the Panzer III armoured observation vehicle was by the machine gun mounted in the middle of the mantlet and a dummy gun barrel to the right (looking forward). The machine gun mounted in the superstructure front was also deleted and the gap filled up. Ausf E to M were used as the basis of the Pz Beob Wg with the earlier models up-armoured with the 30mm plates. These vehicles carried the FuG8 divisional set and the FuG4 artillery control set. The later was portable so could be moved from the vehicle to a forward observation position.

In total 262 Panzer III conversions were carried out from February 1943 to April 1944. They were issued to the Hummel and Wespe self-propelled gun batteries with two vehicles per battery. The Pz Beob Wg remained in service right until the end of the war.

Armoured Recovery Vehicle

Late in the war a limited number of Bergepanzer III or recovery vehicles were produced to support the panzer divisions. In January 1944 units were instructed to return all their Panzer III to be converted into Bergepanzer. The intention was that output would start with fifteen in March, thirty in April and thirty in May.

The conversion was a fairly crude affair and consisted of replacing the turret with a wooden box-body on top of the fighting compartment for the mechanics and their tools. Mountings were also installed on the rear engine deck to take a derrick crane for engine lifting (similar to the Bergepanther). The Bergepanzer was designed to employ the Panzerbergeanker or armoured recovery anchor that would brace it when recovering a stranded tank. When not in use the anchor was towed on its single two-wheeled axle. The wider Ostkette tracks were fitted to give the Bergepanzer greater traction when towing. Armament consisted of the normal machine gun in the front superstructure and another for dismounted use and air defence. The vehicle took a crew of just three, comprising two fitters and a driver.

Around 150 Bergepanzer IIIs were converted from old tanks from March 1944 to December 1944, compared to just 36 Bergepanzer IVs. It is likely that others were produced unofficially as field conversions from damaged tanks or those under repair. Bergepanzer IIIs and IVs were issued to Panzer IV and StuG III/IV workshop companies. By February 1945 about 130 Bergepanzer IIIs were still operational, but this was probably due to panzers being largely impossible to recover from the battlefield by this stage of the war.

Ammunition Carrier

While some Panzer IIIs returned from the front were converted into command and observation vehicles, between May 1943 and May 1944 some were converted into much less sophisticated Munitionpanzer or ammunition carriers. The turret was removed and the old fighting compartment used for ammunition stowage. Sledges were also employed to tow additional loads.

The carriers were employed to support both the panzer and self-propelled gun units. It is not clear how many of these were produced but by May 1944 110 turrets with 50mm guns were listed available to be used for fixed emplacements. Once the Bergepanzer III was given priority no further ammunition carrier conversions were carried out.

Maintenance Vehicle

The Bergepanzers were supplemented by turretless instandsetzungskraftwagen (maintenance vehicles) based on the Panzer III Ausf J or L. This lacked the mechanics' wooden box and the crane. The turret ring was fitted with a round cover to keep out the elements. The former fighting compartment was used to carry extra batteries for starting stranded tanks as well as spares and tools to conduct field repairs.

Pioneer Vehicle

Similarly from 1943 some Panzer IIIs had their turrets removed to serve as engineer vehicles. These were fitted with equipment racks and could carry small assault bridges. They looked largely the same as the maintenance variant and were essentially the same vehicle.

Appendix F

Panzer IV Variants

Self-Propelled Guns

As well as assault guns and tank destroyers, the Panzer IV chassis was additionally diverted to create a wide variety of self-propelled weapon mounts. These either had anti-tank, anti-aircraft or artillery roles. Key amongst them was the Hornisse (Hornet), Hummel (Bumblebee), Brummbär (Grizzly Bear) and Möbelwagen (Furniture Van).

Hornisse

Work on creating a self-propelled platform for the formidable 88mm Pak43 anti-tank gun started in 1942. This led to the powerful Hornisse (Hornet) that was later called the Nashorn (Rhinoceros). It was decided that this and the Hummel, armed with a 150mm howitzer, would utilize a hybrid Panzer III and IV chassis as a 'zwischenlösung' or interim solution until a specially designed self-propelled gun platform could be designed.

A hybrid prototype was presented to Hitler in October 1942. The Panzer III/IV platform utilized a lengthened Panzer IV hull for the central design. This kept the same basic suspension of four pairs of road wheels and four return rollers except for spacing between the components, while the drive sprocket was that designed for the Panzer III. The glacis plate was extended and a small raised armoured compartment for the driver was fitted on the left-hand side. A circular forward-opening hatch that was set back from the driver's position served the radio operator on the right. This self-propelled mount was known as the Geschützwagen III/IV.

The engine was the same Maybach HL120 used in the Panzer III and IV, giving a speed of 42km/hr and a range of 210km. To allow for the open top-fighting compartment at the rear for the 88mm gun crew, the engine was moved to a central position. The compartment was protected on all four sides by slanted armour plates bolted to the hull. These were fairly thin and on the front of the hull amounted to 30mm with just 10mm on the gunshield. The side armour was 10mm on the superstructure and 20mm on the hull.

The initial order with Deutsche-Eisenwerke was for 500 Hornisse, of which 494 were completed between February 1943 and March 1945. After Hitler approved the prototype it was initially agreed to have 100 Hornisse ready by 12 May 1943 in time for his summer offensive and the attack at Kursk. They were first deployed on the Eastern Front with the 655th Heavy Panzerjäger Battalion. Other units equipped with the Hornisse also saw combat on the Western Front and in Italy. Hitler renamed it the Nashorn in 1944.

Hummel

While the Panzer II provided a useful platform for the 105mm field gun, it was decided to mount the heavier 150mm howitzer on the Geschützwagen III/IV hybrid chassis. This was to equip the heavy batteries of the self-propelled armoured artillery detachments serving with the panzer and panzergrenadier divisions. At least four different self-propelled howitzer designs utilizing a 105mm gun mounted on the Panzer IV never got much beyond the prototype stage and did not go into full series production.

The 150mm sFH18/1 L/30 was positioned in the middle of the hull over the engine, which resulted in the Hummel having a higher silhouette than the Hornisse. The prototype featured a muzzle brake but this was dispensed with on the production model. Whereas the Hornisse required a four-man crew the Hummel needed six.

Like the Hornisse an order for 100 Hummel was placed with a view to having them ready for the Kursk offensive. Ammunition carriers were also ordered to support the Hummel batteries. To start with each panzer division only had a single heavy battery equipped with six Hummel plus two ammunition carriers. Later as production increased some had a second battery. The Hummel, like the Hornisse, proved a useful and popular weapon.

The Hummel built from early 1944 had a crew compartment that extended the initial driver's position right across the full width of the hull. Over 600 had been built by late 1944 with 150 converted into ammunition carriers, as lorries were not up to the job. A variant of the Hummel, known as the Oskette, was produced with wider tracks for the winter fighting on the Eastern Front. German self-propelled guns were not coated in Zimmerit.

Brummbär

Also produced in time for Kursk was the mighty Brummbär assault infantry gun. Alkett developed the Sturmpanzer concept while Krupp modified the Panzer IV chassis to accommodate the 150mm StuH43 L/12 gun (StuH – Sturmhaubitze or assault howitzer). This required a fully-enclosed box superstructure for the gunners. Initially the Brummbär utilized fifty-two new Ausf G chassis and eight rebuilt Ausf E and F chassis. Rather than the basic 80mm of armour on the hull front, the first sixty had 50mm plus an additional 50mm armour plate bolted on. The superstructure was also protected by 100mm of armour. Although weighing over 28 tons the overloaded chassis could still achieve 40km/hr.

The initial production models featured a crude sliding-shutter visor for the driver, similar to that on the Tiger I. The middle production version included a periscope for the driver. Both lacked a close defence weapon, which left the Brummbär at risk from enemy infantry. Built from April 1944 to the end of the war the final version had a redesigned superstructure armed with a ball-mounted machine gun in the top left-hand corner of the front plate. A cupola was also installed for the commander.

After seeing Alkett's plans in October 1942 Hitler demanded up to sixty Brummbär be ready as soon as possible. On 7 February 1943 it was agreed that forty should be completed in time for Kursk with a follow-on order for twenty. The initial production run was conducted during April to May 1943; long-term production was then instigated in November 1943 and lasted until the end of the war. In total 289 Brummbär were built at Duisburg with another eight converted from Panzer IV gun tanks.

Before leaving the factory all vertical surfaces on the mid-production Brummbär were coated in Zimmerit. Schürzen side skirt armour was also fitted. They were factory sprayed in dunkel gelb, areas were then oversprayed with small patches of diluted oliv grun. The first unit to deploy the Brummbär was the 216th Sturmpanzer Battalion, which fought at Kursk and was involved in the defensive battles near Zaparozhye ending in October 1943. Three other battalions were formed, fighting on the Eastern and Western Fronts as well as in Italy.

Assault Guns and Tank Destroyers

From late 1943 the Panzer IV chassis was also used as the basis for a series of turretless assault guns and tank destroyers. These consisted of the Sturmgeschütz IV, Jagdpanzer IV and the Panzer IV/70. Combined these represented some 3,120 vehicles with roughly a thousand of each type. These are noteworthy because they diverted valuable tank production just as the tide was turning to what were essentially defensive rather than offensive weapons. Their lack of turret and very limited traverse with the hull-mounted main gun naturally limited their tactical flexibility.

Sturmgeschütz IV, Jagdpanzer IV and Panzer IV/70

The StuG IV first went into production in December 1943 and continued until the end of the war. Krupp-Gruson completely abandoned building Panzer IV gun tanks. The Vomag Jagdpanzer IV was only built during 1944 and overlapped with the Panzer IV/70(V), which remained in production until March 1945.

While Vomag also discontinued Panzer IV gun tank manufacture, Nibelungenwerke built both Ausf J gun tanks and chassis for the Panzer IV/70 until the very end. Notably the Panzer IV/70(A) built by Nibelungenwerke was a stopgap model using chassis intended for gun tank production. As a result the chassis did not have a modified nose, this meant mounting the superstructure half a metre higher than that on the Jagdpanzer IV and the Panzer IV/70(V).

Self-Propelled Flak Guns

Growing Allied air superiority by 1943 made it increasingly necessary for the Germans to divert a greater proportion of their armoured fighting vehicle production to the output of anti-aircraft tanks or flakpanzers. By 1944 the panzer divisions were in need of mobile fully-tracked and armoured anti-aircraft guns that could accompany them into combat. This requirement resulted in the Möbelwagen (Furniture Van), Ostwind (East Wind) and Wirbelwind (Whirlwind), all employing the Panzer IV chassis. These were issued to the anti-aircraft platoons of the panzer regiments. The Möbelwagen was by far the most numerous.

Möbelwagen

The Möbelwagen, or furniture van, was armed with a 37mm FlaK43 L/60 anti-aircraft gun, with the chassis supplied by Krupp-Gruson and proved quite successful. The FlaK43 was designed to replace the earlier FlaK37, which used a two-wheeled trailer similar to the 20mm FlaK30. This newer gun featured a FlaK37 body but also had a gas-actuated mechanism from an aircraft cannon replacing the original recoil-actuated mechanism. This almost doubled the rate of fire. Its effective ceiling was 4,200m. The gun was also mounted in a twin configuration with one gun above the other, rather than the more usual side-by-side. This double configuration was not tried on the Möbelwagen as it would have left the crew permanently exposed apart from the gun shield.

On the Möbelwagen a fighting compartment for the gunners was created by a simple four-sided 50mm plate superstructure, which could be lowered to a horizontal position to permit the gun to traverse 360 degrees at low elevation. The hull had 80mm of armour and the superstructure 50mm. Between March 1944 and March the following year some 240 Möbelwagen were produced by Deutsche-Eisenwerke. It does not appear that the Möbelwagen hull was given an application of Zimmerit on leaving the factory.

Wirbelwind

Whereas the Möbelwagen only had a flat, largely exposed platform for the gun the Wirbelwind was equipped with an open-topped turret into which was installed a 20mm Flakvierling 38 quad. The turret offered just 16mm of armour. This anti-aircraft gun was an improvement on the 20mm Flak 30, which had seen action in Spain and was deployed on a two-wheeled trailer. The rate of fire was increased from 280 to 420 rounds per minute. The Flakvierling 38 was then tried as twin guns and finally a quad mounting was adopted capable of firing 1,680 shells per minute. The gun's ceiling was 2,000m.

The Wirbelwind was designed to supplement Möbelwagen production by using existing Panzer IV chassis that had been returned from the front for factory repair. From July to November 1944 Ostbau converted just eighty-six Wirbelwind before the use of the inadequate 20mm was abandoned in favour of the 37mm gun.

Ostwind

Trials were held in July 1944 mounting a 37mm FlaK43 gun in a turret similar to that used on the Wirbelwind. This resulted in the Ostwind, comprising a six-sided open-topped turret on a converted Panzer IV chassis. An order for 100 was placed with Ostbau on 18 August 1944 but by the end of the war they had produced just 36 conversions.

The majority of the Flakpanzer IV were deployed to the Eastern Front, though some Möbelwagen saw action in France in 1944. Wirbelwind and Ostwind flakpanzers saw combat during Hitler's Ardennes offensive in December 1944 and were also used in a ground support role. Both these type of Flakpanzer IV had their hulls finished with Zimmerit.

It had been planned to replace the Ostwind and Möbelwagen with the Panzer IV-based Kugelblitz armed with twin 30mm guns. Just two Kugelblitz were ever-completed so seven new chassis earmarked for the project was also used to produce Ostwind. Ostbau was looking to produce an Ostwind II armed with two 37mm guns and a Flakpanzer IV armed with a 30mm quad, but loss of their facilities ensured this did not happen.

Submersible Tank

Like the Panzer III, a number of Panzer IVs were converted into submersible tanks known as Tauchpanzer in mid-1940. This was done in preparation for Hitler's Operation Sealion, the proposed invasion of England. In theory it allowed the panzers to operate in water up to 15m deep. But whilst almost 170 Tauchpanzer III were produced there were only 42 Tauchpanzer IV conversions.

This comprised fitting the air-intakes with locking covers and the exhausts with non-return valves replacing the normal mufflers. Also waterproof fabric covers were applied to the hull machine gun, the gun mantlet and the cupola. An inflatable rubber tube encompassed the turret ring. A specially-designed metal cover with a vision block made the driver's visor watertight. A pipe suspended from a floating snorkel connected to the back of the tank allowed it to draw air when submerged and a gyrocompass facilitated underwater navigation.

Trials and training showed that the Tauchpanzer was a reasonable successful innovation. When Hitler finally abandoned Sealion they were made redundant. Nevertheless, the Tauchpanzers did not go to waste as they were shipped to Milowitz near Prague in the spring of 1941 and prepared for another mission. Most of them had a long, rigid snorkel attached to the commander's cupola making them capable of deep river crossings. These Tauchpanzers took part in Operation Barbarossa with the 18th Panzer Division in June 1941.

Support Vehicles

As well as being diverted for self-propelled guns and tanks destroyers, the Panzer IV chassis was employed in a wide range of command and support roles.

Command Tank

The Panzer III had likewise been deployed in a very large variety of roles including the Panzerbefehlswagen or command vehicle and the Panzerbeobachtungs-wagen or artillery observation post vehicle. Hundreds of these were produced but by 1944 they were increasingly in short supply due to the end of Panzer III gun tank production. To make up the shortfall the German Army had little choice but convert existing Panzer IVs to Panzerbefehlswagen mit 7.5cm KwK L/48.

About half the Panzer III command vehicles did not have a main gun in order to create extra workspace. None of the Panzer III observation vehicles had their guns. This meant they were reliant on a single machine gun for protection and were at risk if they got too close to the front. In contrast, the Panzer IV command vehicle retained its 75mm gun.

From March to September 1944 Nibelungenwerke converted some ninety-seven Mk IVs to a command role. This primarily involved the installation of the FuG5 (10-watt transmitter) and FuG7 or the FuG8 radios (20-watt and 30-watt transmitters respectively). These were the standard tank, ground-to-air and divisional link sets. The FuG5 aerial along with a TSR1 1.4m-high periscope was fixed to the turret top. The distinctive star antenna for the FuG7/8 was attached to the rear of the hull on the right-hand edge of the tail plate. These command tanks were issued to Panzer IV battalions.

Observation Tank

The observation post vehicle was essentially the same but with different radio equipment, comprising the FuG4 and FuG8. This provided an artillery control set and a divisional link. This conversion work was conducted by Nibelungenwerke but started slightly later, although it involved similar quantities of tanks. A total of ninety Panzer IVs were changed into Panzerbeobachtungswagen IV from July 1944 to March 1945. These were issued to the Hummel batteries.

Bridgelayer

During the 1930s the emphasis on fixed fortifications in Europe resulted in the German Inspectorate of Engineers concluding that there was an urgent requirement for an armoured bridge layer. Early experiments utilizing the Panzer I and II were soon abandoned as they could not carry a large-enough tank bridge. Instead they came up with the Brückenleger IV.

Four Panzer IV Ausf C chassis were assigned for conversion in August 1939. The following month an additional sixteen Ausf D chassis were requisitioned. By January 1940 it was anticipated that twelve BL IV would be delivered with two employing a Krupp-designed bridge and the rest using a Magirus development. One had a forward pivoting gantry while the other slid the bridge into position horizontally.

The original order had been for fifty 9m bridges, but this was cut by thirty so a new design could be fitted to sixty Panzer IVs. Experience in France and the Low Countries showed there was actually little call for the services of the BL IV and the programme was cancelled. During 1940–1 it was decided to restore fifteen BL IV to the gun tank role. In the end just twenty bridgelayers were issued to five panzer divisions.

Infantry Assault Bridge

There was another design that employed a 50m extending bridge using Panzer IV Ausf C chassis. Known as the Infanterie Sturmsteg or infantry assault bridge, this Magirus construction comprised two bridges side-by-side that created beams for a walkway very similar to a fire-fighting ladder. Just two Sturmsteg were completed in February 1940 and saw use in the invasion of France. One was disabled, losing its tracks and several road wheels. No further conversions were carried out.

Armoured Recovery Vehicle

Late in the war a very limited number of Bergepanzer IV recovery vehicles were produced to support the panzer divisions. This was a fairly crude affair and consisted of replacing the turret with a wooden box-body on top of the fighting compartment for the mechanics. Mountings were also installed on the rear engine deck to take a derrick crane for engine lifting. Just thirty-six Bergepanzer IVs were converted from October 1944 to December 1944.

In contrast 150 Bergepanzer IIIs were produced during that same year. It is likely that others were produced unofficially as field conversions from damaged tanks or those under repair. Both types of Bergepanzer were issued to Panzer IV and StuG III/IV workshop companies.

Hummel Ammunition Carrier

Externally the Hummel ammunition carrier differed from the Hummel simply by having its gun removed and the resulting gap plated over. Internally the fighting compartment was converted to allow for extra ammunition stowage. These vehicles were produced both in the factory and often as field conversions.

Karl Mortar Ammunition Carrier

During the winter of 1940 and the summer of 1941 the Germans produced six Karlgerät, which were enormous 600mm self-propelled heavy siege mortars. These required tracked ammunition carriers and in October 1939 a brand-new Panzer Ausf D chassis was used as a prototype. A new superstructure was constructed, while over the engine compartment were fitted racks that could take four massive 600mm rounds. To get these rounds to the mortar a crane was installed on the front right-hand side of the superstructure.

Once green-lighted it was decided in 1941 to use a newer-model Panzer IV and thirteen Ausf F1 chassis were converted to Munitionsschlepper für Karlgerät. A number of rebuilt Panzer IV chassis were also pressed into service. These carriers saw action on the Eastern Front in support of the mortars, most memorably during the siege of Sevastopol in 1942.

Tiger I and II Variants

Tiger I

Command Panzer

Two command or radio tank variants of the Tiger I were produced, designated the Panzerbefehlswagen VI Ausf E Sd Kfz 267 and the Sd Kfz 268. They carried additional radio sets (the FunkSprechGerät 8 and FunkSprechGerät 7 respectively) which enabled the commander to communicate at divisional level and ground to air. The extra space taken up by the radios meant a reduction in the ninety-two rounds normally carried to sixty-six and also resulted in a slight reduction in the amount of machine-gun ammunition. Just eighty-four of these command tanks were produced in 1944 and were all but indistinguishable from the regular Tiger I. The only give away was the addition of a turret-mounted radio aerial (the aerial for the tactical radio was on the rear right-hand side of the hull).

Recovery Panzer

The weight of the Tiger I meant that recovering disabled tanks was a major problem. In 1944 three Tiger I Ausf Es were reportedly converted to Bergpanzers by removing the main gun, installing a winch inside the turret and fitting a small tubular crane to the front of the turret and a geared winch mount to the rear. These were ad hoc battlefield conversions and in one instance the turret was also fitted with the Panther-type commander's cupola with seven episcopes and anti-aircraft machine-gun ring.

One of these Bergepanzer Tigers was captured in Italy in 1944. Subsequent examination of the latter has shown that the crane was in fact far too light to be used for towing broken-down panzers. It has since been postulated that this was in fact not a recovery tank at all, but an engineer vehicle used for planting explosives to destroy battlefield obstacles or as some sort of mine-clearing vehicle.

Sturmtiger

Amongst the many specialized types of armoured fighting vehicles developed for the German Army was the assault tank or Sturmpanzer. The best-known is the Sturmpanzer IV Brummbär which was developed to help in the street fighting in the Soviet Union's cities. Even more formidable was the Sturmtiger, also known as the Sturmpanzer VI or Sturmmörser. This vehicle arose from the Germans' experiences fighting in the city of Stalingrad when they decided they needed a weapon that could destroy a strongpoint with a single shot. Its full designation was the 380mm RW 61 Auf StuMrs Tiger (380mm rocket projector Type 61 on Tiger chassis) and was the brainchild of Hitler.

The design came about due to the need for a self-propelled vehicle that could carry a massive 210mm howitzer. While the then new PzKpfw VI Tiger Ausf E chassis was chosen to carry the gun no suitable 210mm howitzers were available. Instead the Raketenwerfer 61 L/54, which has originally been produced by the firm Rheinmetall-Borsig as an anti-submarine weapon for the navy, was selected.

On 20 October 1943 a Sturmtiger prototype built by Alkett was displayed for the first time and gained approval. It went into very limited production in the summer of 1944 with Brandenburger Eisenwerke manufacturing the superstructure and Alkett converting the chassis and completing the assembly at their Berlin-Spandau plant. While it could demolish an entire house, by the time it went into production this street-fighting requirement was long gone as the German Army was in headlong retreat on the Eastern Front.

While the suspension, power train, engine and hull were from the basic Tiger Ausf E, the turret and superstructure had to be replaced with a heavily-armoured rectangular body. This was made from welded rolled plates, with the side plates interlocked with the front and rear ones. The joint between the front plate and glacis plate was reinforced with a heavy strip of armour on the outside. The driver's position had the same controls as the Tiger, but the position was much more cramped.

The odd rocket projector, which looked more like a drainpipe than a gun, was mounted offset to the right centre in the front of the superstructure. It consisted of a tubular casting with a spaced rifled liner and cast mantlet. The latter was an integral part of the tube and protected the joint of the mount and the tube itself. The gases from the rocket deflected between the tube and the liner to escape through a perforated ring on the muzzle containing thirty-one holes.

Inside, six ammunition racks were capable of holding twelve rounds. These came as high explosive or hollow charge. The 5ft long, 761lb high explosive 38mm RaketenSprenggranate 4581 (RS-rocket self-propelled) rocket had to be loaded into the breech using overhead rails that took a hand-operated winch, which could run from side to side to place the rockets on the loading tray. The rocket was then manhandled from the loading tray fitted with six rollers into the projector set at zero elevation. Once loading was complete, the tray was folded into the floor when not in use. The winch was also used to help with ammunition storage. Reloading the vehicle was just as laborious. A small hand-operated ammunition crane was mounted on the superstructure to lift the rockets from the supply vehicle and lower them through the roof ammunition hatch into the fighting compartment.

Only eighteen existing Tigers were converted during August to December 1944 and were issued to three Sturmmörser or armoured assault mortar companies, Nos 1001, 1002 and 1003. These were deployed in the defence of the Third Reich and sent to provide fire support for attacks on the advancing Allies. Officially this vehicle had a road speed of 23mph, but with 150mm of frontal armour, 80mm on the sides, 40mm on the roof of the fighting compartment and a gross weight of almost 70 tons it was very slow.

Apart from a few serving with an armoured assault mortar company in August 1944 during the Warsaw Rising, the reality is that by this stage of the war the requirement for the Sturmtiger had long gone. Two companies also saw limited service during the Ardennes offensive. Apart from its lack of mobility, the slow rate of fire of the rocket projector rendered the vehicle a positive liability on a highly fluid battlefield. Most of the Sturmtigers would have been abandoned at the first sign of trouble and few ever had the chance of firing the Ratetenwerfer in anger.

Panzerjäger Tiger (P) Ferdinand/Jagdpanzer Elefant

As part of the Germans continuing policy of seeking to develop successful tank killers, the hunting tank or Jagdpanzer was the next progression from the sturmgeschütz and panzerjäger and had the characteristics of both armoured fighting vehicles. A significant example of this was the massive Elefant (initially dubbed the Ferdinand after its designer Ferdinand Porsche). While it proved to be perhaps the most successful tank destroyer of the war, clocking up a kill ratio of almost 10:1, there were too few of them and it proved to be very unreliable. Ultimately it was a white elephant.

The original designation was Panzerjäger Tiger (P) Ferdinand für 88mm Pak 43/2, but was changed to Jagdpanzer Elefant für 88mm Pak43/2 L/71 (Sd Kfz 184). To produce a self-propelled mount for the 88mm Pak43 it was decided that rather than waste the uncompleted Porsche Tigers, which had been rejected in favour of the Henschel design, they would be used as tank hunters. The gun was also fitted to the Panzer Mk III/IV chassis to create the Nashorn (Rhinoceros) or Hornisse (Hornet).

The 88mm Pak43/2 L/71 anti-tank gun was a development of the earlier 88mm Flak 6 anti-aircraft gun which was adapted as the weapon of choice for the Tiger. This was a longer and much more powerful weapon than the earlier L/56 88mm. The additional barrel length gave it a greatly increased muzzle velocity and it also fired a longer round which greatly improved its penetration ability. While the Flak 41 became the next generation anti-aircraft gun, the L/71 became the very successful Pak43 anti-tank gun. The basic design for the Elefant provided no other weapon, this shortcoming soon becoming a problem and the lack of close protection resulted in the addition of a machine gun at the front of the hull.

In reality the Elefant was virtually a complete redesign of the original Porsche project. It was really a new vehicle that despite its lineage bore little resemblance to the Tiger tank. When the designers had finished only the hull shape and suspension of the original Porsche Tiger remained. The Porsche suspension consisted of three twin bogies on each side sprung by torsion bars. The wheels were all-steel with resilient rims. Notably the original troublesome petrol-electric drive was kept, though in a modified form with the Porsche air-cooled drive motors replaced by two Maybach 300hp HL 120 engines. Rather than in the rear these were positioned centrally, leaving the rear for the crew fighting compartment. The fuel tanks flanked the engine compartment. The slope-sided fighting compartment accommodated the commander, gunner and two loaders. At the rear there was a large circular hatch to allow for weapon maintenance, which included a smaller hatch for ejecting the spent rounds. There were also two roof hatches and pistol ports. The driver and radio-operator were located in the front of the hull forward of the engines. Directional control was provided by a hydro-pneumatic steering system. However, visibility was poor and the driver could only see forward, so cupolas had to be added. To enhance crew protection bolt-on 100mm appliqué armour was added to the nose and 200mm to the front of the superstructure.

The prototype Ferdinand/Elefant first appeared in March 1943 and ninety-one Porsche Tiger chassis were converted at the Nibelungenwerk factory at St Valentin, Austria during March to May 1943. For the coming Kursk offensive they were issued to Heavy Panzerjäger Battalions 653 and 654 that July. Due to the lack of suitable ammunition carriers six Panzer IIIs were converted into Munitionschleppers.

Both units had been formed at Bruck the previous April and the 653 was raised using personnel from the 197th Sturmgeschütz Battalion. The 653 came under the command of Major Steinwachs and the 654 under Major Karl-Heinz Noak. Along with the Brummbärs of Sturmpanzer Battalion 216, they formed the 656 Panzerjäger Regiment commanded by Lieutenant-Colonel Jungenfeld. This regiment came under the XLI Panzer Corps serving with Army Group Centre.

At long range the Ferdinand proved to be deadly and tore great holes in the ranks of Soviet armour. T-34 tanks were reportedly knocked out at a range of over three miles. While the Ferdinands of 653 alone knocked out 320 Soviet tanks for the loss of 13 of their number and the regiment as a whole claimed 502 tanks and another 100 vehicles, the vehicle's shortcoming rapidly became apparent. Many of them broke down, became stranded or were simply overrun by Russian infantry. After just four days of battle almost half of the eighty-nine Ferdinands committed to the attack were out of service due to technical problems or mine damage to the tracks and suspension.

Guderian recalled that the Ferdinand's deployment at Kursk was a liability:

The ninety Porsche Tigers, which were operating with Model's Army, were incapable of close-range fighting since they lacked sufficient ammunition for the guns, and this defect was aggravated by the fact that they possessed no machine-gun. Once they had broken into the enemy's infantry zone they literally had to go quail shooting with cannons. They did not manage to neutralize, let alone destroy, the enemy rifles and machine guns, so that the infantry was unable to follow up behind them. By the time they reached the Russian artillery they were on their own.

Major Noak's crews had resorted to firing their MG34 machine guns down the barrel of the main armament in a desperate bid to keep the Soviet infantry at bay.

In September the German authorities had little option but recall the Ferdinand for modification. This included the installation of a much-needed ball-mounted machine gun in the front of the hull, a modified StuG III commander's cupola to help with visibility and a coat of Zimmerit anti-magnetic mine paste. These modest improvements pushed its weight up from 65 tons to 70 tons. The work was carried out by Nibelungenwerke in Austria and the modernised Ferdinands were perhaps uncharitably dubbed the Elefant. This new name became official by order of Hitler on 1 May 1944. The Elefants were issued to Heavy Panzerjäger Battalion 653 and elements of this unit were shipped to Italy in February 1944. Their weight meant that they were too heavy for most Italian roads and bridges.

The Elefants then saw action at Nettuno, Anzio and Cisterna, but in April 1944 part of the battalion was sent back to the Eastern Front. Then later in the year the 653 Battalion was reequipped with Jagdtigers and the remaining Elefants were issued to a new unit Heavy Panzerjäger Company 614. They resisted the Soviet Army's Vistula-Oder offensive into Poland in January 1945. The last remaining four fought with Battlegroup Ritter south of Berlin in the Zossen area in April 1945.

There can be no escaping the fact that the Elefant was a waste of time and effort, it and the Nashorn were a developmental cul-de-sac, although to be fair the Nashorn was much more successful with 473 produced. However you look at it, the Elefant was a rush job with little thought given to its inherent design faults. The reality was that a good gun was married to a very poor vehicle. Essentially the Elefant was a disaster and was swiftly superseded by much more successful tank hunters in the shape of the Jagdpanzer IV and the Jagdpanther. Likewise, the Nashorn was too small, inadequately armoured and under-powered. It too was taken out of production once the much-improved Jagdpanzer types became available.

Bergepanzer Tiger (P)

Three Bergepanzer Tiger (P) were converted from Porsche Tiger chassis in September 1943. This was carried out in a similar manner to the Elefant tank destroyer. The engines were mounted in the centre of the chassis and a new superstructure was added at the rear. Apart from a small derrick crane, rams and timber beams few other concessions were made for its recovery role. A ball mount was fitted to the superstructure to give it some defence using the 7.92mm MG34. Like the Bergepanzer Tiger Ausf E there was simply too few of them to be of any great help to the panzer crews.

Tiger II

Command Panzer

From November 1944 a number of Tiger IIs were converted to command tanks with the installation of additional radio sets. The command variant of the Tiger II was known as the Panzerbefehlswagen Tiger Ausf B and like the Tiger I command tanks came in two versions, the Sd Kfz 267 and Sd Kfz 268. The first was equipped with the FuG5 and FuG8 radios while the second had the FuG5 and FuG7. These tanks were identifiable by their 2m-long rod antenna mounted on the turrets. To accommodate these radios meant they could only carry sixty-three rounds of 88mm ammunition.

Jadgtiger

The mighty Jagdtiger was the largest armoured fighting vehicle of the war. This Jagd or hunting Tiger was a self-propelled adaptation of the Tiger II armed with the enormous 128mm Pak44 L/55 gun, the largest and most powerful anti-tank gun deployed on any wartime fighting vehicle. Weighing in at a whopping 76 tons it was also the heaviest. With a muzzle velocity of 2,887ft per second (or 880m/sec), the gun could punch through 143mm of armour at 1,000 yards meaning it could kill any Allied tank in service.

Initially it was considered employing either the Tiger I or Panther chassis as a possible mount for the 128mm gun, but following the mock-up of a woodened Panther model these designs were abandoned. The Krupp Panther Gerät-5 designs for a 105mm, 128mm and 150mm gun carrier also all came to nothing.

This limited-traverse tank hunter version of the Tiger II was produced following the Heereswaffenamt policy. Originally designated the Panzerjäger Tiger Ausf B (SdKfz 186) it consisted of the Tiger II hull with a box superstructure to house the gun. A full-size unarmoured wooden mock-up was ready on 20 October 1943 the same time as the Tiger II prototype. The finished prototype was not ready until April 1944. In fact, two prototypes were built, one utilizing the

Henschel nine-overlapping-wheel suspension used on the Tiger II and a version with the eight-roadwheel Porsche suspension.

Attempts were made by Dr Porsche to improve the design with the installation of a torsion bar bogie, suspension similar to that on the prototype Porsche Tiger and the Elefant. Externally it was distinguishable by having one less exterior road wheel either side (four instead of five). Although Porsche claimed that it greatly simplified production only a few vehicles ever appeared. Initial intelligence reports suggested that an experimental version fitted with the Porsche suspension was up and running in April 1945, but the war ended before the project could be taken any further. In February 1944 Hitler ordered that the name be simplified and the Panzerjäger Tiger Ausf B (SdKfz 186) officially became the Jagdtiger.

The vital gun mount was a product of joint design work by Henschel and Krupp and featured a Saukopf mantlet. This offered very limited traverse and elevation, which gave the Jagdtiger a very limited kill zone. The cumbersome box-shaped superstructure to house the gun gave the vehicle a very high and exposed profile. This was fabricated by Eisenweke Oberdonau at Linz and was 250mm thick at the front and 80mm thick on the sides.

Like the Tiger II the Jagdtiger was underpowered, using the V12 Maybach 700hp engine and drive train from the late production Tiger I. Also the driver's station was much more cramped than in the Tiger. Perhaps not surprisingly only 150 Panzerjäger Tiger Bs were initially ordered and they were constructed by Steyr-Daimler-Puch at St Valentin in Austria. The war though intervened with these modest plans as resources and disruption of the supply chain became an issue.

Problems with the 128mm gun meant it was initially proposed installing the 88mm gun used in the Jagdpanther. A Jagdtiger mounting the 88mm L/71 anti-tank gun, designated the Sd Kfz 185, was designed but it never went into production. It is believed that about a dozen of the Sd Kfz 185 variant of the Jagdtiger armed with the 88mm Pak43 gun were built, though they were never completed due to a lack of components including sights.

In total less than 100 Jagdtigers were ever produced. Subsequent factory information indicates that that 11 Jagdtigers were built using the Porsche suspension (eight road wheels) and that the rest had the Henschel suspension. Total numbers vary with reports of forty-eight being built between July–December 1944 and another thirty-six from December 1944–May 1945. Ultimately this matters little, the fact remains very few were ever built. In addition, the suspension was the least of its worries as the weight and underpowered engine meant they inevitably kept breaking down.

While ideally suited for defensive warfare, with a gun that could destroy every other tank, its weight and mobility meant that it was a liability for it crews. Its immense size and firepower could not make up for its slow speed and constant breakdowns. The limited numbers of Jagdtiger saw action from late 1944 until the closing days of the war. They were issued to just two combat units, Panzerjägerabteilung 653 and Schwere Panzerabteilung 512. The 653rd saw action on the Western Front during Hitler's Ardennes offensive, and later with the 512th defending the Reich, most notably at the Remagen Bridgehead on 10 March 1945.

Jagdtigers were captured in the Morsbronn area of France and near Neustadt, Germany in March 1945. While the former, bearing the number 314, was in the standard factory colour of deep sand yellow or dunkel gelb and a hand-painted pattern of olive green, the latter had only received its factory base colour. One of the last ones from the 512th battalion was abandoned on the streets of Obernetphen, Germany in April 1945. Likewise, the US 7th Infantry Division captured one serving with the LIII Panzer Corps at Iserlohn in the Ruhr on 16 April 1945. This Jagdtiger with the number '102' had a very similar camouflage scheme to the one taken at Morsbronn. Jagdtigers also fell into the hands of the Soviet Army. A battle group from Heavy Panzerjäger Battalion 653, which included four surrendered to the Soviets at Amstetten, Austria on 5 May 1945.

Appendix H

Panther Variants

The Panther tank chassis was intended to provide the basis for a whole range of armoured fighting vehicles that would include command, flak, self-propelled gun and recovery variants. Very few of these, however, got any further than the proposal or design stage as time simply ran out in the closing months of the war. Ultimately only the command, armoured recovery and tank hunter versions were produced in any notable numbers to serve alongside the gun tanks.

Panther Armoured Recovery Vehicle

Major problems recovering the 57-ton Tiger from late 1942 meant a dedicated Panther recovery vehicle was vital. This was needed to replace the 18-ton half-track in the heavy recovery role, as it took up to three of these to shift heavy tanks such as the Tiger and the Panther.

In June 1943 the first twelve Panzer-Bergegerät Panther I Sd Kfz 179, better known as the Bergepanther, were produced by MAN using a Ausf D turretless chassis. This though was little more than a towing vehicle, with a limited superstructure consisting of heavy wooden cladding over a mild steel frame built round the former turret opening. The following month Henschel commenced building seventy Bergepanthers from the Ausf D before the company stopped Panther production altogether in November 1943. These were equipped with a 40-ton winch, a spade and a 1.5-ton derrick.

The requirement for Panther armoured recovery vehicles was not fully met and in February 1944 the manufacturers Demag converted their entire production line over to Bergepanthers. This time they utilized the Panther Ausf A chassis with the letterbox machine-gun port still in the hull front plate. An additional 150 Ausf A variants were built until the G variant went into production. Armament consisted of two MG34 machine guns mounted on a gun shield at the front of the hull and the early Ausf A Bergepanthers included the 20mm KwK38 gun.

Perhaps not wishing to detract from Panther gun tank production, Hitler ordered that all subsequent recovery vehicles be constructed from existing Panthers sent for rebuilds. It was planned that thirteen Bergepanthers would be provided in April 1944, followed by eighteen that May, twenty in June and ten in July. This schedule though was never met and only eight conversions were managed in August 1944. In total 232 Bergepanthers were produced from June 1943 to September 1944 using the Ausf A plus the eight conversions. Then from September 1944 to March 1945 Demag produced 107 Ausf G versions.

Panther Ammunition Carrier

Some Bergepanthers without spades later had their winches removed and were converted into a Munitionpanzer Panther to carry ammunition for the gun tanks. Other existing Panthers simply had their turrets removed and were also used as munitions carriers. These vehicles were very much ad hoc field modifications and were not put into formal factory production. Externally they looked the same as the Bergepanther but minus the winch gear.

Assault Panther

Plans for an assault variant or Sturmpanther began in late 1944 with a view to mounting a 150mm StuH43/1 gun on the chassis. This, however, never went into production. Designs were also produced for a Waffenträger or weapons carrier based on the Panther with a turret-mounted 105mm LeFH howitzer.

Panther Command Tank

Two versions of the Panther command/observation tank were produced, the former retained the 75mm gun while the latter did not. The trick with command tanks, which carried more radio equipment than usual, was to make them as inconspicuous as possible or they immediately attracted enemy fire. Deployed by regimental and battalion commander as well as staff officers Befehlswagen Panthers could only be distinguished externally by the extra aerials or the call sign number when visible.

The Panzerbefehlswagen mit 7.5cm KwK42 L/70 had a FuG5 radio installed in the turret and a FuG7 or FuG8 radio in the hull over the gearbox. This Pz Bef Wg was fitted with two additional radio aerials, comprising a 1.4m rod on the right side of the turret and a star aerial in the centre rear of the engine deck.

For designation purposes there were two externally similar models of Panther command tank differing only in the radio installation. The Sd Kfz 267 had the FuG5 and FuG8 while the Sd Kfz 268 had the FuG5 and FuG7. In each type ammunition stowage was reduced from seventy-nine to sixty-four 75mm tank gun rounds. In total 329 Panthers were converted to a command role from May 1943 to February 1945.

Panther Observation Tank

The much rarer observation Panther, designated the Panzerbeobachtubngswagen Sd Kfz 172, was produced by converting rebuilt Panthers in late 1944. Old Ausf Ds were used to create observation post vehicles for operations officers, commanders and staff officers of the self-propelled artillery regiments. To create space for the Blockstelle 0 range-plotting table and other instrumentation for artillery observation the 75mm gun was removed, the front plated over and the turret fixed in place. Instead a dummy gun was installed to give the illusion of a gun tank to the right of which was fitted a ball-mounted machine gun to provide some close-in protection. On the new front plate flaps covered the openings for an EM 1.25m R (Pz) stereoscopic rangefinder. Like the command tank the observation variant was also fitted with two additional radio aerials. Just forty-one observation Panthers were produced by the end of the war.

Flak Panther

Rheinmetall-Borsig started creating a flakpanzer version of the Panther in December 1943 by mounting twin 37mm FlaK43 anti-aircraft guns in a fully-armoured turret on an Ausf D chassis. A wooden mock-up was produced and fitted to a hull but actual production never came to fruition. Other designs included a mount for the 88mm FlaK41 on the Panther chassis.

Infra-red Panther

In late 1944 a number of Panthers were experimentally fitted with infra-red night-fighting equipment with a range of 400m. The Sd Kfz 251/20 half-track known as the Infrarotscheinwerfer or UHU (Eagle Owl) was introduced as the command and observation vehicle for five-strong infra-red Panther platoons. The UHU, equipped with a 60cm Beobachtungs Gerät 1251 infra-red searchlight and Beobachtungs Gerät 1221 telescope, could illuminate and sight targets out to 1,500m. The UHU commander would then direct the Panthers onto their targets using the FuG5 radio once they had closed to some 500m. Although 600 Eagle Owls were ordered in August 1944 only 60 were ever delivered. Likewise, the number of infra-red Panthers was equally limited. Some were used during Hitler's Ardennes offensive.

Jagdpanther

Undoubtedly the most successful and deadly of the Panther variants was the heavy tank destroyer or Jagdpanther Sd Kfz 173, also long-windedly known as the Panzerjäger für 8.8cm PaK43 auf Fgst Panther I. This comprised fitting the powerful 88mm PaK4/3 L/71 anti-tank gun into the Panther hull. Earlier attempts to produce a heavy tank destroyer had largely been unsuccessful and in some cases were little more than bodge jobs. The 88mm anti-tank gun had already been mounted in the Porsche-designed Tiger I chassis to create limited numbers of the Ferdinand and it had also been installed on the Panzer III/IV chassis as the Nashorn. Both improvisations had proven unsatisfactory – the Ferdinand was far too heavy and lacked protection against enemy infantry while the Nashorn was too small and underpowered.

The order for the Jagdpanther development was issued on 2 October 1942 and a wooden mock-up was completed the following October. This was shown to Hitler on 16 December 1943 and he liked what he saw. To house the 88mm gun a fighting compartment was created by removing the Panther turret and extending the upper hull and side plates to make a well-sloped enclosed superstructure. Armour was 80mm on the front and 60mm at the sides. The suspension used was that of the Panther, although the drive train was upgraded with the installation of a heavy-duty transmission to cope with the slight weight increase.

The L/71 was installed in a mount in the sloping front plate of the new superstructure. Initially on the early models the gun mount was welded into place while on the later ones it was bolted. The first production models had a monobloc or single-piece gun barrel while the middle and late production vehicles had a distinctive two-piece barrel.

The driver operated via a periscope in the superstructure next to the gun mount and two hull vision slots (these were reduced to one in later models). The rest of the five-man crew were served by periscopes in the roof. Close defence was provided by a machine gun to the right of the main armament plus the Nahverteidigungswaffe close-defence weapon mounted in the roof.

Production of the Jagdpanther commenced at MIAG in January 1944 and at MNH in November 1944 and continued until the end of the war. It was intended to build 150 per month, but disruption of the production facilities during the last year of the war by Allied bombers made this target impossible. Only 392 Jagdpanthers were built, far too few to have anything more than a local impact on the battlefield. The first units to be issued with it in June 1944 were the 559th and 654th Panzerjägerabteilungen. Only the latter received its full complement of forty-two vehicles. The Jagdpanther saw combat in Normandy, the Ardennes and the Eastern Front.

Panther Tank Destroyer

Toward the end of the war Krupp was working on a prototype rigid mounted 88mm PaK43/1 L/71 in the Jagdpanther. Prototypes utilizing such rigid mounts in the Jagdpanzer 38(t) showed that the Jagdpanther was more suitable. This vehicle was known as the Jagdpanther Starr but it never got beyond the prototype stage.

Weapons Carrier Panther

The Geschützwagen Panther für sFH18/4(sf) or weapons carrier variant was ordered in early 1944 using a shortened Panther suspension. This featured a lifting beam to manoeuvre the 150mm SfH18 howitzer. Daimler–Benz got as far as producing a prototype before the war ended.

Bibliography

This work draws on a number of previous Pen & Sword books all of which are listed below.

Adair, Paul, *Hitler's Greatest Defeat* (London: Rigel, 2004)

Beevor, Antony, *The Spanish Civil War* (London: Orbis, 1982)

Bullock, Alan, *Hitler A Study in Tyranny* (London: Penguin, 1962)

Chamberlain, Peter & Doyle, Hilary, *Encyclopaedia of German Tanks of World War Two* (Wigston: Silverdale, 2004)

Chamberlain, Peter & Ellis, Chris, *The Great Tanks* (London: Hamlyn, 1975)

Chamberlain, Peter, Ellis, Chris & Batchelor, John, *German Fighting Vehicles 1939–1945* (London: Phoebus, 1975)

Clark, Alan, *Barbarossa: The Russian-German Conflict 1941–1945* (London: Cassell, 2001)

Clark, Lloyd, *Kursk: The Greatest Battle – Eastern Front 1943* (London: Headline Review, 2012)

Deighton, Len, *Blitzkrieg: From the Rise of Hitler to the Fall of Dunkirk* (London: Jonathan Cape, 1979)

Dimbleby, Jonathan, *Destiny in the Desert: The Road to El Alamein – The Battle that Turned the Tide* (London: Profile, 2013)

Ellis, Chris, *21st Panzer Division: Rommel's Afrika Korps Spearhead* (Hersham: Ian Allan, 2001)

Ellis, Chris, *Tanks of World War II* (London: Chancellor Press, 1997)

Fey, Will, *Armor Battles of the Waffen-SS 1943–45* (Mechanicsburg, PA: Stackpole, 2003)

Forczyk, Robert, *Panther vs T-34: Ukraine 1943* (Oxford: Osprey, 2007)

Forty, George, *Tank Action: From the Great War to the Gulf* (Stroud: Alan Sutton, 1995)

Forty, George & Livesey, Jack, *The Complete Guide to Tanks & Armoured Fighting Vehicles* (London: Hermes House, 2006)

Forty, Jonathan, *PzKfpw IV Ausf A to J: Panzer IV* (Hersham: Ian Allan, 2002)

Forty, Jonathan, *PzKpfw V Ausf A,D & G: Panzer V Panther* (Hersham: Ian Allan, 2003)

Gander, Terry J., *PzKpfw III Ausf A to N: Panzer III* (Hersham: Ian Allan, 2004)

Gander, Terry J., *PzKpfw VI Ausf E & B: Panzer VI Tiger I & II* (Hersham: Ian Allan, 2003)

Gander, Terry J., *JgdPz IV, V, VI and Hetzer: Jagdpanzer* (Hersham: Ian Allan, 2004)

Guderian, General Heinz, *Panzer Leader* (London: Futura, 1974)

Hook, Patrick, *Hohenstaufen: 9th SS Panzer Division* (Hersham: Ian Allan, 2005)

Jurado, Carlos Caballero, *The Condor Legion: German Troops in the Spanish Civil War* (Oxford: Osprey, 2006)

Keegan, John, *Barbarossa: Invasion of Russia 1941* (London: Macdonald, 1971)

Kershaw, Andrew (ed.), *The Tank Story* (London: Phoebus, 1972)

Kurowski, Franz, *Panzer Aces: German Tank Commanders of WWII* (Mechanicsburg, PA: Stackpole, 2004)

Kurowski, Franz, *Panzer Aces II: Battle Stories of German Tank Commanders of WWII* (Mechanicsburg, PA: Stackpole, 2004)

Lefèvre, Eric, *Panzers in Normandy Then and Now* (London: After the Battle, 1983)

Liddell Hart, B.H., *History of the Second World War* (London: Cassell, 1970)

Liddell Hart, B.H., *The Other Side of the Hill* (London: Pan, 1983)

Liddell Hart, B.H., *The Rommel Papers* (London: Collins, 1953)

Macksey, Major K.J., *Afrika Korps* (London: Pan, 1972)

Macksey, Kenneth, *Rommel: Battles and Campaigns* (London: Arms and Armour Press, 1979)

Matthews, Rupert, *Hitler: Military Commander* (London: Arcturus, 2003)

Mellenthin, Major-General F.W. von, *Panzer Battles* (London: Futura, 1977)

Messenger, Charles, *The Art of Blitzkrieg* (London: Ian Allan, 1991)

Miller, David, *The Illustrated Directory of Tanks of the World from World War I to Present Day* (London: Greenwich, 2004)

Milsom, John, *Panzerkampfwagen 38(t) & 35(t)* (Windsor: Profile, 1970)

Mitchell, David, *The Spanish Civil War* (London: Granada, 1982)

Morris, Eric, *Tanks* (London: Octopus, 1975)

Pitt, Barrie, *The Crucible of War: Western Desert 1941* (London: Futura, 1981)

Quarrie, Bruce, *Hitler's Teutonic Knights: SS Panzers in Action* (London: Patrick Stephens, 1986)

Ripley, Tim, *Steel Storm: Waffen-SS Panzer Battles on the Eastern Front 1943–1945* (Stroud: Sutton, 2000)

Ritgen, Helmut, *The 6th Panzer Division 1937–45* (Oxford: Osprey, 1982)

Schmidt, Heinz Werner, *With Rommel in the Desert* (London: Panther, 1960)

Seaton, Albert, *The German Army 1933–45* (London: Sphere, 1983)

Sharpe, Michael & Davis, Brian L., *Das Reich: Waffen-SS Armoured Elite* (Hersham: Ian Allan, 2003)

Sharpe, Michael & Davis, Brian L., *Grossdeutschland: Guderian's Eastern Front Elite* (Hersham: Ian Allan, 2001)

Sharpe, Michael & Davis, Brian L., *Leibstandarte: Hitler's Elite Bodyguard* (Hersham: Ian Allan, 2002)

Speer, Albert, *Inside the Third Reich* (London: Phoenix, 1995)

Squadron, *Panzer III in Action* (Carrollton, Texas: Signal, 1972)

Strawson, John, *The Battle for North Africa* (London: BT Batsford, 1969)

Taylor, A.J.P., *The Origins of the Second World War* (London: Hamish Hamilton, 1962)

Thomas, Hugh, *The Spanish Civil War* (London: Eyre & Spottiswoode, 1961)

Tolland, John, *Adolf Hitler* (Ware: Wordsworth, 1997)

Tucker-Jones, Anthony, *German Assault Guns and Tank Destroyers 1940–1945* (Barnsley: Pen & Sword, 2016)

Tucker-Jones, Anthony, *Kursk 1943: Hitler's Bitter Harvest* (Stroud: The History Press, 2018)

Tucker-Jones, Anthony, *Panzer I & II: The Birth of Hitler's Panzerwaffe* (Barnsley: Pen & Sword, 2018)

Tucker-Jones, Anthony, *The Panzer III: Hitler's Beast of Burden* (Barnsley: Pen & Sword, 2017)

Tucker-Jones, Anthony, *The Panzer IV: Hitler's Rock* (Barnsley: Pen & Sword, 2017)

Tucker-Jones, Anthony, *The Panther Tank: Hitler's T-34 Killer* (Barnsley: Pen & Sword, 2016)

Tucker-Jones, Anthony, *Tiger I & Tiger II* (Barnsley: Pen & Sword, 2013)

Tucker-Jones, Anthony, *T-34: The Red Army's Legendary Medium Tank* (Barnsley: Pen & Sword, 2015)

Turnbull, Patrick, *The Spanish Civil War 1936–39* (London: Osprey, 1978)

Vanderveen, Bart, *Historic Military Vehicles Directory* (London: After the Battle, 1989)

Vanderveen, Bart, *The Observer's Fighting Vehicles Directory World War II* (London: Frederick Warne, 1969)

Warner, Philip, *Alamein* (London: William Kimber, 1979)

Warner, Philip, *World War Two: The Untold Story* (London: Cassell, 2002)

White, B.T., *German Tanks and Armoured Vehicles 1914–1945* (Shepperton: Ian Allan, 1966)

White, B.T., *Tanks and other AFVs of the Blitzkrieg Era 1939–41* (London: Blandford, 1972)

White, B.T, *Tanks and other Armoured Fighting Vehicles 1942–45* (Poole: Blandford, 1975)

Winchester, Charles, *Ostfront: Hitler's War on Russia 1941–45* (Oxford: Osprey, 1998)

Windrow, Martin, *The Panzer Divisions (Revised Edition)* (London: Osprey, 1982)

Windrow, Martin, *The Panzer Divisions* (London: Osprey, 1973)

Zetterling, Niklas, *Normandy 1944: German Military Organization, Combat Power and Organizational Effectiveness* (Winnipeg: JJ Fedorowicz, 2000)

Index